MW01503861

ART
STARS

LEGENDS OF
PRODUCTION DESIGN

ART
STARS

Interviews by
Tom Lisowski

MASARYK

LOS ANGELES

Masaryk Productions
Los Angeles, CA 90021

www.masarykproductions.com

Permissions and ordering Information:
Special discounts are available on quantity purchases. Please contact sales@masarykproductions.com

Book design by Kristy Jennings www.kjdesign.com

Printed in the United States of America
First Masaryk paperback edition 2023

Library of Congress Cataloging-in-Publication Data is available upon request.

ISBN 979-8-218-33549-6 (paperback)

Interviews have been edited for clarity and length.

Dedicated to my late father
Marek Wlodzimierz Lisowski.

He inspired in me a love of art
and of taking ideas and turning
them into three dimensions.

Contents

Foreword

By Nelson Coates
President - Art Directors Guild
Production Designer
Crazy Rich Asians, In The Heights, Flight

The art of narrative design is a foundational and intrinsic component of visual storytelling, encompassing a vast and often disparate swath of skills, personnel, and resources, coalesced into a team under the creative direction of a Production Designer.

Typically, one of the initial hires on a project, the Production Designer answers to the director, producers, and studio, with the responsibility for the concept and execution of sets, locations, environmental décor, props, costumes, hair, makeup, physical effects, visual effects, color palette, graphics, vehicles... basically all the visible elements of the storytelling process.

No more exciting creative profession exists within the entertainment field than Production Design – leading a design team in forecasting the future, reimagining the past, or creating alternative realities and parallel universes... Every project presents fresh opportunities to assemble and collaborate with unique teams, explore a myriad of tools, and discover fresh methods to convey ideas and engage audiences.

Taking full advantage of world building opportunities; inventing stylistic rules to guide viewers through project narratives; creating a singular visual language, a sense of history, time and place, backstory for characters, and a suspension of disbelief are just part of the vital contributions of the Production Designer to the process of content creation in what ever media capture or distribution form.

The design solutions to storytelling challenges are as diverse as each individual Production Designer, their range of knowledge and experiences, and teams they assemble. The designer acts as visionary, project manager, mediator, benevolent dictator, mad scientist, creative problem-solver – providing methodologies and modalities to deliver a complete concept within the parameters of script, schedule, and budget... creating a visual story arc, much like an actor creates a character arc.

Unlike standard architecture, the narrative designer must conceive how a space can be utilized in a scene to propel a narrative, how those environments work for other departments, and what the space can do to enhance and detail an actor's performance. Whether creating disasters or dystopia, or representing the details of a not-so-known culture, designers have the awesome responsibility and daunting challenge of creating design narratives with the potential to have a lasting impact on the visual lexicon of society.

Since the dissolution of in-house art departments at major studios and the resulting scarcity of training and educational opportunities, fewer organized avenues have existed for interaction with top design professionals – to learn the skills and techniques involved in their design processes, and the integration of those techniques into day-to-day production...

With his book *Art Stars,* Tom Lisowski has created a much-needed mentoring tool and resource for filmmakers and production designers alike. Through his detailed conversations with some of the leading contemporaneous designers in film and television, Lisowski has provided a unique opportunity to learn from the experiences and production insights of these talented creatives in their own voices, and along the way, celebrates the creative contributions of design teams and personalities who are elevating the art of narrative design.

Preface

By Tom Lisowski

A friend asked if I wouldn't mind having coffee with his newly graduated nephew to give some advice about the field of production design. I'd been working as a production designer for a few years and I said I'd be happy to. We had a great meeting–I helped introduce him to the world of designing movies and was reminded of why I love this job so much. After that meeting I asked myself, *What if I were to interview the people I looked up to? The ones who've been designing my favorite films and winning Academy Awards?* It could be a tremendous education for myself and for whomever I could share it with, anyone with dreams of creating amazing designs for movies, like my friend's nephew.

I visited the American Film Institute Conservatory, where I knew the production design department was led by Joe Garrity, designer of the awesome Christopher Guest movies. Even though *Art Stars* was barely more than an idea at that point, Joe agreed to be my first interview. After that initial spark, I continued on from interview to interview, with the lessons from these giants making it into my own production design. I find myself retelling these stories to producers and directors and to my own crews. The enthusiasm and wisdom from these designers has energized my own career and I hope it does the same for yours.

There are now more platforms than ever for releasing our filmed entertainment and stories. And as *Fury Road* production designer Colin Gibson advised, there is no substitute for just throwing tools in the back of your truck and getting your hands dirty out there designing a movie. Let the following luminaries be your inspiration on the road ahead.

Dante Ferretti

When we spoke, Dante Ferretti had just won his third Oscar, for director Martin Scorsese's *Hugo,* after winning one for Tim Burton's *Sweeney Todd* and one for another Scorsese film, *The Aviator.* To date he's designed ten movies with Scorsese and almost as many with the legendary Federico Fellini. He created the look for *The Adventures of Baron Munchausen* with Terry Gilliam and for numerous movies with genius Italian director Pier Paolo Pasolini. He even did two movies at the same time when he worked on *Bringing Out the Dead* and *Titus!* At the time of the interview he was in Vancouver designing *The Seventh Son* for Russian director Sergey Bodrov. I was honored to speak with this legend, learning how Fellini taught him to lie, and the importance of believing a film.

AS: At one of the *Hugo* screenings, the actor Ben Kingsley said his performance was nourished by the set, that he was fed by the set. He said the train station set even smelled like Paris–the coffee, the flowers.

DF: He must have mentioned the smell because he was surrounded by real coffee, real flowers, and many, many other real things. We did everything

from scratch. This is all the set decorator Francesca Lo Schiavo–she did a fantastic job. Everything was shot on stage at Shepperton Studios in London.

AS: How much was in post and how much did you build?

DF: Actually we built everything. Everything is real

scale but we had to do many extensions. Also, in the very beginning they added the first shot when we see Paris. But after we go inside the train station and pass through the big smoke cloud everything was real. It's all real size. We built one floor at almost forty feet high and then we designed all the extensions with Rob Legato, the visual effects supervisor.

> " PREVISUALIZATION IS A SEQUEL TO DESIGN, NOT A PREQUEL.

AS: Did you do a lot of previs? Kim Sinclair, who worked on *Avatar*, described how they would have to build to the previs specs that James Cameron had been working with and how that process made it harder. They would have to make a door three feet high if it was three feet high in the previs.

DF: Yes, we did a lot of previs but the previs based their work on our drawings. I designed the entire movie first and we did all the models for every set and then the previsualization team based their work on our models. Previsualization is a sequel to design, not a prequel.

AS: Do you ever stay after principal photography is finished to work with the VFX team?

DF: No, we do everything during the movie. Then later they send me some of the pictures of what it looks like to ask me if it's okay. Marty always wants to ask me, Is everything correct? Because we did so many movies together. Also Rob Legato–I met Rob Legato when we did *Interview with a Vampire* many years ago. And then we did *The Aviator* and then *Shutter Island* and many other movies. We know each other very well and we know what we have to do.

AS: Scorsese said he met you on the set of the Fellini movie *City of Women*.

DF: Yes, in Rome. I also did six movies with Fellini. Scorsese came to see Fellini when we did *City of Women* and then one day he called me to design *The Last Temptation* but I was busy with Terry Gilliam on *Baron Munchausen*. I had to say, *I can't*, but then when he called me again with *The Age of Innocence* I said, *Okay, I'm coming!* Because it pained me to say no to Martin Scorsese! Because he is my hero. I've done eight movies with him so far. I know him very well, he knows me very well. What can I say, I'm very lucky!

AS: How would you describe the difference between working with Fellini and working with Scorsese?

DF: It's different because with Fellini it's always Fellini's movie. It's always him. You can see it in many ways but it's always Fellini. When he was young, when he was a kid, when he was a teenager, when he was thirty years old. You see all the movies and Marcello Mastriani is always him. When I worked with him it was like I was a prisoner! He would call me at six o'clock every morning and then until nine or ten o'clock in the evening. Also, Fellini was a liar. A big liar. I started to learn to be a liar too! When he asked, *Dante, what did you dream* *last night?* At first I'd say, *Nothing.* Then after two or three times it's like, *Oh my God, now I have to say something!* I started to invent my dreams. He knew I was a liar too but he wanted to hear and understand my fantasy world. Finally he said, *Dante, you are more of a liar than me!*

AS: Would Fellini draw a lot of pictures himself?
DF: Yes, he always made little sketches. He liked to design the women's costumes and some of the sets. But he always gave me freedom. I would do exactly what he liked so we had a very good relationship. I started with *City of Women* and I did all the movies until the last one, *The Voice of the Moon* with Roberto Benigni.

AS: Scorsese said he tried to help him release the last one in the United States.
DF: I remember discussing this with Fellini. Scorsese tried to help Federico but it wasn't easy.

AS: Is Scorsese also a visual director like Fellini?
DF: With Marty it's fantastic. After I read the script we spend many hours together discussing the look. He shows me many movies, sometimes just to see a couple of scenes. I say, *Okay, I understand,* and then he gives me freedom. I do the sketches and the models and they give me all the freedom to do what I think is right for him. I did eight movies with him and every time Marty came to the set and said, *Oh, great, fantastic, this is what I want.* Or sometimes he said, *Is it possible to have a little bit more of this, or that?* But it's really fantastic to work with him because I feel free to do what is better for the movie, what is better for him.

> **❝ FELLINI WAS A LIAR. A BIG LIAR. I STARTED TO LEARN TO BE A LIAR TOO! WHEN HE ASKED, *DANTE, WHAT DID YOU DREAM LAST NIGHT?* AT FIRST I'D SAY, *NOTHING.* THEN AFTER TWO OR THREE TIMES IT'S LIKE, *OH MY GOD, NOW I HAVE TO SAY SOMETHING!* I STARTED TO INVENT MY DREAMS.**

AS: How about Terry Gilliam? I also interviewed David Warren, who was nominated for an Oscar for Terry Gilliam's *The Imaginarium of Dr. Parnassus.*
DF: David was my art director for *Hugo.* He actually started with me, when Terry Gilliam introduced me to him. He also did a piece of *Interview with the Vampire.* And then I called him for *Sweeney Todd.* Then I designed another movie with him, *Defective Detective,* which we never made. I designed five movies for Terry and we did only one! He called me many times. I'm friends with Terry. I'm very close with Terry and I'm sorry it's difficult for him to make movies sometimes. But what can you say?

AS: On *Sweeney Todd* you worked with Tim Burton who's also known to do a lot of drawings. Tim Burton recently had an exhibit of his drawings here in LA.
DF: I went to see the opening at the MOMA. He made many drawings. But with me he made noth-

ing! I'm not kidding! Before *Sweeney Todd* I designed another movie for Tim Burton, *Ripley's Believe It Or Not,* which after four months we didn't make. I designed the entire movie with everything ready to start to build and then the producer said, *Oh, Dante, I'm so sorry. I don't know why.* And then Tim said, *Dante, would you like to do another movie? It's a small movie called Sweeney Todd.* I said, *Of course, anything you want,* and I started to design the movie. And then I came to London with the drawings that I did in Rome and he said, *Good, good,* and we had a very nice relationship.

> **"WHEN I WAS TEN YEARS OLD I ALWAYS WENT TO SEE MOVIES. EVERY DAY, EVERY AFTERNOON, AFTER SCHOOL. WHEN PEOPLE ARE VERY YOUNG AND THEY WANT TO WORK IN THE MOVIES THEY NORMALLY SAY THEY WANT TO BE AN ACTOR OR A DIRECTOR. I ALWAYS SAID I WANTED TO BE THE PERSON WHO MADE THE SET. AND THEN ONE DAY I LEARNED THIS WORD, *ART DIRECTOR.* I SAID, *OH, THIS IS WHAT I WANT TO BE.***

I remember one day Tim came to see me in my office, which was in front of his office in Pinewood. He brought a yellow piece of paper and he said, *You have to do the window like this.* And then he looked at my table and he saw I already had sketches of what he asked me to do and he said, *Oh, my God,* *you already designed this.* I said, *Tim, can you please sign your sketch?* He said, *Oh Dante, I love you.*

He would go to see the set many times without me, by himself during lunchtime. He'd just walk around.

AS: I loved those sets. How much of the London sets were greenscreens?

DF: When Tim first called me about this movie he said, *You know Dante, we have to do a lot of green screen because we don't have enough money. So you have to design all the sets but sometimes you have to not build too much.* And then I said, *Okay, okay, okay,* and then after a few weeks I said, *Listen, how much do you have for the visual effects?* He said, *Something like fifteen million.* I had two million and a half missing so I said, *Why don't you give me part of the visual effects money so I can build something more? And then maybe it's better for the actors than shooting against a greenscreen.* So we agreed and the producers said yes. So we built almost sixty-five percent of the movie. It's a real set. London, the market, the square where he lived, the chocolate shop, where the barbershop was, everything was built to scale.

For the visual effects that we did use, I created a book with all the images with Tim. It was like a storybook for the VFX supervisor. He did a great job.

AS: Do you watch a lot of movies as reference when you're working on a movie?

DF: Yes, of course I do. On *Hugo,* we also had the fantastic Marianne [Bower] who worked with Scorsese on all the research. And the set decorator Francesca Lo Schiavo also did a lot of research.

AS: Does it make things easier having your wife as your set decorator?

DF: Yes, because we know each other very well. We don't have to say too much. She knows what I want, she knows what I like. I know what she can do. For some people it's difficult to work with their wife but for me it's really great. We did so many movies together.

AS: When you're making a movie are you mostly on set or are you in an office?

DF: I'm always on the stage because I like to follow the set, step by step. And then even when we're shooting sometimes I go to the set and look. Then I go look at the next set that I have to do. I'm the first there when we start the movie and the last on the last day of shooting.

AS: I heard you also designed an opera, David Cronenberg's *The Fly.* How was that different from designing a movie?

DF: It's very different. I did that one because Cronenberg was good. But I've done many operas, not just *The Fly.* I worked in London with the Royal Opera, in La Scala in Italy, and everywhere. I've done at least forty operas! The last one I did was *Carmen* in my hometown. For the first time I was the director! When they asked me to do *Carmen* I actually said, *No, I can't.* Then they called me and

said, *You have to do Carmen because it's your home town, you can't say no.* I finally said, *Okay,* and then I asked, *Who is the director?* And they said, *You!* I said, *Me, why me? I never directed!* They said, *There's always a first time!* I had some fun anyway. It was good.

> " A PRODUCTION DESIGNER SHOULD NOT BE ARROGANT. THEY HAVE TO ALWAYS BE LOW-PROFILE.

AS: Did you ever think about directing movies?

DF: No, never, no, no, no. I like to be what I am. I am a production designer. That's what I am.

AS: How did you start? You went to art school?

DF: Yes, I went to a fine art school. I also studied architecture at the university. I started when I was eighteen years old. I was in school and after that I've always worked. Now I'm here.

AS: What do you like about being a production designer?

DF: I like to be in charge of the look of the movie. When I was ten years old I always went to see movies. Every day, every afternoon, after school. When people are very young and they want to work in the movies they normally say they want to be an actor or a director. I always said I wanted to be the person who made the set. And then one day I learned this word, *art director.* I said, *Oh, this is what I want to be. An art director.* And then I studied to be an art director. At that time in Italy we made almost three hundred movies a year. And I'm very lucky because I started with the most important director at the time, Pier Paolo Pasolini. First I was an assistant art director and then I became an art director and then they changed the title from art director to production designer.

AS: What characteristics do you look for when you're hiring crew?

DF: When I'm in New York or in London or LA or in China or wherever, normally I can't bring the crew that I work with in Italy so I have to go outside and look at resumes. But resumes mean nothing. I need to meet somebody. It's what I feel when I look at somebody, I can say this is the right person, this is the right art director, this is the right construction coordinator, this is a good painter or sculptor. Of course I also have to see what they did but so far I haven't made any mistakes this way. Or maybe I did and I didn't know! So far what we did was not bad because we had really good people. This is very important because you can design a fantastic movie and then if you have the right people you can make this movie fantastic but if you don't have the right people it could be a piece of shit!

AS: What are the qualities that a production designer should have?

DF: A production designer should not be arrogant. They have to always be low-profile. They have to understand what the director wants, and the story. Sometimes they call you, waiting for you to give them a good idea. I don't like production designers who talk about themselves. I like to be low-profile. I think that's the best way to do the job and then if you do a good job, create a good look, it's good for you and it's good for the people who go to see the movie. Because when you go to the movie theater to see a movie and you believe what is behind the story, that is the most important thing.

John Myhre

John Myhre has been nominated for six Academy Awards and has won two-one for his amazing work creating an entire Japanese village in *Memoirs of a Geisha* and another for the Best Picture winner *Chicago.* His enthusiasm for design has taken him across genres: he's designed everything from musical blockbusters to period pieces, to stylish action films and he's not slowing down any time soon.

AS: What project are you currently working on?
JM: I'm working on a really exciting project called *Snow and the Seven* which is a live-action version of *Snow White and the Seven Dwarfs* being made by Disney. That alone is really fun–I'm a huge Disney fan and just finished *Pirates of the Caribbean: On Stranger Tides* for Disney and they were really wonderful to work with. But the really exciting thing about *Snow and the Seven* is that it's set in 19th century China. Snow is a colonial English girl. She has a step-mom who's actually not bad at all but who gets possessed early on in the story by the spirit of an evil Chinese queen through an ancient Chinese mirror that they find. And Snow needs to flee from her mother who's out to get her. She flees through the wilds of China and runs into the Seven. But they're not seven dwarfs, they're seven warriors. Warriors from all around the world who are part of this organization and have been around for thousands of years. They keep the world safe from evil. Evil like evil queens. So Snow actually becomes one of the Seven and really becomes a warrior princess. It's almost a superhero movie in a fun way and much more *Pirates of the Caribbean* than a kid's traditional fairy tale story of *Snow White.*

AS: What are you looking at visually as references?

JM: We're doing a really heightened version of the very, very best of China. We're doing beautiful temples and beautiful shrines and the amazing mountains that you only see in China. And we're heightening everything. When we go into a bamboo forest, instead of the bamboo being three inches, the bamboo will be a foot across to make it even more magical and myth-like. And when we go into a temple it won't just be the recreation of a temple we love, it will instead be the best details of every temple we could possibly find in China all put together.

We'll play with the scale of things so there might be a beautiful, round moon-gate–a circular doorway that would normally be seven-foot tall and we might make ours twenty-foot tall. We might take lanterns that are normally two-foot tall and make them twelve-foot tall. We plan to heighten everything and just take the very, very best out of China and condense it into one space.

We did the same thing on *Memoirs of a Geisha* which was set in Japan. I was really lucky to be able to scout Japan on my own for about five weeks. I ended up taking three thousand pictures of details of Japanese buildings. The city that you see in *Memoirs of a Geisha* was actually built in California in Thousand Oaks. We built about fifty buildings. It wasn't about taking a photograph of a building and giving it to a set designer and saying, *Draw this up.*

I'd sit with the set designer and say, *Well, I loved this doorway and I loved this window.* I'd have a picture of a door and a detail of a window and a detail of an eve and a detail of a paper screen and a lantern and I'd say, *Let's take all of these and put it into one building.* And we're doing that now on an even bigger scale because *Memoirs of a Geisha* was a very realistic story, a real world we were creating, but this is a myth-like, almost superhero world that we're creating for *Snow and the Seven.*

AS: You were saying how the color palette is different this time around...

JM: Well, in Japan what we really played on were these natural materials. In our world of Japan we didn't use a lot of paint. It was all natural colors. It was the real color of the cedar they used and the real colors of the bamboo they used. These very beautiful, natural colors. Working with Colleen Atwood, our costume designer, the color in the film really came from the costumes. Now, in the world of China, what we're looking at is a whole different world which is much more ornate, much more detailed, and much more colorful, which will be really exciting.

AS: On the *Memoirs of a Geisha* set, not only did you have to build the entire village, but the set had to go through four seasons...

JM: In *Memoirs of a Geisha* the seasons were a very important part of the design of the movie. As they are in Japan. And we really needed to be able to show the seasons, and control the seasons.

We needed a city with a river, bridges, tea-houses, okiyas, and homes. We needed a city that could one day be winter and the very next day be spring and the very next day be fall and then summer for a couple days and the next day back to winter. So we needed a place where we could absolutely control everything.

We had twenty-four foot tall cherry trees all along our riverbank and all through the city and we actually made four sets of these matching cherry trees. So we had the spring cherry trees which were all in the beautiful cherry blossoms, we had our summer trees with green leaves, we had our fall trees with the beautiful fall colors, goldens and oranges, and then we had the bare-limbed trees that you'd see in winter. They were all on big bases and they all had crane hooks in them and when we'd get the call-sheet and see what we were shooting the next day, what season it was, we'd make sure at night-time two or three cranes came in to lift these giant trees out and carry them through the set and bring the correct season in.

And then a lot of things that could be man-handled by people were moved around and we re-dressed. They actually changed the type of screens on houses for different seasons in Japan so there are even architectural changes we made constantly throughout. The schedule was never really set up in such a way that you could shoot one season out and move to another. We had to be very flexible and it was really fun.

It was amazing watching the crew's faces when they walked into the set because it was the size of about two football fields and it was all designed in a very maze-like pattern. It was like building an old-fashioned back-lot. We didn't want to have any straight streets where you'd shoot off and need a blue-screen in the end. We made everything very curved and maze-like. Which became again part of the design of the film where you never know what you're really seeing, and things are masks. So when you walked into the set you could actually walk for about five minutes through the various alleyways and streets and never leave a three-hundred-and-sixty degree world.

We had a two hundred-and-fifty foot long river that actually recycled its water so that you could throw cherry blossoms at one end and they would float through and come back around. We could also raise and lower it for the different seasons. Rainy season it was up high, eight feet, and other times it was down to just six inches. So the whole thing was super-flexible.

Dion Beebe, who is an amazing cinematographer, was thrown the challenge of the seasons as well. We were shooting in California in the summer which is constant California summer light, but we needed to do fall and winter, with very flat winter light. So he devised the biggest silk that was ever used in Hollywood. The silk was basically two football fields. You could never make one piece of fabric that big because one piece would just be un-controllable. It's like a ship's sails in a funny way.

So he and his key grip devised a very simple idea where he took that whole field and divided it into twenty-five by two-hundred-fifty foot strips and ran cables between each of them so the silk was actually composed of all these little fingers that could be pulled across individually. So you didn't have to use all of it, you could use part of it. When the winds kicked up, as they did, that made it much more manageable. We lost a couple pieces of silk in the course of the shooting but it really did the trick.

AS: How long did it take to build the village and about how many people did it take?

JM: It physically took sixteen weeks to build and we had about three hundred people working on it. And true to the way movies go you never really have enough time in prep. You really can't just go start building a city without having done a lot of drawing. And we did not get an official green-light on the film until about fourteen weeks before principal photography so I wasn't able to put on a big crew until about fourteen weeks before we started shooting.

At one point we had twenty drafts-people on, just to draw every detail and every building and figure everything out. We came up with an idea that we would start at one end. So we started at the north side and we drew up one building that was going to be on the north side and then we started drawing the second building and the third building. While we were building we were still drawing what was in the middle. When the north side was completely built and when the woodwork was all up and it was

sandblasted and it was stained we started dressing before we even finished drawing the buildings that were all the way to the south. And then they changed the schedule around a little bit and pushed the city up a couple weeks. So we were still busy, busy, busy building and dressing on the first day of photography. And Rob Marshall, the director, changed the schedule a bit to give us a little breathing room with it.

AS: You did interiors there also?

JM: We did a couple of partial interiors. We probably had ten exteriors incorporated within our city that were characters in our film: Mameha's and the okiya and the tea house. For each of those locations we had a cutting-piece room so you could go through a doorway and enter into a room instead of it just being a doorway that would open into a piece of black. And then we repeated that doorway on a soundstage, in our set. All of the major interiors were done back at SONY. We wanted to make it as nice an experience for the actors as we could. Being warm and comfortable and allowing Dion to light was important for us.

AS: I heard you made a little scale model and flew a little camera through...

JM: Yes, I work a lot with models and I find it's a really good way of communicating what we do. We can always show people illustrations but it's only from one view. We look at a blueprint but a lot of times it's hard for people who are not used to blueprints to really understand them. So I never build a set without having built a model first.

We normally start with very, very simple, foam-core models. A long time ago John Boorman taught me a trick and I can't thank him enough. Build a simple, little, foam-core model of what you're proposing. Then get a video camera, these little tiny lipstick cameras, and, while they're not absolutely accurate, you can drop it into the set with a couple of figures and see the view on a monitor. What's also fun with the monitor is you can make mattes to show what the different film formats could be. Because I've actually been on films where they're going, *Well, do we do wide screen or not widescreen?* And if you have the two mattes or the variety of mattes for the different formats, you drop the camera into a set, a little foam-core set and it's really interesting how much you can learn. You can move the camera through and look in all directions.

I always make sure I do it with not just the director but with the DP. The DP can go, *Well, you know what, I'm really gonna need more light through here so we'll put a window there.* Or, *This is a wall I'll need to wild out.* Or look at it and say, *You know what, I can tell from the model I don't need any ceiling panels.*

With the John Boorman film we wanted this feeling that the family was always captured and so we always wanted to have walls on both sides of the frame. Never wanted to have something that felt open. That's why we did this at first. And we literally took the walls of the model and just moved them in or out to get to where we wanted them to be. So I learned to be very sacrilegious with the models!

Rob Marshall, Dion Beebe and I have done four or five films together. We all know we're gonna do it every time–we'll have the X-Acto knives and the extra foam core and white paper and marking pens, and we'll change the shape of the set, we'll make it a little longer, we'll make it narrower, we'll add doorways.

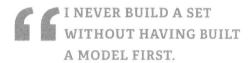

I NEVER BUILD A SET WITHOUT HAVING BUILT A MODEL FIRST.

What's wonderful about it, besides being fun and very creative and helping you think about everything in the movie, is that it also makes the set belong to everybody. So that when the director walks on the set and the cameraman walks on the set and I walk on the set it's all our set. We know exactly what it is. And they've had a chance to think about it. Because also many, many times two days later I might get a call from the cinematographer or the director saying, *You know I've been dreaming about that set and wouldn't it be great if we did this?* And so I'm very big on communication and everyone understanding everything that's going on.

And there's another trick I learned from a director in England, which is also really fun. Usually on movies we'll get an empty soundstage and just with masking tape, we'll tape out the rooms. If you have a house where you're building five rooms that are connected, for example. You bring the director in and let them walk through. And I'd done that probably a dozen times and then this one director, Peter

Hewitt, asked for us to bring in cardboard boxes. And just line the perimeters. And so we did that and it was really interesting because suddenly you were standing in the room. So we got just refrigerator boxes that are six foot tall and we started getting more sophisticated where we'd get different sizes to make window openings and doorways. It's astonishing how helpful that is. Especially when you work with a director like Rob Marshall who is very precise in what he wants to do.

After we look at the model and come up with the basic idea of what it will all be, then we build it out of cardboard boxes where you can, in two seconds, push a wall out three feet if you want to. Or create a window, or move a door. On *Nine* there was one set where we probably spent twenty minutes really locating the doorway down to the inches. And the room down to the inches, because it was a small room that they wanted to shoot as a small room.

AS: In *Memoirs of a Geisha* did you also map out the whole town?

JM: We didn't have the luxury of doing a completely detailed model before we started building the town, because it was such an unusual situation where we had such little prep time. We very quickly, in a very simplistic way, mapped out the buildings and routes and alleyways. We went through those with Dion Beebe, the cinematographer, and Rob Marshall the director. Then we just kept it going and every time we designed a building it went into the model and we kept the model as up-to-date as we possibly could. We kept a really good

dialog with everybody and to be honest it was almost scouted with the model. The model became a much more sophisticated, complex model than I normally do. We ended up doing full-color and getting into more details.

We really specifically wanted to get into really narrow corridors and narrow streets and crooked little passageways and we wanted to be able to see the eaves of the buildings and shops so Dion really, really used the model to help plan shots. And it was fantastic because the model was in the art department but every day there was some department in looking at it–special FX, figuring out where they could be to lay snow in, Dion and visual effects figuring out shots. It was really, really well-used. We did have to laugh because even though it was just a quarter-inch model and even though it was with a little video lipstick camera it was astonishing how accurate it was, in a funny way.

I think there's even a DVD that shows Dion moving the video camera in for a big shot he was planning with a crane which then dissolves into the actual shot he used in the film. Time and time again it just felt like we had already been there. You saw the colors, you saw the buildings, you saw the angles of the street, and you saw the characters in the street, the rickshaws. You knew where the river went and how high the bridges were. And Dion and Rob and I used that model for two months while the town was being built. And when they all showed up at the town, they were familiar with it. They knew they'd walk and there'd be a tea-shop here and a fish store here and a little alleyway here, and Oh, that's the big tree. Look at the great shot from the big tree if you just turn around the corner. And it was all there. It was invaluable and it was really fun.

AS: On *Nine* did I hear that you had a fully-built, alternate set that the dancers would work on?
JM: Rob Marshall is the choreographer as well as the director on all these musicals. Rob and John DeLuca acted as choreographers. And Rob comes from a Broadway background which is very precise, so I've just been trained up by the very best people to do musicals. And he creates the dance and the musical numbers. My favorite thing in the world in movies is to work on musicals because it's pure film and pure design and pure creation.

Normally as a production designer the first thing you do is set up an art department with drawing tables and get in illustrators and computers. The first thing you do with Rob Marshall is set up a dance hall. So you bring in a sprung dance floor, you bring in a hundred-foot wall of mirrors, you start bringing in rehearsal props. I get to be really involved with the creation of the dance working with Rob. He's constantly calling me down and saying, *Well, the proscenium opening that we thought would be thirty feet is actually going to need to be a little wider and I'll show you why,* and he'll have one of the dancers dance. And I'll pull out my tape measure and he says, *That doesn't fit into thirty feet does it?* And I go, *No.* He says, *Okay, how small can we make it?* So it needs to be thirty-five feet, okay.

I get to work with him on the artistic creation of the visual look of the dance and then I get to respond to physically how the dance has been choreographed and laid out. And he will lock in a dance number two months before we shoot it and he'll count on me that everything is not to the inch but to the quarter-inch. Because the dancers he works with are so trained that if they are doing three flips and land on a chair they could do it blind-folded. But that chair better be exactly seventeen inches tall and the top of the chair better be exactly the size it was and the chair needs to be exactly where it was in that dance hall. Sometimes you're dealing with three hundred items that have to be locked in and marked that carefully. On *Chicago* we made it all work on a stage that we had the flexibility of making deeper if we wanted to, or wider if we wanted to, so Rob was really free to create anything he wanted in terms of the dance and we'd respond to it.

What was interesting on *Nine* was that we needed to make each of the musical numbers work on one set that didn't change its basic structure. There were ten or twelve of them so it was very complicated. So we had to work out exactly the size of each of a series of canted platforms and ramps and scaffold structures. The idea was that it was a set under construction, an unfinished set that became the playground for all of the musical numbers. So Rob created the first musical number and we got a sense of how big the various areas needed to be and started drawing that up. And then when he created the second musical number it didn't quite fit so we had to go back and rework the first number and the second number together so that they both fit in the same basic geography. The same thing happened for the third number and the forth number and the fifth number.

> **JUST BEING AROUND DANCERS AND SINGERS IS MAGICAL. IT'S JUST SUCH PURE, CREATIVE FILMMAKING BECAUSE AS YOU'RE CREATING EVERYTHING YOU'RE AROUND HUMAN BEINGS THAT ARE REALLY PHYSICALLY SINGING AND DANCING.**

The basic bones of the set had to be altered continually until we got to a place where we had a stage that we could then, with dressing, change into each of the worlds that we wanted it to be, and at the same time have it still work for each of the dance numbers.

So that ended up being very complex. You can't just show up on a huge, complicated set like that, that has probably twenty different levels based on the floor and our different ramps and scaffold structures and stairwells. It had to be rehearsed in advance. So we had to build a giant rehearsal set that again was exactly to the inch of what the finished set would be.

AS: With all the twenty platforms…

JM: Yes and all the canted platforms and levels and rakes, and staircases and spiral stairs.

AS: You essentially had to build two sets.

JM: We basically built the set twice. Once, out of plywood that didn't look like anything. And that set we would physically alter during the rehearsals because if Rob found out he needed an extra five feet on the side, at night we would go in and extend it five feet. And then once it was established that that was the right thing to have done, we then would go to the real set that we were building simultaneously and extend that. But extend it in a very beautiful way so it looked like this old, Italian set being built.

We had a staircase on *Chicago* that we built as twelve steps and they started rehearsing on it and it was decided it would be better to have it be eleven steps so at lunch time we cut a step off. This was all built out of wood. Then later on that afternoon they went back and said, *No, it probably should be thirteen steps.* So we quickly built two new steps. Once Rob locks it in, it's locked in and I have to take that and turn it into the visuals that tell the story. But all of the physical spaces and planes are defined by the dance. It's so much fun. I mean just being around dancers and singers is magical. It's just such pure, creative filmmaking because as you're creating everything you're around human beings that are really physically singing and dancing.

AS: And they're involved in the creation of the set, unlike the normal process where you build a set and the actors show up…

JM: Well it's kind of the ultimate version of what we talked about with dropping the video camera into the model and laying the set out full-size with cardboard boxes. In *Nine*, the one main set was something that the dancers and choreographers and Dion the cameraman had been working on for six weeks before we started shooting. He actually shot each of the musical numbers on video because once the routines were finalized by Rob Marshall and John DeLuca they would present them to us. The costume designer Colleen Atwood, Dion Beebe, and I would all come in. We'd all been through it in terms of what made sense for each of our departments but they would then present the whole number and they'd run though it a few times. Dion would actually film it on video and do a little rough cut. So even before going in to shoot the number Dion was pretty confident in terms of where he needed to be with the camera, where he needed to be with lights, and I was confident with what I needed to wild out and move.

What's also really fun working on a musical with Rob and John is that when we design a musical number, because they have a Broadway background, we build it all for real. Meaning what you're seeing on camera is all physically happening in real time like it would be in a Broadway show. So if a drape comes up and then a ramp comes out and a staircase drops in from the skies and set pieces come in from the left and the right, from the wings, it's all physically happening in real time. We always have run the number all the way through. So the first time we film it's the entire number run all the way through from beginning to end just as though you were sitting in a Broadway theater watching a Broadway show. And that's really unusual but it's also just been great training. You know the fun thing about being a production designer on movies is that you get to learn all these new things, every show you learn something new. And to have this sort of background in how a Broadway show is run and lit is very exciting and all comes from Rob and John.

> " THE FUN THING ABOUT BEING A PRODUCTION DESIGNER ON MOVIES IS THAT YOU GET TO LEARN ALL THESE NEW THINGS, EVERY SHOW YOU LEARN SOMETHING NEW.

AS: Is Rob Marshall a very visual person?

JM: Extremely visual. So when we sit down in the rehearsal hall we'll just start talking and I'll come in with ideas. He did something which was, I thought, really, really clever. The first feature film he directed was *Chicago* and he cast the crew exactly the same way he cast the cast. With as much effort. So he put together a little team that included Dion Beebe and Colleen Atwood and myself that were all people that had an absolute meeting of the minds with him. We have incredibly similar tastes. And when we come together to talk about something we generally are coming in with the same frame of reference and the same sort of ideas and if not we get excited about something new and we sort of riff off of one another. So it's a really nice, creative team.

AS: Do you ever do any previs with SketchUp or other software using 3D models?

JM: Absolutely. All the new technology is just fantastic. And we do a little of everything. I do still keep with some of the old foam-core models. Because I find that it's something that people have fun with.

I had a really interesting experience. I did the film *Wanted* in the Czech Republic. The director is Timur Bekmambetov and Timur owns a giant visual effects company in Moscow. And he brought his team with him. They were absolutely amazing in that I could do a little floor-plan sketch on a cocktail napkin, like the worst thing you're ever supposed to do, with elevations, take a picture of it with my phone, email it to Moscow, and the next day we'd have a beautiful 3D model you could walk through. It was just brilliant. And that's how he worked. Everything for him was in that 3D world. And we were doing a set and I explained to him that I was going to build a foam-core model of it and get the video camera and put it in and he just looked at me with a smile on his face. Like I was a caveman. And he goes, *Really? You're going to do that?*

And I said, *Let me just do one and see what it's like.* It was an extension onto an existing building so we built the side of the building, and again, the simplest model you could ever imagine. And then we built what we were going to be building onto it. There were going to be some very big, wide-shots that linked into helicopter shots. So I set up the model in the middle of the big central meeting room with the big-screen TV and with the little video camera and the little figures and I actually made cars and all the little action props, and I brought him in and showed it to him. I showed him how the helicopter shot would work. I held the little video camera in my hand and moved it very primitively through doorways and over towers. And he just looked at me again with that smirk on his face like I was just a caveman. So here is the guy who owns the biggest visual effects company in Moscow sitting with this guy from America with his little pieces of foam and his little video camera and we just all laughed because he's such a nice guy.

Well, the next day I walked by the conference room and inside the conference room was Timur Bekmambetov with ten of his people from the visual effects company from Moscow and they were all using the video camera on our foam-core model and loving it! And Timur goes, *John! John, come in! John, this is really good technology! We need to do this on every set! Can we do this on every set?* And I said, *Yes, absolutely!* And so I won them over to the idea because there's something just so tactile about being able to hold the camera and move it just a little inch there. I know it sounds silly but you can even light these things. For some reason, I think because it's physically there and you're physically touching it, it gets everyone around it really involved and aware of it. And absolutely you can do the same thing on a video screen with a 3D model, and we do, but there's something about it, I don't know whether it's just that it's fun or that it's this idea that you're all there together and you feel part of it. You're not having just one guy at the keyboard.

So again we won over Timur who is the most high-tech gentleman in the world and he demanded that we do our foam-core models for every one of the sets and he used them. Production meetings we'd be using them when we had everybody there together: special effects and visual effects, producers and studio people. We're all there with the little cameras looking at the screens and having a great time.

AS: Are you involved with post visual effects at all or are you done when principal photography wraps?

JM: It's all changing now. Production designers are becoming, as we should have been all along, more involved with post. On *Snow and the Seven* what's been worked out is that I'll be very involved with the post. And I think that's important. We're always the ones leading the design and we always work very closely with visual effects and we try to use the same systems that they're using so that they can take our work and just add onto it directly. It's becoming so interconnected now that my hope is that it soon becomes just one department.

AS: How involved are you with the locations department? Do you end up finding locations yourself at all?

JM: I'm very involved with the location scouting because it's all part of my job as well. And some locations are critically important to what we do. I love being able to go out with the location scouts. Generally we'll send location scouts to do a preliminary scout and have them see a lot in a short period of time and then I'll respond to photos and go with them. We don't just go look at what they've seen, if we get excited about something we'll keep moving and finding more. So yeah, I love being able to go out and find locations. In Japan they called it *location hunting* and I loved that so now I call it *location hunting*.

AS: Do you ever do any sketching yourself?

JM: I'll do super rough sketches and then I've got some great guys on this project that then make them beautiful. I'm lucky enough to be working with some wonderful illustrators.

AS: Is your background an art school background? Or did you go to film school?

JM: I'm really sort of a mutt, I've got a little bit of film background, I've got a little bit of schooling, a little film and architecture. I grew up in Seattle, Washington, and I was taking film programs there and studying a little bit of architecture but I was making my living working as an art director for theaters. And I got involved with the Seattle Film Festival. At the Seattle Film Festival they were lovely people and although they weren't able to pay us much money to do the work, to do the programs and the posters, they were really wonderful about letting you meet people that you admired. They were one of the first film festivals that would bring in directors and writers. So if they knew that there was a director that you really wanted to meet they would make sure that you got hooked up. And in the course of two weeks for the first time in my life I'd met real filmmakers. And as I was able to talk to them and have dinner with them, they'd always be very nice and they'd hear that I was interested in film and interested in architecture and in the course of two weeks eight or ten of these real filmmakers said, *Well, why aren't you a production designer for movies?*

And it's embarrassing to say but I never really knew what a production designer did in the movies. I guess I'd seen a thousand movies that had the title production designer/art director listed on them but up in Seattle it just didn't really click what it was. And the moment a real director said to me, *Well, the production designer designs the visual look of the film. The production designer chooses the style of architecture, the color palette, the scale, and uses the visuals to help tell the story,* I was like, *Oh, my God, that's me. That's what I want to do.* I mean, the moment I heard that, I knew that I had to be a production designer.

So like a week after the film festival ended I just packed everything up in Seattle and drove down to Los Angeles and just knocked on doors for three months until I got my first job as a PA in the art department, the lowest level entry position. And then, doing all non-union work I did literally every position in the art department. I was a PA, I drove the prop truck, I was assistant props, I was a prop master, I was an on-set dresser, I've been

a painter, a plasterer, a sculptor, a graphic artist, lead man, set decorator, assistant art director, art director, and eventually production designer. And at one point I started art directing bigger films and production designing smaller films simultaneously. Finally one of those films, *What's Eating Gilbert Grape?* went union and I was able to get into the union and at that point I started to work on bigger films. So I worked for eight years on films that no one in my family had ever heard of. And then finally after *What's Eating Gilbert Grape?* I started working on bigger films that became real movies.

AS: I interviewed production designer John Muto who did *Night of the Comet*...
JM: My first film. I started as his PA. On that film they needed to add on an assistant prop person so it was probably a week or two into shooting when the propmaster Paul Ahrens went to John Muto and said, *Is there any way I could please have John in my department?* And it was a little bit of a promotion to go from PA to the assistant props. But it also involved driving the thirty foot prop truck to work each day!

AS: Do you tend to work with the same crew every time?
JM: I've been lucky over the past three or four years to be able to work with the same team. Which, when you're able to do that, is an absolute joy. Because I've met some really talented people that are really fun to be around and when you know everyone's strengths and weaknesses that's fantastic. I've been very lucky with that. Previously I've

just been thrown into a brand new city or a brand new country where, because of the budget, I need to hire a whole local crew. Which is exciting in its own way. I mean travel is one of the most important things. New experiences and seeing how people make movies differently in different parts of the world is all fantastic. But there is something really lovely when you're able to work with a set decorator that you've worked with before or with an art director you've worked with before. It's terrific.

AS: In *Wanted* was that a whole Eastern European crew?

JM: I was able to bring two or three people over but it was ninety-eight percent a local Czech Republic crew.

AS: And for your upcoming movie you were debating shooting some of it here or in China...

JM: I think one of the reasons Disney brought me on so early and wanted to do a real development of what the visuals of the movie would be so quickly, was the big question they had: *It's set in China, but are we shooting it in China?* I sat down with Francis Lawrence, the director, and we started talking. We both had this ideal that it would be this kind of heightened reality. And it is a fairytale. It's almost a super-hero fairy-tale the way we're approaching it and it seems like everything we're going to need architecturally is so specific and so heightened and so changed in scale that I've a feeling there's probably not a huge amount of architecture that we'd be shooting in China. So the architecture will probably be built on stages.

But I'm sure we'll end up going to China for some of the landscapes which are just amazing. I mean for years and years I've been wanting to go and look at some of these amazing mountain ranges that are in China that I've seen in picture books. So doing the research on it has been fantastic. There are some landscapes that you can only get in China and we'd actually love to go to China to shoot those. So we'll see but that's what part of this whole development process is–we'll look at all angles. The fun thing about this project right now is that we're going at it just visually and creatively. We're first coming up with what we want it to look like and then seeing what's the best way to make that happen.

WE'RE ARE NOT ARCHITECTS, WE'RE VISUAL STORYTELLERS.

AS: Lately with the tax incentives going on in other states it seems that most film production is leaving LA. What are your thoughts about LA losing film production?

JM: It's really sad that Hollywood is losing films. And there are some films, like *Memoirs of a Geisha*, you had to have made in Hollywood. You needed the skilled craftspeople. You needed the metal-workers that are only in Hollywood, the sculptors, the painters, the plasterers, the prop people, the set decorators. When you have a crew of three hundred people in construction you can't train everybody up. And it's here in Hollywood. It's also in London but it's only in a couple places in the world. So it's really tough when I'm hearing that really big, designed films are leaving Hollywood and going to

Detroit or going to Santa Fe or going to Shreveport. It's just really, really tough on everybody. It's tough on the families that live here and people who want to work here and it's tough on the filmmakers that are being asked or told to go to places where you don't have the resources.

Hopefully that will all change. It affects not just filmmakers but it affects the whole economy. If we can find a way of getting some of these tax benefits here in California that seem to be able to happen in so many other states it's not only going to help filmmakers and the families of filmmakers in Hollywood, it's going to make everyone's life in California better. So much money is spent. It makes such a big difference. When we had the writer's strike three or four years ago it was amazing that there were restaurants that closed, there were people that do landscaping that went out of business because just the money that the film community brings in wasn't being spent. So if we can get that money back I have to think that it would be a huge blast to the economy.

AS: Guy Hendrix Dyas mentioned how at one point everyone was talking about moving to Canada for film, but that never ended up happening...
JM: The economy changed. When I did *X-Men* in Canada you took a US dollar and changed it into a Canadian dollar-fifty and the Canadian dollar-fifty bought you three dollars. It was just crazy. So everything for production, I mean hotel rooms, beautiful hotel rooms were a quarter of the cost and we built a lot of scenery for very little money at that

time. I went there a year ago on something and my US dollar bought me ninety-eight cents. The economy has completely changed and it's really hurt Toronto. I think Vancouver's still doing okay because it's so close to LA. The only reason people are taking movies to other areas is to make them for less money. Anything I can do to fight to get films made in LA I will.

AS: What qualities would you say a production designer should have?
JM: I think you just need to be aware of everything and look at everything. Every life experience I've ever had has influenced my work. Even just us talking together, having this interview, maybe I'll use something of this in my job at some point. And I just feel I'm the luckiest person in the world. Because this is what I've always wanted to do. When I was a kid I didn't know if I wanted to be an architect or I wanted to be a director and now I found a way that I can be both. Because I get to design the visuals, the architecture, and tell stories with it the way a director tells stories with the actors. Being creative, being open, being excited about what you do, I think those are all great qualities.

AS: Do you look for those same qualities in the crew that you hire?
JM: I would rather get a young person who's full of enthusiasm and full of new ideas than someone who's done the thirty biggest movies in the world and is just sort of tired to come into work anymore. I mean I think enthusiasm really means a lot. What we do is hard work. We work really long hours. We

work six or seven days a week. We work fourteen hours a day and it's important to keep the enthusiasm and the fun and realize that we're doing something very special and we're lucky to be doing it.

AS: Say someone was starting out in this business, how would you advise them to avoid pitfalls?

JM: I had a philosophy and I can only say what worked for me and I don't know if it would work for anyone else. I just took any job I could possibly get to get in the art department. I knew I wanted to be a production designer but I didn't wait until somebody offered me a job to be a production designer because to be honest with you, I'd be working at McDonald's now. I fought for a job as an art department PA and if I was asked to be there at six in the morning I was there at five-thirty in the morning. And if I heard that they needed someone to come in even earlier to get coffee my hand was the first to go up. And I just tried to make myself invaluable and just tried to take any job I could get in the art department because you learn so much. I remember that on my first week on *Night of the Comet* I felt I had learned more than I learned in two years at film school. You learn being around on a set and seeing how things are done, how movies are shot, how the business end works as well as the creative end. You meet people and a lot of it is meeting people.

As a production designer I make sure I'm really nice to all the PA's because that PA over there could be the producer of my next movie! It just happens that way. When I was an art director and Steve McEveety was a first AD, he said to me, *I'm going to be a producer and the first movie I produce you're going to be the production designer.* And lo and behold, four years later I got a call from Steve McEveety saying, *I'm producing my first movie, you're the production designer.* Steve McEveety, who went on to be a big producer with Icon and did *Braveheart* and these fantastic movies.

> " **I FEEL THAT I'M THE LUCKIEST GUY IN THE WORLD TO DO THIS AND I'M ALWAYS HAPPY WHEN I COME INTO WORK EVERY DAY. NOTHING WORSE THAN WALKING ONTO A SET AND HEARING PEOPLE COMPLAIN ABOUT SOMETHING. AND YOU GO, WELL, GOODNESS GRACIOUS, WE'RE WORKING ON A MOVIE! ISN'T THAT FANTASTIC?**

So just keep enthusiastic. And for me it was just the working, taking the jobs. I designed a lot of really low budget movies. I designed movies where the art department budget was fifteen thousand dollars, but it was a chance to design. And it was a chance be treated as a designer and interact with other departments as the department head. And I know that some people have rejected that route because they want to do more serious, substantial films but for me getting the experience was really important.

AS: Do you feel that production design should be visible or invisible?

JM: I don't think you'd ever want to feel like you're being hit in the face with any element of the movie. You try to make it a very cohesive whole. For me it's about story-telling. We're not architects, we're visual storytellers. And when I read the script for the first time I see the movie in my mind. What can you do to help define the characters? I often try thinking of it like it's a silent movie. And if you don't have any dialog how do you tell the story? It's gonna be the visual setting you see. It's gonna be the lens, how wide are you, how tight are you? The lighting, the clothes, the architecture, the set-dressing, the colors. That's how we look at it.

AS: How do you feel about the future of production design? You were saying earlier about how sometimes you'll build ten feet of the set and the rest of it will be visual effects. Do you see that happening more?

JM: Completely. That's absolutely the future and it's really exciting. And the fact is, there have been some amazing movies made that have been virtually all against blue-screen. But there's still somebody designing all that. There will always be production designers. And now we have these amazing new tools that can extend sets in the ways that we never have before. It's fantastic but it's still the same job.

AS: Any final words?

JM: I feel that I'm the luckiest guy in the world to do this and I'm always happy when I come to work every day. Nothing worse than walking onto a set and hearing people complain about something. And you go, *Well, goodness gracious, we're working on a movie! Isn't that fantastic?*

Mark Friedberg

Mark Friedberg's beautifully gritty design was the dark soul of Todd Phillip's *Joker* movie. The film is an unconventional, uncompromising blockbuster that easily surpassed one billion dollars in the box office. Not all of Mark Friedberg's movies have made over one billion dollars, however. His heart's in the indie world and he's designed a long list of indie classics from Wes Anderson's *The Life Aquatic with Steve Zissou* and *The Darjeeling Limited* to the more recent *Selma* and *If Beale Street Could Talk*. And for Darren Aronofsky he created the giant biblical ark seen in the big budget epic *Noah*. Below is some deep insight into this design genius' process.

AS: How do you go about creating the specific universe of a movie like *Joker*?

MF: The way I design is I want to understand the world before I make it. I'm not making a world and then trying to understand it. I'm not making sets and hoping they go together. I like to work from concept. There was this sense of the city being an oppressive force bearing down on Arthur [Fleck, the Joker] that was in the script.

But there were also strong references to *Taxi Driver* and that era of filmmaking and to living in New York City at that time. It took a while with Todd [Phillips, director] and I driving around to figure out what our Gotham was, what was Arthur's Gotham really. Everything in the visual world of the story advances the plot but also cues us emotionally, in the way the score helps us understand what to feel and the costumes help us better understand the character.

AS: Production designer Bo Welch talks about "cracking the code" of a movie. Is that what you're talking about?

MF: My process is about balancing the two lobes of my brain. The logical and the emotional. I'm a painter in my heart. But when I start a painting and say, *I want it to be like this*, it's never good. And when I just throw paint around a room it's never good. The trick is to find that Buddhist moment where you're leading the brush and the brush is leading you. I'm building a world and it might be set in a period and require visual effects to support it, but I'm also telling a story which is usually more about emotional logic than historical veracity. I usually start on the literal side and start making lists, both in words and images. Then once I have a strong structure I let myself go and find the character, both in the world and the world from their point of view.

AS: When you first get a script is it a matter of coming up with that structure?

MF: I used to be very scientific about it because I didn't want to get it wrong. Partly because I didn't know that I knew how to do it, because I hadn't done it for very long and didn't completely trust myself yet. It's funny, the older I get and the more experienced I get, the more I've learned not to rely as much on process and to simply trust my instincts. I remember there being a point when they asked what I thought it should look like and I real-ized that the only wrong answer was not to trust what I instinctually thought. They hired me because they wanted it to look like how I felt it should look and that was the right answer. It wasn't about getting it wrong or right, it was about, *What do you think? How do you feel?*

When I was younger and prepared for interviews I used to just want to get the job, so I'd try to make sure I got what I thought they'd want. And now I'm like, *This is me. This is how I see it.* If that is not what they wanted, great, glad we found out early. There will be another job.

AS: When does the process start?

MF: The first reading of the script, which is usually before I've met the director, is the most critical. That's the tabula rasa, the blank slate. Usually I'm seeing the movie as I read it so the first time I see/read it is my purest interpretation and often the most interesting. I've learned how vital that part of the process is and to trust what I feel first.

AS: Are you taking notes as you go through it?

MF: No. I used to take notes and now I don't do it. I read it and I try to see it because I don't want to get in the way of the primal experience of the story, much like a viewer. I want to see what I see. The first reading I just try to read it. I might read it with a Hi-Liter and jab at a few set names as I go but I don't want to stop. And I try to read it all the way through. Then I go back for a second reading, sometimes right away, and then I start hitting the keys on the computer.

AS: And start making notes...

MF: Visual notes.

AS: And breaking it down?

MF: Not breaking it down. Visual notes. I try to re-write the words and create a script of images that tell the story of what I saw. Usually I pull photos and art, rarely do I use movie references. I usually don't like to reference movies with movies. Although in this case the *Taxi Driver* reference is built into the script.

AS: *Taxi Driver, King of Comedy...*

MF: Yes, Todd and Scott [Silver's] script directly referenced those films. So does casting De Niro in the Jerry Lewis role. But the real reference for Gotham was my childhood in New York City at exactly this time.

AS: So you read the script, make some notes, then you meet with the director...

MF: I read the script and I try to write the story again in pictures. The quick pass. *Boom, boom, boom*–that's what I saw. And bring what I saw to the interview.

AS: Pictures you collect from various sources...

MF: What's in my brain is pictures. I live in pictures.

AS: Are you sketching anything yourself or are you just finding pictures at this point?

MF: For the meeting with the director I'm not drawing the sets yet. Sometimes I pull out a pencil in the meeting if it helps to illustrate a point. Once we get going we start to do a lot of concept art. But in that first conversation I'm looking for the tonal. Spacial and tonal. And cultural. I'm an American History major. And in a story like this, cultural history is completely relevant. In most stories it's relevant. What's the culture of the world you're making? To me the culture and the way the world looks go together. And it's more interesting if it's a visual world built on ideas and considerations rather than just, *what does it look like?* In this case the culture was dissonance. The social fabric was torn. Cops are corrupt. Subways don't work. Rich are getting richer and being horrible. There's a meanness in the world.

> **THE TRICK IS TO FIND THAT BUDDHIST MOMENT WHERE YOU'RE LEADING THE BRUSH AND THE BRUSH IS LEADING YOU.**

AS: Trash is out on the street.

MF: Social services aren't working. Garbage as a metaphor and as a reality. It happened. If you look at pictures from the 70's they look worse than my sets. And my sets were pretty bad. So that's a visual thing but it's also culture. It's part of that world and in this case it's also story. And Arthur says it, *Is it just me or is it getting crazier out there?*

AS: That's another reason this movie resonates in our current political climate.

MF: The protesters in Beirut are wearing Joker masks! Certainly in this country there's a meanness, whether it's the polarized politics or how we're not civil with each other. Or how the wealthy are taking everything and the dream is dying.

> " THE WAY THE MOVIE LOOKED AND THE WAY ARTHUR ACTED ARE THE SAME THING. ONE IS A MANIFESTATION OF THE OTHER.

AS: How do you feel about comic book movies in general?

MF: I don't disparage them but I don't go see comic book movies. That's not my interest. I didn't even want to read the scripts. In fact, I didn't want to read *Joker* when it was first sent.

AS: I remember you production designed *The Amazing Spider-Man 2*...

MF: It's not me. Three hundred million dollars for that movie. What I spent just in my budget I could have made three *Selmas*. I want to make the kind of movies I want to see. I'm more of an indie person. I love movies that generally don't come out of studios. The movies that come out of people scraping it together, figuring it out, often that come from other countries. The cool thing about *Joker* is that it was an independent film that just happened to be financed by a non-independent studio. In the beginning they were even worried, *Is Joaquin the right guy for this?* They wanted somebody even more famous. It's a business. They're laying out fifty, sixty million bucks–they want it back. On the other hand Todd Phillips has made them a lot of money. And

I guess they trust him. Enough to give this a shot. It seems to have worked out pretty well for them.

AS: How involved was Todd Phillips with the production design?

MF: Very. I sat with him at the interview and I said two things. I said, *It should look like you, a camera person and the actor tumbled out of the van and started shooting. It shouldn't be dutched angles, noirish comic angles. The stakes are real and so should the visuals be.* I wanted to go far away from the comic version of this story. And he's like, *I'm already there.* And then I said, *If you go halfway it won't make it. You gotta go for it and risk ruining your career to maybe do something brilliant. It's a great script and you have a great actor and a great point of view and if you're uncompromising and resist the urge to make it pretty, it'll be stronger.* It wasn't like I had to convince him of that. It was more like he had to convince me that he was there. And he was.

AS: How does working with him compare to working with Wes Anderson on *The Life Aquatic* and *The Darjeeling Limited*?

MF: Wes' movies are stylized. Wes' storytelling is stylized. There is very little that they have in common as storytellers.

The director is the conductor. He's Leonard Bernstein. He stands in front of the whole orchestra. The orchestra is made up of sections–the strings, the winds, the percussion. A movie is similarly orchestral. The director conducts, the sections are the various departments: camera department, art department, lighting, costume, sound and music departments. The best movies, in my opinion, are when the director has everyone playing in the same key, in harmony. In the director's control we are synthesized into this story's telling and hopefully it all works together to propel our character through the plot and on the arc of their journey. Each harmony makes each department work better. It's phenomenal how much better my sets look once the music gets put in.

AS: Everyone talks about how Wes is so specific about details, like the colors of props for example.

MF: Todd's a little bit like that. Todd was pretty involved. I'm a communicator. I want to be on the same page with the director. I'm going to work four months on a set that he's going to see the first time the day he shoots it, a lot of times. I want to make sure he knows what he's getting. If he gets there and it's not what he thought he was getting, those are very unpleasant mornings.

AS: Are you constantly sending him pictures?

MF: Always sending him pictures. Starting with locations, then with drawings of locations, then the concept art, then photos of the set dressing, then with the palette, then as it's being built. And Todd, while directing a movie, responded to every email within a minute. The way the movie looked mattered to him. Not just because that's his instinct as a director but because the way the movie looked and the way Arthur acted are the same thing. One is a manifestation of the other.

AS: Would you say that the city was a reflection of Arthur's character?

MF: I don't know about a reflection. Maybe an extension. Or an influence. Is Arthur the way he is because of the city or is the city the way it is because of Arthur? It's arguable that none of it ever happened. That the whole thing is in Arthur's mind. That he's in a cell somewhere and this is something he dreamed up. Either way in this story the city is Arthur. It even erupts like he does at the end.

WHAT'S IN MY BRAIN IS PICTURES. I LIVE IN PICTURES.

What's real, what's not, what's funny, what's tragedy, what's awful, what's beautiful? People keep telling me, *Mark, your work is so beautiful in this movie.* All I can think about is the ten trucks of garbage I had everyday. And looking for the worst of the worst of what's left in the city–so beautiful.

AS: After scouting and research do you end up with a giant wall of pictures?

MF: We always have a wall. It helps our department to see all the research and how we want it to go together. It helps other departments all get on the same page. I particularly like that it allows us to see it all together in one look. But it's not the only way the research and concepts are used.

This is the way I work: that document I make when I first read the script evolves and evolves and evolves. It starts with scans or photos that I have of things that are in my computer–a painting, a poem, whatever it is that inspired me. I translate the script into my visual language. Then let's say I get hired. I start to work on the story with specific references. It could look like this and this could be his room. It could be this tone and this could be the kind of photography and this could be the palette for each scene. I map out in a visually poetic way what it could look like. And we go to work. And we start to pick locations. I put my references and the locations into the document. Then if you shuffle those two piles of cards you'll start to get the sense of what the sets in those locations might look like. Then we draw our concepts right onto the location pictures that we liked. We keep refining that document. The location pictures become drawings, become concepts of the sets. The set dressing gets picked and approved and that gets into that document. The costumes start getting designed and approved. Then the DP gets hired and starts taking pictures, showing how they might see the sets and that gets into my document. My document becomes a synthesized previs of how the visual components of the film would go together to rewrite the story. A version of the harmony we are striving for. What I started with, my first impression in that document, is now a pretty detailed book version of what the movie can be, wants to be.

AS: And this is all with a team–you have people doing research, you have people doing set design?

MF: We have a room full of designers. I always have a researcher. We have concept artists. It depends on the scale of the movie what size art department you get. On *If Beale Street Could Talk* it was me and two people. But there were much fewer sets. On *Joker* we had a lot of people going.

AS: Do you ever do your own sketches or you leave it to the set designer?

MF: You can't do this work without being able to work a pencil. Or now an iPad. First, on location photos, I use my iPad and Apple pencil and then Hugh Sicotte, the concept artist I work most closely with, spends days refining these sketches into detailed concepts. Sometimes I get jealous because I don't have time to spend days on a drawing. I sketch, Hugh renders. He did so much on this film, including the first image of what Joker looked like.

AS: Do you build scale models?

MF: We build physical models, digital models and sometimes full-scale sections of sets. I want to be very clear on what I'm proposing so all departments understand and can plan accordingly. If I just drew this room for you in plan it would not necessarily convey what this room means. So it's my challenge to communicate that.

AS: How do you use the design book you create?

MF: Right before shooting I publish that book. For Joker it was like four hundred pages. Like a phone book. A beast of a book, 11" x 17", a giant spiral-bound thing which I could barely lift with my bad back. The whole movie under my arm. Usually we take it on the tech scout, the first time we are all together as a production team. *We've been prepping* *and this is the result of our prep.* As we shoot I then put the pictures of the finished sets into the book and at the end of the job I have another book–the "what we made" book. I gave Todd that book on the last day of shooting. The pictures of the thing we made. Which was similar to what we said we were going to do but also kind of different. That's the best part. How the rock solid plans evolve into something else, the movie, the magic.

AS: On *Joker*, how many sets did you end up building?

MF: We built the apartment, the two-hundred foot long hallway, the elevator, the stairways, the hospital room, Arkham hallway, Murray Franklin. For Murray Franklin we had to build a stage to put the set in because the show audience is in the soundstage. We wanted it to look like they were in an older soundstage so we built the period stage around the set. It was like a Russian nesting doll. We also built the Murray Franklin hallways and the dressing rooms. Some of that got cut but the dressing room connects–it was a whole world. We built the fancy bathroom with Thomas Wayne. That was also a much bigger scene at one point. We built the bathroom where Arthur does that crazy cello dance after he shoots the Wallstreet guys. We did the subway car on the stage. There was a significant amount of stage work. The trick was for the viewer never to know what I made and what we found.

AS: For the subway car did you use a kinetic backdrop?

MF: Yes, for the subway scene with the Wallstreet guys we used massive VR walls.

AS: Big screens?

MF: They are giant stadium monitors made up of panels so they can be any size. They are now programmable and modular, you build them with video tiles. We had a subway car set in the middle of a stage with giant walls on each side that both give you something to look at, but also create interactive light. That's the most important part. What in most of the movies I worked on until the last ten years was called poor man's process–mostly spinning lights to give the impression of movement. Now we are in a brave new world.

AS: How big exactly were those VR screens?

MF: For the subway car they were twenty-five feet tall by like one hundred feet long. It would be a sports fan's happiest day to get that TV!

AS: In contrast to *Joker*, what is your process when you're building sets for a movie like *Noah*...

MF: In that case the instructions are in the Bible. Literally, the dimensions are described in cubits (the distance from the elbow to the finger). Darren [Aronofsky] is a great director with great instincts. Most good directors don't start by saying, *I don't know, what do you think?* Especially if they are a writer/director. In that case Darren had a clear vision. His first comments were, *It ain't a boat. Whatever it is, it ain't a boat. It floats but it's not being sailed.* And I agreed. Why do we always depict Noah's Ark like a boat? Where were they navigating to? There's no land! Where the hell are they going? It's a raft. It's a box. It's a storage container. And that's what the Bible describes. It's x' high, x' wide, x' long. Three decks. It's all right in there. But the Bible doesn't say anything about how there's a little house on top and there's a keel. That's just us interpreting. And that's all assuming that it happened. The Bible's also a story that we sometimes get a little confused about, whether it's science or whether it's myth.

AS: Besides the Bible, what else were you looking at for inspiration?
MF: My heart is as an artist and with that movie I went to Anselm Kiefer. He can make beauty out of road tar.

AS: I can see that! You have all the black pitch on the wood outside the ark just like Anselm Kiefer's paintings.
MF: The thing that is similar to *Joker* was this ugly and beautiful continuum. A box made of cut logs and tar–how beautiful can that be? But it was kind of cool. Noah was a real conceptual movie that was leaning into the mythology, whereas Joker was moving away from myth. Almost deconstructing myth into our own personal experience. Myth is there to make sense of things we can't understand. But we all know what's going on in the Joker's world. It's kind of rough out there. But do we know if there's a God or not? My big fight with Darren was that I didn't think God should be in the movie. There is a moment where Russell [Crowe, who played Noah] asks Him something and God turns the rain off. I

was so mad. I wanted to leave the question open. I think Darren would tell you that there's nothing we put in that movie that's not in the liturgy, the Bible. Everything he did came from somewhere. Even the Watchers, the giants. Although it didn't say how they looked.

AS: People always say that a set is like a character in a movie, like for example, the Ark is a character. Do you ever feel that? And how do you feel about production design in general being invisible versus visible?
MF: I don't have a rule about that stuff. You could say that of anything, "That's a character in the story". I don't know what that means. In the case of *Joker*, our Gotham is either an extension of Arthur–something that literally came out of him, or it is the thing that is bearing down on him and causing him on some level to act the way he acts. Being hit and beaten up and running through the streets and almost being hit by cabs. Lying there panting in the muck and the mire he's breathing it. He's tasting the city.

AS: In contrast to *Joker*, your work on Far From Heaven with Todd Haynes was highly stylized.
MF: It was meant to be. Todd Haynes is a very conceptual director. He's one of my dear friends. We wanted to design it as if Douglas Sirk made that movie. Which means that to be a proper melodrama that movie was meant to look like it was shot here in Brentwood, trying to be Connecticut. It's a story about artifice. About the difference between what we see and what is true. The melodrama

heightens feelings until they end up hiding the real feelings. You have to get under the stylized skin to find that. You have to look inside yourself.

AS: How involved are you with visual effects?

MF: Very. I'm designing the movie. The way it looks is my responsibility. In the old days before we knew what visual effects were or could be, you'd hand the movie off and some other concept artist somewhere would do it. But it's gotta all work. In the case of *Joker* the visual effects were in the set design. It's just about how much I build and how much Edwin [Rivera, VFX Supervisor] builds. Most of them were extensions. It's just adding more city or making it more period. So we design the entire world and then divide up what is built practically and what is virtual.

AS: Adding more seedy theaters...

MF: I built a lot of the porn theater marquees. Most of Gotham Square was practical below twenty feet, thirty feet. Very proud of my porn theaters.

AS: And you shot Gotham Square in Newark?

MF: We were having a hard time finding Gotham Square. Because in the beginning Todd was saying it doesn't have to be Times Square. I said, *Yeah it does!* And then every time we showed him something he said, *Yeah, but it doesn't look like Times Square!*

Wait, but you said it doesn't have to be Times Square! He'd say, *Yeah, it doesn't have to be exactly Times Square!* But there's nothing really like it left. Not

in the Northeast. Not in this country. I grew up on the border of Harlem as a kid and I wasn't nervous about going up there but I was terrified about going to Times Square. Seedy fucking shit.

> **WHAT'S THE CULTURE OF THE WORLD YOU'RE MAKING? TO ME THE CULTURE AND THE WAY THE WORLD LOOKS GO TOGETHER.**

And finally I looked at the producers and said, *I know where it is!* And they're like, *Where?* Jersey. For the last ten years [Chris] Christie was the governor of New Jersey and we weren't allowed to film there because he got rid of the tax incentive. I'm in Georgia right now, my home away from home, because that's where the economics of cinema happens. Thirty percent of fifty million dollars is a lot of money. But just as I'm starting to say that Jersey is where Gotham Square is, the new governor of New Jersey, Phil Murphy, put the tax incentive back in and we got it!

AS: How did you first get into production design? Did you study the arts in college?

MF: I did. I went to Brown University where I was a contemporary American history major and a sculpture major. My thesis was Martin Luther King and Viet Nam. While I was at Brown my mom died. She was sick with cancer. She was forty. Up to that point I figured I'm young, I'm a nice Jewish boy, an American History major. I'll get some dumb job and then by the time I'm forty I'll switch over and be the artist I really want to be. But she got sick and it inspired me to say, *You know, maybe I'm going to reverse that. I'm going to try to be more of what I want to be now.* My mom had given everything to be a mom and was just starting to do the things she wanted to do. I'm not waiting. I always in my heart of hearts wanted to be an artist and I thought I'd give it a shot after that. Making art also helped me process a lot of confusion and grief. Still does.

AS: This is when you were at Brown?
MF: At Brown and Rhode Island School of Design. When you go to one of the schools you can study at the other. I spent a lot of my time at RISD.

AS: Did you start studying painting?
MF: At RISD I was mostly doing photo and at Brown I ended up being a studio arts sculpture major as well as an American history major, a dual major. But my dad's a landscape architect and I worked for him forever. In fact, that's why I didn't want to be an architect. Because that wasn't for me. The technical design part of design is less interesting to me. The storytelling part, the visual storytelling part, the art part of it is what I love. Totally different worlds. I'm in the process of redoing my own house and I'm terrible at it. No story.

After Brown I spent years aimlessly living in the back of my pickup truck trying to be a beat poet. Any time someone would call me I'd drive to California and then drive back. It didn't make me wealthy but I had very little overhead. Getting that lost was the way I found myself in this work. If I hadn't done that I never would have even known that this world existed. Driving aimlessly is still a big part of how I find the movie now. So yeah my first year out of school was about getting lost.

AS: Just roving around or doing something related to the industry?
MF: Manual labor. Striving. I guess it was a gap year from life. But it was also what people did once, before everything became corporate and before Americans forgot how to read. I wanted to be a beat poet, I just wasn't a good poet! My model was those guys who'd say, *Let's drive to Denver!* and off they'd go. But I landed in Cape Cod and ended up working for Ralph Nader. Canvassing door to door, then being promoted to campaign manager. A lot of it was learning about leadership. Mostly trying to keep people from quitting! And figuring out ways to inspire them.

In the middle of all that I have lunch with a friend in New York who's working in the production office of Woody Allen. And in the middle of lunch she gets a phone call and she just starts shaking and crying and you hear the yelling voice on the other line. The costume designer Jeffrey Kurland's driver quit and he's upset. He needs someone and she's like, *Would you do it, would you drive him?* She's like, *Just go do it today and I'll find someone for tomorrow.* So I take the minivan and go pick the guy up on 63rd Street and 3rd Avenue where he lived and drove him to 63rd Street and Lexington Avenue where Bloomingdales was. And then sat in the car all day. And then drove him home. He's like, *So you want the job?* And I'm like, *No!*

And he said, *What do you mean you don't want the job? It's a movie job!* And my excuse was, *I can't leave my dog home all day!* And he said, bring the dog! *Really? I get the car and I can bring my dog?* Pay? *Three hundred dollars a week!* I became a PA.

And shortly after that, sitting in a car on a movie called *New York Stories* there was some emergency, something needed to be made. This happens in the movie business. Everybody was flipping out–they needed to make some masks for a scene with Julie Kavner. All of a sudden the dial pointed to me. They're like, *Kid! Aren't you an artist?* And I'm like, *I am...*

Well, would you make these masks? And I'm like, *If you let me out of the car I'll make masks!* So I went and made the masks. I made something that got in a movie and I was like, *Whoa!* That was cool. And some friends of mine went off to make a low-budget indie film called *A Matter of Degrees* and I went up to help, as the most experienced crew member on the team because I had made a mask. And I became the designer of a million dollar movie.

When I came back to New York I went to Woody's designer Santo Loquasto and said, *I want to do this. I think I can do it. I have the skills. Can I work for you?* And he said, *Nope.*

I said, *What do you mean?* He said, *You know how to do it.*

I said, *No, I don't know how to do it! I just did it once!*

And he said, *Yeah, you're a designer now.* And he helped me. I grew kind of like a single cell amoeba, then my cells divided...

> ❝ **THE THING I'M MOST PROUD OF IN MY CAREER IS NOT THE MOVIES NECESSARILY BUT THE HUMANS THAT I'VE WORKED WITH.**

AS: You found another feature to design?
MF: Little this' and that's. I did a pilot. I did a short with Joaquin [Phoenix] when he was ten years old. He doesn't even remember it. Some vanity project for someone else. Then I did *In the Soup.* That was a four hundred thousand dollar movie but it won the Sundance Audience prize with Seymour Cassel and Steve Buscemi. It was a good film. And all of a sudden I'd made a movie now that a few people saw. And then I got going and grew up in the indie thing that was happening "in New York in the 90's.

AS: Nowadays does your agent get you your jobs?
MF: My agent is my dear friend, Ann Murtha. She has been one of my great collaborators and sources of support in my life so I have nothing disparaging to say about her. At all. She's the most awesome and if it wasn't for her I don't think I'd still be doing this because sometimes you just keep banging your head against the wall.

But it's not like anyone calls an agent, *Who do you think should be in this movie?* A casting director does that. If it comes from an agent usually it's somebody calling for a designer more senior than me or more famous than me. If they're not available why not try out this guy?

In my case I was in the streets in New York and it's a small community there. I stumbled from place to place. The guys at Good Machine were doing some of the small stuff. And then they said, *Maybe you can meet Ang Lee.* Ang wasn't as famous when we started *The Ice Storm.* He became really famous in prep because *Sense and Sensibility* came out. He'd done a couple of Chinese language movies in New York and that was it.

AS: What was Ang like to work with?

MF: Ang's my dear friend. I started *Gemini Man* with him. But ended up having back surgery and having to leave the film. I did *Billy Lynn* with him recently. And we did two movies a long time ago. He went to film school with my wife. Ang Lee is a terrific man. He is not as particular about every detail of the set compared to Todd. He's a little more bigger picture. Right now he happens to be obsessed with technology. And he's very particular about that. But doing *The Ice Storm* with him was a turning point with me. Both as a designer and as a career it was a notch up from the little indie things I was doing. *The Ice Storm* was the first period movie I didn't have to research. It's about a thirteen-year-old in 1976, which I was one. And I put some of my Dad's furniture in Sigourney's house!

We did *Ice Storm* together then we did *Ride with the Devil* together. And then Ang went on to start *The Hulk* and I was like, *Great, now I'm going to become a Hollywood designer! Isn't that what's next?* And I didn't get to go. I was crushed. Rick Heinrichs got to do it. Because he knew how to do those movies and I didn't. Computers and effects and all that was just starting. Nobody knew what they were and I'm just some upstart kid. And I was crushed!

Except Todd Haynes called me. Todd and I had gone to college together. I had sculpture class with Todd at Brown. He had such an advanced idea of what art could be even then. He didn't hire me on some of his really indie, out-there stuff early on. I wasn't wild enough for him but I was too artsy for everyone else! But we did come together on *Far From Heaven.* That was the sea-change moment for me when I realized I didn't want to be only a Hollywood designer. Nothing against Hollywood. But it was the moment I realized I wanted to make the kind of movies I wanted to see. And my taste is more indie. Strange, challenging dramas.

Industry friends then suggest that I go do this superhero movie. *Go do* SpiderMan! *You'll make more money next time! Go do* The Amazing Spider-Man 2, *you'll get more famous!* It's against my instincts but it's in New York. *Okay I'll do it.* And Marc [Webb] was lovely to work with as a director. I have nothing bad to say about anybody that was part of that movie. But it just wasn't right for me. And then I reverted to being myself and went back to doing films like *Beale Street* and *Selma,* the movies that mattered to me.

AS: What do you like about the job of production design?

MF: The collaboration is the part I love. The thing that is the opposite of being a painter is that as a painter I sit in a room arbitrarily experiencing my bad childhood over and over again. There's no other point of reference but me. And no particular challenge except to keep going. But when you step into campaign mode in cinema it feels a lot of times like it's life or death. It's terrifying. You know if your set's one minute late you're done. And if it's not awesome you're done. It's got to be awesome, and on time and cheap and brilliant. It's terrifying! So you join forces with a team and that's the coolest part. The working together part. The fact is that the efforts of two people who work apart from one another is much less than the efforts of two people who join forces. In the collaboration world one plus one can equal four.

AS: When you're hiring your crew what do you look for?

MF: It depends. If I'm in New York I know who I'm hiring. The people I worked with on Joker I've been working with twenty years. There's a loyalty and an artistry and a trust and an economy and a kindness. They're my family. I spend more time with them than anybody else. But because I started as an untrained, inexperienced young guy and the youngest guy on my crews for the longest time, I hired old guys, or girls, to help me. As the movies got bigger I hired older crew to make sure that I was covered, to make sure that the stuff I didn't know, somebody knew. And I found that I kept making the same movie that everyone else was making. That a lot of people who do this and do this and do this, certainly in art departments, reference other movies. Not so much the world that inspires the movies. And little by little I started relying more on the PA's and the young people for inspiration. And trusting my instincts about them.

> **CINEMA MEANT SOMETHING THAT YOU COULD ONLY EXPERIENCE COMMUNALLY AND SOMETHING THAT MADE YOU THINK AND FEEL AND TALK. YES, FOR SURE IT WAS MEANT TO BE COMMERCIAL BUT IT WAS NOT *ONLY* MEANT TO BE COMMERCIAL. IT WAS MEANT TO BE IMPORTANT.**

Over time I've brought some of them up, like Alex DiGerlando, a great designer now doing important work for a lot of great directors. He was the PA on *Far From Heaven* and now he just did Jim Jarmusch's last movie, *Dead Don't Die.* He did *The OA*, he did *Fosse/Verdon*, he did the last *Oceans* movie. I just knew he was smart. He wasn't the draftsman guy, he hadn't worked on every movie that had ever been shot in New York, he was just a smart young kid. As I became one of the old guys my point of reference started shifting to the young people who knew what was going on in the world and brought that energy in, and who were a little more visceral. I think that the thing I'm most proud of in my career is not the movies necessarily but the humans that I've worked with.

AS: The people you've brought together?

MF: And the young people that I've been able to help the way that Santo Loquasto opened the door open enough for me to get through it. If he hadn't done that I don't know what I'd be doing. Driving a cab? That's all it took. I have a rule that if anybody asks I'll meet with them. Any young person who wants to discuss their career. I'll do that. Because it's terrifying. And nobody will help anybody. It's so competitive. That's the part I'm most excited about, young talent.

AS: How different is working on a series from working on movies?

MF: Well, I've done *Mildred Pierce* and this one, Barry Jenkins' *Underground Railroad*. *Mildred Pierce* was just like working on a movie. This one is like you're working on a movie but you're working twice as fast every day. You're covering a lot more territory. More pages each day and for longer. So you're working twice as fast for twice as long. So it's pretty intense. It's a lot of story to tell. It's like making three features at the same time. And we're not like, *Oh, because it's TV we'll do it less quality.* That's not the Barry Jenkins way and not the way with this material. We're making it as if it's an extraordinary feature.

Technically it's not that different. But six one hours is a very interesting format. Feature cinema is essentially a short story. It doesn't have the ability in the way that a novel does to divert course. To jump off plot line. To be in a chapter setting. What I'm not that interested in personally is open-ended

story-telling. *We'll keep making this series as long as you keep watching it. We'll just keep trying to think up another plot so you'll keep watching.* I don't mean to disparage it. It's just not what I want to do. As a designer I want to be able to know what the end is, to help me understand what the beginning is. They relate–it's an arc, it's a journey. It goes from here to there and therefore the transitions or the comparisons, those things all matter. They are all vital to the telling of the story.

I was hesitant about the limited series thing just because I'm a movie snob. But also because I'm a child of the 70's and cinema meant something to us. TV meant *F Troop* and the cinema meant something that you could only experience communally and something that made you think and feel and talk. Yes, for sure it was meant to be commercial but it was not *only* meant to be commercial. It was meant to be important. And I'm defined by the movies that I saw as a young person in that time. This new world is something that I'm adjusting to. My kids think I'm out of my mind. They don't distinguish one hour, two hours, ten seasons. And they'll also sit down and watch ten seasons of something over two days.

AS: What direction do you see the field of production design going in? There's virtual reality now where you can be inside the experience...

MF: I can't do it because I can't get the damn things over my glasses!

AS: Do you see there being fewer big screen experiences in the future?

MF: What's amazing to me is that you can't find a crew anywhere in America right now because there is so much getting done. Maybe cinema's down but content is up. There's a film crew working on every corner of every city, everywhere. There's a lot of work going on. I don't even know how it's possible for people to process it all. But the economics of it work in the streaming world where you don't only have two weekends to establish yourself. So many movies were up against the wrong movie that opening weekend or some event happened that weekend and they didn't make it and that's it. They're out floating face down somewhere and that's a shame. And in this streaming digital world there are other ways for a story to get out there and I think that's cool.

My TV is 4K at home. You go to the movies it's 2K right now. Some people would say the quality of writing on TV right now is better than what you get in a lot of what's in theaters. To justify the economics of having a theater, the kinds of movies that get made are bigger and broader. That's just what's happening. Ang said movies will become like Broadway. It used to be there was a dramatic theater on every corner. That's how people got their entertainment. And then TV happened and that stopped. Then Broadway became something that you could do twice a year that cost a lot and was an event. That feels a little bit like what's happening to cinema. But it's not just cinema. It's sports. The stands are empty. Because why go? I can watch five games at home, in my underwear, and it costs me nothing. Or I can spend two hundred dollars

and get on the subway and go to the Bronx and get beer poured on my head. It's a bigger issue than just cinema.

I live in New York and I can't function here in LA because I need to touch people. I need to bump into people. I need to be knocked down a little bit. I need that friction energy to live. That's how I'm raised. The world is not that way right now. We've retreated into our phone world and fortressed ourselves in there.

Technologically the theater's got to figure out how to do something that the LCD screen at home can't do if we're going to keep going. *Joker* is cool because I think that the fact that it's in the theaters is what's making it successful. People are experiencing this story collectively. We're both tearing away the myths of ourselves–how good we are or how base our animal instincts are, and also exposing this sense of rage we're feeling because of the fraying of the social contract we're all experiencing.

AS: Any advice for people just starting out?

MF: Play the long game. Look for people you respond to, to collaborate with regardless of how famous they are at that moment. I chose to focus on trusting my own taste and being true to myself and the films I have gotten to work on have lived on and people eventually did see them even if they weren't big box office successes. Most movies I've designed did not make it the first weekend. But I don't want to win the weekend. I want to win my life.

ADVICE

What advice do you have for beginners?

A compilation of excerpts covering the subject of advice, taken from the interviews in this book

How do you succeed in the business of production design? How do you set yourself apart from the masses? How do you become invaluable to a production? How do you become inspired to create genuine works of art that will be remembered forever as classics? And how do you raise the bar with every subsequent film? The following is a selection of advice to people who are starting out, but also to anyone at any level who needs to be reminded of how to avoid the pitfalls–or how to seek them out! Open your eyes wide... Use all of your life experiences... Play the long game... Smile...

EVE STEWART

Learn to smile all day! Be positive. And learn to draw. For God's sake learn to draw! It's the only way you'll ever get your own way . . . If you're sitting in a meeting and there are twelve people sitting around looking at you and you're all talking about a chair, unless you can draw the chair that you think is right, they'll all be thinking of something different. You've got to be very clear and communicate very well.

JOHN MYHRE

I just took any job I could possibly get to get in the art department. I knew I wanted to be a production designer but I didn't wait until somebody offered me a job to be a production designer because to be honest with you, I'd be working at McDonald's now. I fought for a job as an art department PA and if I was asked to be there at six in the morning I was there at five-thirty in the morning. And if I heard that they needed someone to come in even earlier to get coffee my hand was the first to go up. And I just tried to make myself invaluable and just tried to take any job I could get in the art department because you learn so much. I remember that on my first week on *Night of the Comet* I felt I had learned more than I learned in two years at film school. You learn being around on a set and seeing how things are done, how movies are shot, how the business end works as well as the creative end. You meet people and a lot of it is meeting people.

As a production designer I make sure I'm really nice to all the PA's because that PA over there could be the producer of my next movie! It just happens that way. When I was an art director and Steve McEveety was a first AD, he said to me, *I'm going to be a producer and the first movie I produce you're going to be the production designer.* And lo and behold, four years later I got a call from Steve McEveety saying, *I'm producing my first movie, you're the production designer.* Steve McEveety, who went on to be a big producer with Icon and did *Braveheart* and these fantastic movies.

So just keep enthusiastic. And for me it was just the working, taking the jobs. I designed a lot of really low budget movies. I designed movies where the art department budget was fifteen thousand dollars, but it was a chance to design. And it was a chance be treated as a designer and interact with other departments as the department head. And I know that some people have rejected that route because they want to do more serious, substantial films but for me getting the experience was really important.

ROBERT STROMBERG

You want to be someone who says, *I did this, this and this, what do you think?* As opposed to the person who says, *Is this what you mean?* It's a huge difference because it's the difference between a free thinker and someone who's just getting by. Someone who's contributing and someone who's just keeping pace.

ADVICE

There's also an old saying that I always stick to, *Luck is being prepared when opportunity arrives.* That's kind of what it is. Also, you can generate your own opportunity by not being overly aggressive, but still by pushing.

HANNAH BEACHLER

The thing that I always say to young people interested in design is the best thing you can do for yourself is learn every job in the art department. Because that's what I did and that's why I succeeded. You talk to these older guys and they did the same thing. And because of that, you become more valuable to a producer. I understand how much work it takes and how much money it costs because I did all these jobs.

Don't ever feel you have to jump right into the production design or art director position. Learn everything. I came up set dec side. If you want to come up art director side, start in construction. Move to a set designer. A lot of architects are coming out of school saying, *I've got this degree, what do I do? I don't know that I want to work in an architectural firm, I'd like to work in film.* You're going to need to start as set designer. Or as an assistant art director.

With something like that, it really is about starting as a PA for a big designer and letting them know,

I'm really interested in art direction. Find out who the art directors are that you like and call them and talk to them or send them an email. People really do want to help people and give them advice. Look on the ADG's website–they always have events and who are at these events? All kinds of people. You don't know who you're going to run into. I was at an event and ran into Rick Carter for God's sake! Guy Dyas! Jess Gonchor!

Get all the information you can and then you just have to take the leap. Find the tax incentive states. Georgia. New Mexico is coming back. Louisiana. Those are great ways to get involved. If you really want to be a production designer and you're serious about that, give yourself time.

K.K. BARRETT

Two things: Take every job. Never worry about money. Take ones where you can learn from something that you've never done before, especially if you're scared of it. And then do everybody else's job in your head. And know everybody else's job. Know what they do and how they contribute and how it affects you. And think it out as if everybody's gone home and you've got to do it all yourself. Don't have preconceived notions when you go into a film. Be able to change. Be able to go with it. Be able to discover every day. The last week of the film you should still be able to discover new things.

What advice do you have for beginners?

Make yourself invaluable. Take a job–*I'll do it for free.* Hang around until you have to leave. And then hopefully they'll go, *No, no, no, we need you. We're so used to you solving problems with us we need you now. Will you stay for five dollars?* And then you have to leave again. *Will you stay for ten dollars?* Just make yourself invaluable. Find somebody else that you can help.

GRANT MAJOR

Try to have a life that exposes you to a lot of experiences. Travel and go to design exhibitions, go to plays, go to see lots of movies, go to fashion shows. You subconsciously pull away good ideas. You give them a neural address and they stay there for years sometimes.

I suggest for people wanting to train up to get into this sort of thing, that they should get a degree in architecture. Or go to film school and learn to be a production designer with all the requisite drafting skills. You must be able to draw. A lot of art schools these days don't encourage drawing or don't actively teach drawing. But I think drawing is very, very important. And computer skills now. The young kids are overtaking me now with the ability to use 3D Studio MAX and Rhino and these sorts of things. Having experience in those sorts of programs also gets you in the door. You can be brought in for a specific job, to design a 3D set or

something like that, and then once you're in the art department, at least in New Zealand, you can move around within that. Coming to the project with skills is really important.

And lastly what I tell everybody is just to make your own films however you can, shoot them and get friends to act in them, edit it yourself and just sort of hone that manufacturing business of filmmaking. And make it your own way.

Hands-on skills in visual effects is important for production designers because the vis effects world is currently being colonized by technicians. We need to move into their world majorly with creative skills and film design skills. Being able to design the sets and design the film and follow right through to the visual effects is the future of what we're doing. As a profession we need to be there every step of the way.

JACK FISK

Use all your mistakes and pitfalls to become better. You're going to make mistakes. And it's all in how you react to it. A lot of it is slight of hand. Don't let other people know you made a mistake if you can avoid it! Just go forward.

I would say anyone starting out in the business ought to find young directors that are strong

ADVICE

and imaginative and work with them for very little money. Grow with them. If you want to be a designer you're going to need to work with a director who's going to get scripts made. I started working with Terry Malick just as he finished film school and he's made me a better designer.

EUGENIO CABALLERO

Continuous work. That's the most important thing. And you have to do a lot of reading and watching films. With the internet you have access to a lot of materials. What you're doing with *Art Stars* is very cool. These interviews help a lot of people who are interested in the craft. In LA you can attend certain seminars and master classes but in a lot of places people interested in this career are all by themselves.

No matter where you are, it's important that your experiences feed into your production design. For example, when you go to an art exhibition, think about what visual decisions were made in order for the art pieces to work. Look at how they chose to do the framing, the lighting, the dressing. Every visual art piece has art direction, the artist decides which objects will live in the space that is shown. In film you're constantly making those same decisions.

But the most important thing is to work constantly. On small things, on big things, on things that are

maybe not ideal, not necessarily the films that you aspire to do. But everything adds to your career and suddenly the addition of all those things gives you the tools, the opportunity, the knowledge, and the experience that you will use later. Doing short films, one of the things that is very easy to lose is the joy component. But you have to try to give the complexity that we were talking about to everything, even if it's something small–and you have to really enjoy what you're doing!

RICK HEINRICHS

You need to set yourself apart from everyone else. It comes from what you were interested in as a kid or what you were interested in as a young adult. The travels that you did in life. The things that made you curious growing up. You want to be considered a professional who can do the job but at the same time all of these things help distinguish you as a designer.

I would also tell anyone to learn SketchUp because it's such a great, easy program. If they feel that they are going to be a set designer and draftsman they should probably get into Rhino. But for an art director or even a production designer it's good to be able to really study the scale of things in three dimensions.

What advice do you have for beginners?

ADAM STOCKHAUSEN

The big thing I would say is if you think that you're going to design this set all on your own and come up with this brilliant thing and never need to talk to anyone about it and that they're just going to show up at the end and it's going to be amazing, you're making quite a large mistake. Involve your collaborators in the process early and often.

MARK FRIEDBERG

Play the long game. Look for people you respond to, to collaborate with regardless of how famous they are at that moment. I chose to focus on trusting my own taste and being true to myself and the films I have gotten to work on have lived on and people eventually did see them even if they weren't big box office successes. Most movies I've designed did not make it the first weekend. But I don't want to win the weekend. I want to win my life.

LEE HA-JUN

Production designers should open their eyes wide. Never close your thoughts. When you open your eyes to small things, you'll see the details that could make an amazing library. You can draw inspiration from this library. Do not try to look only for good or cool things. See everything you can. You will see the story and what it contains. When you keep looking at the people on the street, you can sometimes tell their character from their walking style and fashion. If you train yourself to look into the things around you, you'll have a very good quality library of your own. Also, you need to be physically healthy so that you can have the strength to run around to work. Sometimes you need to win the fight with stamina. Do not give up easily.

Do not only watch entertaining films. Watch lots of films so that you can compare them to each other.

MICHAEL NOVOTNY

I hate to say it but it's true you should probably shut up and listen to the director. I think a new designer might tend to get out and think he's the greatest thing since sliced bread. The danger there is that very quickly somebody's going to realize that he's not the greatest thing since sliced bread. His talking is going to overshadow the conversation at hand. So the bottom line is that sometimes it's better to simply listen.

PATRICE VERMETTE

There are two ways [to get into production design.] You can start out being the apprentice and production assistant and go the feature film route. Or you could go into music videos. That route goes faster because you shoot different projects and you meet different directors. And every director in music videos and commercials has a hidden script

ADVICE

somewhere that they want to write eventually. They all wish that eventually they'll be recognized as feature film directors as opposed to commercial directors. They all dream of that. And by meeting these people on commercials and music videos eventually you're going to make a good connection. You're going to meet a guy like I did with Jean-Marc Valée. Someone that you click with and you have basically the same philosophy with about filmmaking. And that person will take you onto their feature film project. It might take four, five, or six years to write it and to finance it but eventually they will finance it. One of the directors that you work with will get their project on the road. Might not be a great budget but you just do it. Do it with your passion.

DAVID WARREN

Be creative, be imaginative. Learn the current technology to the highest level you can because you'll move a lot faster. Old guys like me look at people that are twenty-five who are very, very fluid in current software and say, I need that guy with me on the next job because I haven't got a clue how that works. You know it is as simple as that.

The art department still has so many different pathways within it. I think designer's obviously what everyone wants to be but still you can make a good career out of being a good sketch artist or a visualizer. You can make a career out of being a set decorator. You can make a good career out of being an art director. You have to make that decision at some point. Because the trouble is any one film only needs one production designer or possibly two, like we had. But you'll always need more art directors and you'll need a lot of set designers and you'll possibly need two set decorators. You know, the further down the pile the more possibility you've got of getting a job in the beginning days.

KIM SINCLAIR

These days I have to say that it's essential that you have computer skills–but don't get seduced into thinking that's the be-all and the end-all. You can learn Maya but then maybe you're going to sit behind a computer the rest of your life doing modeling when you could actually be a really good art director. Computers are just tools, you need to know how to use them and be familiar with the applications. But I still think it's much better to get a bit of life education. Get out there and watch movies and do things. Travel. Get experience.

GUY HENDRIX DYAS

I'd say to young designers just love what you do. There is good karma out there and if you work hard and if you develop your craft you will get a

What advice do you have for beginners?

chance. But no one's going to open the door and say, *Hey, come design!* You're gonna have to get out there and practice your art and your design and eventually someone will see you. If you don't love designing, if it's a chore to pick up a pencil or paint something, then do something else. But if you love it and become as good as you can as a craftsman, the job will find you.

JESS GONCHOR

You just gotta do it. You gotta work. You can only learn so much and then you just have to start doing something and making mistakes. The cliché is so true: How do you get to Carnegie Hall? *Practice, practice, practice.* You have to get out there and do something. If you're in school you should also be doing something at night or on the weekends. If you want to be a DP just start shooting stuff. For everything you do there's a lesson learned, whether it's good or bad. It's every single thing that you do. You know to be in this business you have to be out there and aware and absorbing information all the time. I just keep my ears and my eyes open, seeing what's out there.

SARAH GREENWOOD

You just have to be really persistent. Particularly when I'm just starting this project and everyone gets a sniff of it and I have twenty emails a day,

or phone calls or texts. Somebody might have texted me three months ago and I go, *I'm not doing anything.* You need to be at the right time, at the right moment.

And just be open-minded and interested. If you want to be an art director and you're starting as an art director assistant then be interested in what set decs are doing, be interested in construction, be interested in the whole process. Get out onto the floor. See how films are made. It's such an amazing business. Again, why do it if you're not interested?

LAURENCE BENNETT

I usually advise people to first watch as many movies as they can. We have now a hundred year history of film from all over the world. When I'm not working I spend a lot of time watching movies, trying to continue my education about film. And it's an exciting thing for me. A lot of great stories have been told on film in the space of that hundred years. And being familiar with it and learning from it is really key.

I would also advise people to find designers whose work they admire and pick their brains. Find someone who you respect to work with if possible. If you're studying in film school, I can't imagine there's much substitute for actually making films.

ADVICE

In addition to being a student, sign up and design small projects for people for free or whatever you need to do to get as involved as possible in the process because that's where you really learn your craft.

DENNIS GASSNER

Having the strength of a strong mentor is important. In my case it was Dean Tavoularis. Production designer Rick Carter and I are good mates and we talk about this a lot. His mentor was Dick Sylbert. Dick and Dean were the two top guys when I was coming in. *The Godfather, Chinatown* and so on. Both interesting minds. And bravo to you for doing the *Art Stars* blog because it's also like a great mentorship.

NATHAN CROWLEY

If I was starting out with the knowledge I have now I'd be looking for young directors with great stories. I think those guys are usually writer/directors. You need to find people you want to work with and help them. Many directors starting out have no idea how a designer can help them. Young directors that have never had a production designer open their eyes. You have to make yourself be invaluable.

DAVID WASCO &
SANDY REYNOLDS-WASCO

DW: I'd say to get as much formal training as you can and then try to either intern or get an art assistant job where you can be in the middle of an art department and see how it works because it might not be what you really want to do.

SRW: If you've got the passion for it then maybe the formal stuff is okay but if you're going to do four years of film school I think going out and doing the work is better. Even more of a liberal arts background is good, so you have a variety of tools in your belt. You then have literature and philosophy and music and painting. You need all those references to be able to say a night sky is like a Munch painting, or describe a camera angle in a photograph or know that all the lighting in a Civil War period film will be by flame.

DW: In contrast to when we were starting there are just more people trying to get jobs and there are just fewer jobs. A lot of really good production designers have done theater work and I think that's always a good route. My friend Carl Sprague, the production designer, is also a great theater designer.

SRW: Just do it. It's really about your connections and who you're meeting and keeping in touch with and broadening those connections.

DW: You've got to use *everything*. If you know or

What advice do you have for beginners?

your family knows somebody, keep the connections alive. When I meet with people I usually like to hand off one or two names for them to contact and then I ask them to get two names from those two people and that ends up being four more people. And you just keep building and building and building the connections and eventually somebody is just going to say, *Are you available? Can you just start?*

PATRICK TATOPOULOS

Don't be afraid to be humble. Don't be afraid to say, *Hey guys, I've done this in the past but I haven't done it to this level, what do you guys think?* When I did my first movie as a director I had no directing experience whatsoever. Len Wiseman [*Underworld* series creator/director/producer] came to me and said, *At the beginning of my career I had no idea about lighting, I barely knew what kind of light a 10K was. So I took my little sketch pad and sketched my idea and said, "I would like this, I just don't know the term for it."*

I've done the same thing for my movies and people reacted in a very positive way. You have a vision and they respect that. You don't try to make believe you know everything. When I designed *Independence Day* with Oliver Scholl we both started as concept artists. We both came from nowhere and then suddenly we're production designing a movie of that scale together.

What we did was, we hired James Teegarden, who was one of the top art directors at the time. He's one of the best I've ever met. The director knew Jim was the backbone of the art department. He knew that the set would happen because that art director knew what he was doing. We never tried to make people believe we were in charge out there, you know what I mean? We designed, Jim made sure it happened. Stay humble, people will respect you for that.

COLIN GIBSON

You don't have to start as an art director. You don't have to draw. You don't have to go to art school. Like Jack Fisk, throw a hammer in the back of a ute and head off and the badlands will shape you.

Jack Fisk

Jack Fisk has an amazing career designing the films of auteurs including Terrence Malick, Paul Thomas Anderson, David Lynch, and Martin Scorcese. He designed every Terrence Malick film including *The Thin Red Line, Days of Heaven, The New World, Badlands* and the more recent *Tree of Life*. He received an Oscar nomination for Paul Thomas Anderson's *There Will Be Blood* and Alejandro Iñáritu's *The Revenant*. For David Lynch he designed the dreamlike *Mulholland Dr.* and for Martin Scorsese, *Killers of the Flower Moon*.

AS: Did you go to art school?

JF: I went to Cooper Union here in New York for a year then I went to Pennsylvania Academy of the Fine Arts in Philadelphia. In 1970 David Lynch and I went out to California to seek our fortunes–or at least find a job.

AS: Did you know David Lynch from before?

JF: David and I have been best friends since high school and we went to art school together. He'd been accepted into the American Film Institute and I decided to go to California too. After a few months I got my first job as an art director. I had only worked on a couple of films, but Jonathan Demme hired me to be art director on a Roger Corman film *Angels Hard as They Come*. Steven Katz, the cinematographer, was a friend, I called Steven and said, *What does an art director do?* and he says, *I don't know!*

So I started doing everything. I didn't know the boundaries or what they expected so I did everything I could think of. I've been doing that ever since. When you don't know what you are doing, you're reinventing the wheel, but I didn't have any options. I didn't know how to make flats but I had a pickup truck and some tools and a lot of energy. At that time working for Roger Corman's company was like going to film school. On-the-job training.

In 1972 I met Terrence Malick. He was going to AFI the same time that David Lynch was there and was about to make his first feature. I'd heard through mutual friends he was doing this period film. I thought, *Oh, I'd love to do a period film.* A friend introduced us and Terry was like, *Can you start? Can you go out to Colorado in May?* And I said, *Sure.* I rented a van, put all my tools in it and drove to Colorado and on July tenth we began shooting.

AS: Was that *Badlands*?

JF: Yes, *Badlands.* And it was an exciting film for me because it was the first time I saw that film was an art form equal to painting or sculpture, or music.

AS: You've had a career working with directors who are artists.

JF: Yes, I've been very lucky, and I've done two films recently with Paul Thomas Anderson, and it's the same thing, he's an artist.

AS: Did you hire a local crew when you went out to do *Badlands*?

JF: I hired a kid named Kenny Hilton who lived in La Junta, Colorado and I called a friend who'd met at Pratt when I was going to Cooper Union

and asked him if he wanted to work on a film. He was doing nothing so he came out. And that was Ed Richardson. He went on to become an art director.

The first film I remember having an art director on was *Thin Red Line*. On a lot of them I didn't even have decorators! I was doing what I could. Bill Paxton was a part of my team on the Corman films and up through *Carrie,* but he later gave up the art department for acting and directing. I was always grabbing anybody I could. Anybody who was willing to stay up all night and work could be part of the team.

> " I CALLED STEVEN [KATZ, THE DP] AND SAID, *WHAT DOES AN ART DIRECTOR DO?* AND HE SAYS, *I DON'T KNOW!* SO I STARTED DOING EVERYTHING. I DIDN'T KNOW THE BOUNDARIES OR WHAT THEY EXPECTED SO I DID EVERYTHING I COULD THINK OF. I'VE BEEN DOING THAT EVER SINCE.

I used to measure how passionate I was about a film by how many nights I would be up all night. *Oh, that's a three-nighter film!* I got ten days in a week because I figured I could work during the day and during the night. *We're going to shoot in four days, but if I get in trouble I've got eight days.* I can't do that anymore. But I just finished a film with Paul and I had one day that was thirty hours. We were prepping sets in LA and shooting in San Francisco. So I flew down to LA at six o'clock in the morning then back to San Francisco for a night shoot. We shot all night and in the morning we drove to the country outside of San Francisco and shot there until ten-thirty a.m.

As a production designer I like to be on the set as much as possible, protecting everything we've created. It's hard for me to come up with a plan and then not be there for the execution of it. I think affects the design of the film. Most of the directors I work with are changing things constantly and I like to be around to make the appropriate adjustments.

AS: Would you say the ability to stay up all night is a key quality that a production designer should have?

JF: I would say passion. And I think if you have passion about what you're doing you may end up staying up all night. Once I hear about a film, my mind starts working and there's no way of shutting it off, even if I'm not physically up all night. Once I tune into a project I don't think about anything else.

AS: What types of preparation and research do you do? Do you watch a bunch of other films?

JF: I try not to watch films except maybe documentaries because I don't want to use film as a reference for making a film. It seems like inbreeding. You might come up with a weird baby! I research as much writing as possible. I love personal journals from the period I am designing.

AS: Like for *The New World*.

JF: I read all the Jamestown narratives. Then I started to suspect that they weren't truthful because the Jamestown Company was a business. They were trying to promote the colonies so they edited the journals before they were published to make Jamestown look better. John Smith's journals were sent to England and published without him even knowing it. I got suspicious when I read about the fort. The fort was built in thirty days. And one colonist described the wall construction as wide boards. I knew they weren't boards. Because to get a board in those days they would have had to cut two sides off of a log. There's no way, in thirty days, you're going to cut boards for over a thousand linear feet of palisade. When I got suspicious of that I got a little skeptical of everything they said.

Then I met Dr. Bill Kelso, the archaeologist who discovered the real Jamestown fort in 1996. I talked to him about the fort we were planning to build and I said, *Well, we're going to simulate the fort*, and I saw on his face he completely lost interest when I said *simulate*. And I said, *What I meant was we're going to build it exactly as they did in 1607!* And then he perked up. And he started giving me all this information. He had found soil stains where every log was. Where each post was set, it left a stain. So it was logs, it wasn't boards. I learned a lot about the first English settlement from Dr. Kelso.

It became fun to build the way they did with wattle-and-daub. In my mind, I was making a documentary about Jamestown. But Terry is a philosopher and he was making a film about Pocahontas being the mother of us all. In reality Pocahontas at the time of John Smith was nine years old and she had a shaved head! Things were so different back then, but you can't always put reality on film because it can be so bizarre. Queen Elizabeth's teeth were all rotten. King James never bathed so his hands were black. People described them as feeling like black velvet. I was in England looking for locations and at Knole they have a little museum set up where they had the last bed King James used. It had an upholstered back and there was big grease spot on it where the king's head had rested. He was against smoking because he thought it was unhealthy but he was also against bathing because he thought it was unhealthy.

Someday it would be nice to recreate the world as it was. It would shock a lot of people! Thomas Eakins, who also studied at the Pennsylvania Academy of the Fine Arts, had done a lot of paintings of doctors performing surgery because he loved anatomy. Back then the surgeons wore wool coats and they got so saturated with blood they were like cardboard. If they set them on the floor they would have held their shape. Such a different time.

I researched everything I could find on Jamestown. You immerse yourself so much into the period but then at some point you just let it all go and start working intuitively. You've got a foundation and then you just start working.

AS: Do you do a lot of sketches during those early stages or do you have someone do sketches?
JF: I've never had an illustrator work with me and

I only do sketches when necessary. I'd rather build and change it. When I was younger I started with models of sets because the carpenters that I was working with didn't all read blueprints. So I'd cut my drawings up and make white-board models and then everybody understood what I was thinking and they'd work from those.

> " I USED TO MEASURE HOW PASSIONATE I WAS ABOUT A FILM BY HOW MANY NIGHTS I WOULD BE UP ALL NIGHT . . . I GOT TEN DAYS IN A WEEK BECAUSE I FIGURED I COULD WORK DURING THE DAY AND DURING THE NIGHT. *WE'RE GOING TO SHOOT IN FOUR DAYS, BUT IF I GET IN TROUBLE I'VE GOT EIGHT DAYS.*

AS: Do you still do models?
JF: Yes, but I use SketchUp a lot. I think in SketchUp. Because it gives you good proportions and scale. It's replaced physical models and sketches for me. Most of the directors I work with never ask to see drawings. Once David did a little sketch on a paper bag of how he thought the apartment in *Mulholland Drive* would be laid out, but I looked at it and I couldn't figure out what he'd drawn. I kept it because it was just so beautiful. Terry likes to be surprised by locations. I've never seen Terry look at a storyboard or a sketch. He'll look at paintings or photographs. Usually I have so little time in pre-production that I just start building.

AS: During preproduction do you have a wall of pictures?

JF: Yes. That's normally what I do. Those walls seem to benefit everyone on the film. They help them understand the place and the period. For me it started on *The Thin Red Line,* one of the first times that I had an office. We Xeroxed our research and put it up. I do all my photography digitally and print very little but I'll use iPhoto if I have to show somebody a slideshow.

AS: When working on *The Thin Red Line* would you ever show Terry pictures of bunkers or anything?

JF: We would look at research. I had so much research on *The Thin Red Line.* When we left Australia to shoot in Guadalcanal I had thirty-five boxes of documentary tapes, research books and government pamphlets and so on. I left it all to the WWII museum in Guadalcanal. That was an easy film to research. I live right near Washington DC and I went to the military museum there and the military bases in Virginia gathering information on the period.

I found the original manufacturer of the army uniforms and some of the original fabric. We used the same patterns the military used during the war. We even ordered the uniforms the same way the army did, not knowing what size the actors were going to be. I asked, *What would the army normally order? sixty percent medium and ten percent large?* We outfitted like a real army.

I got to Australia and they didn't have period airplanes. We found one DC-3, but I needed some fighting planes. In a museum in Queensland they had a Bell Cobra and they allowed us to come in and make a rubber mold of it which we cast in fiberglass. And that gave us our Bell Cobra. The welders built a frame for it and landing gear. We actually put motors in some of our airplanes and had props that would spin around.

We needed some Wildcats because those are the planes coming off aircraft carriers so we got a big, wooden kit for a radio-controlled Wildcat and we just enlarged it to full scale. We built them just like a model airplane, but at one hundred percent. We built five of those.

We built landing craft, the Higgins boats, out of plywood and Styrofoam. In the end we were able to get two real landing craft to complete our fleet. You'll see a lot of them out there. Some of them are CGI and some of them were plywood with Styrofoam bottoms with an outboard motor hidden inside. We built half of a landing craft that we put on a gimbal and set out in a field in Port Douglas. Whenever an actor was finished or going back to the States, Terry would get them into the half landing craft and he'd shoot a scene with them. We'd be throwing buckets of water over the side. It was really analog, old-timey but it was fun.

We built a pillbox for the Japanese up on top of a hill but it was so steep that we couldn't get a backhoe up there to dig the hole. Art director Ian Gracie found a guy who'd won a competition with one of those little Bobcats. He got him to come up and dig the hole because the Bobcat was much smaller and he wasn't afraid of falling off the mountain. He would dig and dig, smoke a joint, and then go back to digging. He could pick a coin up off the pavement with his Bobcat bucket. And he didn't even use a ramp to get it on the truck. He was gifted.

AS: Did you bring any crew from the States?

JF: The art department was all Australian. And when I went to Guadalcanal I used people from Guadalcanal. We built a village there. Today's villages have evolved and changed, so we built a period village. The drawings would be made with a stick in the dirt. I'd say, *Well, we should put a house here and the center lodge here.* The first day probably fifteen people showed up to help build. Half of them were men. After we'd built our first structure the men got in there and started chewing betel nut. That gets them a little bit high and from that day on they just sat in there and chewed betel nut. The women did all the construction. They would be carrying rocks down the beach, collecting materials and thatching the houses. They were great workers.

On the way to work, I would stop at the open-air market and pick up three or four live chickens and throw them in the back of my car. I'd drive to set and one of the women would take them out and go to a stream and get them ready for lunch while the other women were building. We'd go up in the jungle and get sago palms. We built it just like they used to. On some days I'd see grandparents bringing little children into the village to show them how they used to live.

Ian Gracie was there the first day and we went hiking up in the mountains looking for all the palms and wood we needed. There was a beautiful stream and it just looked like heaven and he said, *Oh, I'm going to drink some of that.* I said, *I don't think you should.* And he said, *No, no, I think it's okay, look how far up it is.*

> " AS A PRODUCTION DESIGNER I LIKE TO BE ON THE SET AS MUCH AS POSSIBLE, PROTECTING EVERYTHING WE'VE CREATED. IT'S HARD FOR ME TO COME UP WITH A PLAN AND THEN NOT BE THERE FOR THE EXECUTION OF IT.

Well, the next day he was really sick and ended up having to go back to Australia. But it timed out well because he and his wife were having a baby in a couple of days so he got to go back home and be there when his son was born. We had to be careful, Guadalcanal is the malaria capitol of the world. The studio did not want us to shoot in Guadalcanal. But it's just such an exquisite place.

We shot the ship approaching Guadalcanal off Santa Catalina in California. It had been a rainy winter and the island was lush and green and it looked amazing.

AS: Do you mostly build 360 degrees and avoid using set extensions?

JF: When I started to work with Terry I saw it was hard to know what he was going to shoot because when he gets behind the camera he just goes! So I started building 360 degrees. I just do as much as I can. And then it sort of became the way I like to work because it creates a world. It creates more work for the art department but it really helps the actors.

AS: Was *There Will Be Blood* a huge build?

JF: We rented a fifty-five thousand acre ranch and built just about everything in that film. We shot in Marfa, Texas, within twenty miles of where they shot *Giant*. The derrick we built was ninety feet tall. I went to Taft, California and started going through the files at an oil museum there. They were selling a print for ninety-nine cents, of an 1896 plan of a derrick. So I bought a couple and those became our plans. They even included a lumber list. We pretty much built that 1896 derrick and added a staircase. How are you going to design a derrick better than the original?

Paul and I spent a couple of days walking around the ranch to find a place to erect the derrick. We decided on a hill. I did a SketchUp drawing of a foundation that I thought would hold the derrick but then I got a little scared, because of the responsibility–the derrick is ninety feet tall and big and heavy and you're out in the plains and you get high winds. And the actors are going to be up there. So I got a local engineer and he looked at the drawings

and he says, *Well, that's more than you need. That's what we use for those hundred and fifty foot wind towers.*

So we brought a truck out and it drilled holes about fifteen feet deep and three feet in diameter, and we filled them with rebar and pumped in cement. Once we got the concrete pilings up to level we started building our deck. The derrick was really built by two carpenters, plus one operating a cherry-picker. You get too many people up in the air and they get in each other's way. We'd have to stop if the wind got to thirty mph. Safety people would pull them off. It took us about three weeks to build that derrick.

AS: You have an eye for the authentic sources…

JF: When I did the interior ship at the beginning of *Thin Red Line* I went to see the ghost fleet on the James River in Virginia. Where they keep all the old military ships. I was able to get permission to go out and board some of those ships. There was this old troop ship that was built before WWII but it had no electricity on it. I went out with flashlights and went through it and shot a lot of pictures and videos for research on how to build this ship. I took a neighbor, a friend of mine from Virginia. He found these bunk covers, these canvas covers that the guys slept on and underneath they had done all these drawings on them. He got real excited and he took pictures of those. He ended up arranging with the military to get a lot of those covers before they destroyed the ship and he did a museum display and wrote a book about them. I believe some of those covers are now in the Smithsonian. All from that one trip. I talked to the people at the harbor and they gave me the original plans for the ship I documented. I was able to take those with me to Australia and we built off drawings of a real government troop ship.

We needed M1s and machine guns for our film and I found them in the United States. The U.S. Army had over ten thousand M1s in Kentucky. They had a program where they would give them to sixteen-year-old boys. If you were in the Boy Scouts you could write a letter to receive one. Well, I tried to get five hundred of them and they wouldn't give them to me. They don't want any military films made unless they're DOD-approved. They wouldn't help us. I made a preliminary trip to Australia and made arrangements with an Australian armorer to get all the weapons we needed. I had about a month off before we really started prepping the film and I went back to the States. I would call him and I'd write him notes but he never wrote me back and I started getting a little worried. I got back over to Australia and I found out that in the two months I was gone there'd been a mass killing, somebody'd gone crazy. As a result, the Government had outlawed guns in Australia and they were buying them back and our armorer had sold all his guns for five hundred thousand to the Australian government.

We were there making a WWII picture and we had no weapons. So I started searching around and thinking of where weapons would be. The United States wouldn't give them to us. Somebody told me about all the weapons we'd left in Viet Nam and I believed it because I had seen all the stuff that was left in Guadalcanal from WWII. So we contacted some armorers in Viet Nam and we ended up buying all our M1s and cannons and other American weaponry from Viet Nam. We couldn't ship them directly into Australia, we had to ship them to Canada and then in Canada they had to fit them so they could only fire a certain blank. Then they shipped them to us in Australia. The rule was, we had to ship them out of Australia when we were finished. So it got real complicated. You know, our job is solving problems. Sometimes designing sets is the easiest part of it!

AS: Is the ability to solve problems on your feet another requirement for production designers?
JF: Definitely. I think that's what we do. No matter what is written in the script we've got to figure out how the company with their budget and resources can get it on film. Sometimes it's building the sets and sometimes it's greenscreens. Sometimes it's making something else work. There's never one set answer.

AS: The challenges are always different.
JF: I love shooting on location because you move into a little community and start working with them. To go to Guadalcanal and build a village with Solomon Islanders, there's no way you could do that as a tourist. You get to know people so well. You're eating with them, learning about their culture. I'd read studies of the cultural differences of the Solomon Islanders in advance so it was easier

for me to work with them. Men don't work, they're warriors. They used to be headhunters. They look very fierce.

I was there by myself at first. I had gone up to one of the battlegrounds and was walking back through the hills late at night. I heard people in the villages, children laughing. I was walking up the road and there were three huge Melanesians who looked very fierce approaching me. They all carry these three-foot machetes. I'm probably the only American on the island and I'm thinking, *If I was in New York right now I'd be very scared.* But they were so fierce-looking that when they smiled it was just like a thunderbolt. It was even better than a normal smile because you don't expect it.

There was one cave that had some thousand-year-old drawings on the walls and I wanted to take Terry to show him. So we drove out in a little car and there were three Melanesians at the entrance. It was a Sunday and they were pretty drunk. I said I wanted to show Terry the cave and they said, *That'll be a million dollars.* I said, *I don't have a million dollars.* We negotiated and got down to us going in but we had to give them a six-pack of beer. From a million dollars to a six-pack of beer.

They were still discovering bodies from WWII when I was there. A couple of Japanese soldiers were revealed where the sand had washed away and the Japanese came to negotiate to get the bodies and build a little memorial. But the negotiations always started at a million dollars! In the end maybe they'd give them a wheelbarrow or something.

AS: How involved are Terrence Malick, David Lynch and Paul Thomas Anderson in the production design?

JF: With Terrence you might think that he wasn't involved but he knows everything. He's been to all the locations before you start looking at locations. I always feel he's guiding me towards the location but not saying he knows about it. With Terry the challenge is coming up with something he hasn't found, something that he hasn't thought about. He writes on some films for years. He'd written *The New World* before we did *Badlands.* He'd started *Tree of Life* back at that same time. For him looking at locations is part of the writing process. On most films Terry will give me a couple of books that have clues to what he is visually looking for in the film. But Terry doesn't like to have shots and even locations planned out, he is looking for a natural spontaneity. He'll often move the location of a scene just to destroy any predictability that comes from scenes being overthought. He works to create situations where the actors are not performing.

It's easier to build for David because he's got his own view of the world and he has most of the film in his head before we start filming. David understands construction and building because he started building sets in art school. He designed and constructed all the sets for *Eraserhead* and his earlier films. We can talk in short hand. He likes to build and paint on the sets. He has a great shop at his house and he'll build sets in his yard and shoot little things for his web page. With David it's like talking to another art director.

I first met Paul at the Burbank airport to do a location scout in Texas and New Mexico and we got along instantly. He's very enthusiastic about film and has a great sense of humor. We spent a lot of time walking around on ranches looking for locations for *There Will Be Blood*. I would put stakes in the ground and stick PVC pipes on them to show him the scale I was thinking in. *Here's the church, we'll make it this big.* He'll say, *Maybe you should move it over a little.* So it was a real creative process. Paul had done extensive research on oil rigs and the oil business while creating the script and he passed all his research on to the art department.

The one thing Paul said to me about the look of the picture when we first started was, *Let's not use any signs.* I thought that was a great idea and we didn't have any signs in the film. I have so much respect for his understanding of character and I see how much he struggles with himself putting a script together–that's one thing that makes him such a great filmmaker–it's his writing.

At one point we'd been shooting *There Will Be Blood* for a while and he says, *You're getting to pick all the colors.* So I gave him a Benjamin Moore color swatch book and he carried it around, but four days later he walked over and handed it back to me

and said, *Okay, you pick them!* Paul's favorite color is white. Terry won't allow white on a set.

The only time that we had a disagreement on *There Will Be Blood* was on the direction of Daniel Plainview's office. Daniel Day Lewis' character had an office and I placed it so he could look at the well pumping, but that put the church directly behind him. And Paul said he would never let that preacher be behind him. We had the building on stilts and I figured out a way that we could just turn it without moving the piers. We had to bring a crew in on Sunday but we were able to just pull it around in a couple of hours and Paul got what he wanted.

> ❝ YOU KNOW, OUR JOB IS SOLVING PROBLEMS. SOMETIMES DESIGNING SETS IS THE EASIEST PART OF IT!

AS: How about with DPs? Do they ever ask to see sketches?

JF: Usually I find DP's and Gaffers want a floor plan of each set or location. With Chivo [Emmanuel Lubezki] we look at locations and talk about light. We look at paintings. On The Tree of Life he showed me a book he had on Vermeer. He loved that window light and dark backgrounds. I worked with him on color. I would paint a wall and he would take some pictures. *Can you make it darker?* I added windows for him. In the house in *Tree of Life* we added more windows because we were shooting only with natural light.

AS: Was it a Terrence Malick decision not to use any studio lighting?

JF: Yeah, he and Chivo set up a couple rules for themselves in the beginning and one of them was to use natural light. Let the blacks really be black. No underexposed film. As much depth of field as possible. To do that they used wider lenses. I think that the narrowest lens they would use was a 27. Anything between 8 and 27.

The boy's bedroom, which we created in our main house, didn't work in the morning. There was no window light at that time. So we had another house three blocks down the street that was similar but faced east and we recreated the bedroom there. We changed the woodwork to match the original. So we had the kid's bedroom here and the kid's bedroom there. But we didn't have the budget to duplicate some of the dressing so if Terry decided he wanted to shoot the boy's room in the morning the dressers and anyone that was kind enough to help would be moving it quickly over to the other location.

That's the way it was with a lot of Terry's scenes. Everything was around the light. Most scenes were shot near windows. I put a translucent roof on the porch to let more light in, but if it was too dark to shoot inside we'd just move outside and shoot that scene or another scene that Terry would think up.

AS: That movie looked beautiful.

JF: I loved working with Chivo. He's such a pleasant person. He taught me that a "light-sandwich" was when you have light coming from two different sources, and it's not as flattering as one strong source. So we would black out other windows and just concentrate on the one the sun was coming through.

When we're not using lights I can look at the set and know what it's gonna look like on film. I've had sets destroyed by over-lighting. Or false lighting. It drives me crazy. Then you get DPs that are great– our work sings.

AS: Chivo's amazing.

JF: With Chivo I go out with my camera and shoot stills and I can show him, *This is what this window looks like at two in the afternoon,* and we are able to discuss the possibilities of a location. I also worked very well with the cinematographer on *There Will Be Blood,* Robert Elswit. I don't envy the daily pressure on the cinematographer.

AS: What is your style when leading your crew?

JF: We are a team. For crews my first requirement is that they can do whatever they do better than I can do what they do. And hopefully, better than anybody else. And the second is that they're as pleasant as possible. You know I work with David Crank a lot and he's just so happy. He's just a happy person. And Ruth De Jong, my assistant art director, is always enthusiastic. Any time you give them a challenge it's like, *Let's do it!* And that's really important in our work. It's a stress-filled job that, if you know you're in it together somehow you're going to make it work. Failure is not an option. And that's why I look for people who are positive and passionate in a crew.

AS: You directed a few feature films yourself. How was that different from production designing?

JF: I enjoyed directing but I love designing for films. The thing that was difficult for me about directing was you'd first have an idea and then you'd talk to a writer and get a script together and then go to a studio and try to get money. And then get actors the financiers would approve. The whole process took a couple of years. I found that I would rather get called when the studio already has the money. Work hard in a creative position and leave the day shooting ends.

AS: Do you ever oversee visual effects that go on after principal photography?

JF: On *Tree Of Life* there were a lot of visual effects but I really wasn't involved. Terry knew what he wanted so I had no concerns. On *Water for Elephants* we were shooting the desert in California for New York State so all the backgrounds were put in with CG matte paintings. I worked with the people at Crazy Horse Effects during shooting. I made some models and gave them my suggestions, but I knew I wouldn't be around when they were working on the matte paintings. I did do some work planning a scene on the Fox lot's Mulberry Street to illustrate to the director how extensions could work there.

AS: Does it bother you not to be there when they're working on the visual effects?

JF: That's just the nature of the beast because they're not going to pay us to hang around for months. The solutions that I come up with are to do as much physical, practical work as possible to avoid CGI and when there is extensive CGI just to figure it out as much as possible before shooting is completed. If you're shooting a scene where you know there's going to be a lot of CGI you really have to have an idea of what the extensions are going to be before you even shoot it. And then you just pray. It's never quite up to your standards but that's just the limitation of the business.

> **FOR CREWS MY FIRST REQUIREMENT IS THAT THEY CAN DO WHATEVER THEY DO BETTER THAN I CAN DO WHAT THEY DO. AND HOPEFULLY, BETTER THAN ANYBODY ELSE. AND THE SECOND IS THAT THEY'RE AS PLEASANT AS POSSIBLE.**

The best situation was *Avatar* where Rick Carter and Robert Stromberg were working together. Because Robert was in, years before Rick Carter and years after, with an extensive knowledge of visual effects, the art department was represented throughout. Rob loves to paint and he's got a good eye. So they had the best of both worlds there. Stromberg did some of the matte paintings for us on *Water for Elephants*. Most of us need an education on how the process works and the options available.

AS: Like Robert Stromberg and Rick Carter you shared an art director credit on *Carrie* but I understand it was a different scenario...

JF: When I did *Days of Heaven* in 1976 I wasn't in the union but Canada said, *Sure, you can work here.* But when I did *Carrie* we were in Culver City and the producers ended up having to pay a union art director to do nothing. We never even saw him. They just said, *Pick a name. Pick somebody. We've got to sign off on it.* For all the days I worked on *Carrie*, a union art director was getting paid and he never came to the lot. That's how the union worked for a long time.

But now my hopes are that the union becomes a place that has some way of raising the standards of everybody's work. By having a knowledge-base that we can all pull from. A program where people can come in and apprentice and learn from the best. I'm hoping that the union can become an organization that makes us all better.

AS: What do you like most about production design?

JF: The thing I like about production design is the idea of illusion. The magic of it. We're creating worlds that don't exist. When I was a kid I saw a *Little Rascals* show on television. They'd built a fort and when you were outside the fort and looked across the fence you saw people marching by with guns. You go inside the fort and it's these two little kids marching with a broken ladder. One rail was missing and the rungs of the ladder were sticking

up so you thought it was a platoon of kids marching with guns. That image just stayed with me. I thought, *That's magical.*

And having financial limitations makes us more creative. You need some sort of parameters or limitations to know how to work. I came up with that realization early on, working with Roger Corman. I was just thinking, *If someone told you to create the most expensive, beautiful dining room that ever existed, where would you start?* You start asking yourself, *Would they have gold inlay? Marble floors? What kind of molding would they have?* But then if they said, *Build it for fifty thousand,* suddenly it's easy. Because you know what you can do with that amount of money. If they said, *build it for five thousand* it becomes difficult and easy in another way. Scripts and budgets set up the parameters for our imagination to start working, because without some guidelines we might just sit and fantasize forever.

AS: Fellini said once that if he didn't have a producer telling him what he couldn't do, he would never do anything.

JF: I love for people to say you can't do it and you figure out a way to do it. Never say to a director it can't be done, instead figure out how to do it. As quickly as possible!

AS: Do you feel a set can be a character?

JF: Definitely it can. Sets are characters. The house in *Days of Heaven* was a character. One of the producers and I had a disagreement because he thought it should have been a ranch house. You know, a Texas ranch house. But Terry wanted a belvedere. He had shown me a picture of a Victorian house and then I looked at the Edward Hopper picture of *The House by the Tracks*–it's just so pleasantly bizarre to put a belvedere out in that environment. It was so big that you could see it for miles away. I think that house became a character. And with the fort in *The New World* I wanted it to grow and evolve.

AS: Evolve through the progression of the story...

JF: Yes. So in *The New World* I built a couple of buildings to add over time so it looked like the settlers had been there for a year. I installed them one weekend and then Terry wanted to shoot something that was from the first year. And I said, *Okay but we can't shoot that building because it's not up yet!* And he said, *Don't worry, I won't see it, trust me!* He started shooting and there's no controlling Terry. I borrowed an orange parka and I went and stood in front of that building. He was shooting the scene and getting excited and they were moving around with a Steadycam and the ADs said to me, *Get out of the shot! Get out of the shot!* But I just stood there. And then Terry comes around and the camera locks on this orange parka and he starts laughing. He knew he'd been caught.

Terry always says, *I will never embarrass you, you'll have final say. If there's something you don't want in the film I'll take it out.* And he says that to Chivo too. So I don't really have to fear.

AS: With your main residence in Virginia do you find it hard to be away from Hollywood?

JF: For the kind of films I do I could be anywhere. I go back and forth. When I lived in California, in Topanga Canyon, I found I was only there three months out of the year. I like being away from Hollywood because in Hollywood you're exposed to the business so much you lose track of the real world. Where I live there's nobody in the business. We live on a farm.

I was painting some barns on a cherry picker with my airless-sprayer the other day and I started thinking, *I could paint a town with this thing in three days.* I'm still always thinking about film. I use all the tools that our construction people use. I'm familiarizing myself with solutions to problems that may come up. Our farm is this big art project.

> ❝ THE THING I LIKE ABOUT PRODUCTION DESIGN IS THE IDEA OF ILLUSION. THE MAGIC OF IT. WE'RE CREATING WORLDS THAT DON'T EXIST.

AS: Do you have a bunch of animals?

JF: We have less now. We have a few horses and dogs. But at one time we had chickens and we had up to fifty-five horses. When we had all those animals I wasn't designing very much. And now, as I'm getting older I'm more excited about design. I want to do more films. I'm back at the farm now but I've been gone two years working three films back to back. And the first of the year it's gonna start up again and it could be another year before I get back.

AS: What's the next one coming up?

JF: My wife [actress Sissy Spacek] is directing a film in Arkansas in the spring. And Terry's got two films coming up. And I know Paul wants to do another film. And I've been talking to some other directors about films. I don't know exactly which ones are going to follow Terry's but there are a lot of films out there. A lot of films I'd really like to do.

AS: How is it with both you and your wife being in the industry? Does that make it hard or is it easier?

JF: Much easier because she understands the commitment and the passion that you have for a project. And when you get home at two o'clock in the morning or you're gone on Sunday she understands why. That you're making the film better. We met on a film and have worked a lot on the same films. We have an unusual life. All of us that work on films are like circus performers or the military. You pack up and ship off.

AS: Any advice for someone who is starting out in the business and wants to avoid any pitfalls?

JF: It's impossible. I would use all your mistakes and pitfalls to become better. You're going to make mistakes. And it's all in how you react to it. A lot of it is slight of hand. Don't let other people know you made a mistake if you can avoid it! Just go forward.

I would say anyone starting out in the business ought to find young directors that are strong and imaginative and work with them for very little money. Grow with them. If you want to be a designer you're going to need to work with a director who's going to get scripts made. I started working with Terry Malick just as he finished film school and he's made me a better designer.

I'm just starting to see people realize how powerful the contribution of production design is to film. Reviewers more often consider the design of a film in their reviews.

Such an exciting job that we have. It's so unpredictable and I just love it.

Hannah Beachler

Hannah Beachler made a name for herself designing critically-praised independent films like *Creed, Fruitvale Station*, and the Best Picture winner *Moonlight.* Now she oversees thirty million dollar art department budgets for films like the blockbuster *Black Panther*, for which she won an Academy Award. When I spoke with her she was preparing to design *Black Panther 2: Wakanda Forever.*

AS: Going from lower budget indie films to the Marvel movie *Black Panther* did it feel like the same kind of job or is the process totally different?

HB: It is and it isn't. The biggest challenge was that it's a marathon, not a sprint. I approached it with a lot of naiveté regarding how much it was really gonna take out of me!

AS: How long were you on *Black Panther* for?

HB: I was on it for thirteen months. And then I spent a month in South Africa and a week in South Korea. That's something that I never got to do with the indie films. It was awesome.

I went everywhere in South Africa, not just Cape Town and Joberg. I flew into Cape Town with my assistant and the location scout and we scouted from Cape Town all the way north past Lesotho and then back up the coast to Ladysmith. It was like two weeks. In thirty days I was in twenty-six airports and seventeen hotels! And at one point they actually did put us on private planes.

When we were flying in, the pilot was like, *We gotta go it's gonna get dark!* I'm thinking, *What's the big deal about it getting dark?* Well, here's what the big deal was. We're flying in as it's getting dark and I see people on the ground holding up cell phones and I realize we're literally landing on what's comparable to a driveway. And there are animals everywhere. People were holding up cellphones so he knew where the end of the runway was! And I was like, *Okay, so that's crazy.*

> ## EVERY SINGLE TIME YOU HAVE TO UP YOUR GAME.

As far as the budget goes, I handled it the same way that I would have handled any budget. It's a lot more people but you either know how to manage people or you don't. That wasn't really different. It was really the mental challenge, the length and the level of sets that we were doing. I knew what the expectations were. The biggest challenge was being scared to death the whole time that I'm not doing honor to the cultures that we were representing or to the people of Africa. And you just had to be like, *Okay, they're gonna love it or they're going to hate it. This is what came out of me. And I gotta stand by my work.* The high level of research we did was so that we did get it right. We needed to make it feel real.

AS: How did that compare to your experience on a movie like *Moonlight*?
HB: *Moonlight* was such a small, beautiful little story about one person in three chapters. A tight little story in one little city. For something like *Moonlight* you don't want people to notice the design so much. If it's standing out then you did not do your job. And the same with *Creed*, even though that was bigger–about thirty-five million dollars at that point and my first studio project. That was the first time I was doing big builds and augmentations and had a much bigger crew. It was very helpful to have *Creed* before *Panther*. It prepared me to go in and speak to Marvel to even get the job. It was a coup that I got that job and part of it was Ryan Coogler [*Creed* and *Black Panther* director]. He's the one that went to bat to get me the opportunity to walk in the door.

That's very important for every professional to remember, it's not necessarily getting someone a job, it's getting them in the door. And that's exactly what Ryan did for me because we already had a working relationship. And he's a very loyal person. You see that he has had most of the same key crew since *Fruitvale Station*. And it'll be that way for Ryan. I would never not want to work with him! I'm always scared when he's around other designers because I'm like, *No, he's mine!*

So that was a big reason I got in the door. I knew I had to go in there and get the job because I couldn't have Ryan say my name to the likes of [producers] Kevin Feige or Victoria Alonzo and then not come in and represent exactly why he mentioned my name! Every single time you have to up your game. I knew I had to bring it. That was challenging.

AS: Is Ryan Coogler a visual person? Is he very focused on how the sets look?

HB: For sure. He's super visual. That's pretty much the only way we work. Visuals and storytelling. And it has been that way since *Fruitvale Station*. Ryan is also his own writer so our process is that after he starts writing he will get on the phone and tell me the story. And he'll tell me what's important to him about the story. For *Creed*, Philadelphia was really important as a character. The gyms were really important to him. And we talk about color. He pretty much was the one who came up with the colors in *Black Panther*, as far as the River Tribe being green, Nakia always was in green, the Dora Milaje in red. He told [costume designer] Ruth Carter and me that the royal color was purple and black. The Border tribe was blue.

When he was in Africa he texted me a picture. He was staying in a hut out in Lesotho with some of the shepherds he met in Cape Town. He just met these guys and they said, *Hey, come to our hut!* He went up to Lesotho and stayed with these dudes and sent me a picture outside their hut that was like ten feet in diameter, in the middle of nowhere. There's a picture of Ryan with one of the Lesotho blankets on and he's like, *This is the Border tribe!* That was a couple months before we even started the movie! He sent me that picture and it never changed. That was all Ryan. He was like, *They're blue!* You know he'll say those things and then Ruth Carter and I will add our perspective to it.

But there's also stuff like the heart-shaped herb where I'd be showing him different visuals every single day. *What about this? What about this? I think this is really cool.* Finally it was like, *This is it! This is what I'm doing! You're just going to have to trust me, Ryan! It's gonna be great! This is the heart-shaped herb and this is the whole story behind this plant.* He's finally like, *Okay! All right, all right!*

He really sets the mood, the tone for everything. There are times when I'd have the fabulous illustrator Tani Kunitake go in and I'd say, *Tani, take a couple hours with Ryan.* He'd go in with his paper and pencil and Ryan would tell him what he's seeing in his head and Tani would draw it out and bring it to me. I'd look at the sketches and be like, *Okay, this is cool. Let's do this. Let's add this. Let's create an aircraft for the Jabari and have it coming up over this hill.*

Ryan and I have our way and you know there's not a lot of words. Sometimes we don't have to say anything. We'll just look at something and I'll be like, *I got ya. Yeah, I see your face. I know what that means!* I think everybody in the film industry wants that relationship.

There are so many famous director/PD relationships like Martin Scorsese and Dante Ferretti, David Fincher and Don Burt. Jess Gonchor and the Coen brothers although the Coens have also used Dennis Gassner and Rick Heinrichs. They have always worked with Nancy Haigh and no other set decorator. Those are very coveted relationships. And I got to the point where I was like, *I'm never gonna find that!* And then here came Ryan. I know how lucky I am to have that relationship.

AS: How closely were you involved with the visual effects department on *Black Panther*? Did your team do a lot of set designs and illustrations that VFX then based their visuals on?

HB: Ryan and I made a pact that visual effects were going to be background as much as possible. *Black Panther* is maybe the only Marvel film that had as much building as we did. But there are certain things that you can't build. VFX came in maybe two months after I started so I already had illustrators going. We had illustrated and designed everything.

I created a five hundred page bible that talked about the history of Wakanda, the demographics, the land, the topography maps. It talked about each tribe, it talked about the metallurgy and mining of Vibranium, the heart-shaped herb, and all the different provinces in Wakanda. It was pretty dense with information, illustrations, and reference images of what the buildings were in each part of Golden City, the capitol of Wakanda, which is what we were focused on at that time. Of course in the sequel you'll see other parts of Wakanda.

So that bible then went to the ILM and The Third Floor visual effects houses. What I would do in post is go into the Marvel offices and sit down with the visual effects supervisor Geoff Baumann. He'd say, *Okay here's what they've done with Golden City,* and

I'd go through and say, *Okay, this needs to not be that. Let's go back and look at the city.* I had one person working on building Golden City in 3D. Which took about eight months. We dumped it onto a ginormous hard drive and that went to ILM so they had our 3D digital city.

When we created the palace in 3D we were able to go inside the models, so when we built the sets it matched when you're looking from inside the set at the outside. And my art directors also built sets in VR so I could stand inside the set and walk around and say, *Okay let's move this here, move that there.*

We did the same thing with the Royal Talon fighter aircraft. That interior was all built. We built some of the exterior as well. And we built the front window using a huge piece of glass. It was really expensive and I was shocked they let us do it but because of the way Ryan wanted to shoot it, we had to. We designed all of the aircraft and we dumped all of those files to ILM and they did the VFX on them.

And the great mound where T'Challa comes back in the third act was all a huge build. That was probably half of a football field and we constructed two stories of the actual building. The VFX was the background and the extension of the building. Everything else was practical and built. We cut the top of a hill off! And we had about a hundred feet in diameter poured concrete, probably fifteen feet deep, because that's the hole they fall into. So it was a real situation!

AS: Did you ever put up scaffolding to show scale to the director in prep before starting a build, like Rick Carter does?

HB: We didn't put up scaffolding for height anywhere but what we did for every single set was tape it out. We taped the whole Nigerian road out, which was like eight hundred feet long, so they could do the action and gain speed. Many times we taped out Warrior Falls. We did it for every single set.

AS: Do you do a lot of sketches yourself? Do you have a background in art?

HB: Originally, when I was young and dumb, I went to school for fashion design. My father's an architect, my mother's an interior designer. I grew up with it. My dad designed the house I grew up in and I have his drawings for the house hanging above my mantle. I do sketch, although I don't as much anymore. I will always sketch what I want and give it to the illustrators, along with a thousand references.

Sometimes I'll just grab a piece of paper and illustrate a room and then say, *Okay, this! It wants to be this and then there's a thing that comes out here. And then it goes over like that and in plan view this is what it looks like. And then this is the elevation and they walk in here.*

We'll sit down with each illustrator and say, *This is the texture. I'm thinking something like this.* I'll have a very specific idea, like for Hall of Kings the idea was puzzle pieces put together. The influence for that was very much Mpumalanga in South Africa and Angkor Wat in Cambodia. Once I hand that to

the illustrator they'll go off and do their thing and then we sit down again and I'll say, *Let's do this and take that away.* And then I'll draw some more while sitting there. And after illustration it goes to set designers and the set designers have to make things that actually work in real life.

> " MY MOTHER'S AN INTERIOR DESIGNER. I GREW UP WITH IT . . . WHEN MY MOM WOULD BE PISSED THE HOUSE WOULD GO ALL DARK BLACKS AND GRAYS. SUMMER IT'S ALL GRAY–AWESOME! I REALLY UNDERSTOOD EMOTION THROUGH THAT.

AS: Do you start with a very long wall with reference images up for all the scenes in the movie?

HB: It's the first thing I do. It's funny, I've done pretty much every movie with Jesse Rosenthal art director and he'll tell my crew, *She's going to spend a week having you guys put up pictures and reference images.* It's intense!

This fabulous decorator I was working with on the Soderbergh film, Merissa Lombardo, was like, *This is intense, man!* Because it is. I get into that in a way that's over-the-top. I do boards not for every scene but for the character's life. I'll do every board for their world. Sometimes every character's assigned a color. I'll talk to the director about what this means to them. And then I'll find a shape for them and that shape then gets carried through. When different characters are occupying the same space you get to work with the shapes and colors that come with their worlds colliding. You can have an impact on the psychology of their motivation, whether it's violent, whether it's passion, whether it's empathy, by using this psychology of color along with how those shapes interact with everything.

Maybe this is the most difficult way to do things but then that's sort of been my motto for my entire life! When I was little my dad was like, *Everything you do, you do it the hardest possible way!* And it hasn't changed my entire life! It's helpful for me to do things that way. Because you know I'm a big fan of Ferdinando Scarfiotti. He changed production design, especially if you watch his early work with the Italian filmmakers. You see the shapes and colors and the collision of those when different characters are together. That's my aesthetic.

I put my sketches up in my office and reference images are everything, but when the illustrations start coming out and the renderings start coming out I'll pick a room and put all the illustrations up. And the hallways are always filled with the reference images.

I've probably done that for every single film. I did it for *Moonlight.* You do as much as you can depending on the size of the production. For *Moonlight* I could only have so many images because it was printing off of my little tiny printer! We didn't have a lot of time and I was one of the painters, the carpenters, set dressers, decorators, and graphic people, as well as the production designer!

But I always make sure to do those walls of imagery. It's something the directors really appreciate because they get a sense of what story it is they're telling.

AS: You mentioned Ferdinando Scarfiotti, are there specific sets of his that inspired you early on?

HB: I did a viewing at the Egyptian Theater in LA of *Il Conformista* [*The Conformist*] and did a talk about it afterwards for the ADG. Basically everything in that film influenced me! And it drew me towards more of his work like *Empire of the Sun, Scarface,* and also towards reading interviews with him and interviews with [director Bernardo] Bertolucci about him. For him the design was very much about the things that felt like they didn't make sense but were still important to the character. He pointed out one example which was in *Il Comformista,* a scene where the main guy goes up to the office of the fascist dude that he's working for. He walks into the office and there are all these walnut shells all over the desk and covering the fireplace mantle. When Bertolucci walked in he said, *What's with all the walnuts?* Ferdinando was like, *That's him showing his power.* Bertolucci said, *Very good. Keep it!* It wasn't like papers and pencils and an in-and-out box and a phone. All of the things you think you have to do to make it understandable. It's just this beautiful scene and it becomes a texture.

Or when they go away to Paris for the dance scene. The lead character is standing in the middle and they're doing a sort of serpentine conga line and they tighten around him and it becomes these concentric circles that are tightening and tightening and tightening because that's what's happening to him, he's getting squeezed. In this very joyous moment the life is being squeezed out of him. You know he's going to die and it's like, *That was so beautiful.* And Scarfiotti was like, *I want this room to be glass because of this dance that's happening,* and he had everything to do with the reds and the blues that were in that room.

Production design is not just about the walls, the brick and mortar. It's about those types of things. The leaves that blew when the camera's really low and it's tracking across to the car when he pulls up to the mother's house. As the camera tracks, the wind blows and the leaves go off to the side and the colors they create mixing with the suit and the car, that to me is production design. That's just beautiful. And everything that it means for that moment in that scene for him psychologically. Scarfiotti does some of the same things in *Scarface* as well and *Empire of the Sun.* What he taught me more than anything is that it's more than just walls, it's the details that make all the difference in how we understand characters. That's something I consistently do and that's because of Scarfiotti for sure.

AS: Do you always have to have a personal connection to the values of the films you work on?
HB: I don't think you can do those types of things if you don't have some connection to the material or if you're doing it for the wrong reasons.

But you do have to make a resume in the beginning! I did these little one million dollar horror movies forever here in New Orleans and Baton Rouge. I used them as a place to learn as a designer. It was a good place to learn how to work with a crew and to learn what everybody expected from me as a designer. That was my first time building anything on stage and managing budgets. I still threw myself into it, like, *I hate this project but it still has to be perfect!*

> **" IT'S MORE THAN JUST WALLS, IT'S THE DETAILS THAT MAKE ALL THE DIFFERENCE IN HOW WE UNDERSTAND CHARACTERS.**

AS: How did you first get into production design?
HB: I went to school for fashion design but I realized I didn't want to do fashion design and I dropped out of college. My friends were all in bands and they were like, *Hey, we should make a music video.* The kind that was sort of grunge and SubPop and 4AD. We just listened to every kind of thing back then and I was like, *Sure, I'll do that!* And they said, *Okay, well, we want you to bring stuff to dress up the place.*

I was like, *Okay, I'll bring the stuff!* I didn't know what it was called! And then we told a little story with it. It was like, how about there's this party and then the cops come and break it up. And I'm like, *Oh my gosh, this is really great! I should go to film school!* And so I was in my late twenties and I went back to film school. I thought I wanted to direct like everybody who goes to film school and I remember on one of my projects one of my professors said, *I don't know if you'll be a great director or anything but your art direction is really amazing!* I was like, *Art direction? What are you talking about? I kind of took it as an insult like, You don't think I can be a great director?* But then I started to realize that's really what I'm paying attention to when I watch films. My whole connection with the story and the characters is through the art direction, period.

I don't know if that's because of how I grew up, with my Mom changing the interior of the house every season. And going to job sites with my Dad and seeing things transform. When my Mom would be pissed the house would go all dark blacks and grays. Summer it's all gray–awesome! It was weird. So I really understood emotion through that. And I realized that there's a bigger connection to this art direction idea, still not really knowing what production design was, but knowing that there's a bigger connection from me to it.

And a friend of mine who graduated from my film school called one day and said, *I'm doing this really small Lifetime movie and I need someone in the art department. Do you want to come and help?* It was me and two other people. I was like, *Okay.* And she said, *We'll pay you.* And I was like, *Oh, for real? Okay!*

I was scrubbing floors and painting and stuff and that was when I told myself, *This is what I want to do!* And from that moment on I have not done anything but art department.

AS: Any advice for beginners wanting to get into production design?

HB: The thing that I always say to young people interested in design is the best thing you can do for yourself is learn every job in the art department. Because that's what I did and that's why I succeeded. You talk to these older guys and they did the same thing. And because of that, you become more valuable to a producer. I understand how much work it takes and how much money it costs because I did all these jobs. On a director's scout producers want to know instantly, right away, *What are you going to do and what is it going to cost?* And I'm able to say, almost to the dollar, how much a set's gonna cost just by looking. I know what I think it should be, I know if it's gonna work, I know the amount of work, the materials, and what departments are gonna need to be involved. Do I need fixtures in here? Do I need welding in here? Am I gonna need a plasterer in here? Are we gonna use industrial foam?

All of Warrior Falls in *Black Panther* was industrial Styrofoam. We bought all the industrial Styrofoam in the United States of America at one point Between *Black Panther* and *Avengers.* There was no more. We had to get it out of Canada!

So I can always give them a number. Even on *Black Panther* I was able to give them numbers. When we were talking about seventy foot by eighty foot sets I was still able to give them a number and it's only because at one point I painted, at one point I was a carpenter, at one point I welded, at one point I was a set dresser. I was a set decorator. I was an on-set dresser.

Learning all those things served me when I was working on small projects because I knew how to do a lot myself. I could get people who maybe didn't know everything to come and help me and cost the producers less. You know, working on a non-union film, a little six hundred thousand dollar film like *Fruitvale Station*, it's like me and Payam [Imani, set dec PA]. Two people. That's how many people I had in the art department and we built and we plastered and we painted and we sanded and it was the two of us doing everything.

Don't ever feel you have to jump right into the production design or art director position. Learn everything. I came up set dec side. If you want to come up art director side, start in construction. Move to a set designer. A lot of architects are coming out of school saying, *I've got this degree, what do I do? I don't know that I want to work in an architectural firm, I'd like to work in film.* You're going to need to start as set designer. Or as an assistant art director.

With something like that, it really is about starting as a PA for a big designer and letting them know, *I'm really interested in art direction.* Find out who the art directors are that you like and call them and talk to them or send them an email. People really do want to help people and give them advice. Look on the ADG's website–they always have events and who are at these events? All kinds of people. You don't know who you're going to run into. I was at an event and ran into Rick Carter for God's sake! Guy Dyas! Jess Gonchor!

> ❝ AS THE CAMERA TRACKS, THE WIND BLOWS AND THE LEAVES GO OFF TO THE SIDE AND THE COLORS THEY CREATE, MIXING WITH THE SUIT AND THE CAR, THAT TO ME IS PRODUCTION DESIGN.

I recently did a Master Class at the Chicago International Film Festival and one of the people who were putting it on was like, *Hey, Adam Stockhausen is coming in to do a Master Class.* I said to them, *I would like you to set up coffee with Adam!* It was like meeting a rock star. It was so awesome. I just asked him all kinds of questions like I'd never even done the job before! And he was like, *You're a designer! What's your process? Tell me about this movie, tell me about that movie.* I was just taking notes and staring at him awkwardly!

Usually I'm surprised when people are like, *Are you Hannah Beachler?* People reach out to me on Twitter. People reach out to my agent who always sends me emails and I try to get back to people. Take those steps and what's the worst they can do? Not talk to you? Get all the information you can and then you just have to take the leap. Find the tax incentive states. Georgia. New Mexico is coming back. Louisiana. Those are great ways to get involved. If you really want to be a production designer and you're serious about that, give yourself time. That's another thing, I gave myself time because I never really wanted to be a designer. I wanted to be the next Nancy Haigh. It was a director who suggested that I design and I was like, *What are you talking about? I'm a decorator!*

> " ONE DIRECTOR SAID TO ME, *WHENEVER SOMEBODY TELLS YOU THEY THINK THE CINEMATOG-RAPHY IS GREAT THEY MEAN THE ART DIRECTION IS REALLY GOOD!*

You just have to put yourself out there. Learn everything and make yourself valuable to producers. Because for a while they're the ones who are going to be hiring you. Once you meet the director that you have this kismet with, then it's directors hiring you. But in the beginning when you do small budget stuff it's gonna be producers because the director's gonna be a crew hire like anyone else. It's not going to be a director-run show when you're talking about a six hundred thousand to a million low or no-budget show.

AS: What do you do when someone first sends you a script?
HB: The first time I read a script I just read it. If I read it all the way through without stopping, I'm interested. If I put it down at some point and go make dinner and then don't pick it up until the next day then I'm probably not interested in it. I'll gauge myself to see how I'm reacting to it. The Steven Soderbergh one, *Kill Switch*, I picked it up and did not put it down until I was at the end. I realized this is something I really want to do.

The next thing I'll do is a deck. I'll go through the script, break down the sets, and then I'll put together a deck or a look book. I'll pull images of ideas that I have that feel the tone, the mise-en-scène, of a particular moment. The colors. Every one of these decks is different depending on what the mood is or what the tone is of the script. That goes to the director and if they're interested they'll talk to me. And then we'll have a conversation.

Steven [Soderbergh's] so funny because I did this deck, put it together and we got on the phone. In fifteen minutes he was like, *Yeah, great, let's do this.* I was like, *Really? You don't need another five hours to talk about this?* He said, *I looked at your decks, I saw* Dark Waters. *I talked to Todd Haynes. I'm really impressed with your work.* Steven's really fabulous. He's really pragmatic. He's not done anything else but be a director his entire life. He started doing it when he was, like, eighteen. He's got a sense of filmmaking that's much different than anyone else I've ever worked with.

It's quite lovely and he knows what he wants. He's his own cinematographer and his own editor. Which makes it a lot easier to work with him because I don't have to wait for the cinematographer to show up, he's here! The cinematographer isn't going to throw a wrench into anything! And he lights very efficiently. He lights the set. Not for the shots, he lights the set. It's every designer's dream.

AS: He's also a visual guy?

HB: Oh, yes, absolutely. He sent me a little one-minute trailer with music that he edited of some of the references I sent him. Just to give me a sense of the tone. It was great! I'd never received something like that from a director. It was only like sixty seconds but it was an idea of where we're going and how the music will sound.

Ryan also always plays the music for me. Todd Haynes also did that. The Coen brothers do it. I've not worked with them but they also send the music first. You start to see the patterns of these masters. Martin Scorsese does the same thing.

So that was really a lovely experience with Steven Soderbergh. We were like two weeks out from shooting when we had to stop because of coronavirus. I haven't been able to shoot with him which I was really looking forward to. And hopefully that still happens.

AS: As part of your process do you feel you have to "crack the code" of a script?

HB: Absolutely. You have to figure out what the theme is that's stringing the whole thing together. That's what the director is going to lean on you for. They have their own ideas but they also want to know what you think the themes are. What you think this whole thing is about. How you see it and your point of view. If they don't see it like you do then it opens up conversation. So now you're having a conversation.

> **❝ I LOOK TO GIVE PEOPLE OPPORTUNITIES AS WELL. PEOPLE WHO MAY NOT BE ABLE TO GET THE OPPORTUNITY BECAUSE THEY'RE A WOMAN OR THEY ARE A PERSON OF COLOR. THEY HAVE A HURDLE TO GET OVER BECAUSE THERE REALLY ARE NOT A LOT OF WOMEN OR PEOPLE OF COLOR IN THE ART DEPARTMENT, IN THE INDUSTRY.**

Not every director knows how to articulate what they're thinking. You have to become a psychic! Sometimes it's like pulling teeth! Sometimes they'll say, *I like this movie,* and you have to decipher what they mean by that. They say, *I like Se7en.* Okay, let's watch it together. When we do that I watch them and see what they're responding to. It's like, *Oh, that's what you like about it! It's not that you want it to be those colors, it's the fact that it's desaturated. That's what you're reacting to.* They're thinking of what the cinematography is gonna look like. One director said to me, *Whenever some body tells you they think the cinematography is great they mean the art direction is really good!*

AS: What kind of characteristics do you look for in your crew?

HB: You know now I have a crew, the same people keep coming back in the department head positions. Jesse Rosenthal [art director] I've worked with since *Creed*. Allen Hook is the supervising art director for *Panther* and he'll be back again. Merissa Lombardo is a decorator I'll be working with pretty consistently from here on out.

> " I'M VERY LUCKY IN THAT I GET TO TRAVEL FOR THE FILMS THAT I WORK ON . . . THOSE EXPERIENCES INFORM MY DESIGN. MEETING PEOPLE AND HEARING THEIR STORIES INFORMS MY ABILITY TO CREATE A WORLD . . . YOU CANNOT CREATE ANY WORLD IF ALL YOU KNOW IS THE BUBBLE THAT YOU'RE IN.

I look for skill. I look to give people opportunities as well. People who may not be able to get the opportunity because they're a woman or they are a person of color. They have a hurdle to get over because there really are not a lot of women or people of color in the art department, in the industry. And so I will look at that. You get the opportunity to come in and talk to me. Doesn't mean you get the job. You have to have the skill. I'm very clear about that. I'm also very clear about firing people. I don't play around with anything. My expectations are high. Everyone knows this now! They are really, really high. My father set almost impossible expectations for us as children. For everything. That's a character flaw to some extent. And as I get older

I'm learning to work with the idea that my expectations can't be everybody's expectations. Right now they are. I expect extremely hard work from people. And good references. And bring me your portfolio and show me what skill you have. Or if you don't have a portfolio yet, tell me why I want you here.

When I was on *Kill Switch* I put it out on Twitter to send me resumes. *I need a PA in Detroit, you have to work as a local but you'll get paid and you get to be my assistant.* I got a ton of resumes. I thought I would get maybe a few but it blew up! I went with a young man who hadn't had any film experience, just graduated from college. He was very young but very passionate, you know? That was the thing. He was very much a self-starter. He took the initiative every single time.

AS: That passion and enthusiasm helps people.
HB: It really does. Show me that you want to be here, right? Show me that you want this! I may need you to organize the paint samples, you organize those paint samples like you ain't never organized paint samples in your whole life! The gods come from the heavens and shine down on the paint sample organization! That's what you have to bring to it. You have to bring that drive! Because there are hundreds of thousands of people who want it too. In order to get in you have to be better than those that are already there.

Some of the people I worked with on *Panther* are third generation Hollywood crew. My charge scenic Franco Ferrara is one of the best scenic painters and I swear I'm going to jump off a building if I can't get him for *Black Panther 2*. He was the scenic charge, his father Gio was his foreman. You look at Gio's IMDB credits and he's got every award-winning film you could think of over the last forty years. His son came up under him. My propmaster Drew Petrotta, his father was a propmaster for Tim Burton and his first job was prop assistant on *Pee Wee's Big Adventure* when he was seventeen. I remember standing in line at catering in the morning and there's this kid in front of me with a walkie on who looks like he's like twelve or thirteen. I was like, *Where are your parents?* Drew said, *That's my son!* Third generation. His first job at thirteen is on *Black Panther*. Think about that. And that's what you're competing with. These kids don't have to go to film school because they're getting master classes in these crafts on the job. And by the time they're of working age supporting themselves they've had a whole career in the film industry, with every connection.

AS: What do you like about production design?

HB: I'm very lucky in that I get to travel for the films that I work on. I get to meet all kinds of people. When I was working on Beyonce's *On the Run II* tour we were in Jamaica for two weeks and the whole crew was Jamaican except for my art director from LA. We had a blast. And one day I was like, *We're going location scouting!* And we spent the whole day in the ocean. We went out to the bush in Jamaica because one of the guys we needed to paint these speakers for the dance hall scene actu-

ally made the pigment for the paint himself. And he lived on the beach. He built this compound on the beach and we hung out drinking Red Stripes and watching the water come in.

Those experiences inform my design. Meeting people and hearing their stories informs my ability to create a world. Whether I like it or I don't like it, whether I'm in a situation that makes me nervous or not. You cannot create any world if all you know is the bubble that you're in.

> **" I'M A TRAVELER. I'M AN ADVENTURER . . . YOU CANNOT BE A DESIGNER IF YOU DO NOT OPEN YOUR WORLD TO THOSE TYPES OF EXPERIENCES.**

Like when I was on *Dark Waters* we spent a week in Parkersburg, Virginia which is very, you know, Red. I was like, *This could be scary.* But it was lovely. When I was in Des Moines, Iowa, working on a film I felt the same way. People had different opinions but we were able to discuss it and the people were lovely. Spending the time in South Africa and South Korea and scouting in London, just having all these different opportunities. Going to Zaha Hadid's DDP in Seoul, Korea, seeing that masterpiece, seeing her masterpiece in Italy, the MAXXI museum in Rome. She's a huge influencer for me to this day and inspiration for the next *Black Panther*. Her designs were the first I was drawn to for possibilities for Wakanda. And to actually be in one of her buildings and walk up and down the stairs that you only see in pictures was an amazing experience. Just to hear the people who run the building tell you about the construction of it and the idea that led to its inception, and how the government reacted to it.

Or in Ladysmith, South Africa, speaking to a young man who is part of the Zulu tribe and who told me about all his struggles and his dreams of coming to America to become a filmmaker. Talking to the bellboy at the hotel and then going back to the township where his family lives and hangin' out. I'm a traveler. I'm an adventurer, although maybe sometimes a reluctant one! You cannot be a designer if you do not open your world to those types of experiences.

But it's not always easy. There are days when I'm like, *I hate this! I'll never do this again!* That's never true, I just say it. My friend and I were talking about retirement the other day and I said, *Maybe when I'm seventy-five!* You look at people like Dante Ferretti, he's in his late seventies and he's still going!

I can't think of a job where I get to be around people like Ryan and Ruth and Rachel [Morrison, *Black Panther* DP] and get to travel and get to meet all kinds of people, eat all kinds of food, and then end up at something like the Oscars! I just don't know of another job where that can happen!

Lee Ha-Jun

Lee Ha-Jun designed arguably the greatest film of the 2020 Oscar season, the Korean movie *Parasite.* He was nominated for the best Art Direction Oscar and won the Art Director's Guild award for Best Contemporary Production Design. The film itself won four Academy Awards, including Best Picture. His team built and dressed almost every set in the movie from scratch, including an entire city street that was flooded. I was elated to discuss production design with this artistic visionary.

AS: Director Bong Joon-Ho told me that you built a section of the city for the amazing flood scene in *Parasite*. What was it like designing that exterior set?

LHJ: There is an actual location in Seoul that has a similar look but since we had to flood the street in the scene we built the whole neighborhood in a water tank. We went location scouting where there are still apartments that have history. I designed the set by looking at the photos from the location scout and also referred back to the semi-basement where I used to live as a university student. When I was living in the semi-basement I hated having a toilet full of mold but later I realized I could draw from that experience!

We built the street set knowing it shouldn't look like a set. We thought it should be a character in the film. So I told my art department team not to fabricate every single detail but instead to get set dressing and props from the real places. We got our ideas from where redevelopment has started.

We got old bricks from there and used them to make silicone molds. We also collected old tiles, doors, chassis, bug screens, windows, gates, pipes and even electric wires. The art department crew, set decoration crew, and also the production team all worked together to collect the materials we needed. It took months to gather all of it. And then we started to fit the materials into our pre-designed set. When the dimensions of the materials we collected didn't exactly fit, I redesigned our set. This process created an environment greater than what we had planned. In those old places people fix and maintain their houses over decades and it makes their houses very different from how they were in the beginning. Watching all of these very specific elements being added made me push myself even harder to create the perfectly detailed neighborhood for the film.

After a certain point my production design team started to really have fun with it. In the poor neighborhood, there were almost twenty buildings and almost forty houses and we tried to create specific stories for each of them. For instance, this house is for an old granny who collects recycling after her son and daughter got married and moved out. Her back is very bent so she needs to use a stroller when she picks up the papers for recycling. Another house is where they do milk delivery for the neighborhood, another is an electronic shop run by a proud, retired Marine. There's a family with many kids that lives on the first floor. Another family runs a snack car so they have many boxes of the ingredients in front of their house.

There's a psychic where all the neighbors go for relief, there's an unemployed YouTuber, and so on. The stories we created helped direct the departments and added more narrative to the film.

AS: And what was the process for designing the rich family's house in *Parasite*? Where did you get your inspiration?
LHJ: The design of the rich house was based on the actors' blocking, the movement of the actors which came from director Bong's plan from when he originally wrote the script.

There are actually not that many big houses in Seoul that have huge gardens, and the ones that do exist are hard to get into. So we researched the design of the rich house using many books and architecture magazines from the library and papers about architecture on the internet.

The concept of the Park's house is that it is built by a well-known architect, so the approach wasn't easy because I'm not an architect. The space an architect can imagine and those a production designer can imagine are different. As production designers we focus more on the movements of the actors or on the camera angles, while architects focus more on the people who live there, because real people have to live in there. The approaches to design are different. We actually heard that comment from an architect when we showed him the floor plan that director Bong came up with during the script-writing stage.

We designed the whole house in the reverse order of a normal architect's procedure. We first designed the inside of the house to accommodate the movement of the actors. And then we planned the outside using many domestic and international architecture references. However, we had to link the inside and outside since we didn't shoot the inside and outside separately. We had to build a whole house. Director Bong and my team gathered many reference images to be able to incorporate his ideas into the rich house. It had to be minimal, flawless, big, and straight rather than being cozy. It had to contrast with the poor semi-basement neighborhood, with moderated color, materials, and designer-made furniture. We needed a big living room with a window that had a panoramic view of their huge garden. We also made the glass window dimensions the same as the camera's aspect ratio, 2.35:1. It is a house designed only for a film shoot. I tried my best to design as minimally as I could by using specific colors and materials because the most important element of Park's house is the garden, rather than the exterior architecture or interior. We actually built the set outside [and not on a stage] so we could incorporate the garden.

Director Bong once mentioned that the fictional architect in the film, Namgoong Hyeonja, built the living room on the first floor to be able to appreciate the garden. That was Namgoong Hyeonja's philosophy. Therefore there is no TV in the Park's living room. We wanted the audience to see the living room and the garden as one unified artistic composition, like a fine art painting or photograph.

To emphasize the contrast of the inside and outside, I used dark wood and materials with a gray tone for the interior.

> **I TRY TO WATCH AS MANY FILMS AS I CAN THAT HAVE A SIMILAR TONE AND MANNER. I FIGURE OUT WHAT IS GOOD TO TAKE AND USE AND WHAT NOT TO TAKE. THERE IS NO LIBRARY AS GREAT AS OTHER FILMS.**

AS: How did you initially meet director Bong Joon-Ho?

LHJ: There was film titled *Haemoo* [*Sea Fog*], that he produced. I was the production designer of the film and that was the first time I met him. When we were having dinner together during the production of Haemoo, Bong told me the basic synopsis of *Parasite*. After that, we worked together first on *Okja* and then on *Parasite*.

AS: How is working with Bong Joon-Ho different from other directors?

LHJ: Director Bong always explains all the details to us. Sometimes we have to guess the parts that are not explained and while this is hard, I'm never worried because the whole process always yields amazing results. Assuming that I tend to use ninety-eight percent of my ability when I work, director Bong always encourages me to use the last two percent and he drags that two percent out of me very well! It feels like he knows everything. I guess that's his skill. He always communicates with his crew, often texting and sending great reference images. He's like a highly skilled captain of an enormous ship. He knows how to compromise when dealing with what's possible and what's impossible. He deals with the variables very well. Most of all, he doesn't shout at all on set. He's very much the ideal director. And his script is very detailed as well. Everything he wants to express, all the underlying meanings, are in the text of the script. The ingredients are very important when cooking, right? Director Bong cultivates the ingredients in his world very well. We just take those ingredients and cook them with nice tools, great decoration and a great chef. I hope to continue working with him for a long time.

AS: What do you do when you first get a script?
LHJ: What I do first after receiving a script is research. I go through books at bookstores, libraries, the internet, research papers. I figure out the characters of the film and this helps me to design the environment. For instance, Ki-woo (the poor son in *Parasite*) sleeps on a couch in the semi-basement apartment without his own room, and Yeonkyo (the rich wife) has a big shelf with expensive dishes in her kitchen. Those choices are all influenced by their characters.

AS: Do you use other movies for reference?
LHJ: Of course. I try to watch as many films as I can that have a similar tone and manner. I figure out what is good to take and use and what not to take. There is no library as great as other films.

AS: Do you do a lot of your own sketching and drawing for your movies? Or do you have a set designer who does all the sketches?
LHJ: I sketch the basic idea myself. When I explain details to the designers, I draw. Before we had such advanced computer applications, we drew from the beginning to the end of the process. Nowadays everything is a fight against time. We often use 3D programs as the sets are developed but we do not have a concept designer in my art team. All of us can handle 3D programs and use Photoshop. For *Parasite* we designed the sets in 3D and made sketches based on those models.

AS: In addition to the 3D computer models did you also build physical scale models?
LHJ: We only used 3D programs when we designed. But there was one more procedure that we used while in pre-production for *Parasite*.

Normally during pre-production director Bong will go to the locations often. But for *Parasite*, we built all the main sets. Since they didn't already exist in reality, we needed to provide him the something that he could use to visualize the locations during prep. Based on the 3D designs and renderings my team created, the visual effects team made a 3D virtual environment that, when using a keyboard like a game, one could wander around inside the houses. It was a totally new experience for us too.

AS: How involved are you with visual effects on your movies?

LHJ: Basically the concept art and 3D models that my team generates become a blueprint for post CGI. The work of the visual effects team should be based on the content of the production design team. The mountain in the background of the rich house's garden and the neighborhood background for the poor family's apartment were shot separately and were later composited during post production. Our team views the results and discusses any fine-tuning that might be needed.

AS: You also worked with Bong Joon-Ho on the movie *Okja*. Were you involved in the CG animal design?

LHJ: There was a character designer who worked separately. Looking at several submitted design options I helped to improve and finalize the design in discussions with the director.

AS: How was your process working on *Okja* different from Parasite?

LHJ: For Okja, the principal photography was in the US. For those of us who are used to the Korean system, it was a very unfamiliar experience. Every crew member had a very specific profession and predetermined hours, and the set was full of blue screen. There were so many things to learn.

Meanwhile, *Parasite* was built practically from beginning to end. It was an impressive depiction of a very authentic Korean subject. One will be able to use the film to look back and study current Seoul and see the reality of Korea today.

AS: How did you get into production design? Did you go to art school or film school? Have you always been an artist?

LHJ: I graduated from Korea National University of Arts, and majored in Stage Art. At the time I worked on the set design of plays, musicals and operas. Then I took part in a senior's film thesis. That was when I was blown away by film production design. I remember that I was treated as an outsider when I worked in film for the first time. This made me work even harder.

" BASED ON THE 3D DESIGNS AND RENDERINGS MY TEAM CREATED, THE VISUAL EFFECTS TEAM MADE A 3D VIRTUAL ENVIRONMENT THAT, WHEN USING A KEYBOARD LIKE A GAME, ONE COULD WANDER AROUND INSIDE THE HOUSES.

AS: What do you like about designing movies?

LHJ: Visualizing a script for the first time is exciting. It's also a job where you can really leave a mark in history. There are classic films that are still honored today and I imagine one day my work will be included among those classic films. I do my best to make my own mark.

AS: Do you always work with the same crew?

LHJ: Yes, my crew has worked with me for five to six years on average. The longest one has worked with me for ten years. They are family rather than crew for me. We know each other very well, encourage each other and enjoy working together.

AS: What characteristics do you need in your art dept crew?

LHJ: While individual technique is important, I believe the basic mindset of collaboration is the most important characteristic for my crew to have. There is a separate division for 'Art Department', but the entire film crew collaborates: Directing, Producing, Photography, Lighting, Props, Costumes, Make-up, and so on. Many different teams need to think together and figure out what's best for one film. There should be a lot of communication, collaboration, and compromising if needed. Within the overall team, we lead and follow each other to visualize the film as written.

AS: How did you work with the DP on *Parasite*?

LHJ: We determined the angle of the house based on the angle of the sun and based on our 3D-rendered set designs. Sometimes we discussed widths and lengths to accommodate the required angles. I always go over the production design not only with the director but also with the DP. Our DP Hong Kyung Pyo loved to take reference photos. We went over many stories and ideas based on his photos. And we discussed practical lights and camera angles by looking at the 3D virtual environment created by VFX. Our DP is a real master who is always really invested in the project. I always learn a lot from him and respect him.

AS: How do you get your jobs? Do you have an agent? Or is it all through people you know?

LHJ: I get my jobs from directors, producers and sometimes from other acquaintances. We don't have agencies for crew in Korea, just for the actors. We all work independently.

AS: Are you on the set during shooting?

LHJ: I'm on set most of the time except when I have to build another important set in advance.

AS: You mentioned earlier that certain sets can become characters in the movie...

LHJ: The set seems like it's in the distant background, behind everything, but when the crew and actors come into the set and become one with each other's inspiration, the place becomes the main character.

AS: How do you feel about people saying the design of a set should be "invisible"?

LHJ: I don't think it's always good to design a set that stands out. Except for the cases where you need to emphasize the expression, it is better to be in harmony with the character of the film.

AS: How do you see the future of production design? More and more greenscreens and VFX?

LHJ: I was kind of anxious when I was doing *Okja* because it had a lot of CG compared to my previous work. But the production design team's job still requires creativity. There may be fewer sets to build but won't there still be infinite imagination and details required?

AS: What project are you currently working on?

LHJ: I'm working on the biggest blockbuster in Korean film history. It is the first time for a Korean film to have two production designers.

AS: I'll look forward to checking that one out. Do you think you'll ever be interested in writing and directing a feature film of your own?

LHJ: Rather than directing or writing, I'm more interested in cinematography. I study cinematography now too.

AS: Do you have any advice for people just starting out as production designers?

LHJ: Production designers should open their eyes wide. Never close your thoughts. When you open your eyes to small things, you'll see the details that could make an amazing library. You can draw inspiration from this library. Do not try to look only for good or cool things. See everything you can. You will see the story and what it contains. When you keep looking at the people on the street, you can sometimes tell their character from their walking style and fashion. If you train yourself to look into the things around you, you'll have a very good quality library of your own. Also, you need to be phys-

ically healthy so that you can have the strength to run around to work. Sometimes you need to win the fight with stamina. Do not give up easily. Do not only watch entertaining films. Watch lots of films so that you can compare them to each other. But even as I say this, I know I'm unable to watch that many films because of my work schedule. I have a wish list of films to binge watch later when I have time. I hope that time comes soon.

> DO NOT TRY TO LOOK ONLY FOR GOOD OR COOL THINGS. SEE EVERYTHING YOU CAN. YOU WILL SEE THE STORY AND WHAT IT CONTAINS . . . DO NOT ONLY WATCH ENTERTAINING FILMS. WATCH LOTS OF FILMS SO THAT YOU CAN COMPARE THEM TO EACH OTHER.

AS: Anything else you would like to add?

LHJ: Thank you to everyone who loved the Korean film *Parasite*. I am so grateful for the love and for the film to generate so much interest during the Oscar campaign. It was an unforgettable experience.

FIRST

What do you do after you receive a script?

*A compilation of excerpts covering
the subject of first steps, taken from
the interviews in this book*

The job of production design consists of a maelstrom of activity every day and night for months on end, but what do you begin with on the first day? What are the initial steps after they send you a script? How do you crack the code and create a unique visual interpretation of the script, one that will inspire the director and motivate the rest of the crew? Do you start with extensive research? Find the elements that strike a chord with you in the script? Or fill a book with sketches?

GUY HENDRIX DYAS

The first thing I do is I start sketching; actually I start a new sketchbook for every film as it's the easiest way to keep ideas organized. Research is very important to my process as well but it usually comes into play slightly later, when we have an art department set up and are starting to put presentations together.

SARAH GREENWOOD

Well, if there's a book that goes with it like *Anna Karenina,* you read the book. I'm reading another fantastic book which is by Orlando Figes called *Natasha's Dance* which is all about Russian society from the 1600's. Why they built St. Petersberg, what Moscow was like, what society was like at the time. Frankly, if you don't know that I don't see how you can understand how *Anna Karenina* in Tolstoy's mind worked. You have to know that. Whether you choose to use it, to apply it, is up to Joe and myself. But you have to know as much as you can know about the subject. That's even before we start.

And then for me I just get as many visual references as I can. When we came back from Russia we had to buy another suitcase. It was way overweight: forty-two kilos of books I bought in Russia. I can't read any of it because it's all in Russian–they're all visual, pictorial, photographic. So then you go through that and then you start trying to figure it out.

EVE STEWART

I'll always read it and start drawing all over the script. And I buy a new sketchbook and start drawing. I'll sit in a room with the director drawing and thinking. Looking at research and pulling out books and images.

RICK CARTER

The first thing I do is to let it wash over me so I can just experience the first reading, which will be the freshest I'll ever have. Just experience what the movie means to me and what comes out to me. In your interview with Guy Dyas he talked about sketching what he saw along the way, but however one does that, whether one makes notes or doesn't make notes, sketches or doesn't sketch, one gets a feeling from the script.

Now let's just say, as it's been numerous times for me, and as it was on the Star Wars movies, there's no script when I'm starting. Concepts are just being developed. *Polar Express* was that way, there was just the children's book. And *Avatar* was only partially developed. I'm looking for the feeling and what flickers and the little glimpses and associations I make. I try to note what they are without interrupting the flow because I'm not only looking at it moment to moment as though it's a series of stills, I'm looking at it cinematically, in motion. Then I see what aspects of characters or scenes I associate with something else in a script. They are either connected literally or are not connected but should be.

FIRST

ADAM STOCKHAUSEN

I start with imagery. I start pulling references for things. A lot of it starts online now because there's so much there and every year there's more. But then you start watching films as reference and you start looking into books. And stuff that isn't always online. And then you start going places and looking at the real thing. So it grows.

EUGENIO CABALLERO

I believe a lot in one's first intuition. I'm a Latin, I'm Mexican, so my approach is not on the cold side, it's very visceral.

When you first read the script and make notes, it's like a switch flips in your head. When you read a script you start that dream. You find answers to a lot of questions just by walking or by reading. You're looking for things and creating, but mainly you're just getting into a mood where you're more receptive to the things around you. I love that process. It's one of the things that I enjoy the most.

HANNAH BEACHLER

The first time I read a script I just read it. If I read it all the way through without stopping, I'm interested. If I put it down at some point and go make dinner and then don't pick it up until the next day then I'm probably not interested in it. I'll gauge myself to see how I'm reacting to it. The Steven Soderbergh one, *Kill Switch,* I picked it up and did not put it down until I was at the end. I realized this is something I really want to do.

The next thing I'll do is a deck. I'll go through the script, break down the sets, and then I'll put together a deck or a look book. I'll pull images of ideas that I have that feel the tone, the mise-en-scène, of a particular moment. The colors. Every one of these decks is different depending on what the mood is or what the tone is of the script. That goes to the director and if they're interested they'll talk to me. And then we'll have a conversation.

MICHAEL NOVOTNY

It varies script to script. Some scripts require a lot of very specific sketching, some scripts require none. A lot of it's just conceptual. I read the script once, very briefly, just to get an overview. That's mostly to send an emergency message to the location manager saying, *Here's the big one this time.* Then we tackle that part together first. This is for episodic–features are very different. The episodic process is the most fly-by-the-seat-of-your-pants and run-'til-you-drop-dead process that there is in filmmaking–which is why I like it so much. And it's a question of reading the script and then pulling out the elements, making the breakdown. The breakdown sort of gives you a sense of the quantity. Once the quantity's assessed you allocate areas

What do you do after you receive a script?

of responsibility. And this is where you're close to being a scientist because you really have to quickly assess what the ingredients are. Once you do that you can start to allocate areas of development to other people. When you do that, and you have good people, you have a good project. So I think half the battle is to let those good people do their job. And I have been working with my team for years. They're like an extension of me. I can sketch on the phone, talking about past creations that we've done together, and I will know that we're all talking about the same thing.

It's very different when you're dealing with someone who's entirely new to you and it's a new team. I went off to do a series in Canada and I was able to bring nobody. So I approached it very differently. I did a lot more very specific sketching and so forth. It depends on the show.

JOHN MUTO

It is different in each one. In the olden days, when they knew how to make movies, the script would go to the supervising art director. It would go to Cedric Gibbons, or Anton Grot or one of these guys. Because the first thing you need to know is how you're going to make this movie. But now someone will decide they're going to make a movie and the first thing they'll do is hire a production manager who will go out location scouting. So you got a guy who's not a scout and not a designer scouting locations that may or may not be necessary. Just because the script says "swimming pool" doesn't mean they need a swimming pool. They could have scouted *River's Edge* based on the script and they wouldn't have found a single location that I was going to use. So the first thing that you have to do is convince them to throw away all the work that they've put in so far.

COLIN GIBSON

I read [the script] and then go back and start over again almost immediately. I break down the ideas that are in it. If it's a good script I can find three or four arresting images. You come up with those three or four arresting graphic moments and then you go back to the director or whoever's offered this to you and say, *What about this? This is how I imagine you could get that across. Does this tap into something?* Then you start to come up with a visual language to go with the written language. I'm wedded to the word as much as I am to the picture. If you discover something that strikes a chord with you, usually it can echo with an audience as well.

Robert Stromberg

Robert Stromberg won an Oscar as production designer of one of the highest grossing movies of all time, *Avatar.* His second Oscar came from Tim Burton's *Alice In Wonderland,* which has also made over one billion in the box office. A leader in visual effects, he began as a traditional matte painter and now directs.

AS: You've said that production designers don't need to feel threatened by visual effects these days because they're involved during the physical production of a movie, unlike how historically visual effects would only happen in post and the production designer would be long gone...

RS: Sometimes you'd get a kind director that would keep the production designer involved into post but most of the time the production designer would leave the show right after the physical production was done and then the design part of it actually fell to the visual effects vendor, the visual effects supervisor and the director. They'd create

what went into those greenscreens and so on. But with the new technology, you're seeing what will be there on the day you're shooting the physical set. It gives the production designer input and they have a say in what the design should be.

Because I come from visual effects I know how much stuff that I personally designed for movies well after the production designer was gone. That's why on *Master and Commander* I created this new role which I called *visual effects designer.* That was the person who would take over when the production designer left the show and be the mouthpiece for the director and the visual effects supervisor and the vendor. So there would be a creative entity still continuing along into post.

AS: Keeping one design vision.

RS: Yes, and of course respecting what the production designer had done. I was talking to Rick Carter about this. He's great because not only is he interested in knowing how it all works but he also knows the value of what the new technology can do for you. He's an old school production designer who obviously knows the nuts and bolts of traditional production design. After our working together Rick can now go to another project and have a greater toolbox to play with. It's not only about what's going to be inserted later, it's also about how much to build as a physical set or not.

AS: It affects the resources that you spend on the physical set…

RS: A lot of times the physical sets can be overbuilt. Especially in these days when budgets are constantly being scrutinized and getting smaller, we need to find ways to streamline and accommodate these budget changes. So one way you do that is have a better understanding of exactly how much you need to build or not. It makes a lot of dollars and cents to the studios as well.

AS: You mentioned working with Rick Carter, what was that like?

RS: Rick came on *Avatar* a year after we'd been designing this world. I was working with Jim [Camer-

on] directly a year, maybe a year and a half, before Rick came into the picture.

AS: You were designing during that year?

RS: Yes, the whole world itself. Of course there were other needs after that. For example, the Hell's Gate and the ships really hadn't been designed yet. At that time I was still called the visual effects designer and Rick was coming in as a production designer. He had the right to come in and stick a flag in everything and do what he wanted. But he doesn't have that personality. He loved what had been designed. Jim was also on board with the design already so Rick, being the personality that he is, decided to bring his knowledge of production design to what had already been done. He went along with the idea that there were two creative entities that were going to come together.

Maybe six months or so after Rick came on I had a meeting with Jim at his house. I'd been on it about two years at that point and we had designed almost all the organic side of Pandora–the floating mountains down to every little detail of the planet. Jim said, *I know Rick's on board but I really think that you also deserve production design credit.* We just needed to run that by Rick, and Rick was supportive of that from the beginning. There are some people who would feel a little funny about sharing that credit but in this particular case it actually helped the film because in the film itself there's an invasion into the organic Pandora by this man-made force. It's kind of a collision of two different design elements.

That's what's happening in the movie and that's what was happening behind the camera. So that actually helped the feeling of being an alien force in a pure world. By the way, Rick had a tremendous task in front of him of building all the physical sets in New Zealand.

AS: The fact that James Cameron stood up for you in receiving a production design credit speaks for him as well.

RS: There actually are three production designers because the other one is Jim. We've all heard people tell those stories about Jim but the thing that they don't know about Jim is that he has tremendous heart and soul and passion for things. And a lot of great artists, because they're so passionate about things, have short fuses because they want their product, their artistic vision, to be something exceptional.

AS: Uncompromised.

RS: Yeah, and I don't think that relates just to Jim. Any critical artist would feel that way. You have all of the guns pointed at Jim and all the pressure on him to deliver. Because you have to remember up until December of 2009 we had no idea what *Avatar* was going to do at the box office or whether it would be accepted. As a matter of fact it was the opposite. Around July or August, when the first trailers came out, it was being criticized a great deal. And so it took a lot of courage from Jim. He continued on with all of this bad criticism coming very early on and he stood tall because he knew, like we all knew, that it was going to be good.

Doing a movie with Jim is like going into battle. If you're not going to pull your weight you're going to get yelled at. And with good reason, because there's a lot on the line. That being said, once you make that connection and show that you can pull your weight and that you're a good soldier then you're treated with respect. You're treated with dignity and you're more of a collaborator at that point. It's the people who don't show the same enthusiasm, or don't come through, or don't listen, or don't follow the plan, those are the people that get yelled at. But generally if you're doing your job and you're contributing and you're collaborating it's just like working with anybody else.

AS: You mentioned that he's almost a third production designer. Is he very hands-on, doing sketches and so on?

RS: I think he had more input on the creature designs and the mechanical machines. Of course he had input on everything but less on the environmental stuff. He would of course comment on things, but he saw that cool things were happening and most of the time he did pretty much leave me and a small group to do what we would at will.

AS: How different was it to work with Tim Burton on Alice in Wonderland?

RS: I've been fortunate enough to work with a lot of great directors from James Cameron to Tim Burton but also with Steven Spielberg and Peter Weir. The thing that always strikes me as interesting is they all do the same job, they all direct movies, but it's just that the way they do it is so different. I always find that when I meet a director for the first time I quickly try to figure out what their personality is and then adapt my approach to that. Because every director's different and the way to present things to them is different.

Early on in *Alice in Wonderland* I would go over to Tim's house and office in England with [visual effects supervisor] Ken Ralson. For the first three months or so it was just Ken, Tim, and myself pretty much figuring out what we were doing, just through pencil sketches and doodling and ripping and throwing paper away.

AS: And Tim Burton is also an artist...

RS: Tim could be a production designer tomorrow himself. And he has a very specific style that everybody knows. Going into something like that, the first thing I did was re-look at all his films, going back all the way to *Beetlejuice,* just to get the vibe before I met him. But on *Alice* he was trying to invent a new style in addition to keeping his traditional fingerprint on it.

It was more a bunch of guys drawing on tablets and saying, *What do you think of this, and this, and this?* Whereas with Jim I would do something and then we'd get together and he would either like it or not and contribute or not, but if he liked it, it just went on through the process. Whereas Tim would constantly perfect design. Not that Jim didn't. They're both artists in the traditional sense but one of them is really down the art trail and the other is down the art-tech trail.

It was an interesting experience with both but I think because I grew up drawing and doing matte paintings and being an artist myself, it was a unique experience to go through a process with an artist of the caliber of Tim.

> " I GOT FIRED FROM MY JOB LOADING TRUCKS. I GOT FIRED FOR DRAWING ON THE JOB ... THERE'S A GREAT LINE IN *AVATAR* WHICH RELATED TO THAT MOMENT FOR ME, *WHEN ONE LIFE ENDS, ANOTHER BEGINS.*

AS: Did you go to art school?

RS: I had dreams of going to art school and I actually applied and was accepted to Art Center in Pasadena. I moved to Los Angeles from Carlsbad and after that was pretty much penniless and sleeping on a friend's couch. Of course before I left Carlsbad I was doing tons of artwork. I was doing matte paintings down there.

So I spent a couple of years on loading docks, you know, loading boxes. I don't think I've ever told anybody this but I can pin one point as my change in direction–it would be when I got fired from my job loading trucks. I got fired for drawing on the job.

AS: Really? So you were sitting there with a sketchbook—

RS: Yes, sketching, and someone fired me! There's a great line in *Avatar* which related to that moment for me, *When one life ends, another begins.* Jake says it as he's coming off the transport.

What that did was it opened up a window where I was able to meet somebody who knew somebody who knew a cousin of somebody else who worked on commercials. That opened up a production assistant job where I literally started at the very bottom. I swept floors. As a matter of fact, I remember literally sweeping out an entire auditorium for a commercial one time. Stayed up all night. Everyone had gone home, the lights were out.

And the next morning I was still there and the producer came back in and he saw me still sweeping and he said, *Hey come here. He sat me down and said, I like you're enthusiasm. What do you want to do in this town?* I told him about visual effects and matte painting and so on and somehow that led to the next thing and all of a sudden I had an illustrating job. And then I had a job doing an actual matte painting for something. The first time someone paid me for a matte painting I thought I'd hit the jackpot. It was about twelve hundred dollars or something. I thought there's nothing higher than this.

AS: And this is the traditional matte painting on glass . . .
RS: Yeah, old school. As my former boss used to say, *Animal hair and sticks.* I was probably like nineteen or twenty years old and I ended up in Canada, in Toronto, and I'd never been out of the country. I ended up doing glass shots right on the set which is even worse because you actually set up a piece of glass in front of the camera and there's a partial set that you're blending a painting into. So that was my first set experience. It was on a Saturday morning kid's show called *Captain Power.* I was starry-eyed and again thought, *It can't get any better than this.*

And, long story short, that led to the next thing and then the next thing and then I was hired by a company called Illusion Arts. I met Syd Dutton and Bill Taylor and they were part of a group from Universal Studios run by Albert Whitlock who was probably the most famous matte painter of all time. He was, by the way, the reason I started matte painting–I saw an interview with him. Albert Whitlock and Syd took a liking to me and gave me advice so then again I thought I'd reached the top and it can't get any better than this. You can see where this is going.

So I worked there for seven years and then had a rough patch for a couple of years where I got very sick. During that period of time where I was lying there sick I told myself, *If I ever get out of this jam I'm going to do something really special with my time.* I said, *I need to push harder.* I got married that same year, had a kid a year after that, and career-wise I really pushed for the big time. I got some investors in and started a production company called Moving Target and I became a commercial director for a couple of years. I got in the DGA. And during that period of time I was really pursuing directing which is why I started to begin with. I wanted to be a director.

Moving Target went on for a while and then I decided to start another company parallel to that which was a visual effects company called Digital Backlot. Digital Backlot started to really sail and we were doing a lot of commercials. Things were looking pretty good but that company, as a lot of companies do, fell apart.

At that time I met Peter Weir and he asked if I could help him through the visual effects process. This was *Master and Commander*. I ended up spending a year with Peter, traveling with him. Being his voice for the film to ILM because he's old school and didn't really understand visual effects. What that gave me was a bigger handhold into design. After all the years of designing and doing matte painting, this was a slightly bigger-scale design issue. It started to give me the experience which would eventually lead me to production design.

AS: How did your transition from traditional matte painting to computers come about?
RS: We all saw the computers coming and to us that was like the army of Satan coming. Because we all thought, *Well, this is it, I don't know computers and I'm going to be out of a job. Obviously this magic box is going to rule the universe.*

AS: Some of the old school production designers might be thinking that now, seeing visual effects coming in...
RS: It's the same situation. I finally bought a computer. It was 1994 so you can only imagine how slow it was. I bought it and it literally sat in the corner of my apartment and I didn't turn it on. But I had one, you know? I would walk by and give it the stink eye every once in a while.

> " WE ALL SAW THE COMPUTERS COMING AND TO US THAT WAS LIKE THE ARMY OF SATAN COMING. BECAUSE WE ALL THOUGHT, *WELL, THIS IS IT, I DON'T KNOW COMPUTERS AND I'M GOING TO BE OUT OF A JOB. OBVIOUSLY THIS MAGIC BOX IS GOING TO RULE THE UNIVERSE.*

The reason I bought it in the first place was that I used to do what were called original negative matte paintings. Which is a matte painting but you're sort of blending blindly. I did a matte painting of the Bonneville Salt Flats and I needed to blend through a white area which was nearly impossible. One day somebody said, *You know they have this new machine, a digital visual effects toolbox.*

I had spent about three weeks trying to blend this thing together and then we went to this place and the guy said, *What do you want to do?*

I want to blend this so that you don't see a line. And the guy says, *Oh, like this?* And he literally blended it in three seconds. I said, *Okay I need to buy a computer.*

Once I started to work on the computer I realized that there are some pretty cool things that you can do. And by the way, bringing all of the old school experience to the computer put me way ahead of a lot of people. Because what happened was, the people who created them were technicians and not really artists. The early examples of art on computers were not that great because you have technicians trying to be artists. It only started being something really valid when artists got into the mix.

It was a very small group of people back then and I very quickly became one of the main, top people that did digital matte painting. I can't even remember what year the last physical matte painting I did was. Probably around 1996 or something.

> " YOU WANT TO BE SOMEONE WHO SAYS, *I DID THIS, THIS AND THIS, WHAT DO YOU THINK?* AS OPPOSED TO THE PERSON WHO SAYS, *IS THIS WHAT YOU MEAN?* IT'S A HUGE DIFFERENCE BECAUSE IT'S THE DIFFERENCE BETWEEN A FREE THINKER AND SOMEONE WHO'S JUST GETTING BY. SOMEONE WHO'S CONTRIBUTING AND SOMEONE WHO'S JUST KEEPING PACE.

Of course production designing these movies is a huge accolade, it's really great, but you're managing a huge group of people and there's a lot of political entanglement and everything else that comes with something that big. That's why I still love to go back to matte paintings because it's just me and maybe one other guy. In a way it's a very fast satisfaction, you know what I mean? A lot less stressful.

AS: On Alice in Wonderland, how did you overcome the difficulties of the actors mainly working with greenscreen?

RS: I had walls full of artwork every day on the set related to what scene we were shooting. I had a full digital MotionBuilder set with which we could do an instant composite. I had a whole crew of SONY Imageworks guys who had a command center that was feeding in and doing real-time composites. We were tracking camera and everything. That was what I invented on *Avatar*–we call it Simulcam. We used it again on *Alice*. But at a certain point Tim actually preferred to just stare at the actors. It was interesting because Jim wanted every detail of the background whereas Tim wanted to focus on the performance.

And the third thing I did was I hired four model builders. We had a miniature set of every scene in the movie. So if there was a question of what was going to be there, Tim could go over to the model with Johnny Depp and say, *You're going from here to here.* Then you could go to the physical set and you could see a playback with the composite. That was not possible during the times of *Skycaptain and the World of Tomorrow* and I think the performances are better now because of things like that.

AS: Do you plan on continuing to do production design alongside visual effects?

RS: For me personally there will be more design and more matte painting. I like to mix it up. I don't want to be just one thing. I just find it's an exciting time and with my knowledge of what's possible I'm also trying to push into directing.

AS: Do you have any advice to people just starting out in this business?

RS: You want to be someone who says, *I did this, this and this, what do you think?* As opposed to the person who says, *Is this what you mean?* It's a huge difference because it's the difference between a free thinker and someone who's just getting by. Someone who's contributing and someone who's just keeping pace.

There's also an old saying that I always stick to, *Luck is being prepared when opportunity arrives.* That's kind of what it is. Also, you can generate your own opportunity by not being overly aggressive, but still by pushing.

AS: The people you want on your team are–

RS: Innovative and pushing the envelope even further out. Because we're still in the infant stages of all this digital technology. Even after doing what we've done, it's still early on. We're just really less than twenty years deep into this. If we can do *Avatar* today just think what we can do fifty years from now. And it's just increasing exponentially. There's the success of *Avatar* and *Alice in Wonderland*'s box office is through the roof. I honestly feel *Avatar* changed the game–it'll be that spike in film history like *Star Wars* was. That's the first spike of many coming in the next twenty years. So I'm excited.

John Muto

John Muto designed one of the biggest live-action comedies of all time, *Home Alone.* His extensive list of features also includes one of my own personal favorites from the 80's, *River's Edge.* He worked with director James Cameron on *Terminator II/3D* and visual artist H.R. Giger on *Species.* We grabbed lunch while he was co-teaching production design at AFI with the late Hitchcock art director luminary Bob Boyle.

AS: What brought you into production design in the first place?

JM: You know for me, my training is entirely in writing–I have no design training whatsoever. I got out of college and I always wanted to be a writer. I don't know if I wanted to be a comic book writer, or a movie writer, just some kind of writer. Which I think, by the way, is a better preparation for production design than most art schools. Because movies are about story. And of course that's the biggest problem we have, is getting good stories. Working with lousy scripts, believe me, in

film school that's a big problem. So that's what I studied in college. I went to Berkeley. I got out of college and I actually applied to film school and I got in but I just couldn't bear to go. I'd had it with school and I didn't know what I should do. But I had a strange desire to get into show business and of all things I got mixed up with a theater company that was really a dance company.

And I had this sort of odd fantasy of being a dancer, because I loved dance films. I had no talent but I was young and I was very strong and very thin and so I could actually keep up with people who had talent. A little bit. Enough that I got into a dance company. Which just recently had a revival of one of their ancient pieces from the 60's at the Redcat downtown. It's actually a famous piece of avant-garde choreography that they rarely did. When I was with them they decided to do it because a film company was going to document it. And the guy who did our lights was sick. So I wound up doing the lights. I was the natural choice. I wasn't in the dance really but I was doing the lights. Although I wound up moving with the lights as if it was a dance. But the upshot of the whole thing was that I got involved with the film company. These guys did commercials and one thing let to another and I got into animation.

I did some animation for them because even though I didn't have any particular talent as a dancer I had learned so much about movement and I had kind of an intuitive way of dealing with drawing and animation so it was all very natural. Then out of the blue, dumb luck, I got a call from the Oingo Boingo people who I'd known slightly in college. They were doing a feature film and they wanted animation and they knew that I was a friend and that I knew something about animation. It just came at a perfect time for me to just cut loose. So I did a piece to just show them what I was thinking about and they were very excited about it. It was for this movie called *Forbidden Zone*. It was an underground feature directed by one of the Oingo Boingo guys, Richard Elfman. His brother is the composer Dan-

ny Elfman. Susan Tyrrell is in it, Joe Spinell is in it. The Kipper kids, Viva, the Andy Warhol Superstar. A lot of these people are still around. And this movie's been revived in the last few years. They made a great DVD of it, it was in black and white and they colorized it, which I thought was just a total commercial, grasping way to squeeze more pennies out of it. But the colorizing is beautiful. Lovely. It really enhances the film. The posters were done in the 80's with that kind of punk graphics, skateboard graphics, very garish colors. Which is what I assumed they would do with *Forbidden Zone* but they did it more with pastels and really sensitive colorations.

> " MY TRAINING IS ENTIRELY IN WRITING—I HAVE NO DESIGN TRAINING WHATSOEVER. I GOT OUT OF COLLEGE AND I ALWAYS WANTED TO BE A WRITER. I DON'T KNOW IF I WANTED TO BE A COMIC BOOK WRITER, OR A MOVIE WRITER, JUST SOME KIND OF WRITER. WHICH I THINK, BY THE WAY, IS A BETTER PREPARATION FOR PRODUCTION DESIGN THAN MOST ART SCHOOLS.

AS: The movie combined animation with live action?

JM: It's a live action picture. In fact the picture was done before they had any animation but they realized they needed it. The animation comes when the action starts to lag a little bit, almost at regular intervals. Some of my stuff sort of pretends to be live action because I do cut-out animation from cut-outs I make of the characters.

AS: Kind of like *Monty Python*?

JM: Some of it's very Monty Pythonesque, some of it's very much like Fleischer Brothers animation. You know–weird, rubbery things. We were working with an animation place in Hollywood. They had worked out what they call a photo-roto process– where you put a lamp into the camera to shine down and you can trace frames. Well they took it a step farther and used photographic paper and used it as an enlarger in a way. And then you had pegged frames that you knew related to the film.

So we did a scene where you fly into this girl's mouth. She's screaming and you fly down her throat. And you know I was able to pick up on the camera zoom and match that in the animated zoom. In fact Bob [Boyle] did a very similar gag in one of his movies called *Nocturne* where you zoom in on this window in LA. Once the window fills the frame it becomes part of the footage filmed on stage. And it matches. Very clever. It's a matter of measuring things. Taking a one hundredth inch ruler and measuring and doing it with your brain. Because the computer wasn't smart enough to do it in those days. It was a wonderful experience.

So we did this picture and it got me to LA and it got me a place to live and it made a few bucks. From the animation I wound up going to work for Roger Corman which is a whole other thing. It was great because [James] Cameron worked there in those days. I just worked on these two space movies, *Battle Beyond the Stars* and *Galaxy of Terror*.

AS: James Cameron was on *Battle Beyond the Stars*, wasn't he?

JM: Yeah, he started out as a model maker and wound up basically designing the picture. And then we did a second movie, *Galaxy of Terror*. It was a sort of *"Ten Little Indians*, in space" kind of movie and Jim was the Second Unit Director and the production designer officially and, except for the fact that it's not a very good movie, it looks a lot like *Aliens* and we did it for nothing. There was Jim, there were the Skotak brothers, whom you may have heard of. They picked up a couple of Oscars working with Jim. And they are incredibly interesting guys who taught me how to do perspective miniatures and all those kinds of things.

AS: So you were doing miniatures on that film?

JM: I was around it. I wasn't really doing it. On the first film, on *Battle Beyond the Stars*, I was hired as an animator. The guy who was running the visual effects for Roger Corman was a guy named Chuck Comisky, this strange visionary guy. He's still around, he worked on *Avatar*. He would see qualities in people that no one else would really see. He looked at this crazy, underground animation I'd done and said there's no reason you couldn't do effects animation and hired me. So that's another lucky break that I ran into him.

So I did those two movies and then this Comisky guy started his own company. So I went with him and we worked a variety of pictures, some good, some bad.

AS: You were mostly doing visual effects then?

JM: That was all I was doing. I was like an art director there. They ended up putting me in contact with Dick Sylbert and his crowd on a movie called *Strange Invaders* which was written by Bill Condon, the guy who did *Dream Girls*. I was around this and saw that the people doing art direction and production design didn't really understand the visual effects. In the olden days it was the same department. I did visual effects on several mainstream pictures that convinced me that there was a big need for someone like me in production design. I foolishly thought that I'd make more money and have more power. The tail that wags the dog now is visual effects. Visual effects wags everything else. I really thought production design was more important.

The last movie that the company did, which destroyed the company, was a movie called *Jaws 3D*. Directed by a production designer. Terrible movie. Incredibly frustrating. Although I got to do some really cool stuff because I would draw the original storyboards and people would shoot all these plates. Then I would go into a video studio and composite them in 3D. I'd call out directions so I could adjust where things were in space, you know, looking at things through a World War II map reader. There's a whole article about it in *American Cinematographer* that I had to help write because there

was no one else the writer could talk to that could make sense of it. I was the highest placed layman.

AS: You were determining how close the shark gets to the camera?

JM: On a piece of film if an image is in the same spot on both eyes it's at the window. If it diverges one way it goes behind the window and by the same token if it diverges the other way that brings it off the window.

Our company got fired before we finished the job, I mean it was really a big scandal, but I walked off there with a lot of money. This is probably mid-80's by now. I think a thousand a week. In those days a thousand a week was great money and you could live forever on it. I saved up enough money so when the company blew up rather than look for another job in visual effects I started telling people I was a production designer and eventually some people found me. Another lucky break. They were doing this movie called *Teenage Comet Zombies* but I was so desperate to design a movie that I read the script and said, *You know this is a great picture*. It was really fun. It's cleverly written. It's really a mystery to me how that director/writer has not made a better splash in Hollywood.

The parable that I tell the students is about keeping your mouth shut. Having read the script and met the director, I was desperate for this movie. They basically said, *We'd like you to do it but we have to talk to you about salary*. The producers were these two guys who'd done *Valley Girl*. On my way in from the beach–I lived in Santa Monica–as I passed the 405 freeway I was saying, *Well, I have to get at least one thousand dollars a week, you know that's what I got on my last job.* Past the 405 I go, *Nine hundred! I would do it for nine hundred!* And then I would drive to another landmark–*Seven hundred!* So by the time I got to the studio I thought I'd do it for nothing.

But luckily they came in and sat me down and gave me this big speech about how you know this movie's going to be really tight, but we want to do something wonderful and we like you so we're going to tell you what we have, if you could do it for that we'll be happy but this is not a bargaining thing. It's just you'll do it or not do it. So I'm thinking, *One hundred a week. I'll do it for one hundred a week.* So with that speech they obviously have one hundred a week. So they said, *We'll pay you twelve hundred dollars a week.* So it's like, *Keep calm, keep calm, keep calm!* So I said, *Yes, I guess I could do it for that.* I mean I was smart enough not to jump up like the dog in *Peanuts,* you know.

AS: And that became *Night of the Comet?*
JM: And that couldn't have been luckier. It's a wonderful little movie. In retrospect they just hired me because they knew I would do the visual effects for nothing. They had some matte shots or whatever. It was clear they didn't consider production design very important. Hire this schmuck, he'll do the trick shots and maybe he'll design something. And not knowing any better, I just leapt into everything.

AS: Would you include extensive knowledge of effects as one of the attributes a production designer should have?
JM: A lot of it depends on the kind of picture you're doing. I think everyone who works in movies should know everything about movie making. I teach my students to use lens templates. Because then you can make suggestions like, *You know we don't need to shoot this, we can do this as a trick shot. Or a partial trick shot.*

You should also know about editing. I've done a lot of second unit work and I did a test for second unit on a shot. After we shot the test we crowded into a little room to look at it. And it was very funny. It wasn't supposed to be funny, but looking at it as a long test it was amusing and at the end the director screamed at me. And he went into this big routine about how "this is going to be comedy" and "I'm not going to let you fuck up my movie". I said, *What, are you crazy? This shot required eight or ten frames. This test shows there are a lot of eight or ten frame shots in here.* This is a guy who's a big movie director who makes more money than everyone in this entire restaurant combined. He didn't know what the fuck I was talking about. In fact it was interesting because the producer was a real, way-up-the-butt-of-the-director kind of producer and he jumped in on my side because it was clear to him.

They ended up using footage from that test in the final movie. In fact, I'll tell you the reason that it's in the movie is the editor was smart enough to know that it was working but he didn't open his mouth. He just rolled up the shot and put it in his drawer and pulled it out when he needed it for the movie.

AS: So in the final edit they used the test which at the time the director was screaming about.
JM: Yes.

AS: So it was your knowledge of editing that gave you the upper hand, not just looking at the movie from the design side, you were thinking of the movie as a whole...
JM: What do you need to make this thing work? You need eight frames. It's hard to do more than eight frames that work but it's easy to do eight frames. To me that's what production design is about. And not everyone agrees with me. I mean there are plenty of production designers who don't draw. You know, maybe they know a little bit about interior decoration. Some production designers are producers. They don't really have any artistic talent at all. They assemble a great team.

AS: They bring everyone together.
JM: Yeah. And on some of those movies they do it great. There's a lot of ways a movie can be great. Anybody can do one or two movies and be a genius designer or even a genius actor or anything else because it's such a collaborative medium that just by keeping your mouth shut, if you're working with good guys, you can wind up looking like a genius.

AS: You get in with the right people...
JM: That's why Dick Sylbert is amazing, I mean over an entire career he never fucked up. But you start seeing certain designers that are great designers when they're with a certain director. When they're with another director they're no good. Same with DPs. We think of some directors being very visual then you realize they're always with the same team. So you can't separate it out.

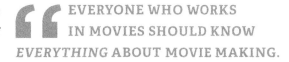

EVERYONE WHO WORKS IN MOVIES SHOULD KNOW *EVERYTHING* ABOUT MOVIE MAKING.

AS: You were talking before about how every designer has that one movie that they're proud of that never got the recognition it deserved–do you have one of those?
JM: Yeah, my lost film is called *Wilder Napalm*. I used to joke about that, saying this is the film that will enable me to steal some of Bo Welch's work because it has a carnival. It's a fantasy kind of movie. Like almost a Tim Burton kind of picture. Written by a very interesting guy named Vince Gilligan who wrote it when he was very young. He created *Breaking Bad* and directs most of it. He was also on the *XFiles* for ten years. And it was directed by Glen Caron, who couldn't be more interesting, the guy that did *Moonlighting* and *Medium*. Just an endlessly interesting kind of a guy. Debra Winger was incredibly cute, sexy, wonderful. Dennis Quaid is in it and Arliss Howard. Jim Varney, the *Hey Verne* guy, was in the movie.

We used to describe it as *True West* meets *Fire start-er*. It's about two brothers who have pyro-kenetic powers fighting over a girl. That's the plot. But we built a carnival which I'd always wanted to do. We did these huge circus banners. We made everything. We built what Vince called a Putt-o-saurus, a miniature golf thing with a Mayan dinosaur theme. Unfortunately it's one of those movies that was the winner of that sort of boobie prize, costing the most money making the least money that year. It cost like thirty million and made like fifty thousand or something. It was only released in a couple of theaters and in my opinion it ran afoul of studio politics. It only got released in a couple of theaters even with these big stars. It's a beautiful film, take a look at it some time.

AS: What is your usual process from when you first get the call?

JM: For every job it's going to be different. It's my belief, and this is giving away a trade secret, but I think most people, including directors of photography and directors, are not capable of visualizing the way you and I do. If you can draw, not just draw something that's real but think of something, put it down on paper, that's a skill that not many people have. It's my observation that if you can draw a good enough picture, or present it in a smart enough way, and then show it to the director or DP, even if they initially say they don't like it, chances are they will shoot it that way. They won't be able to drive it from their head. So that's why I always tell the students, *You've got to learn to draw*. At least draw well enough that you can express emotion in

the drawing. How low the ceiling is or how far off in the distance it goes. This is the point of master shots. You don't need a master shot to be on the screen very long to give people a sense of where they are and how people are supposed to feel. So that's why you draw. You can do the same thing by showing pictures. I had an experience I can tell you about on the picture *River's Edge*. You probably know *River's Edge*.

AS: I'm a big fan.

JM: Well the thing about *River's Edge*, I actually heard about that film from a girlfriend of a girlfriend. Someone I was dating had a girlfriend who was a writer who had read the script and thought it was wonderful and she tried to push me to the director. And I had never done anything like that. I had only done science fiction, fantasy, and this and that. But I read the script and I was knocked out. I had never read anything so great. I'd heard that the director was obsessed with creating the movie that was on the page. The guy that wrote it was crippled and the director felt there was something magical and that this had to be rendered just as it was on the page. Which I though made sense except in the art direction. Because the implication is that the movie was supposed to take place in suburbia. It was based on a real story that took place in Milpitas which is lower-middle class, with California track homes.

This particular director had written and produced a film called *Over the Edge* which is about teenagers running wild, in some ways a similar movie. It was shot in a certain kind of milieu and I thought it kind of killed the movie. Just because it wasn't interesting and it didn't give you anything in particular. So I went in to meet the guy to tell him, *I know you aren't going to hire me, I know you don't have the money, I know that this is a decorator and a location guy picture so I'm here to plead with you, don't shoot it as written. This is about savagery, this is about de--evolution, this is about people losing their civility and becoming savages. The sidewalk should be cracked by the trees, you know, bla bla bla,* and he totally went, *You are the guy. You're going to do this movie. I'll find the dough somewhere.*

I remember when I found the house I talked to the director and I said, *I found a perfect house for these people.* And I said, *But you may not like it.* And he said, *What do you mean, does it look bad?*

No, it looks fabulous but it's gonna be a nightmare, because it's built all wrong. It's like some carpenter, thinking he was an architect, built a modern house. There's no place to put a sofa in the living room, the hallways are the wrong width, the ceilings are too low, it's just a nightmare. But it's perfect for the movie. And sure enough it was perfect for the movie but it was a nightmare to shoot in. Very difficult. But this guy was smart. Tim Hunter. Another guy that I'm surprised hasn't done more movies that we know. Although he's worked a lot. He's done some of the detective shows on TV. Very interesting, smart guy.

So smart that he told me that he would not allow me to do any drawings. Because he knew that I was going to try to get it into his head. By chance I was going through a book of Gustave Doré engravings, and there was a drawing of Adam and Eve. They were sitting on the banks of a little teeny river and Adam was sitting on his butt with his knees up, and Eve was next to him lying there asleep. And they were both naked. And she was asleep but she looked like she was dead. I said, *Wow, this is just like River's Edge.* So I brought it in and I showed it to him and the DP at the same time. The DP was this guy Fred Elmes, very good DP, not a lot to say, never talked very much. And they just looked at it and went, *Ehh, whatever.* No reaction. I didn't think much more about it until I saw the movie. The master shot of that movie is that engraving. Once it was in there heads...

AS: It stuck with them...

JM: It *is* the image. He sits the same way, she lays the same way. The river's on the same side. So that was a great lesson to me about getting images into people's heads.

AS: How do you approach communicating ideas that you have that may be different from what the director and DP are thinking?

JM: Well, as I'm sure you know it's scary communicating ideas because generally they try to shoot them down. And the thing about DPs, because they're the last guy and they press the button, they can basically do whatever they want. So what you have to do is you have to convince them that working with you is going to make them look good. And you can only do that if you're good. Or you're a total con artist I suppose. But I think I've been fairly lucky at getting DPs on my side because I try to be honest with them and I feel like I know enough about what they do that I'm not going to get them into trouble. And I know about diopters and I know about low angle prisms. I just think it's important to know all those things.

On *Wilder Napalm* the director wanted a shot where the three principals wind up in jail. He said, *Can you do a shot where the frame's divided into three and it's the three jail cells and they're sitting in the cells, totally symmetrical?* And I go, *Yes, piece of cake.* I asked Jerry the DP, *What lenses would you shoot this with do you think?* And he goes, *Well, generally I would make it a 40.* And I go, *Okay, good enough. It'll work for a 40.*

Really? he goes. *Yeah, believe me, it ain't that hard.* I drew it up in a minute and very quickly figured out the sizes. We built it on stage, these three jail cells, and then I drew an "x" on the floor where the camera goes. And because it was a cover set they didn't get to it until the middle of the night when I was asleep. The phone wakes me up in the middle of the night, we're in Florida, and it's John and he says, *I can't get this thing to work. It just doesn't work.* And I said, *Do you have a 40 mil lens on the camera? ;And he goes, Yeah.*

Is it four foot six inches off the ground? And he goes, *Yeah.*

I said, *Well you must not have it on the "x" yet.*

And he goes, *What?*

There's an "x" on the floor, it's about twenty-five feet back. Put it on the "x". And he calls back and he goes, *Unbelievable. How did you do it? Did you have a camera?*

No, it's all geometry. It's in your book, buddy. The American Cinematographer Manual *tells you how to do it.*

A lot of DPs you say, *Put it on the "x"*, and that would be the end of the conversation. I mean Jerry was so tickled by this whole process. You just have got to convince them that you're one of the good guys. It's always about that, isn't it? You're not trying to hurt them, you're not going to try to make them look bad, you're not going to one-up 'em. Because you don't need to, really. There's enough glory to go around.

AS: They're making you look good and you're making them look good.
JM: Ideally. You know, within reason. You're bound to get in a fight sometime. Be the good guy. I mean, how do you stay married?

AS: We were talking about *Home Alone* before and about how some people will say, *that house is like a character in the movie.*
JM: I think that's a very glib, bullshit thing that people say because they think it sounds clever. Characters are characters. A character is an entity. Generally it's like a human being that walks around

on two feet, talks and stuff. Maybe it's a ghost. Godzilla's a character, but for Christ's sake, a set's a set. A set's a setting. It's someplace something happens. Maybe if it's the house in the *Haunting* that's a character because it does things and it talks to you.

AS: Do you think production design needs to be "invisible"?

JM: I mean, is the design of this restaurant invisible? We like this restaurant because we like the way it looks, not because it's invisible. If you're on the beach is the beach invisible? The beach is sand and spray. If you're in the desert is the desert invisible? I think it's another way of trying to sound clever. Life is full of sights and sounds and smells. Nothing's invisible really.

AS: In *Species*, H.R. Giger designed the monster. Did you interact with Giger at all on that one?

JM: The first thing we did on the picture was get on a plane and go to Switzerland. It was interesting, we went to his studio, he was building a Sil statue out of Plexiglas and tubes, I think that the face was cast off a girl and he had a bunch of guys working on it. But he clearly didn't understand what was required for a movie. It was sort of like, *Why are you doing this? We can't make this work, it's not a robot.* I suppose once he finished it we could have scanned it and animated it that way...

He's a very interesting artist. He seemed like a very sweet guy. Very pale. Kind of sickly-looking. He took us out to dinner at this restaurant in Zürich that was a very interesting because it had art on the walls from all these different artists who never had money, who would give a piece of art in return for eating there. It's a very fancy restaurant now. And in the middle of dinner this girl showed up who was his Sil. I guess he thought that we were going to hire her to be Sil in the movie. She made the mistake of bringing her boyfriend along, I don't think that pleased him very much.

> " CHARACTERS ARE CHARACTERS. A CHARACTER IS AN ENTITY. GENERALLY IT'S LIKE A HUMAN BEING THAT WALKS AROUND ON TWO FEET . . . MAYBE IT'S A GHOST. GODZILLA'S A CHARACTER, BUT FOR CHRIST'S SAKE, A SET'S A SET.

We went to his house, which was really kind of scary. From the outside it just looked shabby–ratty foliage and stuff. You go inside and everything inside was painted black. Even the insides of the windows were painted black. His paintings, the paintings you know in his books, were zip-screwed to the walls. And he had a Giger table. There was a skeleton there that looked kinda scary. I certainly didn't eat or drink anything. We stayed there several days. I think part of the reason we went was we hoped we could get him to come to California to work with us. He wasn't willing to leave. He said because of his mother he couldn't leave town. Luckily our producer had a pretty good relationship with him. And then it turned out there was this guy named Steve Johnson that Giger actually liked, a guy who he felt could make his designs work. So that was the lynch-pin I think–that we had Steve Johnson. He made a full-size puppet. It wasn't in the movie nearly enough. Really beautiful. Really something special.

That movie happened unfortunately before digital animation really got good. So you know at the end when she's jumping around there's not much of a sense of weight. I mean you can say she's an insect. You know I think it helped kill Boss FX, that film. But the film itself was successful. I'm very proud of everything in it.

AS: What goes on when you get a script and you want to design it? Is it different for each film?

JM: It is different in each one. In the olden days, when they knew how to make movies, the script would go to the supervising art director. It would go to Cedric Gibbons, or Anton Grot or one of these guys. Because the first thing you need to know is how you're going to make this movie. But now someone will decide they're going to make a movie and the first thing they'll do is hire a production manager who will go out location scouting. So you got a guy who's not a scout and not a designer scouting locations that may or may not be necessary. Just because the script says "swimming pool" doesn't mean they need a swimming pool. They could have scouted *River's Edge* based on the script and they wouldn't have found a single location that I was going to use.

So the first thing that you have to do is convince them to throw away all the work that they've put in so far. Maybe it was worth it for them to put in all that work because it got it off the ground.

AS: In *Home Alone* there were all those gags with the doors opening and the laundry chute–were you involved with those things?

JM: The most interesting thing was we had an entire effects sequence for that movie that was planned out. I storyboarded probably two-thirds of it. Chris, the director, storyboarded a bunch of it. The idea was that [Macaulay Culkin] fell asleep eating ice-cream and he woke up but he didn't really wakc up.

AS: Like a dream-sequence?

JM: It was exactly that. A nightmare sequence. On the piano were all those nutcrackers. They chased him around the house and eventually chased him into the trash compacter and turned it on and squeezed him down into a cube with his face on it and then that went down the laundry chute. When he got to the laundry basket he popped up. And then remember the furnace in the movie? That's why I went to all that trouble with that furnace. He was afraid of the furnace. When he pops out of the laundry basket the furnace tears itself loose like a big octopus and starts chasing him. He goes up the stairs and winds up on the roof and there's a battle. He's in the middle of the battle between the furnace and the tarantula. The tarantula comes out of the chimney or something–it's huge. So then they're fighting over him, they're pulling him in different directions–it's wonderful stuff. The guy that did

Night of the Comet with me was going to do it. We hired him, we brought him all the way out there, and then the studio canceled the sequence.

The movie did not start out as a Fox picture. It was a Warner Brothers film and we got in a big fight over the budget. And part of it was they didn't understand why we needed to build a house. Now these are studio executives at Warner Brothers not understanding that in a movie that stars a child, takes place at night, and is nothing but gags, that you need a set. It's like, *Well why don't you shoot it in a house?* You know, a film where the sled has to go down the stairs and out the door.

So we were working on the picture, probably a month out or something. We were using this abandoned high school in Winnetka as a studio, big old high school gymnasium, perfect stage in some ways. And the producers, we had two young producers, you know contemporaries of Chris's at NYU, and they came around and told us that the movie was over, go home. We'd been there quite a while. I had my whole crew working. But as soon as they walked out the door another guy walked in behind them and said, *Just go to lunch and relax.* And when we came back we were employees of Fox. So obviously there was some back-stage maneuvering going on.

We never had a lot of money but that was a movie where everyone was on the same page. Chris and the director of photography and I were like three brothers. I don't remember ever fighting with them

about anything. The 1st AD had done a couple of John Hughes movies and my understanding was that John Hughes movies were always sort of a big mess, you know, because he'd be very capricious in his ideas.

We were having a production meeting and Hughes was invited and we were all a little worried about that and the 1st AD guy said, *Don't worry about it, he'll be here for ten or twenty minutes, he'll get bored and he'll leave.* So we had a production meeting and we set it up on a big u-shaped table. Everybody was there, Chris and the first AD were right in the middle. I was there and Julio the DP was across from me. Everybody could hear what the three of us were saying. And we just . . . made the movie. Described what we were going to do. The three of us knew everything. We had it all figured it out and everyone just listened. Hughes stuck around for the whole meeting and afterwards he chose to collar me and say, *Is this the kind of meeting you guys always have?* I go, *Well, what other kind of meeting would you have? Isn't that the whole idea of the meeting?* 'Cause he had never had that.

I think he's a wonderful filmmaker, by the way, and in contravention to most people I have nothing but good things to say about John. He watched out for me when other people who knew I was out of town all alone, didn't. This guy who was supposed to be a whatever, he was the guy who took me out to dinner, took me to a hockey game. You know it's like me and Cameron.

AS: You often hear that James Cameron was challenging to work with back then.

JM: If you are competent there are no problems between you and Cameron, that's my experience. I never saw him beat up on anyone who didn't have it coming. And when he beat up on them they deserved it. It was a pleasure to see someone in the movie business get beat up for a real thing rather than get beat up for some fantasy. No, I have nothing but good things to say. I wish Jim all the luck in the world. I hope that *Avatar* goes through the roof because that's real film making. That's a film that's totally synthetic and yet I'm sure will have enormous heart and emotion. He's our greatest living feminist filmmaker and he's one of our great romantic filmmakers. Fuck all that technical shit. I mean people don't really look at those films and see how positive the values are. I mean even Scorsese, who I think is just the greatest–his film *Casino* is scary, I mean vicious. There's a meanness in some of that, you know? But Jim is great.

AS: You worked with him on *Terminator 2 3D*...

JM: I got to do great stuff on that. And had very little interference from him. I built a model about as big as this table and I learned a lesson that if I ever worked with him again I would never glue anything down on a model. Cause I had all these sort of "areas" and he just started ripping things up and rearranging them. And eventually he pretty much came back to the way it was in the first place. Which he found amusing. That didn't make him mad. He just wanted to see. Yeah, it was very foolish gluing things down with him.

It's a pleasure to work with people like that in the movie business because there aren't many. I think John [Hughes] was hard to work with because it was all in his head. I guess he didn't trust other people. But look at *Planes, Trains and Automobiles*– is there a better film? Is there a better comedy ever made? Jesus Christ almighty.

I'll tell you another thing that was interesting. When I came out to Chicago and started working on *Home Alone* they always made John Hughes's wife the bad guy. They said John's wife will be here to look at all the sets and everything and when they saw what I was doing they said, *You're going to be fired for sure.* Because it didn't look like a John Hughes movie. Cause his movies were very blue. They were very much about a particular segment of society. But I mean we were making that house like a young Italian American kid's idea of Heaven. That's really what it's about. It's totally warm. There's nothing blue in that house. There's nothing cold in that house.

And when his wife finally saw it she was delighted. She got that we were trying to do something different. I mean that's Chris Columbus directing a movie he didn't write. You know when he directs movies he writes, generally they're awful. And it was Hughes letting someone else direct one of his pieces. And those things came together in a great way on that movie. Because it was a Christmas movie and it needed to be corny. I mean even at the time I thought this movie's really going to be something special.

AS: And then *Home Alone* became one of the biggest comedies of all time...

JM: It was the biggest comedy of all time for quite a long time. It might still be the biggest comedy that's not about effects, that's not *Ghostbusters*. As far as a relatively mundane, down-to-earth thing it was the biggest comedy. I mean what's any bigger? Some of the cartoons. But it is if you're just talking about a regular film shot on stage.

You know how there are stairs that go down to the basement? He goes down and we see him flip and fall. You know that wall there and that stairway down into the basement, does anything seem odd about that?

AS: Nothing really stood out...

JM: Exactly. No one has ever done a stairway like that. Stairways that go down to a basement in snow country go down the side so they can be under the eaves. Otherwise it fills up with snow. It's like you come up with something that's so wrong it's right.

Like the whole house in *Home Alone* is completely wrong. I mean the decoration, the look of it. We never found anybody that lived anything like that. The people that lived in the real house were well-to-do Germans, very nice. We used a real exterior which we altered quite a bit. Their house had no window treatments. A lot of beautiful floors and area rugs, almost a Japanese kind of feeling. I kept them out of the set until it was finished and dressed. Partly because I thought that it would be amusing. Then I brought them into the set. It freaked them

out because they thought people would think they lived in such an ugly place. *Do you think people really think we live in a house like this? It's too garish, isn't it?* I mean a year later they were taking bows in *House and Garden* like it was their house. They're human. No, I knew that their eyes would just fall. They just thought it was so terrible.

> " AS SOON AS YOU ROLL THE CAMERA IT'S LYING. SOMEONE SAID THAT FILM IS TRUTH TWENTY-FOUR FRAMES A SECOND, TOTALLY WRONG. IT'S LIES TWENTY-FOUR TIMES A SECOND. HOPEFULLY GOOD LIES. BEAUTIFUL LIES.

You do the research and then you throw it away. It gives you an impression. Usually wrong. It's like the idea of justifying things by research. You don't justify by research because you can justify anything with research. You can justify that Romans had dreadlocks or something. What you have to do instead is justify it on artistic grounds, *Is this going to help the story or not?*

AS: So it becomes the difference between the reality and what would look good on film.

JM: All that's important is the movie. You can't possibly be right. As soon as you roll the camera it's lying. Someone said that film is truth twenty-four frames a second. Totally wrong. It's lies twenty-four times a second. Hopefully good lies. Beautiful lies.

Grant Major

Grant Major does big movies. He was nominated for Oscars for all three *Lord of the Rings* films and won for *Return of the King.* He also received an Oscar nomination for Peter Jackson's *King Kong.* When he's not doing huge blockbusters, he likes doing smaller New Zealand films close to home, like Niki Caro's Oscar nominated *Whale Rider* and Jane Campion's *The Power of the Dog,* for which he received his fifth Oscar nomination. When I caught up with him for our first conversation he was in the middle of production on an Auckland-based independent feature, *The Emperor.*

AS: How did you end up working on big, epic movies?

GM: A lot of my career was influenced by Peter Jackson's trajectory. I started off doing some moderate-sized films with him back in the mid-90's and then he segued into *The Lord of the Rings* and of course I was there for that. And then after that, *King Kong.* But I've got a family in Auckland and I'm very keen to spend time here so I take on small jobs to be able to stay in Auckland if I can. Which is what I'm doing at the moment. Working on *The Emperor*, a story about the possible war crimes against Emperor Hirohito in Japan in 1945. But I do need to keep my foot in the Hollywood scene as well so that's why I did *Green Lantern* a short while ago.

AS: What skills help you handle those big projects?

GM: With any project you put in the same amount

of effort and the same creative impetus. The big ones are obviously a longer haul with a lot more financial commitment. It's a bigger decision-making process. There are more people looking over your shoulder and more people with an opinion about what you should be doing. You need to be able to fend off that sort of overview. It can work for you but it can also stifle the creative decision-making. It's just being ready and having the strength for the long haul. You need to have a lot of stamina.

There's a certain thrill in making big sets and doing these big production design set-ups. It's great because we have huge teams of people working with us and under us. It's a thrilling way to make a living. On the big films you have a lot more technical toys to play with. The vis effects work and special effects work are amped up so it's a greater roller-coaster ride.

AS: How closely do you work with the visual effects team on a film?
GM: On Peter's work we all know each other because WETA's workshop is literally just down the road from the film that's being made. It makes it very comfortable. I've known a lot of them for years and years so I can't help but work closely with them. On these more modern projects like *Green Lantern* it's a separate contract to the film. They were more divided because SONY Pictures Imageworks was across town. But we had one of their supervisors doing standby visual effects work on set every day.

I do feel there is a problem with post production work going on after the production designers leave the show. I want to be able to move on to vis effects after the film and personally follow though on designs that are being done. Because such a lot of the film's design now happens in this vis effects world. It's kind of awkward leaving something like that to someone who can do whatever they want after me. I prefer having control.

AS: With *Lord of the Rings* was it the case that the visual effects went on for months after you left?
GM: That was the case. It's not good being away but it was such a long project with such a lot of pickups in the latter stages that I was moving very far away from it anyway. I knew a lot of those vis effects people and I knew that it was all in good hands. Also, WETA was a great place to just go in and have a look at how things were going. And Peter's a very visually-oriented guy. He never gives it away completely to a vis effects house.

On *King Kong* I had a visual effects art department, which is a step up from the *Lord of the Rings* arrangement. We had a little art department in WETA Digital and we were still designing things during that post production phase. I was able to keep up with what was going on that way.

For example, a lot of the virtual New York sets that we did for *King Kong* had a lot of graphic work on them. Sign writing and everything New York used to have back in the 30's. A lot of that was going on during that post production phase. It worked out quite well having an art director in there.

AS: You mentioned that Peter Jackson is a very visual director. Does he follow the designs being developed in the early stages?

GM: He's very refreshingly collaborative. He's really into listening to what people think. For example, he'll often have little competitions with previs artists to come up with great little action sequences that help tell his story. But at the same time he's the last word on all the artwork that we produce and everything is done to present to him. He also has a very, very long memory. It's incredible considering the length of time that these projects take to design. He remembers things he's told us a year and a half ago. He's both collaborative and also a micromanager of all aspects of the film.

AS: What has kept you guys working together so long?

GM: Well, I'm not doing *The Hobbit,* that's being done by one of my art directors. But before that it was well over ten years on the same projects. When we met I'd been designing for not even four and a half years and Peter had been doing these small, very cheap "splatter movies". Very wacky horror films. His producer asked me to work on a film called *Heavenly Creatures* which was made on the south island of New Zealand and we got on really well. We basically rose through the ranks together I suppose. *Heavenly Creatures* was really successful so he asked me to do the next one. And that was pretty successful so he asked me to do *Lord of the*

Rings and that was successful so he asked me to do *King Kong* and so on and so forth. He has loyalties to the people he has employed before and we're friends.

AS: You have also collaborated with the director Niki Caro on several films, completely different from the Peter Jackson style.

GM: I like the diversity. I very much like to mix things up for my own sake. But Niki and I have known each other for equally as long. She's a bit younger than me. She went to art school and asked me to help her with some of the student short films she was working on and we've kept on going from there. We socialize together. She's got young kids and I've young kids and we see quite a lot of each other socially so it's been a very fruitful collaboration really.

AS: Did you go to art school yourself?

GM: Yeah. I went to art school in the 1970's. Back then it was called Auckland Technical Institute, now it's out of Auckland University of Technology. There was no film design then and I studied graphic art. But I wasn't really interested in going into advertising. My first job was in television and I ended up doing quite well. I ended up staying on the first job for three and a half years. I went over to study set design with BBC television in London which at that time was quite a big production institution. Studios working on twenty-four hour shifts. There were one hundred set designers, assistants, buyers, librarians, and so on within the art department back then. Going from such a tiny industry here in New Zealand to the BBC was just fantastic. That was my true apprenticeship. And then I came back here and the film business was just starting up. I called myself an art director back in the 1980's and then segued into production design in the 1990's.

AS: What was your first job title in the industry?

GM: Assistant set designer. It was pretty much on-the-job training. I was given shows to design straight out of art school. Having a graphic arts background at the time was very useful because back then the set designs were a lot more painterly. The other good thing about starting in that situation was that I could experiment with things that are actually being seen by the public. Within about three weeks of getting the job I was sent down to an island in the very south of New Zealand called Stewart Island to design a television film based on castaways. Here I was, straight out of art school, on an island both propping and designing and building sets for this drama series. Starting on the deep end, but it was really a fantastic learning experience.

AS: How did you get that first job?

GM: Back then they guaranteed everyone a job who went to the institution. Long gone are those days. It was based around the end-of-year exhibition. They would have a lot of people from the advertising industry, publishing, and interior design companies come to these exhibitions and meet us and hand-pick the people they wanted. I was offered several jobs out of that, including advertising, but I didn't really want to do that. What I actually wanted to

do at the time was move on to fine arts. I thought I would earn some money for a year or so before going back to university and getting a fine arts degree. But when I went into TV at that point it was such a good way to earn a living. And since I was earning a living at it I just kept at it.

AS: After working at the BBC you returned to New Zealand to get into the film industry there?

GM: I actually came back to New Zealand by accident rather than by design. I had a full-time job at the BBC back then. I came back to New Zealand on a holiday to catch up with my family. I've ended up staying here because a lot of my friends who I'd been working with in TV back in the 70's were now in the film business. Television was sort of disintegrating. They didn't have in-house design departments anymore and they didn't have drama departments–all those things were split off from the TV companies I had worked for. It coincided with one or two very early New Zealand films that hadn't done badly. *Sleeping Dogs* was one of them, by director Roger Donaldson who's still up in Hollywood directing films. It attracted peoples' attention to the possibility of making films in New Zealand. The government responded by doing this sort of tax dodge. Tax dodge schemes financed films back then.

So there were a certain amount of films being made. Not a huge amount. I wasn't able to make a living out of doing films all the time. I had to diversify–doing a little bit of graphic work, doing some event design and things like that. I worked on the New

Zealand pavilions for the world exhibitions in Australia and in Spain. Things like that helped supplement the beginning of my film career.

AS: Now that you've worked in both places, what would you say is the difference between working in New Zealand and working in Hollywood?

GM: Immediately the scale difference is apparent. Hollywood is the capital city of this sort of thing. In New Zealand when a Peter Jackson film is being made it consumes pretty much everybody who's in the industry here. Which is good because I know everybody–we've worked with each other years and years. In America the stakes are a lot higher. I am competing with a lot of people who are way better at designing than I am. All I can do is learn by looking at overseas publications and at films that come in from overseas. In America it's brilliant because it's got this film making culture that is so much deeper. For example, I ran into people there who are second, third generation standby props people. There's that sort of history there. There are also the guilds and the unions there that promote the industry side of things. They have lessons on the latest IT and CGI techniques in filmmaking and they run art classes. While I was up there I managed to socialize with other production designers who have done the most incredible films, the most awesome projects. You can imagine someone coming from a place like Winchester, Illinois and going to New York, it's the same sort of experience. It's really amazing and I hope I get the opportunity to be invited back.

AS: Did you do the film *The Ruins* to branch out?

GM: I was looking for an American film to do and it was my first American film done off-shore. It got me out of the Wellington set. And it was an adventure. It was nice to turn to something wacky like horror with poisonous vines.

AS: Was it hard to convince production to build the entire Mayan temple?

GM: It was a decision to go to Australia and they don't have that sort of thing there. For practical reasons we made it in two halves. We made the bottom two-thirds and then the top third was made that rose up off the ground by quite a long way. We also built various interior sets which you didn't see much of because there was not enough light.

AS: Do you feel a set can be a character in a movie? In *The Ruins* that temple almost becomes more than a set.

GM: Absolutely. Absolutely. It's not just a temple, it has to be part of the storytelling narrative. That's really important to me. All the decisions are made in terms of the story and the drama.

AS: Do you have any thoughts about sets needing to be visible versus invisible?

GM: Neither one of them. Where it needs to tell a story it's got to be seen for what it is. For example, the great big underground laboratory in Green Lantern has to be seen because it's very much described in the script. Other ones, like people's offices, rooms, bedrooms and so on, they want to play a support role to the drama that's being played out by the actors. So it really depends on the brief in a way, on the script. At the end of the day people are really taking in a lot by osmosis. For the osmosis to be readable it still needs to impress itself on people's imagination even if it's indirectly.

AS: On *Lord of the Rings* you worked with illustrators Alan Lee and John Howe. How involved were they in developing the look of the films?

GM: Majorly so. With regular American films you hire a production illustrator or concept artist and they are incredibly skilled but they often have a sort of a style and an imaginary vocabulary that's quite recognizable. You see it come through a lot on films. But Alan Lee and John Howe came from the publishing world and had both independently developed idiosyncratic styles to their illustrations. Alan's been around for way longer than I've been designing for. They had been used by these publishers for a lot of classic English stories, including *The Lord of the Rings*. They developed the look of the book. Alan had illustrated *The Lord of the Rings* for years before this film project even started, likewise John Howe had been doing these ancient old English and old European sword and sorcery stories for a living for a long time. They were picked up by us in the very early days and as a way of staying very close to the established look of the book. When they came over it was fantastic because with the book illustrations they just did a moment in the story but this time we were doing what Rivendell really looks like, for example.

We did have other artists who were working on the films and past a point an illustration is just what it is, it's something that has to be made into something that's filmable and buildable and buyable. We had to be able to make the business side of it work, we had to be able to physically manifest these things on a location or a studio. We had three hundred to four hundred people in the design department but Alan and John were key roles in the sharp end of the look of it. It was a brilliant choice for them to be on.

AS: When working with illustrators like that do you start by giving them a napkin sketch? Do you tend to do any sketching yourself these days?

GM: I used to do all my own stuff in those earlier films but on these bigger films being able to sit down and spend a day drawing is well nigh impossible. There are just too many projects going on at the same time to be able to do that. My drawing skills have dropped away a little bit, I must say! I do still draw quite a lot on the smaller projects but when it comes to projects like *The Green Lantern*, I had a huge amount of time and people to do concept work and it worked really well. Having the drawing skills is great, to be able to sit down and draw with the illustrators and do napkin sketches and things like that. But I don't end up working on finished illustrations that are pitch documents for the director and producers.

AS: In those early stages of conceptual design what kind of references do you look at? Do you look at a lot of other films?

GM: I tend to want to dash things out. Sometimes the first ideas are the best ideas and sometimes they catch. I try to get the first ideas out without a lot of research and reference. After that phase, I immerse myself in the world of whatever it is I'm designing. The one I'm designing at the moment is Japan in 1945. There's a huge amount of visual material that exists. You're able to just sit and flip through images and read books and look at movies that are to do with that. I immerse myself in the world and then try to revisit these early ideas and see if they're any good. I dash out early stuff and then do studied stuff in time.

> " I TRY TO GET THE FIRST IDEAS OUT WITHOUT A LOT OF RESEARCH AND REFERENCE AFTER THAT PHASE I IMMERSE MYSELF IN THE WORLD OF WHATEVER IT IS I'M DESIGNING . . . I DASH OUT EARLY STUFF AND THEN DO STUDIED STUFF IN TIME.

AS: K.K. Barrett said that sometimes when he's doing a romantic comedy he'll look at westerns, instead of just using all the standard romantic comedies as reference. Or he'll go for a walk around the block and be influenced by what he sees.

GM: You're continually taking things in. Even for movies that haven't even been made yet. Try to have a life that exposes you to a lot of experiences. Travel and go to design exhibitions, go to plays, go to see lots of movies, go to fashion shows. You sub-consciously pull away good ideas. You give them a neural address and they stay there for years sometimes.

In those early stages, before you get swamped by the practicalities of the whole film process, you're grabbing things that can be quite original. Oblique ways of looking at something. You try to get original ideas out first.

AS: Are you involved in a lot of the character design? For example, in *The Lord of the Rings* or *Green Lantern*?

GM: In *Lord of the Rings* that was really done by WETA workshop as a sort of contract. Although having said that, Alan and John and I developed a lot of them on pencil first and then they got made by the WETA workshop. But on *Green Lantern* Ngila Dickson, the costume designer, and I invented all of those. They were based on existing comic book characters. Neville Page and Aaron Sims were the illustrators who worked to our brief. It always involves character design up to a point but we played a much bigger role on *Green Lantern* than on *Lord of the Rings*.

AS: What would you say are the attributes of a good production designer? Having that inspiration and at the same time the practicality of making it filmable?

GM: I try to stay fresh and stay young. It's a competitive business, it's a speculative business. Try to not pull out the same ideas over and over again. Try to be original and be your own person. Learn how to sell ideas. Ideas go nowhere if you can't get people to buy into them. A lot of it's how you frame ideas and how you pitch them to directors and producers. I've learned a bit of that along the way as well.

Over time I have been getting a lot more confident. I experimented a lot in the early days and learned a lot of lessons and made mistakes and had successes. There's no equivalent to just doing it and getting better at it from a technical point of view. People get more confident in you. Your reputation grows so people now can come to you knowing that you can do a project of a size and that you can do it of a standard.

AS: When you are pitching one of these ideas is it a matter of presenting really good set design sketches?

GM: And telling the right story, putting it within context of the greater film. But, yes, the visuals are really important. For example, I've been noticing a lot recently how when location scouts go out and take photographs, well, they're not photographers. You could end up with a good location that may suit you, but you've got crap photographs. You have to go back and shoot it yourself. Everything has to be as best as it can possibly be. It has to tell the story you want to tell. So it's just upping the ante on not just yourself but all the people that work for you as well. Whip them! Whip them hard! (laughs)

AS: How do you go about finding good crew?

GM: All the people I've worked with before I seem

to hand-pick myself. I'm working on a project in Auckland currently, it's the second small project I've done in Auckland since I've been back in the country. And I'm having to look around for who's hot at the moment. I tend to want to work with them first and give them a chance. If they can maintain a standard and bring me what I need, they get to stay on the next film. These films have a certain lifespan and then you move on to another film so it's an opportunity to keep people or find new people as I go. Of course in New Zealand there are a lot of people who I know already so that makes things easier. In America I rely a lot on having a good art director who's got a good team of people he or she can bring in and work with me.

> **"LEARN HOW TO SELL IDEAS. IDEAS GO NOWHERE IF YOU CAN'T GET PEOPLE TO BUY INTO THEM. A LOT OF IT'S HOW YOU FRAME IDEAS AND HOW YOU PITCH THEM TO DIRECTORS AND PRODUCERS.**

AS: So for the films you've done in America, you've worked with local crew as opposed to bringing in New Zealand people?

GM: Absolutely. Like I say, the skill base of most of the people I've worked with there is phenomenal, brilliant. So it's worked out pretty well.

AS: As principal photography is going on, do you spend a lot of time on the set?

GM: I start the day on the set, way before call time.

I'm the first one there if I can be. But by and large I tend to not hang around on set. It depends a little bit on what's going on that day. If it's a very complex day then I'll hang around for that. In New Zealand and Australia and England we have a Standby Art Director role. The person who leads my on set crew is my standby art director. He keeps me informed on what's going on and what's coming up and how the day went. It's more flexibility for the director on the day without me having to be there.

AS: I heard that Peter Jackson often changes things at the last minute.

GM: Absolutely. He stays flexible right through. Right until the button's pressed on the camera.

AS: When he does make a change like that would that go to the standby art director or would you get a call?

GM: It would be a bit of both. If it's something that can be handled on the day by the art director, all well and good. But in that case that person would call me and if I'm close by I'll probably drop by anyway. We do things a wee bit differently here. Things don't tend to be quite as locked down as in America on a daily shoot. A bit more invention happens on the day.

AS: You directed your own short film (*Undergrowth*, 2009). Are you thinking of transitioning to directing films?

GM: I've got to earn money! (laughs) To feed my family and things like that! I don't think changing to directing now is really going to be that beneficial

to that. At the same time it's only a short film but it took up six months of my time, which was in-between projects. I learned a lot from it. To be able to write, direct, and edit my own film was fantastic. I'd been very lucky to raise one hundred grand to put into the project, so it was all shot on 35 mil and had all the bells and whistles. A lot of vis effects, a lot of favors pulled in.

I like to keep on the edge of risk with what I do because it keeps me vital. Making a short film was a venture into the unknown. I'd like to do it again with another sort of short film, or maybe a longer film. But I'm not wanting to become a director per se, it's just a way to stay creative.

AS: How do you feel about not doing *The Hobbit*? Is that something that you wanted to do or you were glad not to do it?

GM: Both. I was asked about doing it when I was in the middle of another project. And I sort of felt like I'd been there and done that. I'd spent years and years of my life on *Lord of the Rings* and it sort of felt like it would just be doing it again, really. Also, I wanted to spend time back in Auckland with my family. *The Hobbit* was in a different city and I'd just become a commuting dad again for another three or four years. So I was happy to turn it away but at the same time I would love to have done it as well. It is what it is. I was offered the work and I was empowered enough to turn it down and work on other things. I don't like to put all my eggs in one basket. I like to work with other directors and take other opportunities and different sorts of risks.

AS: Speaking of working with different directors, how was working with Niki Caro different from working with Peter Jackson?

GM: Niki's not such a visual director, she's more of an actor's director. So I was given pretty much a free hand with all the art directing and the production design. At the same time it's a different flavor of film. It's a lot more to do with love and more of a gentle style of filmmaking. She's really family-friendly as well. Doing *Whale Rider* my boy was very young and he was able to hang around on set. She had her kiddie back then and they both liked hanging around. So it's a different way to go about making films and I really appreciated it.

AS: I interviewed Kim Sinclair a while back and he mentioned *Whale Rider* as one of his favorite New Zealand films.

GM: Kim's good; oddly enough I've never worked with him. I've known him as part of the film business here. I was pleased to see he's on your site.

AS: On *Whale Rider* you had to build several whales?

GM: Yes, we made all the beached whales for that. We also made a part of a whale which Paikea rode when she went into the sea. Quite tricky actually. All the smaller ones were made of silicon and had aqualung divers that could animate them from inside. They worked the blow-holes with compressed air. The big one was really difficult, it was right on the tideline where all the waves come crashing in. Of course it was a very tidal beach so the tideline

would shift all the time. We had ballast tanks in the big whale that we had to fill up to keep it stable. We had to continually empty the ballast tanks to move it. We had to winch the thing up and down the beach in between shots to keep the thing in the right place. We had a sea anchor and a land anchor. It was a hell of a piece of maritime engineering to make that work. Of course it was a huge sculpting and casting job as well.

> "I'VE BEEN NOTICING A LOT RECENTLY HOW WHEN LOCATION SCOUTS GO OUT AND TAKE PHOTOGRAPHS, WELL, THEY'RE NOT PHOTOGRAPHERS. YOU COULD END UP WITH A GOOD LOCATION THAT MAY SUIT YOU, BUT YOU'VE GOT CRAP PHOTOGRAPHS. YOU HAVE TO GO BACK AND SHOOT IT YOURSELF. EVERYTHING HAS TO BE AS BEST AS IT CAN POSSIBLY BE.

AS: Weren't there some creatures in *The Lord of the Rings* that you had to move around with cranes as well?

GM: The Oliphants. Likewise they were huge, huge sculpts and they had these sort of backpacks which had all the soldiers on top. They were huge and we also needed cranes to move them around.

AS: In *King Kong* was the whole ship a set?

GM: The ship itself was built several times. We had an actual ship which was hugely modified. We rebuilt the bow of the ship. We changed the whole superstructure on top of it. That was the Venture that you saw when it was at sea. And then we built the ship again on the backlot on a big sort of tilting mechanism to tip the thing up for when it hit the rocks. And then we built the interior pretty much all in one piece except the bridge was built in a separate set. And that was a whole interior build at a stage.

AS: It gimbaled back and forth?

GM: The exterior, backlot one did. The huge, big steel structure. Actually we made it again a forth time in miniature as well when it was touring around the rocks. And there was a digital version as well.

AS: Say someone is just starting out in the business. Do you have any advice for them to avoid any pitfalls?

GM: I suggest for people wanting to train up to get into this sort of thing, that they should get a degree in architecture. Or go to film school and learn to be a production designer with all the requisite drafting skills. You must be able to draw. A lot of art schools these days don't encourage drawing or don't actively teach drawing. But I think drawing is very, very important. And computer skills now. The young kids are overtaking me now with the ability to use 3D Studio MAX and Rhino and these sorts of things. Having experience in those sorts of programs also gets you in the door. You can be brought in for a specific job, to design a 3D set or something like that, and then once you're in the art department, at least in New Zealand, you can move around within that. Coming to the project with skills is really important.

And lastly what I tell everybody is just to make your own films however you can, shoot them and get friends to act in them, edit it yourself and just sort of hone that manufacturing business of filmmaking. And make it your own way.

AS: Making your own films is so much cheaper these days.

GM: And there are more and more venues to get them screened as well. More and more ways of showing them. They have this 48 hour film festival where these kids get together and they've got a weekend to write, shoot, and edit and present their film. It's a fantastic sort of competitive way to just sort of get in there and do it.

AS: How about the future of production design? Do you see more and more greenscreens and fewer practical sets?

GM: In the early days we were doing 360 degree builds but it's getting harder and harder to justify that sort of build when the cost of doing CGI work is coming down and becoming more competitive. Hands-on skills in visual effects is important for production designers because the vis effects world is currently being colonized by technicians. We need to move into their world majorly with creative skills and film design skills. Being able to design the sets and design the film and follow right through to the visual effects is the future of what we're doing. As a profession we need to be there every step of the way.

AS: What do you like most about designing movies?

GM: The whole thing is pretty amazing. But in terms of a phase, the phase I like best is the "blue-sky thinking" phase at the beginning of a project where the film can be anything. The middle part of it you've just got your head down dealing with the day-to-day making of the thing. But those first ideas that come out go full-circle, sometimes taking years. Then you're sitting in the cinema and you're looking at the film and here it is on the screen. It's taken this long to get there. I like how where we begin influences where we end.

GM 2

UPDATE: When the coronavirus pandemic was gripping most of the world, I caught up with Grant Major a second time as he worked steadily in his native New Zealand. Here are his thoughts on more recent projects and also on the current state of our industry...

AS: Is all film work shut down for you now because of coronavirus?

GM: New Zealand's fared pretty well, actually, notwithstanding the mayhem that's going on. We're all back to work here. We got over the coronavirus a couple weeks ago. We have the odd person coming into the country with the virus but they get stopped at the border.

AS: Great to hear you're all working. What are you currently designing?

GM: I'm working with Jane Campion on *Power of the Dog*. This is the first time in thirty years that we've worked together and it's been great. Before she went on to do *The Piano* I had worked with her on *An Angel at My Table*.

AS: Have you been mostly working in New Zealand since we last talked?

GM: Predominantly, but not exclusively. Mainly I've become a New Zealand go-to person for the movies that come here.

AS: Were your movies like *The Meg* and *X-Men: Apocalypse* shot there as well?

GM: *Apocalypse* was shot in Montreal but *The Meg* was shot here in New Zealand.

AS: Do you still tend to bounce back and forth between big budget movies with extensive visual effects to smaller, local movies?

GM: Yes, as much as I can. I have predominantly been doing these larger films but I also try to support the New Zealand film industry here.

AS: With the importance of visual effects increasing does it ever seem like a VFX house might take over the actual design of a movie?

GM: The production designer normally comes on very early and ought to be involved in and designing those visual effects. If they are going to appear in the movie it's really the production designer's responsibility. We have to really wrestle that into our own camp. Production designers need to be able to actually work on visual effects. We need to be able to produce these things. I know it's a different skill set but it's essentially part of the production design process.

AS: When we talked before, we discussed how a lot of visual effects can go on after the production designer leaves.

GM: The way I work is that I hand over to the visual effect supervisor a turn-key design so everything's been conceptualized and modeled in 3D as required. All research files go with that, all the texture files, color choices and everything else. For example, on *Mulan* the art department produced the complete visual effects set extension work that was required. Now, I expect some things to change and some things to be massaged as they go, but with all the information they've been given they have more than enough material.

AS: Hannah Beachler talked about doing the same thing on *Black Panther*. Designing the whole city of Wakanda before the 3D models were handed over to visual effects.

GM: That's our job, you know? The design needs to be cohesive. Everything in proportion to each other. It's important that we sort of stamp our personality and our techniques on the visual effects area. It's a tool, really. It's a tool for visually expressing time and place and what have you, so we need to take control of that.

AS: On a movie like *The Meg* were you involved in the design of the Meg creature itself or was that a whole different team?

GM: It was a mixture of both. Because it interacts with the submarines and it interacts with the big marine biology lab in the middle of the ocean, we had to have an understanding of what the Meg is, what its actual size is, what its look is and how it functions. So yes, we did model that up and ultimately those designs were taken

to visual effects. They developed the skin texture and all the finer points, but we started the ball rolling with what it actually looks like. We're not creature designers but we had to do it for the sake of knowing how it interacted with things. It had direct implications on how we built the boat, and how the boat was all geared up to tip over. We also built a big Meg head piece that was suspended on the back of the boat.

> **CINEMA TO ME IS LIKE THE CLASSICAL MUSIC OF THE WHOLE MEDIUM. IT'S THE HIGH ART FORM.**

AS: And you constructed water tanks for these sequences to be shot in?

GM: New Zealand at that point didn't have a water tank for filming. We looked around a lot of coastal areas to see where we could put it, but because we would have had to commute too far from Aukland, we ended up building it in our backlot. And we built a huge greenscreen wall behind it. We built the whole thing from scratch. It's still there actually! *Avatar II* used it a little while ago. We also built a huge indoor tank for all the underwater sequences. They had to be built because we needed access to the top, access windows through the bottom of the tanks, and we needed to be able to get all the way around the tanks to be able to light them. We also had to be able to control the temperature for the actors.

AS: Any advice for production designers who have been designing smaller movies and then suddenly get to design a film with a huge budget?

GM: An equal amount of creativity goes into a big-budget film but the organization and the stamina is different. Small movies tend to be fairly short and sharp in terms of the prep and the shoot, because of the budget. You don't tend to travel far from home. On the big shoots you have to be able to take on the right people to be able to divvy up the work load. The supervising art directors are great at organizing studios and taking on crew. On a small movie you do all that yourself. On these big, sprawling movies you need to bring on more crew and you have to be prepared to travel. You have a lot of different jobs going on in different parts of the country or different parts of the world. So you find yourself commuting a lot more between these places. You have teams of people here, there, and everywhere. There are a lot more logistics involved, in terms of getting on top of mountains and out into the middle of lakes. The canvas is way bigger with more interesting and extreme environments. You need to be able to focus on just the most important production design elements and then bring on people who can take the weight of the organizational side.

> **AN EQUAL AMOUNT OF CREATIVITY GOES INTO A BIG-BUDGET FILM BUT THE ORGANIZATION AND THE STAMINA IS DIFFERENT.**

AS: Often I'm impressed with the sheer number of art directors on bigger movies.

GM: You have to divide up the film, don't you? On *Mulan*, for example, we were splitting ourselves between the studio and China and the South Island of New Zealand. We had three geographical areas that we were working in. And then within that there were big sets to be built at various places so I had a different art director dealing with each of those areas and within those areas, assistant art directors doing specific things.

AS: What was your experience like working in China?

GM: It was interesting. They have quite large backlots that all specialize in particular time periods for their movies. Our film was based in the Tang dynasty so we were looking at the Tang dynasty backlots. But the backlots over there are not exclusively for filming. They often have them as theme parks and it's a way a lot of the Chinese learn their own history.

They have different ways of working up there. Just the way that they divide up labor, the way they cost things out, those sorts of practical things are a little difficult to get your head around. Just takes some working out, you could say. We found in the end that we were pulling things back to New Zealand because it was more of a known quantity. New Zealand is actually quite good geographically for a lot of other places in the world. We're quite lucky, it's quite a diverse landscape. In China there are iconic landscapes like Guinlin but a lot of the regular "in between" locations we shot back here in New Zealand. Obviously for production and political reasons we had to have a reasonable footprint there. We're expecting a large Chinese audience and they have to be able to buy into the story and feel national pride seeing their country looking great on screen.

AS: Of the directors you've worked with, would you say Bryan Singer is one of the most visual?

GM: Bryan is quite an interesting guy. Through the prep

of *X-Men: Apocalypse* he didn't come up to Montreal. So we were communicating long distance and that worked out okay but it did have its problems. Just the technicality of explaining creative ideas via Zoom was a little tricky. But you know it all worked out pretty well. He's an incredibly talented man and knows what he wants. He is a visual person. In *Apocalypse* we were picking up on what John Myhre had done before me on *Xmen: Days of Future Past* and trying to keep in the same realm of the world he'd created.

AS: Did you bring a lot of people to Montreal from New Zealand?

GM: No. That would be nice. But there was a terrific bunch of people in the art department there. The art department there had all gone through architecture school and they were quite a tight bunch of people who had gone from one X-Men film to another. So a lot of them had done *Days of Future Past* as well. They're a very, very talented bunch of people. I made a lot of good friends up there shooting that film.

AS: What do you think of the world of episodics versus film? Production value seems so high these days in the episodic world.

GM: I just did the first couple of episodes of *Cowboy Bebop* which is still in the throes of being made. It was my first television series in years, decades probably. It's been really interesting looking at that as a medium. There's a different sort of framing and a different pace of production and that's a new experience for me.

AS: Do you prefer one over the other?

GM: I like them both. I must say I like the sort of pulpy

nature of TV, and it's a lot faster turnaround. The immediacy of TV is quite interesting. I'm looking forward to working in that format again but at the same time cinema to me is like the classical music of the whole medium. It's the high art form. The audience is in a totally black room with a massive screen, seeing all this detail. But both are really exciting to me as a production designer. Both mediums are essentially using the same tools just in a different sort of way.

> " THE STORY'S THE MOST IMPORTANT THING BUT THE STORY ITSELF IS A VESSEL AND INSIDE THE VESSEL ARE CHARACTERS. IN THE BEST STORIES THESE CHARACTERS HAVE PERSPECTIVE, THEY HAVE BACKGROUNDS AND HAVE PSYCHOLOGICAL REQUIREMENTS. RECOGNIZING ALL THESE SUBTLETIES IS TREMENDOUSLY IMPORTANT BECAUSE HUMAN BEINGS ARE A SOCIAL SPECIES. WE GO TO THE MOVIES TO INTERACT WITH OTHER HUMAN BEINGS, NOTWITHSTANDING THAT THEY'RE PROJECTED ON A CINEMA SCREEN.

AS: How do you see the future of production design changing?

GM: Good production design is all to do with the narrative. The narrative overrides all these other technical inventions that come along. The story's the most important thing but the story itself is a vessel and inside the vessel are characters. In the best stories these characters have perspective, they have backgrounds and have psychological requirements. Recognizing all these subtleties is tremendously important because human beings are a social species. We go to the movies to interact with other human beings, notwithstanding that they're projected on a cinema screen. Technologically production design's gonna move on, but the fundamentals of storytelling won't change. We still are creating environments and worlds within which we tell stories. It's the best job in the world I reckon.

SKETCHES

Do you do your own sketches?

A compilation of excerpts covering the subject of sketching, taken from the interviews in this book

How important is it to be able to wield a pencil, or a stylus, in this business? Do you need to be able to create giant, charcoal masterpieces or simply scribble a floor plan on a napkin? In what ways is the ability to draw going to help you in this intensely competitive, visual medium? Each one of the production designers interviewed has their own style of communicating their visual ideas. While a large number of them are amazing traditional artists, others are able to make it all happen with taste, knowledge of the filmmaking process, and an intense passion for the medium.

GUY HENDRIX DYAS

[I draw] as much as possible because I enjoy it and it's such a great communication tool. Sometimes my schedule means that I have to do my own illustrations during off hours but it's always worth it as it enables me to quickly show a director an idea and then be able to hand off sketches to an art director. I guess the only thing nowadays is that I rarely have the time to take my illustrations into color, I mostly have sketch books filled with pencil drawings.

Sketching is all I do when I start a project. I've got this routine now where I'll read a script and get an 8.5" x 11" sketchbook and basically sketch the entire film. This sketchbook becomes my bible. It becomes my go-to place when I'm thinking of handing out projects to my staff to develop.

DAVID WASCO & SANDY REYNOLDS WASCO

DW: Sandy's a better sketch artist than I am. A lot of the concept illustrations that are done for the movies I hire a concept illustrator for only because it's a time-consuming thing. A full-time thing. It's not something that you do in an hour. You hire somebody and they're on it for days. Sometimes the doodle on a napkin is what jump-starts it.

Sandy's a very good perspective illustrator. The design of Jack Rabbit Slims started with a thumbnail that Sandy did.

SRW: That kind of sketching is really helpful and that's just a pencil on a napkin. If you're in a car

with a director and then you think, *We can't find this theater for* Inglourious Basterds *so let's do it this way.* You draw a little sketch and it's like, *Okay let's put it on the backlot.*

JOHN MUTO

there are plenty of production designers who don't draw. You know, maybe they know a little bit about interior decoration. Some production designers are producers. They don't really have any artistic talent at all. They assemble a great team. And on some of those movies they do it great. There's a lot of ways a movie can be great.

It's my observation that if you can draw a good enough picture, or present it in a smart enough way, and then show it to the director or DP, even if they initially say they don't like it, chances are they will shoot it that way. They won't be able to drive it from their head. So that's why I always tell the students you've got to learn to draw. At least draw well enough that you can express emotion in the drawing. How low the ceiling is or how far off in the distance it goes. This is the point of master shots. You don't need a master shot to be on the screen very long to give people a sense of where they are and how people are supposed to feel. So that's why you draw.

JACK FISK

I've never had an illustrator work with me and I only do sketches when necessary. I'd rather build and change it. When I was younger I started with models of sets because the carpenters that I was

SKETCHES

working with didn't all read blueprints. So I'd cut my drawings up and make white-board models and then everybody understood what I was thinking and they'd work from those.

But I use SketchUp a lot. I think in SketchUp. Because it gives you good proportions and scale. It's replaced physical models and sketches for me. Most of the directors I work with never ask to see drawings.

PATRICK TATOPOULOS

It's beyond true [that you need to sketch on spec to get a job]. My competition is fierce. You need to attract a client in some way. When a client comes and visits you and you've read the script before and you show a couple of images it's a big, big, big deal, even if they don't go with you.

I've gotten movies in the early stages of my career as both a designer and creature person by just showing my excitement for the project, showing my passion for the concept. People come and sit down with you and you drop three drawings on the table that you've done yourself–you didn't hire a concept artist, you've done them yourself–and they look at that and they can tell right away that you care about the project. So they see that and they go with you.

Some designers are very much just coordinators of the art department–very strong at making things happen but maybe creatively speaking not the people who are going to take a pencil or even a computer and create images. And that's okay, that's one type of designing. But there are also designers who are concept artists.

Directors are the same. Some directors are storytellers and can work on the screenplay. Writers who come and direct may not have a practical vision of something but they have the concept. I come from the other side. Look at people like Ridley Scott and James Cameron, they're people who actually draw their movies before they even start preproduction. For me it's about putting visuals together and starting to design my world in preproduction.

EVE STEWART

I'm quite quick. I do tons [of sketches.] I did a whole sequence of watercolors and paintings for *Les Mis*. It gives you something to talk about with directors. Even if something is wrong at least it's a starting point.

I sometimes get [set designers] to do a visual if it's a big street scene or something because studios like that sort of thing. But no, primarily with Tom [Hooper, director] he will happily work from my watercolors.

Do you do your own sketches?

KIM SINCLAIR

We joke that nobody in my New Zealand art department can draw! There are so many talented conceptual artists and illustrators whom I employ. A little sketch on the back of a napkin is about as far as I get these days, if you're lucky!

HANNAH BEACHLER

I will always sketch what I want and give it to the illustrators, along with a thousand references. Sometimes I'll just grab a piece of paper and illustrate a room and then say, *Okay, this! It wants to be this and then there's a thing that comes out here. And then it goes over like that and in plan view this is what it looks like. And then this is the elevation and they walk in here.*

We'll sit down with each illustrator and say, *This is the texture. I'm thinking something like this.* I'll have a very specific idea, like for Hall of Kings the idea was puzzle pieces put together. The influence for that was very much Mpumalanga in South Africa and Angkor Wat in Cambodia. Once I hand that to the illustrator they'll go off and do their thing and then we sit down again and I'll say, *Let's do this and take that away.* And then I'll draw some more while sitting there. And after illustration it goes to set designers and the set designers have to make things that actually work in real life.

SARAH GREENWOOD

I scribble. It's called "The Art of Sarah Greenwood". It's basically crap. They photocopy my sketchbook with scrappy plans and ideas. So no, I very much rely on the artistry of my team! I have an amazing illustrator that I work with called Eva Kuntz. She's German and she is brilliant and I've worked with her on the last three or four films. The illustrations we do, they're slightly more "montagey"–do you know what I mean? They're not polished. I really don't like polished, finished illustrations. They're atmospheric, they give the mood of the scene. They're not detailed as such. Maybe they're slightly disproportioned or the perspective is slightly off but you know I quite like that. They're atmospheric, to give a feel. They're not these perfect, glossy, finished pieces. They're done from my initial location photographs, from references, they're the juxtaposition of all sorts. You play with the color and the texture of things. That's a strong tool.

GRANT MAJOR

I used to do all my own stuff in those earlier films but on these bigger films being able to sit down and spend a day drawing is well nigh impossible. There are just too many projects going on at the same time to be able to do that. My drawing skills have dropped away a little bit, I must say! I do still draw quite a lot on the smaller projects but when it comes to projects like *The Green Lantern*, I had

SKETCHES

a huge amount of time and people to do concept work and it worked really well. Having the drawing skills is great, to be able to sit down and draw with the illustrators and do napkin sketches and things like that. But I don't end up working on finished illustrations that are pitch documents for the director and producers.

COLIN GIBSON

I draw badly. But I can also draw with words. I can draw with passion. I can sell anyone a used car if I have to.

ADAM STOCKHAUSEN

I do have an art background. When I have time I'm extremely happy to get on a drawing board and be sketching. Reality being what it is I end up not doing as much as I would like to. I was a set designer for theater and worked for a while in New York as a freelance set designer for regional theater and opera and that was great fun. In theater you're doing all your own sketches! And all your own drafting. It was because I was drafting that I came into the movie business. I started working in the art departments just doing a couple days here and there drafting.

DENNIS GASSNER

I'll do little teeny sketches. I don't draw elaborately anymore. There are people who do that so well. I do a two minute sketch and give it to a concept artist and have him work on it for three days. It comes back and it's amazing.

JOHN MUTO

It's my belief, and this is giving away a trade secret, but I think most people, including directors of photography and directors, are not capable of visualizing the way you and I do. If you can draw, not just draw something that's real but think of something, put it down on paper, that's a skill that not many people have. It's my observation that if you can draw a good enough picture, or present it in a smart enough way, and then show it to the director or DP, even if they initially say they don't like it, chances are they will shoot it that way. They won't be able to drive it from their head. So that's why I always tell the students, *You've got to learn to draw.*

RICK HEINRICHS

It's really important to be able to draw. To do some of the work yourself whether it's drawing a plan or an illustration. I do a very rough version of most of the illustrations I want people to work on. They're shitty, they're not rendered, but they say every-

Do you do your own sketches?

thing I want them to say and it gives the illustrators enough to get going. Excellent illustrators help because what you want to do is communicate to the director both the fundamental spirit as well as the particulars of a given set.

MARK FRIEDBERG

You can't do this work without being able to work a pencil. Or now an iPad. First, on location photos, I use my iPad and Apple pencil and then Hugh Sicotte, the concept artist I work most closely with, spends days refining these sketches into detailed concepts. Sometimes I get jealous because I don't have time to spend days on a drawing. I sketch, Hugh renders.

DAVID WARREN

Production designers are all human beings–they're all different. Some of them draw, some of them don't. Some of them have got tireless energy and excitement. Some of them are much more quiet. I don't think you can write this on a piece of paper and say, *Well, that guy can draw so he'll be a great designer*. I know that John Myhre for instance doesn't draw a lot but he still has two Academy Awards. He's obviously got a fantastic eye for references and he knows exactly what looks good when it's built. He knows how to dress a set. [Dante Ferretti] does draw and he does it in the Italian way. Doing these big, charcoal sketches of the sets. Lots of color, lots of lighting. He does them very quick. He just gets out his colored paper and draws these beautiful visuals from his imagination.

I come from a background of illustration so the first thing I reach for in any situation is a pencil. And in the early stages we were hammering out drawings on the drawing board. When Terry likes it he comes over and puts his fingers all over it and it gets messy. Then he grabs a pencil and he starts scribbling on your drawing. That's the language that we used to make decisions.

K.K. Barrett

K.K. Barrett has created unforgettable art working with some of the world's most original filmmakers: Spike Jonze on *Where the Wild Things Are, Being John Malkovich, Adaptation,* and *Her* (for which Barrett was nominated for an Oscar); Michel Gondry on *Human Nature;* Sophia Coppola on *Lost in Translation* and *Marie Antoinette.* He had just finished the Stephen Daldry-directed Tom Hanks movie *Extremely Loud and Incredibly Close* when I met him in the DUMBO section of Brooklyn where he was prepping Karen O.'s psycho-opera *Stop the Virgens.*

KK: I always wish somebody would win an Oscar for production design and talk for just a minute about the simplicity of the most purely correct, but minimalist, piece of production design of the year. A film where people edit out visually what doesn't belong until everything is pure and correct for the film, rather than the bells and whistles and the over-the-top and in-your-face design where you forget who the characters are. You can art direct a film without painting anything, without building anything, and still control a palette, still control a mood and make it a very strong statement.

AS: Reducing until you get to the essence...

KK: There's only so much space in a film. A good example is when a book gets edited down to a script. Subplots are lost, characters are lost. You can only make so much of a statement in the hour and a half, two hours you have for the film.

Production design is often the same way. You can only do so much. You don't need to show the world that isn't discussed or isn't affecting the characters. Even though it may exist down the street. Sometimes the biggest process is saying, *No, that has nothing to do with them, it distracts from them, let's take that away*. It would distract or confuse the character's existence, or their dilemma, or their happiness. You just have to take things away until you're concentrating on the character and the affected environments.

AS: The sets shouldn't overshadow the characters...

KK: That's a given unless you're making a summer thrill-ride. There's design for entertainment and then there's design for drama. Sometimes it works hand-in-hand. Sometimes it's dramatic and it's entertaining. It doesn't mean it shouldn't be entertaining but it should always be engaging. Sometimes entertaining is not engaging. I like to think that you can help the audience have an experience on their own by absorbing things rather than telling them what to think all the time. A summer film usually tells the audience what to think and is very nervous about not telling them what to think. They don't want them ever to get bored. Don't get me wrong, I buy a lot of popcorn and enjoy those movies, I am just trying to give thought to the more unsung statements of design.

I like to find my own way into films. I like to have my own experience of it. Just like when people listen to songs. The lyrics mean different things to different people. Of course some people don't listen to the lyrics. And some people only listen to the lyrics and couldn't tell you anything about the melody.

I like to find my own version of the movie and not be told this is what it is and this is only what it could be. Just like a book. When you read a book you can see so many more versions of what the world is with the few descriptive words that you're given. In a movie unfortunately you can only take away what's shown or at least hinted at, so you have to be very careful how much information you give.

> " **THE BEST IDEA WINS. IF THERE'S A BETTER IDEA IT SHOULD BE IMPLEMENTED AT ALL COSTS.**

AS: Some people say that a set can be a character in a movie.

KK: I suppose in Hitchcock's *Psycho* the hotel was a character in the movie. Because it embodied the past. Usually it's a character support rather than a character itself. It's more like a coat, you know? Sometimes it's like when an actor can't really find themselves until they put on the character's clothes. I like to walk the actor through the sets early on in the process. I'll show them the pictures of what we intend to do. They have really good feedback because they've thought a lot about their character.

AS: In the films that you've done with Spike Jonze the sets are stylized but at the same time still feel

like a real places. On *Being John Malkovich* was that an augmented location or did you build the whole 7 1/2 floor?

KK: It was a real place. It was a location. As written, everything was half-sized. Furniture was half-sized. Everything was half-sized. Spike had a great idea to ground everything. Because we were going to go fantastic with the physics of the world. We found a real location so we could really look outside the windows. And we lowered the ceiling. Put new crown molding on it.

AS: You used the existing doors but put new crown moldings on?

KK: We built a lot of hallways and doors–tunnels within the space. We used existing windows so we could take advantage of fire escapes, the details connecting to the outside world. And we added the T-bar drop ceiling like it had been remodeled in the 80's. We said it had been around a long time but there were things that we modernized like office buildings always do. So you weren't just stepping back in time, you were stepping through a number of times.

The tunnel that Craig Schwarz goes through was written as big, gelatinous, and vibrating. I thought it was just as absurd to have it be dirt on the 7 1/2 floor, as if you're on ground-level. You have something that's extremely tactile and familiar from the physical world. Even if it's in the wrong place at the wrong time. If Schwarz opened it up and it was a wormhole then all of a sudden you said to the audience, *Okay, anything can happen now.* So the audi-ence isn't curious any longer. It's like, *Okay they can fly so why can't they do this, why can't they do that?* They start doing the logic for you if you give them too much room to move.

AS: Are you involved a lot in CG nowadays or does it end up just being a post production thing?

KK: I'm involved in it. I'm very frustratingly involved in it. So many things can go wrong. It's done at the end. It can be farmed out to five or six different places depending on how important it is. Those five or six different places may not have their best man on it. I did a lot of interviewing on the last movie for special effects supervisors and companies and what I realized was that what you really want to do is have a relationship with the artist who's actually doing it. Just like you would with an illustrator who's working under you. To be able to correct things and see things that they don't see, because you're more familiar with the project.

AS: You mean the individual CG artist modeling the environment?

KK: Yes. They're the ones you have to trust. You could actually save a lot of money by dealing with them directly because you could decide what was important and what was not. And know when something's done. I would take direct interface with the renderers. Often changes are translated through others.

The first time I worked with greenscreen was 1980. It was the first film I ever did. No budget. Everybody learning. Bluescreen and greenscreen.

Because we had something in frames side-by-side and we didn't know if we could key them in and separate them. It wasn't so easy to make windows and mattes back then. I was coming from working on film motion graphics which was the early predecessor to the computer work. So you could just do a straight key but you didn't have a computer to do it. You were just keying out blue and keying in your image. If you wanted two things to key in into the same frame you had to have different color channels to replace. So it was a little bit trickier.

AS: Did you do that film before your commercial and music video work?

KK: I did that film before I did anything. Because the band I was in hooked up with a director and he wanted to do some musical projects. This was before MTV. There really wasn't an outlet for musical short films. It got rebuilt into a linear story and then we shot connective tissue to put the different song bits together. And I had built a recording studio that was like a soundstage in an old vitamin factory. I just volunteered to do the work. I said, *Well, who's gonna design it?* And he said, *I don't know.*

I said, *I will.* I'd never designed anything for film. I'd studied art in school as a painter and a sculptor. I wasn't afraid of it. I didn't really know what an art director did. I didn't know what a production designer did. Somebody told me that that's what the name of the job was. But I was always a voracious reader and I looked it up and figured it out. And then, because I had done that at that time, six

months later videos started happening and they were so cheap that anyone who said they could do it got the job. So I did a lot. And then those video directors started making commercials.

> "YOU SHOULDN'T GO INTO A WESTERN BY LOOKING AT WESTERNS. YOU SHOULDN'T GO INTO A SCIENCE FICTION MOVIE BY LOOKING AT OTHER SCIENCE FICTION MOVIES. YOU CAN BE AWARE OF IT BUT YOU SHOULDN'T TAKE YOUR TABLE OF CONTENTS FROM DESIGN WORK THAT SOMEONE ELSE HAS DONE.

AS: Is that when you met Spike Jonze?

KK: Yeah. I did a commercial with him. His producer Vince Landay knew I was doing work for someone else in the building and he kind of hooked us up. We met and started talking. Found out that we'd been a lot of the same places years before. Sat across the room at the same party, knew people in common, things like that.

The first thing I did was a commercial with him for Coke. He wanted me to try all different animation styles. Computer animation, pixelation, puppetry. But he was doing something else at the same time so he just said, *Figure this out.* And we did a couple of other commercials after that. And he started picking up really fast. This is when he was with the Satellite Films division of Propaganda. I was doing other commercials for Stéphane Sednaoui and Simon West. So it was a good place to be in the halls of.

> " PRODUCTION DESIGNERS HAVE TO OBSERVE THE WORLD. THEY HAVE TO KNOW HOW IT WENT TOGETHER. SEE WHAT WENT INTO IT. *HOW DID THIS BUILDING SURVIVE THE BUILDING NEXT TO IT? HOW HAS IT CHANGED? WHY IS IT STILL HERE? WHAT HAPPENED?;*

AS: Then when you did some work with Michel Gondry was that a connection through Spike Jonze?

KK: It was. He was there too. It was a very incestuous time. In fact I've had a very incestuous career. Hanging out with Spike I met Michel. Michel had done a little short, a black and white film where a boy becomes a camera. And Sophia [Coppola] had done a short film called *Lick the Star.* Another black and white film. And we were watching them all on one night. I knew Sophia because she was with Spike, and Michel was there so I met him too. After that I did some music videos and some commercials with him. And then when his first film came along I did his first film.

AS: *Human Nature?*

KK: Yes. Also Charlie [Kaufman] wrote it. I met him through Spike. On *Being John Malkovich.* Coming to the set and hanging out.

AS: Michel Gondry and Spike Jonze come across as very visual. How involved are they with the design?

KK: They are visual to different degrees. Michel is extremely visual. He could tell everything with visuals alone. When we did *Human Nature,* which was very low budget for the seventy or so sets we had, he storyboarded every set to within an inch, in his cartoon style. He'd say, *We only need from here to here.* So we had a stage with sets lined up, fifteen feet wide, ten feet wide, twelve feet wide. We'd just go to the next, to the next, to the next, and then tear those down and build the next set-ups. They were very, very tight. It's a very funny film.

Spike is visual in a bigger picture kind of way. In an emotional way. *What kind of emotional impact does this space, this environment have on you? How do I feel in this space?* And Michel is less emotionally attached to the visuals except through joy. For both of them in different ways, it's like going into your house and opening your closet. Or your medicine cabinet or refrigerator. Your desk. Say you open your closet and everything falls down. Because they say if you look at someone's closet that's how their mind works. Cluttered or uncluttered; organized or unorganized.

Michel likes to see how things were thought out. The process of how something was made. He's very observant. Production designers have to observe the world. They have to know how it went together. See what went into it. *How did this building survive the building next to it? How has it changed? Why is it still here? What happened? Why did they put that door in there?* All of these different details that make up the history of the place. And Michel's very interested in that and then he kind of takes it apart. *What if it happened like this?*

AS: You were saying that in *Being John Malkovich* the drop ceiling was designed to look like it had been added in the 80's, but the rest of the building had more history.

KK: You can't do a historical piece and only start at the year it's taking place. You have to know where it came from. How did it end up there?

AS: What would you say are some of the characteristics that a production designer should have?

KK: I'd say number one is curiosity. Number two is observation. Curiosity, observation, and decisiveness. That belongs, that doesn't belong. We don't need that, we need this. It's the same as being editorial. Making decisions quickly doesn't mean you can't change them. It means it unclutters the way so you can concentrate on things you haven't solved yet, that aren't so obvious to deduce. Setting aside all the quick, easy answers may inform the ones that aren't clear yet.

Then you may go back and say, *That's not going to be in our movie any more. We've grown so much since then.* You start to see the tone and you start to see what belongs. You start to see how it's shot. I have to be on set for the first month or so of a film as much as I possibly can to see what the camera's editing. What's being found and what's not being

included. So that I know how to steer it. What to give it. What it's missing. I'm not talking about key props. Sometimes it can be claustrophobia. *They shouldn't be claustrophobic. You know the scene where he's in yet another restaurant in yet another room somewhere? Let's take that outside. Let's get down to the dynamics of the film and let it breathe. Let's not be in someone's tormented head in a small space for the whole movie. Let's have a dynamic, so if you really want to make a point with that, you can take it out and then you bring it back.*

In *Where the Wild Things Are* there were so many scenes written in a forest. And we knew we were going to get tired of it. The DP got really tired of it and decided that one expedition had to be somewhere completely palate-cleansing from that. And I already had made three different forests because I knew that problem existed. One of the forests we painted all the pine trees white.

AS: These forests were all done at exterior locations?

KK: Interior and exterior. We had to do both because we were working with a child that can only work until nine PM at night and we had a lot of night scenes that go on and on and on so we had to build the forest on stage.

AS: Where did you shoot the movie?

KK: Outside of Melbourne, Australia. And I'd always wanted to go to the sand dunes and we finally did that at the end of the movie. It was a long ways away. And I knew that would be a palette-cleanser from all this forested interior as exterior. Mind-clearing in a way. You want to feel like you've gone a long distance and in a forest you really can't get that. We all became aware, after we'd shot for a while, that we couldn't do that scene in a forest. We had to change it.

Often when I break down a script I'll understand that they keep going back to the same place. But there's no reason they have to go to that place. Sometimes it's not really necessary. It's convenient. Or nobody had thought about it up to that point. And it's your job to think about it. *Why are they there? Why can't they be someplace else? What does it do to the character? How else can we know something about their past or about another facet that makes them more complex?*

AS: Did the fantastic nature of *Where the Wild Things Are* feel very different from the other movies you've worked on?
KK: I went from *Marie Antoinette* to *Where the Wild Things Are* the next year. It was completely different. There are almost no props in *Where the Wild Things Are*, almost no set dressing. I just wanted big environments. I didn't want tables and chairs or anything silly like that. I wanted to keep it about the internal neuroses of the characters. Every time you strip everything away what you leave behind is very, very important.

We didn't leave nature alone. We modified nature quite a bit. We planted trees. We did a lot of things just to give it a little bit of specialness but to still keep it grounded. We changed seasons so it was spring and fall at the same time. We took all the green out of the movie. The first thing I decided was no green. Because everybody says, *Where are you going for this? Are you going to the jungle?* I had been looking at the forest and every time I was there I didn't feel wild. I felt comforted. And it had no depth. Very shallow. By taking out green, the color everyone relates to healthy nature, it all of a sudden became more exciting to me. I'm sure there's some green in there. But we made the decision to not have green and to have yellow and orange leaves instead when they showed up. You've already got giant people in half-fur and half-feathered costumes. You can mash up the outside world a little bit as well without having to go to CG.

AS: What was it like working with Sophia Coppola on *Lost In Translation* and *Marie Antoinette*?
KK: She's very trusting. And very specific. With any director you just have to get in sync with their mentality. Their sensibility. What their sensibility for the project is and what their natural, inherent sensibility is. The sooner you figure it out the better off you are. She was very concerned about palette. And quality.

One thing that all the filmmakers I've worked with have in common is they don't want to make movies about other movies. They don't want to reference other movies. They don't want to have the design reference other movies. Every movie should be its own. And I think this is extremely important to production designers. You shouldn't go into a

Western by looking at Westerns. You shouldn't go into a science fiction movie by looking at other science fiction movies. You can be aware of it but you shouldn't take your table of contents from design work that someone else has done. It's a wonderful chance to make it not like anybody else's. Just decide what it can be. It's such a great opportunity to create a vision and support a story and a cast. It's just a missed opportunity if it looks like another dirty spaceship or another exact same type this or type that. Science fiction is probably the worst abuser of it, eating itself.

AS: Someone comes up with the idea of doing a dirty spaceship and then everyone's doing a dirty spaceship.
KK: Yes, there was the original one, which might have been *Dark Star,* and then it's the norm. But you know, *make another norm.*

AS: When you get hired on a movie and get a script do you end up watching a lot of movies for reference?
KK: I watch movies that probably don't relate. Movies that maybe have the same emotional mood but that are not in the same genre. See how the mood affected the characters and how the mood that you settle on affects the characters. You could watch a Western for a romantic comedy, or a romantic comedy for something else.

AS: And that relates to the characters?
KK: Always. It's their journey. Not yours. And the viewers' journey through them. So I always try to

think of it from the viewers' point of view. *What wakes me up again?* Just when you think you know the film. You constantly re-attune the audience to paying attention. And steer them in the right direction. Or just put them in a room and open the door and let them look.

I do all kinds of research but it's not specific to what the film may be about. It could be as banal as the place around the corner from your house. You get in the mindset of the film and then you go out and look at the world again. And you see how it bounces off. You keep applying it. It's a long kind of "research by procrastination." The film is constantly with you and you're trying to figure out what it is. Everything you look at may have a clue.

I take a lot of pictures all the time. Maybe a couple hundred a day. And I'll print out my favorite pictures. They may not be about the film. I'll do it like I'm playing cards. I'll take twenty of my favorite images out from whatever day or week it was. And I'll start saying *Oh, I like that, I like that, I like that, I like that.* If you find things you like they may find a way into affecting your design. And then you end up with maybe twenty images that do apply to the film in abstract ways. Then there will be one that really sticks out–I really *like* that but it has no place in the film. You take it out but then you go, *This is too homogeneous now.* It needed that wildcard. That belonged in there. It was the wrong color that I never used anywhere else. It needed that spike of color.

So it's looking at the design problem-solving di-lemma in a very abstract way. You take that and go, *What if that picture was that character and that picture was this character?* And it's not a room for a room. It could be a car for a room. A smiling face for a room or an abstract bridge for a room. Anything like that. It's part of the "procrastination-process". Constantly exploring.

AS: Laying out a picture for each character reminds me of the playwright who set up a little plastic animal for each of his characters as he was writing his play.

KK: Just make sure that you're looking at it from another side. Rather than just landing on: *Oh, well then it's got to be this. It's a bathroom, I know what a bathroom looks like. It's a bar. I know what a bar looks like.* Like if you told somebody to make a sports bar. It seems like an obvious thing, full of touchstone clichés. *What can we not do? Can we take the TVs out? How can we turn it on its head and still say what we want to say?* Or you take a sports bar and you populate it only with women.

AS: Rather than just printing out clichéd stills of what you know and expect from a place.

KK: The pictures can be totally unrelated. Sometimes it's for composition. Sometimes it's for color. Sometimes it's for intrigue. There is a story in the picture, *Why is there a story? What made it a story?* When somebody says, *What happened just before this picture? What's gonna happen with the elements that are in it?* Then you've really got something. So if you can get that in the design then the story can

be added to, and the set can be a character. Because it can have a past and a future. Potential tension. Tension's very important. To keep everybody alert. Even on films that aren't thrillers. It heightens the senses.

AS: Did your being a musician have an impact on your film work?

KK: I was an artist first and I discovered when I became a musician that it was the same as being an artist. I approached everything the same. The same decision-making process exists in music as it does in film and design.

I used to compare a live set-list of songs to a song itself. You've got an introduction, you've got some alternating balances, verse/chorus, verse/chorus, you've got a bridge. A cliff-hanger. Film is exactly the same way. Instead of the songs there are scenes. And if you blow the ending–if you don't have the ending then they'll never remember the wonderful things that you've done to them on the way. If the last note is off they'll forget the whole song. All they remember is the thing that stuck out. Rather than the dynamic journey.

It's the same type of thinking whether it's musical or it's artistic. What's your first glance? What's your discovery after you look at something for a while? What's the thought after you think about it tomorrow? I certainly hope that everyone walks out of the theater arguing at least. Because then they'll keep thinking about it tomorrow. They might change their mind. They might hate it again.

They might love it afterwards thinking they hated it at first. You don't want them to just go, *Yeah, that's . . . good. What do you want to eat?* And the design is just one cog in that.

AS: Would you describe the project that you're currently working on with Karen O., *Stop the Virgens*, as an opera?

KK: It's a psycho-opera. Karen recorded some music five years ago when I was off doing *Marie Antoinette*. She was a neighbor in Los Angeles. Between my doing *Marie Antoinette* and *Where the Wild Things Are* she wrote this whole album of music that she thought of as a musical or a song-cycle. She wanted to make it into small vignettes with different directors doing each piece. That never happened and we talked about making a film out of it. I tried to write a script with her on it and we realized that we didn't really want to have any other words besides the lyrics. And we didn't want anyone talk-singing like they do in musicals. So it was not a musical whatsoever, it was an opera. It was story delivered emotionally through music. Not narratively, through music.

She moved back to New York and since I've been in New York for the last year [working on *Extremely Loud and Incredibly Close*] we had time to really start thinking about it again and everything fell into place. We started interviewing directors and then we got funded by the Creator's Project which is a combination of Vice Media and Intel. And all of a sudden we said, *Okay, we gotta do this. We gotta do this right now.*

I had made models for it maybe two years ago. Trying to figure out if it was to be staged or if it should be filmed. The models could have been for either one. And then I had to quickly re-organize them to be specific to this New York stage presentation. I've never really done actual theater before but if you've done enough music videos you've pretty much been doing theater in some way. It just kind of fell together and a lot of our friends are creatively involved with it. It's got an orchestra, the people who actually recorded the songs, and her costume designer Christian Joy is doing the costumes. Everybody's able to get outside of what they normally do and play.

> **" YOU SHOULD ALWAYS THINK AS IF YOU HAVE TO LIGHT EVERY SET. AND AS IF YOU HAVE TO PHOTOGRAPH EVERY SET . . . IF YOU'VE DONE YOUR JOB WELL, THE CAMERA WILL COME IN AND GO RIGHT TO WHERE YOU WANT IT TO.**

AS: Karen O. did some music for *Where the Wild Things Are*. Was she part of the Spike Jonze circle?

KK: Yeah. She just kind of like swam into the circle. You know how friendships are. I think it's your job as a friend to bring in new blood to your other friends. And hopefully they do the same. So it's constantly expanding and contracting.

She can do anything she wants. She can just sit down and spontaneously make something up and it's great. She was just so good at doing *Where the Wild Things Are* songs. And this music is completely different. She and I had done another side project that was a live presentation about three years ago here in New York at a small club called Union Pool. Just seven songs that she had nothing else to do with. So we just made this little nautical scene.

> **" YOU SHOULDN'T *TALK ABOUT* VISUALS. YOU SHOULD ALWAYS *REFER* TO VISUALS. BECAUSE PEOPLE SEE DIFFERENT THINGS AT THE SAME TIME IF IT'S JUST VERBAL.**

AS: A little nautical set?

KK: Yes. A little jewel box. A little Fabergé egg that you just kind of look into. A one-time performance. So this is an expansion on that mentality.

AS: You mentioned doing models of the sets in *Stop the Virgens*. Do you do a lot of physical models when you do movies?

KK: Yeah. I do a lot of physical models to figure things out for myself. I work with sketch artists too. I'll sketch a little bit and have them run with it. And play with the model and try to see spatially what happens and then sometimes the photographs of the models take the place of illustrations. I just find it easier to work in those dimensions. I find it very, very hard to work in SketchUp because there's no romance to it. It's very hard to show it to anybody. Even in fly-throughs. By the time that you've rendered in to the degree that someone can

be enchanted by it then they go, *Is that exactly what it's going to look like?* And you go, *No . . .*

So it's hard. It's always that problem of how do you present something so that they can still use their imagination? More and more with computer tools we can show exactly what it is. But it's time-consuming, it's laborious. So at the early stages it's better so show something that still has some romance left in it.

AS: So ideally when you're going to build some sets and you want to show the director and producers something you'll build some physical models and show some sketches?

KK: It's different every time. I also use reference images. But usually there's a photographed model involved. And sketches. Often I'll Photoshop alterations to locations myself. But sometimes there's something that's intangible and you want to make sure everybody's on the same visual page. And you shouldn't *talk about visuals*. You should always *refer* to visuals. Because people see different things at the same time if it's just verbal. It's a great way of getting everybody back on the same page.

If you're doing your job you're thinking of all the direction choices, you're thinking of all the DP's choices, you're thinking of all the costume choices. You've really got to wear all those hats. So when you start to have discussions with those people you'll at least have been running into some of the problems. You'll have a logic-stream of how you arrived at it. You'll also be able to accommodate and understand their version of it so you can meld the two together without starting from scratch. You should always think as if you have to light every set. And as if you have to photograph every set. As if you have to put the directors through it and where you would put the camera.

AS: You can create a beautiful set but if you have no way to get light in there, it's impossible to shoot.

KK: If you've done your job well, the camera will come in and go right to where you want it to. There are sweet spots. You'll find the sweet spots. Kubrick used to light his sets to the point that he didn't need a gaffer around. *Leave me with the camera and the actors.* They were in a constant environment. It works with over-lit sets or brightly-lit sets. But more and more with the technology we have now with cameras, you don't need to over-light. Choosing practical light sources, soft and hard lighting, can be more important than painting.

You should interview Jack Fisk. On Terence Malik's *Tree of Life* they found matching houses, one facing morning sun, one facing evening sun. Depending on the time of day they went from house "to house and shot naturally.

I'd like to hear from production designers grounded in the pre-digital era but who are still working and learn how that transition has affected them. Not job-security-wise. Just taking advantage of the tools of the trade. There's a lot of things to be learned from the earlier methods because they were simpler. A lot of times the more tools you have doesn't mean you'll use them. It's like a city. You can live in the biggest city in the world and only use your neighborhood. Your store, your recreational spot. Your house. Your connective tissue. Even if it's just a corridor the full length of the city, you never walk to the sides. There's a lot to be said about stripping away things. And the new cameras are doing that.

> " A LOT OF TIMES THE MORE TOOLS YOU HAVE DOESN'T MEAN YOU'LL USE THEM. IT'S LIKE A CITY. YOU CAN LIVE IN THE BIGGEST CITY IN THE WORLD AND ONLY USE YOUR NEIGHBORHOOD.

AS: How closely do you work with the DP?

KK: Extremely closely. I think you have to. Because they need you and you need them. You need to know how each other thinks. I work right next to the DP constantly. That's why I want to be on set so much.

AS: Do you also work with them closely in prep?

KK: Absolutely. Try to show them stuff as much as I can.

AS: You didn't work with your usual DP, Lance Acord, on *Extremely Loud and Incredibly Close*.

KK: The original DP, Harris Savides, was a friend of

mine. We had done a lot of commercials together in the early days when we were both starting out. But I'd never done a film with him. He had a style that was completely different from Chris Menges, who took over the film. I had to adjust. Because I'd built for illumination in one way, but then had to completely adjust to Chris's way. Soft ceilings to hard ceilings. It's just a different mentality. They're both really dramatic lighters but come from opposite ends of the spectrum. It was really interesting. I had to completely switch gears. It was a really fun process to do that. To one day just go like, *Okay, I have to completely rethink all of this.* I had to talk to Chris and figure out what his sensibility was. I was already a big fan and I'd singled out some small films that he did that I thought were gorgeous.

AS: Did that transition happen during preproduction?

KK: Just before we started filming. I'd been there for five months. But films are about change. You've got to be able to change constantly.

AS: Is that adaptability another characteristic one needs as a production designer?

KK: It is. The best idea wins. If there's a better idea it should be implemented at all costs. You don't want to go limping in with, *Well, that was our first idea but now it really doesn't work. And there's a great idea that we're missing.*

So you've got to constantly be ready to change things. *What can we sacrifice to make it happen?* I make rules but sometimes I break them.

AS: Like "No green"?

KK: Like no green. But I break them. The next film I'm doing with Spike I've already made a lot of rules. It's a very specific environment. And I know I'll break them. But all of a sudden I start to see the world because of the things I'd taken away and the things that I've constrained.

AS: What kind of a film is the new one with Spike?

KK: I can't say. Because it's a very specific environment. (Grins.)

AS: You mentioned once that no one really controls a film, they simply channel it.

KK: You have to allow for whatever might happen and be able to be loose enough to take advantage of it. Even if it's a disaster. You've got to be able to spin it. An analogy was when I was playing music and somebody would make a mistake and I realized if you repeated that mistake it became a part. You go from taking something that sticks out because it's wrong to doing it twice and then all of a sudden you've celebrated it. It's like taking someone who can't sing very well but putting their voice up front in the mix. You'll get emotion out of it. Filmmaking is very much like that. It's a constant discovery process.

AS: Say someone was starting out in business, any advice to avoid pitfalls?

KK: I think you should find every pitfall you can find! I think you should fall into every hole you can possibly find!

Two things: Take every job. Never worry about money. Take ones where you can learn from something that you've never done before, especially if you're scared of it. And then do everybody else's job in your head. And know everybody else's job. Know what they do and how they contribute and how it affects you. And think it out as if everybody's gone home and you've got to do it all yourself.

Don't have preconceived notions when you go into a film. Be able to change. Be able to go with it. Be able to discover every day. The last week of the film you should still be able to discover new things.

Make yourself invaluable. Take a job–*I'll do it for free*. Hang around until you have to leave. And then hopefully they'll go, *No, no, no, we need you. We're so used to you solving problems with us we need you now. Will you stay for five dollars?* And then you have to leave again. *Will you stay for ten dollars?* Just make yourself invaluable. Find somebody else that you can help.

AS: How do you see the future of production design? Do you see it becoming more and more greenscreens, fewer actual environments?

KK: No. Will we be thinking about 3D films in four years? It went away before. What I'm surprised at is that there are not more people making films for nothing. Because the technology is there. You could really make films for the price of the access to a camera. To be competitive you just have to have good stories. Engaging stories. And characters. And you need good sound. But all of those things are very obtainable for five thousand dollars. And a lot of free time. But I think it's because there aren't enough good stories.

FILMS ARE ABOUT CHANGE. YOU'VE GOT TO BE ABLE TO CHANGE CONSTANTLY.

So I don't think it's about CG or not CG, or greenscreen or not. Those are just tools. They're not ideas–they're just tools. A hammer can lay sitting on a table but it's not going to help you unless you have something you decided to do with it. Tools are just tools. You have to have the idea and make something out of it.

David Wasco + Sandy Reynolds-Wasco

Production designer David Wasco and his set decorator wife Sandy Reynolds-Wasco could be the hippest team in Production Design–they have done almost all of Quentin Tarantino's movies, starting with the iconic *Reservoir Dogs* and *Pulp Fiction,* and have worked with many other greats, including Wes Anderson on the beautifully designed *The Royal Tenenbaums* and *Rushmore.* More recently they collaborated on *La La Land* for which they won their first Oscar. I caught up with them right before their trip to England where they were headed to conduct a London Film Festival masterclass at BAFTA.

AS: Tell us about your latest project, *Seven Psychopaths...*

DW: With *Seven Psychopaths* we were given an opportunity to showcase L.A. We had similar opportunities with *Pulp Fiction,* with *Reservoir Dogs,* and with *Collateral* and feel lucky because we love to explore the city. Every neighborhood feels different. We have a specific interest in L.A. architecturally.

People think the city has been shot out and there's nothing left to shoot but there are places that haven't been seen and there are things that are untapped, and those are the places we took director Martin McDonagh. Martin wrote a big scene for Joshua Tree National Park east of here in the desert. You're not allowed to shoot guns at the real Joshua Tree and you're not allowed to do fire so we actually built a sizable visitor's center in the middle of Lancaster which was far more film-friendly. Lancaster is north but feels just as remote. Locals kept pulling in, happy to see a sign of civilization but perplexed–they said they had no idea Joshua Tree came all the way out there! It was funny. They watched it being built, shot in a day, then disappear.

Working in LA is great and *Seven Psychopaths* was a lucky, dream opportunity, written for L.A. and shot in L.A. With a lot of work going out of state, so much art direction time and money is wasted by turning, say, New Orleans into California.

Before *Psychos* we did *Rampart,* also L.A. for L.A. and by another brilliant writer/director, Oren Moverman. I liked that film a lot too. It had a short release date but is worth looking out for.

SRW: After watching Martin's previous film, *In Bruges* we reacted like so many of our friends... *Bruges? It's beautiful! We have to know more about Brussels!* And that's the reaction we hope to see happen after people see *Seven Psychopaths,* especially non-Americans. We want everyone to go, Wow, L.A.! The California Desert! What a crazy, great place.

DW: Bruges tourism actually increased after Martin's movie.

SRW: The story is about a writer who's been asked to do a screenplay but he's been struggling against it, against the requested action and the guns–the

typical American fare. He's researching psychopaths and we get to go back in time to visit a few of them.

DW: But he wants to do a different psychopath movie that is more about peace and love! It's very funny. Martin attracted an incredible cast, part of his entourage of acting talent: people like Colin Farrell, Chris Walken and Sam Rockwell who have been in some of his plays. You have no idea where the movie is going to go.

SRW: I also think it's wonderful that theater directors like Martin make every individual feel equally important. It's a team-effort and he really respects all the crafts. When you're on the set everyone is equally valuable.

AS: You were saying earlier that *Seven Psychopaths* might be like the next *Pulp Fiction*.
DW: It might be the next *Pulp Fiction.* That was my take on it while doing it. We only saw a rough cut but from what I saw it has the same sensibility. Not that Martin is trying to copy Quentin because Martin is his own writer, but it's got so much great dialogue, so many short stories that add up to an interesting whole and a fun ride.

AS: Speaking of Quentin Tarantino, how have things changed with him from the early days like on *Reservoir Dogs* to the most recent films?
DW: Well, it's been twenty years. We started with Quentin with *Reservoir Dogs* and nobody knew who he was then. Although he'd penned two scripts,

Natural Born Killers and *True Romance*, he wasn't a known name. We got the script and we interviewed just like every other project. Even with directors I've worked with multiple times I think it would be naïve to think that I'm the only person that they would want to hire. There are so many uncontrollable elements. A new producer might come on and be pushing their guy to be production designer. I met Quentin at an interview at an apartment Lawrence Bender was renting south of Wilshire and it was very relaxed. He liked the fact that we were doing period films. *Reservoir Dogs* wasn't a period film but it was supposed to be in this nebulous era of Los Angeles. That was why he told me he hired me.

> **THERE ARE A LOT OF PEOPLE THAT DO WHAT WE DO AND DO A GOOD JOB. IT'S JUST REALLY ABOUT HAVING THE DIRECTOR FEEL COMFORTABLE BEING ABLE TO COMMUNICATE WITH YOU. THEY JUST WANT TO HAVE THAT EASE OF COMMUNICATION AND BE ABLE TO RELY ON YOU.**

There are a lot of people that do what we do and do a good job. It's just really about having the director feel comfortable being able to communicate with you. They just want to have that ease of communication and be able to rely on you.

When we started with *Reservoir Dogs* it was really fun filmmaking. He had so much fun making the picture that his joy was contagious. In many ways he was the same as he is today–almost like a big kid–which I'm saying in a nice way!

SRW: He loves writing and filmmaking.

DW: He loves filmmaking and he truly has an encyclopedic memory. He can remember everything. I think he truly has looked at every single movie. I don't know how anybody can do that because he's only so old and if you looked at every movie without a break every day for life you can't even look at every movie. But he has! And he remembers everything. And that was how he worked with us from the very beginning until most recently.

But on *Reservoir Dogs* there was this sense of wonder and glee with being given the opportunity to do this movie and he was so thankful and thankful for all of us. And so happy. And he expressed that to everybody. In describing what he wanted he would act out these scenes and flop around the floor and everything. That was so funny! He almost never used storyboards or for that matter concept illustrations because he felt that locked him into a structure. We all are of the mind that making a movie is like doing a painting. You kind of have an idea of what you're going to do when you start but you don't know exactly what you're going to end up with until it's done. You want to keep it open for ideas and contributions. He really was just fun to work with and attracted a really great cast.

Monte Hellman was the original director of *Reservoir Dogs* and Quentin was going to produce it but when Harvey Keitel put his name on the project it boosted the budget and Monte was asked if he would not mind if Quentin directed it. And Quentin then took over directing while Monte remained on as the producer. We had been scouting with a Spanish cameraman Josep Civit who had just done a couple movies with Monte but Josep was tired and he just didn't want to do a third movie straight in a row. This new cameraman was brought from Europe, Andrzej Sekula. I think this was his first job in America. He did *Reservoir Dogs* and *Pulp Fiction* and he came in with a new way of lighting and helped the art department create this whole colorful, bright, and harsh-lit look that then became a Quentin thing.

AS: Is Quentin a super-visual guy?
DW: Yes and no. He is an artist. He is a visual guy but not like Wes Anderson. Wes Anderson is to me a super visual guy. And I think I would say Michael Mann is a super visual guy. Quentin is more concerned with the geography of a set that would allow his actors to move around and have enough space to be able to say a line before they can reach a door and exit. In contrast, Wes would be ultra-concerned with, for example, the shade of the color of the wall. And we would change that color a few times. For instance in *Royal Tenenbaums* it was anguish to get to the final pink inside the house. The minutiae of the props were also anguished over by Wes. Quentin is equally concerned about props but, in true B-Movie mode, he has mentioned that cardboard backdrops would be enough for him in most situations.

SRW: Quentin loves the characters and his are definitely character-driven stories. He's not so interested in specific art direction. As long as it has some grand elements that will allow his camera to move in a certain way and his actors to move in a certain way as they speak, he's content.

> **WE ALL ARE OF THE MIND THAT MAKING A MOVIE IS LIKE DOING A PAINTING. YOU KIND OF HAVE AN IDEA OF WHAT YOU'RE GOING TO DO WHEN YOU START BUT YOU DON'T KNOW EXACTLY WHAT YOU'RE GOING TO END UP WITH UNTIL IT'S DONE.**

As guides for us, both in the script and in conversation, he will reference a lot of films and TV shows with set details or camera moves that he likes. He'll say, *Okay, we need this space but we need the staircase from this movie and we need this vista from this other movie...*

Wes, on the other hand, specifies sets that often describe the character, add to their backstories, give texture to the scene. His actors appear in a space and the space itself talks to the audience, adds to their personalities and the tone of the story. His ideas really helped us create some beautiful environments in *Tenenbaums*.

But whereas Wes' interaction with actors seems more restrained, Quentin's very garrulous and likes working with the actors.

DW: Both Wes and Quentin would have us look at movies. I remember Wes showed us a few Fellini movies that were more for tone and feeling and there were a few things that he specifically showed us in his New York City apartment. Whereas Quentin really directed us to lift certain elements. Like for instance he had us look at Elvis Presley's *Speedway* when we were doing the Jack Rabbit Slims set. *Speedway* had a nightclub scene in it where racecar drivers were hanging out in this club and they were dining in cars that were cut in half and they had banquet tables in them. We lifted that idea. Then in Howard Hawks' movie *Red Line 7000* they had this other nighclub set where racecar drivers hang out that had a slotcar track in the bar. So we lifted that and put that in Jack Rabbit Slims. *Pulp Fiction* was modestly budgeted but we spent a good deal of our budget on this pretty big set. It struck a note with the audience. People would come to LA asking to visit this restaurant. Disney, who had released the film, contacted us and asked us if we would help them build that club in Disney World. However, it ended up not happening for whatever reason.

We gave a mid-century spin to this race-car-themed nightclub because we had recently been asked to contribute to a museum exhibit in downtown LA called *The Legacy of The Case Study House*. For the exhibit we build three full-sized recreations of the Case Study houses and then we decorated them to the vintage period that the houses were built. We built the Pierre Koenig house full-sized, the Eames frame house full-sized, and the Ralph Rapson house full-sized. We had just finished this between

movies so we had this kind of modernistic theme going through both of our heads. We thought, *Let's weave this into the style of the Jack Rabbit Slims thing.* We actually even chose as an exterior a closed bowling alley that was designed by Armet & Davis. They were the Googie-style designers who did all the very famous 30's and 40's roadside diners. It had this kind of lunar, modern, zig-zaggy roof. John Travolta pulls in with Uma Thurman and they park and walk up to it. Not only did we have this mid-century Googie look going on inside but we were able to marry it with this exterior and it really struck a note with the audience.

AS: One thing I sometimes ask is can a set become a character in a film and it feels like that one did.
DW: I think that one did. And maybe the house in *Tenenbaums*. I think any set that you're in for a long period of time can become a character. Traditionally the rule of thumb is we really are trying to do something that's going to support what the actors are doing and help the director tell a story. Plain and simple. Quentin specifically requested this to be over-the-top and when that's a director's request it's your opportunity to do something interesting.

Something happened in the middle of shooting that knocked two days off of shooting in that set. The cameraman Andrzej had a very bad car accident. He was almost killed. He ended up coming back to the set and we ended up finishing the movie but there were all of these plans to shoot top shots above the dance floor that would show that the dance floor they're dancing on was a working tachometer but none of that was done. So it would have even been more of a character in the movie if they were able to capture more of that. But we were lucky that Andrzej was okay.

AS: You work as a husband and wife Production Designer/Set Decorator team. Dante Ferretti's wife is also his set decorator. He said it makes things easier.
DW: We do this all the time and it makes a big difference. It's like having two production designers.

AS: Does it feel like you can never get away from it?
SRW: When we take the job, we don't set the movie aside at dinner to catch up on real world events. It's never set aside! Good or bad, we're absorbed and it's 24/7 when we're doing it. It doesn't matter that it's sort of overwhelming because it gives you piece of mind in the long run. You've got the jump, you're organized and it also really helps with all the compressed prep time lately. Even in the interview process, working closely helps because we're able to break down the script together, share research and ideas or questions to offer a director. What's good is that we both fill in where the other one's weaker. After we're hired and as locations begin to be chosen, that cord is broken. David really becomes the director's liaison to the art department and I focus on managing my department.

AS: When you go into a meeting do you go in together?

DW: No. The interview process is me alone. But I exploit Sandy's contribution in prepping. I use the benefits of having two art directors like we are, having two people there that can visualize and figure out the project. When we go in and start working on the project Sandy will have her own meetings to discuss the set decorating, talking about all this ephemera that you surround the actors with that help the director tell the story and I'll have my separate meetings about the art direction of the movie. But in describing the physical office I like to have a bull-pen situation where of course Sandy and the art director will have their own offices, and I'll have my own office, but we'll all function in a big, open area where when you get these little bits of lucky time when the director comes in and sits at a table we're all listening to what he or she is saying. It's a nervous hour or so and then when they leave we can all compare notes on what they said because everybody hears different things.

SRW: Everybody's focused on something they need to hear but it's always good to hear what everybody else has to say. Anyone can contribute in that situation. P.A.'s can add, illustrators can add their two cents and it's all good.

DW: Absolutely. I really am a collaborator and I like to solicit from everybody. First of all I try to crew up my art department with almost everybody being overqualified and really, really talented. Even in an art assistant or for that matter an intern that's not getting paid anything, I like having somebody that's really sharp. And I let them listen also when the director comes in. They can be doing Xeroxing or something but they're listening. I encourage a free and open environment that's not all just David Wasco talking, *Well, this is what we're going to do!* Instead it's like, *Guys what's the best idea?* If the best idea comes from the intern we're going to use the best idea. And I'll give credit. It's truly the most collaborative art form of our time. I liken it to an architecture firm that has to build a skyscraper. You have a thousand people working on this building and a lot is riding on every individual person.

AS: Do you always hire the same crew?

DW: I almost never do one movie and then the next week start another movie. I struggle to find really good, script-driven projects that often are written by the guy or girl that's gonna direct the movie. Almost everything I've done, the director wrote the project. That sometimes means there are long strings of time in between projects so it's hard for me to have a core team of people that I like to work with that are standing by ready to start something.

AS: Because they jump on something else...

DW: They may not be as concerned about the material as I am. I don't have these crews that I can carry from show to show so the time in between movies I usually spend routinely meeting people, once or twice a week. People contact me via email, they'll call me, they'll write me a letter. I get letters from all over the world and I try to just meet all these people. I try to hire people that have strengths that balance out my weaknesses. I am not a tech-savvy guy so I will hire people that are good at doing CAD or computer assisted drafting. However, I'll still have lead set designers working side-by-side with CAD people.

I first try to hire some people I've worked with before and if they're not available it's a mix of some people that have worked with me and some new people. I get people that are really enthusiastic and that want to really be an art director or production designer and see how the art department works. The immensely talented production designer Andrew Laws started as one of my art department assistants, then he worked as an assistant art director and then he worked as an art director and now he's production designing.

AS: Do you often have to crew up in distant locations?

SRW: When we started in the late 80's with *American Playhouse* we'd go out of town a lot and the entire crew was local to the film location. We'd be in Minnesota doing a movie about Scandinavian Lutherans and then in Montana doing a farm story. And then in Virginia doing a Civil War story. In all those places we took an art director but crewed up locally. In many ways, It's a wonderful way to weave local flavor into a film because they have a built-in knowledge of the culture, the people, the local auction house, the Masonic lodge with tables and chairs to rent... They've got resources and they know where things are and that's all really helpful.

DW: We continue to work with some of the people we've met in these places. In Virginia on James Purdy's *In A Shallow Grave* we worked with Brett Smith fresh out of high school. He is now one of the best leadmen in the business. We gave him his first job and then he decided he wanted to move to Hollywood. He's worked with us multiple times. *Reservoir Dogs, Kill Bill.* In Germany we worked for almost a year on *Inglourious Basterds* and also met some wonderful people.

SRW: That was a great pool of talent.

DW: We had no notice when we started on *Inglourious Basterds.* We had the script sent to us on a Friday and we were on a plane on Monday to go to Berlin. We were ten weeks from shooting when we were flying to Berlin, which is an unusually short prep-time for a period film. The ultimate deadline was one year from day one of principal photography–Quentin really wanted the film at the Cannes Film Festival. We were the ones who got crunched with having no prep, not knowing anything about the movie. Even though we have a rapport with Quentin we would rarely get a script early on, where we could think about it. It comes to us ten weeks before we're going to shoot! I don't think he quite understands what we do and how it could be better if we had a bit more time to be able to think about things!

But because we had this rapport with Quentin and knew how he worked, that gave us a leg up on actu-

ally being able to pull it off. At first it was like, *Can we even pull this off?* because it was quite a herculean ambition.

What had happened was an opportunity allowed us to get the best team in Germany. Polanski was just starting to gear up and shoot *The Ghost Writer* at Babelsberg Studios and he had Germany's A-team working with him but something happened and the money fell through and they pulled the plug on the project. It freed up this group of people and I was able to get Sebastian Krawinkel and his team of Art Directors and Set Designers. It also freed up all the stages. We had sets in every single stage in Babelsberg. The studio was actually built in the 20's for Fritz Lang. Joseph Goebbels had an office there when it was a propaganda studio.

SRW: But it was a film production studio way before that regime.

DW: Yes, Fritz Lang's *Metropolis* was shot there. *The Blue Angel* was shot there. Recently, *Speed Racer.* Quentin chose to go there because he wanted to be on the same turf as Fritz Lang. He wanted to be standing on the same floor that these actors had performed on.

I ended up getting this really great team and they spoke perfect English. Had I not had this great team it would have been difficult. I was only able to bring Sandy. I did lobby to bring an art director–I wanted to bring an art director that I used on *Roy-*

al Tenenbaums, Carl Sprague, who spoke German and had worked in Berlin. But they only let me take Sandy so all of Sandy's department, the set decoration department, and the art department, the prop department, everyone was local. It was an incredibly talented crew.

SRW: It helped having a crew that was like a machine within itself. They'd all worked together. This was really lucky because had there been ten weeks of prep with the normal number of expected glitches, we would have been fine, but there were three big challenges thrown in the mix before shooting. One thing was that it was originally going to be shot black and white right up until the scene where the Nazi's redress the theater and the premiere begins.

DW: So we were prepping a black and white movie.

AS: Which is different...
DW: It's harder.

SRW: And hard to change mid stream to color. But there were also two other things. Originally Quentin wanted to shoot all locations. It wasn't decided that we were actually going to do all the builds until after three weeks of location scouting.

The third challenge involved the centerpiece theater. Quentin really wanted to build something on a Babelsberg stage and burn it down. He isn't interested in CGI or effects. But these studios are old! The stages had wooden roofs.

DW: All wood, very flammable. And it was a real lobby to the studio to allow us to do pretty big burns within the studio with real fire. Controllable burns were approved right up until the last minute when they decided it would be too dangerous.

SRW: It would have been!

DW: We ended up doing minimal controlled burns in somewhat fireproof sets that were built out of Sheetrock within these very dry wooden timber stages. But then we also found this massive clear span empty concrete factory that Fritz Lang actually used in the 20's. It was a closed, derelict space that had seventy-five foot ceiling spans and it allowed us to build a full-sized duplicate of the auditorium. We were able to do a raging fire burn without burning the building down.

These were the things that Sandy mentioned were the mini-curveballs. Having done virtually all of Quentin's movies we know that this guy really likes working with practical locations and if he wants to shoot in a little, tiny room, *Fine, great.* Some of the sets that came out of Quentin's movies were either because the practical locations didn't work or we were asked to do an interesting nightclub set like Jack Rabbit Slim's. But for the most part the guy really likes to work in practical locations so we scouted and we found the perfect French farmhouse. We found all these great locations but after taking Quentin to them he said, *You know guys, I'd really like to build this instead.* This was then ending up to be five weeks before shooting! We had to scramble to put all this on paper and still find a practical location that we could set the farmhouse in and then duplicate it again on stage. Then we built it yet again where it was cut in half like an ant farm. You could see half-way through the structure and then pan down to see the family hiding.

So there were a couple curveballs but curveballs come in pretty much every movie. That's one of the things that we really like about what we do. Every movie is completely different. You have a blueprint–you do this first and you do that second. You try to get as much ready before principal photography as possible because when principal photography starts it's like a starter pistol goes off. And then it goes from high gear to overdrive and you're working twenty-four hours a day and it's basically chaos.

SRW: Controlled chaos.

AS: Are you on the set during shooting?
DW: Sandy more than me. I deliver the set and walk the director around and have him say, *This is fine, or I'd like to change this*, or *I'd like to do that*. I like to open the set every day and make sure all the elements are there for that day of shooting. At the same time as we're shooting, we're prepping the next set and striking the set from before. I usually don't like to hang around because the environment on a shooting set is a slowed-down pace, like an ocean-liner. It's based around the actors and assistant director and what the director's trying to do with the actors. I make sure that there is a good on-set dresser but I don't like to be just standing around with my hands in my pockets.

> **CURVEBALLS COME IN PRETTY MUCH EVERY MOVIE. THAT'S ONE OF THE THINGS THAT WE REALLY LIKE ABOUT WHAT WE DO. EVERY MOVIE IS COMPLETELY DIFFERENT.**

SRW: I usually stay on every set until the DP has shot all four walls because the minute David has walked through the set with the director and they walk away, everything disappears. The furniture is pulled out so that the lighting can come in, and the camera. I try to document the set as it was when the director first walks in. So I'll have a record to hand the on-set dresser who is so key to our department, a sort of an unsung hero for us. But there are always changes so until the thing gets really locked down I like to be there to help compose the shots. Before I decorated I did the gamut of other jobs and one of them was an on-set. So I know immediately the kind of things to listen for and to prepare for before they have to ask for it. It's good to just watch the crew and see how much care they're taking. Once it's all locked down then I feel comfortable leaving. Because you know if it's not right and you're three hours away at some other location they're going to call you!

AS: You mentioned that one of your early films was *Night of the Comet*. John Myhre and John Muto both also worked on that.

DW: That's the only movie that I ever took set decorator credit on. When you're starting out any morsel of a job is a great opportunity. Again it was the director Thom Eberhardt who wrote the material. It was John Myhre's first job–he was assistant props on the movie. I remember the two of us driving around in a step van together picking up furniture and props. John Muto was the art director–it was before they started liberally using production designer as credit. It was the only zombie movie that I have worked on and it's actually a great zombie movie! It's a wonderful and interesting movie in L.A., shot all here.

It never ceases to amaze me how little the art departments were in the early days. It would be a three person art department on these masterpiece movies. I did a couple of them–on *El Norte,* I was a one-person art department. There's always the emphasis now to try to have as few people in the art department as possible for money reasons but because producers are now minimizing the prep we have to have so much pulled off in such a short time.

SRW: They minimize the prep but then they add all these other things like the previs, that add more money and work.

DW: But even with all of the newer tools of technology it's still this old-fashioned craft that is not that much different than when it started.

AS: Do you ever have a hard time finding good material?

DW: We really struggle to find and interview only on things that my heart can get into or that Sandy believes can be really good. Like when we read *Reservoir Dogs* we were like, *This is really different and really unique.* But there's no rhyme or reason. You can have a masterpiece script, you can have a great cast, and it just may not be a great movie. Or you can have something that is just kind of clunky and it will just strike a note with people. It's what's going on in the world at the time. It's a very funny business. It's a huge gamble. So you appreciate when producers are trying to be frugal with stuff because you don't know if it's going to be this two hundred million dollar clunker that's not going to perform. But we still just try to do these stories that are unique and interesting that we think will be of interest to the public. I try to not do remakes or sequels.

AS: How did you both very first get into the business? Did you go to art school?

DW: Sandy is formally trained, I am not. Sandy is a Vassar art history major and I am informally trained. I have two immensely talented artistic parents. My dad went to Cooper Union. He brought me and my two brothers up to be artists. I actually tried to get into Cooper Union and I didn't get in. My intention was to try again the following year and follow in his footsteps. And I actually ended up getting a few paying jobs in New York City working with graphic design firms fresh out of high school and I was like, *Well, this is what I wanted to go to college for and I'm actually getting paid to do it. I'll just delay it another year.* So I just ended up never getting to that other level. My dad said, *What do you need that for? You just draw every day. If you do one drawing every day that's all you need to do. Keep doing it.*

We were living in Bennington, Vermont, which has a great liberal arts college. My dad was one of the art teachers at the high school there in Bennington and they did a lot of things in concert with Bennington College. He was the set design teacher at the high school and also the art teacher. In the late 60's it was this free-form world between the two schools. I don't have a diploma from Bennington College but I basically went to Bennington College.

My dad also had been photographer's assistant to Arnold Newman. Newman is a brilliant, brilliant still photographer but he actually did these hand-made, animated movies that my dad worked on. I just looked over his shoulder watching him. We had Super 8 cameras, my two brothers and myself. I have these pretty cool movies that I've done so there was always this interest in film.

After living in Bennington I ended up in the San Francisco Bay Area still toting around a portfolio trying to get graphics jobs. I ended up taking a full-time job doing retail store display for a company called Design Research, which is what Design Within Reach copied. I became the display direc-tor and kind of worked my way up with them for a number of years.

These two sisters were also working there, one of whom was the nanny to Francis Ford Coppola's kids, Roman, Gio and Sophia. There were times when I was able to go over to Francis's house and watch films in his screening room. The one sister's boyfriend, Jerry, who didn't work at the store, was given a script and was asked to be a PA and go off to the Philippines to do *Heart of Darkness* with Francis. Jerry said, *David you gotta come out, you can be an "art grunt."* I was offered the job of being a PA on what became *Apocalypse Now* but I was simultaneously offered a promotion at Design Research to corporate display director.

Jerry said to go to the Philippines you have to get this whole series of shots. And I didn't want to do that! So I turned down being a PA on *Apocalypse Now* and Jerry goes and they give him a speaking part in the movie! He was Johnny from Malibu! He was a surfer that Robert Duvall does a whole scene with where he says he loves the smell of Napalm in the morning. He said, *I want you to go surfing.* And that's Jerry Ross! So he has a role in the movie and he was also asked then to become an apprentice editor. Had I gone to the Philippines I would have got to work with my mentor designer, Dean Tavoularis. So I always felt that it was a lost opportunity.

But at the same time if I had not been moved to Boston for the corporate display director job I would have not met Sandy. They put me up in the South End, and Boston is a great architecture city. I worked in Cambridge, Harvard Square, and this Design Research store was an amazing environment to work in. I met incredible people through that. So here I meet my future wife and we end up marrying five years later.

Design Research went bankrupt and they went away so I end up in New York City. My friend Jerry Ross then needed an apartment in the city. I gave him my apartment in New York and I told him to set me up a meeting with Dean Tavoularis. I wanted to move out to the West Coast. He said, *Sure, I'll set you up a meeting with Dean Tavoularis.* I heard that they were going to start up *The Outsiders.* So I move out to Los Angeles. It was a bad timing thing because right when I moved out, Zoetrope Studios releases *One From the Heart,* also one of my absolute favorite movies, and it didn't perform and the studio just tanked, it went bankrupt. Here I gave away my apartment in New York City and went out to LA thinking *The Outsiders* is going to happen and it didn't and my meeting with Dean Tavoularis didn't happen either.

Another friend from Design Research, who's now working as a rerecording mixer, Matthew Iadarola, said, *Hey, this commercial art director is starting up a feature film and he's looking for an assistant. Do you want to meet him?* And I was like, *Sure, I'd love to meet him.* Because it was 1980 and not only was it the bad time for Zoetrope, there was also this massive directors/writers strike. So there was nothing going on in LA. It was just dead so here is this little independent movie that was like *Conan the Barbarian* and it was called *Beastmaster* and I met with the production designer and he wanted to hire me.

It was just kind of being in the right place at the right time, doing things that I learned doing in my previous job. And they were very happy with everything I was doing and the movie was a huge hit! I am just extremely lucky that everything I got onto became a huge, popular thing.

I had this carrot dangled with *Apocalypse* and when I saw the movie I was like, *Now, why didn't I do that?* But when you hear the real story it was really, really hard. The movie was shut down multiple times, they had a hurricane that destroyed the sets, everyone was doing drugs. Would I even be alive after that? Would I be doing drugs? I would probably have not have married Sandy who's probably the best thing in my life.

SRW: I would not have gone into the business unless I tagged along with David. Now there are film schools but back then there were very few of them. Everyone took very circuitous paths to get here to do what they're doing. I lived in a rural, creative area, Concord, Massachusetts. Lots of good history and literature, ponds and forests. I built a lot of forts and tree-houses.

DW: But you did set design.

SRW: Yes, for school theater all the way up from

kids' Christmas pageants to Vassar where I took a couple years of theater design. Only in my senior year did they finally introduce film history. My Dad always accused me of being a dilettante, which was mortifying! But I studied fine art, drafting, photography, archaeology, psychology and they've all been useful! It's just lucky I followed David though. I might never have found the key to putting them all together in such a happy way. I could have channeled it into curatorial work or art conservation but I'm thinking film is way less monotonous.

DW: What Sandy did that I didn't do was when Sandy moved to LA she continued taking classes in perspective drawing, set design.

SRW: In your early movies you're doing everything. You're wearing every hat. I'd say, *If I'd known how to faux-finish, that would have been better.* So I'd go take a class.

DW: Sandy's a very good perspective illustrator. The design of Jack Rabbit Slims started with a thumbnail that Sandy did.

SRW: That kind of sketching is really helpful and that's just a pencil on a napkin. If you're in a car with a director and then you think, *We can't find this theater for* Inglourious Basterds *so let's do it this way.* You draw a little sketch and it's like, *Okay let's put it on the backlot.*

AS: Do you both sketch?
DW: We both do. Sandy's a better sketch artist

than I am. A lot of the concept illustrations that are done for the movies I hire a concept illustrator for only because it's a time-consuming thing. A full-time thing. It's not something that you do in an hour. You hire somebody and they're on it for days. Sometimes the doodle on a napkin is what jump-starts it.

" WHEN WE DID THE THEATER AUDITORIUM IN *INGLOURIOUS BASTERDS* WE BUILD A MASSIVE MODEL THAT WAS BIG ENOUGH FOR QUENTIN [TARANTINO] TO STICK HIS HEAD IN AND ACTUALLY LOOK AROUND FROM WHERE THE SEATS ARE. I DON'T KNOW IF THE COMPUTER THING IS GOING TO OVERTAKE THAT.

AS: Talking about the previs and all the post CGI that comes later, do you see film moving away from the traditional craftsperson thing?
DW: The benefit of working on a movie versus a commercial is that you have the time to really think about something but that time is going away. One of the reasons is there are all these things that are contributing to making everything go faster and faster. SketchUp and all this stuff is not going to overshadow someone who is a really good lead sketch artist like my friend Carl Sprague who is also a brilliant production designer.

Being able to go into a 3D model and move through it on a computer screen is great but I still like even a rudimentary foamcore model. Like when we did the theater auditorium in *Inglourious Basterds* we built a massive model that was big enough for Quentin to stick his head in and actually look around from where the seats are. I don't know if the computer thing is going to overtake that. Even the iPad, which I use a lot, and is a great, helpful tool, has its limitations. When I'm out in the field I whip out the iPad but it sometimes doesn't work because there's too much glare outside so I'll take these 11″ x 17″ Itoya folders with color Xeroxes of location pictures that are in plastic sleeves so that if it's raining out you can still open this book and it works perfect. You get your answers and you can actually sketch on those things.

SRW: There's so much more video content out there and it's used in so many more ways. It's not just film and television anymore–it's on your gas pump, its on your phone, it's everywhere. As the written word gets less and less I think there will be room for everything. Both simple and highly technical modes of filmmaking can exist together and are equally useful because they express things so differently. Primitive methods will always be interesting to some directors like Michel Gondry and his audiences who love the magical look of Méliès.

DW: Or Wes Anderson. Wes does not like CGI stuff and that's part of his success. It still comes down to a good script and good actors and someone like Quentin who's great with actors and you're going to end up with a masterpiece, something you'll want to watch in fifty years.

AS: What advice would you give to people starting out in the business?

DW: I'd say to get as much formal training as you can and then try to either intern or get an art assistant job where you can be in the middle of an art department and see how it works because it might not be what you really want to do.

SRW: If you've got the passion for it then maybe the formal stuff is okay but if you're going to do four years of film school I think going out and doing the work is better. Even more of a liberal arts background is good, so you have a variety of tools in your belt. You then have literature and philosophy and music and painting. You need all those references to be able to say a night sky is like a Munch painting, or describe a camera angle in a photograph or know that all the lighting in a Civil War period film will be by flame.

DW: In contrast to when we were starting there are just more people trying to get jobs and there are just fewer jobs. A lot of really good production designers have done theater work and I think that's always a good route. My friend Carl Sprague, the production designer, is also a great theater designer.

SRW: Just do it. It's really about your connections and who you're meeting and keeping in touch with and broadening those connections.

AS: One thing leads to another...
SRW: Exactly.

DW: You've got to use *everything*. If you know or your family knows somebody, keep the connections alive. When I meet with people I usually like to hand off one or two names for them to contact and then I ask them to get two names from those two people and that ends up being four more people. And you just keep building and building and building the connections and eventually somebody is just going to say, *Are you available? Can you just start?* The whole process of making movies is also the process of getting work in between movies.

AS: What do you guys like about your jobs?

DW: It's probably the most unstructured job that you can ask for now. And we get to work together. Sandy gets asked to work on movies all the time independent from me and it's a choice that I ask her to wait for my next movie, to be working with me, and she honors that. We get to travel together and get paid to do that and we get to meet and be friendly with some very interesting people.

SRW: Every story is different but most importantly every director is different. What they pull out of you is different every time and what you learn in that process is really wonderful. The more demanding they are, the more you learn and grow and go the extra mile. And do things you've never done before.

DW: Maybe the harder the movie, the better the movie's going to turn out.

SRW: It's only a short period of time, eight months give or take, but it can be life-changing.

Guy Hendrix Dyas

Guy Hendrix Dyas is a rock star in the world of film design: he designed Christopher Nolan's *Inception*, Steven Spielberg's *Indiana Jones and the Kingdom of the Crystal Skull*, Terry Gilliam's *The Brother's Grimm*, Shekhar Kapur's *Elizabeth: The Golden Age*, and at the time we first spoke he was hard at work on Spielberg's *Robopocalypse*. After studies at the Royal College of Art in London and Chelsea College of Art and Design he went from industrial designer to visual effects art director to concept artist and finally to production designer where he quickly rose to the top of the field.

AS: I was amazed to hear how much of *Inception* was practical versus CG. And is it true that the foundations of the fortress in the snow were made out of ice?

GHD: To our surprise many people have commented on how they thought the hospital was a real location but this bunker-like fortress doesn't exist. Very early on Chris [Nolan] and I made a crude clay model of this set. Chris wanted to create something akin to what he'd seen in some of his favorite Bond films–that's how we came up with a mix between military, governmental architecture and Panopticon prison design. Very quickly it became apparent to us that this set would have to be divided into two separate builds. The interiors were built on stage in Los Angeles while the multi-level exterior was built at approximately 7,000 feet in altitude. Chris chose an amazing part of the high mountains of Calgary which was quite remote but the final result was worth the effort. Seeing our large set built against such a beautiful natural backdrop really made our construction crew proud. The beauty of this natural site also meant that concrete foundations weren't an option so instead, to anchor the set, we dropped large wood posts into holes filled with water and let them freeze into place. Using ice to stabilize the foundations was something that I'd never done before but it worked amazingly well. We started building the exterior portion of the set in Calgary with a Canadian construction crew in late summer so as to be able to have it completed before the heavy snow set in for the winter. Despite a few blizzards we were really fortunate to have perfect weather conditions and during the shoot we benefited from real snow blowing across the set.

AS: And the train that runs down the middle of the street–that was real?

GHD: Chris Nolan uses CGI very cleverly and for *Inception* shooting in real locations and using practical sets was important whenever possible. We knew from the start that the freight train sequence was going to be shot 90% in camera and require us to have a real train driving through the streets of downtown Los Angeles smashing cars. The art department worked in tandem with the special effects and stunt departments to make it happen. We molded parts from a real freight train and assembled them onto an extended truck chassis. The front was reinforced and weighed down so as to enable it to stay on its course despite obstacles.

AS: What was it like creating those Penrose stairs?

GHD: The Penrose staircase is based on an optical illusion made famous by some of Escher's drawings. It's an ever ascending staircase which can never be built or made functional in the real world which is why it was so much fun to create as a set. However, perfecting it took a lot of research and development and we used traditional models as well as computer models to determine its exact dimensions as well as the camera positions needed to pull off the illusion. We ended up building our Penrose staircase set in the UK inside the atrium of an empty office building, the actors walked up the staircase to its highest point and the final shot was created thanks to clever camera work.

AS: What was it like working with Christopher Nolan? Is he a visual director?

GHD: Chris ordinarily works with the same crew but as his production designer [Nathan Crowley] was unavailable Chris sought out a new designer for Inception and I was lucky to be chosen for the job. I've been a fan of Chris's since *Memento* and there's no question that he's an extremely visual director. Actually all good story tellers are visual people. One of the most exciting aspects of working with Chris on this film in particular is that he has a genuine interest in architecture and film design and he's said that he would've liked to have been an architect had he not become a filmmaker.

AS: I hear you're working on Steven Spielberg's latest–what type of project is it?

GHD: It's a science fiction film, a very ambitious project based on an upcoming novel by Daniel H. Wilson, a talented young writer who also has a Ph. D. in robotics from Carnegie Mellon University. It's great source material and everyone is very excited about adapting it for the big screen.

AS: Kim Sinclair worked with Spielberg on *Tintin* and said his interaction was mainly virtual with weekly poly-conferences–was that also your experience?

GHD: I live in Los Angeles so I'm usually in direct contact with him as I run my art department from his offices. However as one of the busiest people in Hollywood I know he uses the system a lot.

> ❝ ONE OF THE MOST IMPORTANT GOALS OF A PRODUCTION DESIGNER IS TO SATISFY A STORY AND A DIRECTOR'S VISION, SO BY DEFINITION THIS MEANS THAT EVERY FILM SHOULD BE A COMPLETELY NEW EXPERIENCE.

AS: You also worked with Spielberg on *Indiana Jones and the Kingdom of the Crystal Skull*. You designed many elaborate sets–were there many challenges?

GHD: I think one of the challenges was to design a film that fit in stylistically with the others while also showing the passing of time as our story takes place in the late 50's. Like many I'm a huge Indiana Jones fan and beyond the fact that I was really looking forward to working with Steven Spielberg for the first

time, there was the added excitement of being a part of the Indiana Jones adventure. It's definitely an experience that brings out the kid in you and it was fun to express that through our designs.

AS: David Warren worked with Terry Gilliam on *The Imaginarium of Dr. Parnassus* and said Gilliam was very hands-on and provided a lot of visual input–was this also your experience on *The Brother's Grimm*?

GHD: Terry's films are some of my favorite films so I knew that being able to work with him would be an incredible experience, especially since he's been a designer himself. I still remember the impact of seeing *Brazil* as a student at the Royal College of Art. It was being shown as part of a special film series called "Grand Illusions." I think it's the film that first opened my eyes to the art of Production Design. Working with Terry is exactly what you'd imagine, he has endless creative energy, he draws amazingly well and it was fun to be able to exchange sketches with him.

AS: Going from Terry Gilliam's imagination on *The Brother's Grimm*, to Elizabethan England in *Elizabeth: The Golden Age*, to Spielberg's *Indiana Jones*, to *Angora*, to *Inception*, and now to *Robopocalypse*, is there anything in your work that remains constant or is it a radically different experience every time?

GHD: I think one of the most important goals of a production designer is to satisfy a story and a director's vision, so by definition this means that every film should be a completely new experience. Directors are really the ones guiding the way and our aim is to bring their visions to life. I hope my designs appear as different and varied as the films and stories being told. If there's a constant it's perhaps the fact that every film is a learning process and that for designers it's nice to be able to take those experiences, and the things you feel were the most successful, on to your next assignment. After a while you start assembling your own personal bag of tricks.

AS: How closely do you work with visual effects?
GHD: I have a background in visual effects; I was trained as a visual effects art director at ILM and one of my first films was *Twister*. For that reason I feel I have a first-hand understanding of the tools as well as huge respect for the craft and artistry that goes into digital effects. As a production designer I find the interaction between our crafts extremely exciting. For every job you have to find the best tool and this is one more amazing tool at our disposal.

AS: Do you tend to always work with the same crew ?
GHD: I like to work with the same crew whenever possible but sometimes schedules and distant locations make that difficult. However what I always strive for in the art department is a great mixture of talents, skills and experience. Generally it works well to have seasoned crew working with younger artists, there's a nice exchange that happens.

AS: You studied art at the Royal College of Art in London and Chelsea College of Art and Design–is art school a good start for an aspiring production designer?
GHD: People in films seem to come from all walks of life but in my case art school was very useful, if only for the fact that I can draft, sketch, paint, sculpt and make models. These are skills you learn at art school and probably wouldn't have learned in a film school. Learning those basic skills allowed me to have a good foundation for a future in production design even if at the time I was very focused on industrial design and architecture. It's only when I got accepted into the Royal College of Art that I became aware of the film department and started learning about filmmaking and volunteering on student film projects.

AS: Do you still do illustrations for your movies?
GHD: As much as possible because I enjoy it and it's such a great communication tool. Sometimes my schedule means that I have to do my own illustrations during off hours but it's always worth it as it enables me to quickly show a director an idea and then be able to hand off sketches to an art director. I guess the only thing nowadays is that I rarely have the time to take my illustrations into color, I mostly have sketch books filled with pencil drawings.

AS: You went from industrial designer to visual effects art director to concept artist to production designer–how did this transition come about?
GHD: The transition from industrial designer to

visual effects art director was probably the most intimidating for me because it meant taking a leap of faith and joining an industry I knew very little about. It meant leaving a career path that I was starting to forge for myself in industrial design in Japan but l was in my twenties and when the opportunity came along to join ILM it seemed worth the risk.

AS: What's the first thing you do when you get a new script of a movie to design? Do you do a lot of research?

GHD: The first thing I do is I start sketching; actually I start a new sketchbook for every film as it's the easiest way to keep ideas organized. Research is very important to my process as well but it usually comes into play slightly later, when we have an art department set up and are starting to put presentations together.

AS: How closely do you work with the DP?

GHD: Very closely. Creating the look for a film is really a collaboration between the director, director of photography, myself and the costume designer so the sooner you can start the exchange process, the better. DPs don't create the production design but they do shoot it; they are a designer's biggest ally.

AS: What are qualities that you think a production designer should have?

GHD: What I love about our job is that designers can rely on a variety of skills. There really is no one set of qualities that will either ensure you success or failure. If I speak for myself I tend to get excited by projects that are artistically challenging in some way or another. I've realized that for those films you're often asked to create an entire world so it's good to have a strong vision, a good working ethic, good leadership skills as well as enthusiasm. I don't think people always realize how physical our jobs are, when we're preparing for a shoot there's rarely time to breathe. You have to enjoy that kind of pace.

AS: When you're crewing up, what are certain attributes that you look for in your art department?

GHD: As someone who's come up through the ranks of the art department I have the utmost respect and admiration for my collaborators. I enjoy being able to assemble an art department with a wide range of talents and experiences as it helps develop a genuine appreciation for each other's work and contributions.

AS: Do you feel a set can be like a character in a movie?

GHD: If the story allows for it, absolutely. I think this is something that's dictated by the script. While some sets are meant to be more inconspicuous, every once in a while the opportunity arises to be a bit more experimental and exuberant and let a set become its own character, one which demands its own attention. Our work is about treading that fine line between invisible and visible production design and knowing what's best for the story. It should be invisible unless the story calls for more ostentatious visuals. This is what differentiates production designers from other designers. Personally I love both expressions of what we do, the invisible work as well as the more stylized and mannered aspect of production design.

AS: Do you have any books or other resources that stand out as useful for a production designer?

GHD: I'm a collector at heart and I like surrounding myself with things that spark my imagination but I also think that inspiration can come from just about anywhere–books, music, museums, travel, nature. One thing I've learned over the years is that it's important to step away from the drawing board once in a while too, because we're more productive and imaginative when we've had the chance to resource ourselves.

AS: Say someone was just starting out and wanted to avoid any pitfalls...

GHD: If at first you don't succeed, try, try again. As everyone knows there are no rules or guidelines in our business, it's what makes it so exciting but also daunting at times. So much is based on luck and being in the right place at the right time but for those who persevere there are some great rewards.

AS: Do you see Los Angeles ever returning to its days of film production glory or do you see art department crews all taking up residence in places like Atlanta?

GHD: It's an interesting question. I'm guessing film production will always be attracted by out of state and foreign tax incentives but whether this means a permanent relocation of our film industry I don't know. I still recall when everyone was talking about relocating to Canada when so much film and TV production was going there. Things are always changing in our business and all you can do is remain as flexible as possible.

> **" OUR WORK IS ABOUT TREADING THAT FINE LINE BETWEEN INVISIBLE AND VISIBLE PRODUCTION DESIGN AND KNOWING WHAT'S BEST FOR THE STORY.**

AS: How do you see the future of production design? Is it shifting towards fewer sets and more greenscreens?

GHD: Our industry is changing rapidly and it's normal for production designers to wonder what the future holds. I tend to be optimistic and not only because I have a background in VFX but because films will always need the contribution of artists and to me a green screen is a tool, it's not a craft, and tools can never replace crafts, someone still has to envision the environments for these stories to take place in.

GHD 2

UPDATE: When I saw photos of Guy Hendrix Dyas' Oscar-nominated design work on *Passengers* my mind was blown. I had interviewed Guy back when he had his first Academy Award nomination for *Inception* but with *Passengers* he'd taken it to the next level. Here's an update on his process.

AS: Is sketching as important to you now as it was the last time we spoke?

GHD: Sketching is all I do when I start a project. I've got this routine now where I'll read a script and get an 8.5" x 11" sketchbook and basically sketch the entire film. This sketchbook becomes my bible. It becomes my go-to place when I'm thinking of handing out projects to my staff to develop.

AS: After your initial meeting with director Morton Tyldum did you then go off and create a lot of sketches to bring back to him?

GHD: I turned up to the initial interview with many of these sketches. I'd been given the script and was excited by it. This is a script that has no monsters, no guns, just raw science fiction in the greatest tradition of films like *2001* or even *Silent Running*. It's a wonderful film because it makes you think about moral choices. It makes you think about love and life and your own existence. The script had been knocking around in Hollywood for many years and I never thought I'd get a chance at it. But when I was up for it I grabbed it, and ran with it.

The first drawing for the exterior of the ship was done before my initial meeting with Morton. He saw it and he said, *You got the job*. The idea was that we wouldn't just create a large bulky ship moving through space where you press a red button and there's your gravity. We treated our design scientifically. The three hulls rotate around a central core propulsion unit, which would probably be nuclear. A crew halo at the front rotates around the ship at a different speed, creating gravitational pull. It separates the passengers from the nuclear propulsion unit. Otherwise they would die of radiation poisoning before they reached their destination one hundred twenty years later. The halos of light on our hibernation pods are there to feed vitamin D to the skin of the bodies to keep them alive and healthy. We try to think of everything in terms of how this would work scientifically. Still, our designs are perhaps a little more fanciful than some of the films we've seen in recent years that have based their design thread on NASA.

AS: So you relied less on research at places like the U.S. spacecraft facility JPL?

GHD: The project happened at such breakneck speed that we didn't have time to bring in any experts–it really was based on my own schoolboy science and my background as an industrial designer. It was very fast for a film of its scale. We were ten weeks in development of the artwork and then we quickly went to Atlanta. Ten weeks to build everything. And then Chris and Jen turned up for a seventy-eight day shoot.

AS: Do you still make clay models like you did for the fortress in Inception?

GHD: Yes, although less clay and more CAD and architectural models. The spaceship model we developed purely as a 3D model in Rhino. In this ship design it was very important for me to have a link to 2001 and one of the most iconic spaceship of them all, the rotating space-station. Once you've established the frontal view the audience thinks they know what they're looking at and then as the ship turns they start to see the rotation in the side-view which gives the audience a completely new perspective on that concept.

AS: Did you do any 3D printing?

GHD: There was a lot of 3D printing to demonstrate what those shapes were like in physical terms. However, a lot of the interiors were designed as regular architectural models and illustrations. One of the things my team and I pride ourselves in is getting the sets to look as close to the illustration as we can. So many times coming up as a young illustrator and concept artist myself, I'd produce amazing illustrations and then I'd see the set and it would look nothing like it.

I have an inherent connection to the concepts now and a desire to see them reach the screen so I dictate very strongly that the designs stay the course and look the way they do in the illustrations. There's a wonderful thread through these illustrations to the final sets.

A lot of people accuse me of doing the illustrations after the fact. I promise you, the set designs are first! In many cases we will get a still frame of our 3D model and then render over it for the set design. And when we later take that 3D model apart to build the set it matches perfectly.

AS: Did you use CNC routing to industrially print any of your elements? For example, the tiles in the wall of the bar that have the silhouette of the ship in them? Or the curved walls of the observation deck?

GHD: Most of this honestly is wood frame with MDF on top and some very skilled painters giving me beautiful automotive finishes on the top of everything. Some people are blown away by some of the finishes we have. They think it's CGI but it's not.

AS: You mentioned being influenced by the bar in *The Shining*. Is watching films for reference part of your process?

GHD: Not always. However, with Morton we

latched onto *Silent Running* and *The Shining*. That relationship between Jack Nicholson's character and the barman had huge similarities emotionally to what we were creating between Chris Pratt's character and our barman. The Art Deco bar was a beautiful red and gold jewelry box in the middle of this antiseptic spaceship. There was a seductive need to go there. And the barman had to have no legs so he couldn't leave the bar. If Jennifer and Chris want this synthetic relationship they have to go to the bar and meet this guy.

We were lucky we had a script that called for an ocean liner in space. I could indulge with my Art Deco bar, romantic French restaurant, swimming pool, and an amazing, weird-looking observation room for people to look out to space. The amphitheater set looks to me like the inside of a 1930's race-car. A lot of people think it's all CGI, which is a little heartbreaking! I started with this idea of orbiting planets and then translated that into these amazing alloy ribs, all made from wood with amazing paint finishes but you'd never know it. I finished it off with a Japanese Zen garden in the middle. It's really a place of meditation and contemplating life and the universe. It becomes a sanctuary for Aurora to write in when she's going through the horrors of realizing she will die before she reaches her destination.

AS: When we last talked we discussed Christopher Nolan's involvement with production design–how involved was Morton Tyldum?

GHD: Every director's different. You have directors who really want to be involved while other directors say, *This is your thing–you just go design something brilliant for me and I'll tell you if I don't like it!* But because this was Morton's first big budget film he was very excited. I was very lucky to have him spend a lot of time with me in the art department. It was like two little boys encouraging each other to design the most outrageous spaceship they could ever come up with! I'd show him a design and he'd say, *Give me more of this! Or, Can you make this more crazy?* He was always trying to push the envelope. That's food for me. Chris Nolan is the same. I love the challenge when a director pushes me and encourages me to take an idea even further. I attribute a lot of his encouragement to why the sets turned out so imaginative and different to what you'd expect. He doesn't draw. He doesn't stand over your shoulder and point. He would just say, *This is great but can you do anything else?* He was always pushing, pushing, pushing, which is a fantastic trait in a director. He was a champion of what I was doing and I was very lucky. Tom Rothman and his team at SONY were also behind it. It's magnificent to think that a studio will allow us to build these monstrous sets to support two actors just to get the best performance out of them. In this day and age it's extraordinary.

AS: How important was working with the DP, Rodrigo Prieto, on the look of the sets?

GHD: Rodrigo was one of the greatest collaborators I've ever worked with. What I loved about working with Rodrigo was his natural good taste and finesse. His ability to see what I was doing. You need a DP to understand how beautiful these shapes are in order to put lights inside them to give you that glow. And if those lines were highlighted with light in my illustrations they were vigorously followed. Rodrigo came on a little later, as DP's do, but I worked with him tirelessly to make sure the color and feel of the lighting was going to suit the story-points and the scenes. I'm very grateful to him for enhancing what we had done. It was just lovely to have someone with the common goal of, *Let's do something great here.*

AS: How much do you normally think about lighting when you're designing a movie?
GHD: It's a huge part of what I do. That probably comes from painting and drawing. When you draw and paint you're cognizant of where the light is coming from and what it's doing to someone's face, what it's doing to a surface. In our illustrations you'll see a strong indication of light and the color within the light, whether it's a warm light or a cold light. I'd like to think those are inspirations for the DP when he's lighting the set.

AS: Last we spoke you were involved in another science fiction story–an ambitious Spielberg movie titled *Robopocalypse,* that has since been put on indefinite hold.
GHD: The scale of *Robopocalypse* was epic. What we were doing with robots was very unique. It would have been a game-changer. It was a brutal experience to leave it unfinished especially after working with someone I love like Steven, who is fantastic. Two years was a very long time for me to

be out of the game. But that doesn't happen with fast-track projects like *Passengers*. They stay raw and that's the beauty of something that happens so quickly. There's no "design-by-committee". They happen, they come out and there's a beautiful rawness to them.

> **IN DESIGNING THE EXTERIOR OF THE *PASSENGERS* SPACE-SHIP I WAS VERY COGNIZANT OF THE FACT IT WOULD HAVE BEEN DESIGNED AND BUILT AS SECTIONS LIKE THE SPACE STATION, OVER A PERIOD OF SIXTY YEARS . . . AND SO YOU SEE A RANGE OF ARCHITECTURAL STYLES AND MATERIALS ON THE SHIP TO SUPPORT THAT PASSING OF TIME.**

AS: We also talked about the future of our industry last time, discussing the use of greenscreen increasing in the world of production design. This time I'd like to know if you think it will become old-fashioned to see a flat movie on a flat screen? In the future will we be in virtual environments every time, where we can look all around us in a 360 degree world?
GHD: God, I hope that happens. I'm thrilled by immersive environments because I tend to design in a very three-dimensional way. My sets are designed for you to walk around them and explore and make discoveries. Which often you don't get to do when you're looking through a lens in one direction. A lot of designers say that they are only able to capture sixty-percent or forty-percent of

what their sets have to offer. During actual filming you often lose the level of detail and miss the angles where you can find a sweet spot to show something off.

I came up through ILM so my background is in CGI. I see the guys in visual effects as my brothers in arms. They're there to help support the vision. Not everything I design can be realized in the time frame or in the budget that I have. I rely heavily on visual effects to help finish off the look of the film. I look forward to the day when somebody says we're going to do a film and you're going to be in it. That just means more design.

> **" I SPEND HOURS AND HOURS WORKING AND DESIGNING, WHETHER IT BE WEEKENDS OR HOLIDAYS, BECAUSE THAT'S WHAT I BELIEVE I'M HERE ON THE EARTH TO DO . . . WHEN YOU FIND YOUR CALLING YOU NEVER ACTUALLY SEE IT AS WORK.**

AS: When you design, are you in communication with the VFX supervisor from the beginning?
GHD: Erik Nordby, who was phenomenal on *Passengers*, came onto the film about halfway into our period here at SONY. Like Rodrigo he was a true professional, very thoughtful, and a big supporter of the vision. He came in and said, *I want to make this ship work and look real.*

In the huge shopping mall, we build the first three hundred fifty feet of it and had his help topping it up to the five levels above. It was my good friend Erik who completed our vision and worked tirelessly to match the illustrations. And in some cases improve on them. Hats off to them for finishing off the bits of the set we just physically couldn't do because we're not in space! For the exterior of the ship, the design was given to them to implement and apart from two or three airlock sections that I had to build, all of the shots of the ship flying by are attributed to them and their amazing work.

AS: You've spent a lot of time thinking about the future in your design. Do you see human civilization eventually expanding into space?
GHD: It's always that schoolboy dream, isn't it? Every now and then we make huge leaps in terms of space exploration but it still takes time. Even in designing the exterior of the *Passengers* spaceship I was very cognizant of the fact it would have been designed and built as sections like the space station, over a period of sixty years. You'll notice that the core of the ship is designed in an almost traditional NASA style. But as you spread out, the ship becomes more futuristic because over sixty years, design and technology would be moving forward. And so you see a range of architectural styles and materials on the ship to support that passing of time.

AS: Any advice for young people going into the field of production design?
GHD: There's no trickery to becoming a designer.

I was very lucky in that I just love what I do. And I spend hours and hours working and designing, whether it be weekends or holidays, because that's what I believe I'm here on the Earth to do. I've found my calling. When you find your calling you never actually see it as work. You make yourself very available because you're excited. If you do a good job eventually somebody's going to say you should be designing. In my case I was found and given the opportunity by Bryan Singer, the great director of the *X-Men* series and *The Usual Suspects*. He picked me out of nowhere to design his initial TV show, *Battlestar Gallactica*. The show didn't happen for me, although ironically they did use all my designs. And won an Emmy with it! But we went on to do *X-Men 2* together as a wonderful consolation prize. So that was my first film. I've always considered myself very, very lucky.

AS: Did Bryan Singer find you through ILM?

GHD: No, I left ILM after I did *Twister* in the 90s. I had studied industrial design at art school and ILM for me was like film school. After ILM, I just loaded up my car and came down here to Los Angeles to try to become a production designer. I started by illustrating for other designers. And I'd been doing

that for six or seven years, earning a reputation for being fast and good at what I did. Bryan loved my stuff and just said, *You should be designing*. He knew my background. He knew I'd worked for SONY designing some of the last generation Walkmans and Discmans. He felt I'd do a good job on *X-Men 2*. That was my first film and I loved it and never looked back.

> ❝ THERE IS GOOD KARMA OUT THERE AND IF YOU WORK HARD AND IF YOU DEVELOP YOUR CRAFT YOU WILL GET A CHANCE.

I'd say to young designers just love what you do. There is good karma out there and if you work hard and if you develop your craft you will get a chance. But no one's going to open the door and say, *Hey, come design!* You're gonna have to get out there and practice your art and your design and eventually someone will see you. If you don't love designing, if it's a chore to pick up a pencil or paint something, then do something else. But if you love it and become as good as you can as a craftsman, the job will find you.

CREW

What do you look for in a crew?

A compilation of excerpts covering the subject of crewing up, taken from the interviews in this book

You're only as strong as your crew. But how do you pull together this team? How do you assemble a posse in the Everglades, in the Outback, in the jungles of the Amazon? What qualities do you look for in the band you'll bring with you into battle? How important is their attitude and mindset versus their years of experience? How much does enthusiasm and passion count for? If you micromanage or attempt to do everything yourself you'll never experience your design becoming exponentially greater than the sum of its parts...

JOHN MYHRE

I would rather get a young person who's full of enthusiasm and full of new ideas than someone who's done the thirty biggest movies in the world and is just sort of tired to come into work anymore. I mean I think enthusiasm really means a lot. What we do is hard work. We work really long hours. We work six or seven days a week. We work fourteen hours a day and it's important to keep the enthusiasm and the fun and realize that we're doing something very special and we're lucky to be doing it.

SARAH GREENWOOD

You have an art department of fifty on Sherlock Holmes, but I expect everybody to have read the script and to know what's going on in the script. And to go out and see everybody else's sets. Don't just work on your tiny little bit and not ever leave the drawing board. Why do what you're doing if that's where you'll be? Be interested in the whole process and the failures and the solutions that we come up with. It's funny because sometimes you'll have people who've worked on the film and they'll go, *My God, I didn't realize it was going to be like that!* And you go, *Well, hang on a minute, why? You were there with us, you should know everything!*

COLIN GIBSON

[I hire] someone who doesn't look like they're pretending to laugh at my jokes! It never ceases to annoy me how many people it takes to make me look competent. I love to find people who are passionate about what they do and they make me passionate . . . Like all the other jobs you do as a designer you *become* passionate. You become fascinated. You discover that whether it's outer space or scuba gear, you learn a new passion. And you can only do that by finding people who already have that passion who can help pass it on to you. In that way I'm a little vampiric.

HANNAH BEACHLER

I look for skill. I look to give people opportunities as well. People who may not be able to get the opportunity because they're a woman or they are a person of color. They have a hurdle to get over because there really are not a lot of women or people of color in the art department, in the industry. And so I will look at that. You get the opportunity to come in and talk to me. Doesn't mean you get the job. You have to have the skill. I'm very clear about that. I'm also very clear about firing people. I don't play around with anything. My expectations are high. Everyone knows this now! They are really, really high. My father set almost impossible expectations for us as children. For everything. That's a character flaw to some extent. And as I get older I'm learning to work with the idea that my expectations can't be everybody's expectations. Right now they are. I expect extremely hard work from people. And good references. And bring me your portfolio and show me what skill you have. Or if you don't have a portfolio yet, tell me why I want you here.

When I was on *Kill Switch* I put it out on Twitter to send me resumes. *I need a PA in Detroit, you have to work as a local but you'll get paid and you get to be my assistant.* I got a ton of resumes. I thought I

CREW

would get maybe a few but it blew up! I went with a young man who hadn't had any film experience, just graduated from college. He was very young but very passionate, you know? That was the thing. He was very much a self-starter. He took the initiative every single time.

Show me that you want to be here, right? Show me that you want this! I may need you to organize the paint samples, you organize those paint samples like you ain't never organized paint samples in your whole life! The gods come from the heavens and shine down on the paint sample organization! That's what you have to bring to it. You have to bring that drive! Because there are hundreds of thousands of people who want it too.

EVE STEWART

[It's important that art dept. crew is] really good-humored, mainly! That you can have a laugh. And that everybody gets on. The people that I tend to use also have a very theatrical background. They're very skilled. They've not only done film. They have an appreciation of real life and real characters.

DANIEL NOVOTNY

They have to be really good politically. Especially on a TV show. On a feature you know you're going to work with a person for a few months and then you're going to leave. And with a commercial, really who cares because you're just going to be done with them in a week or two. But on a TV show when you're going to be working with someone for ten months it's really about finding a good family member that's a good fit. On CSI in particular, the politics on this show are playground politics. Everybody's been there a long time so nobody really cares who you are or where you came from, they just care if you can get along with everybody. And then obviously secondary to that, or equal to that, is their skill, what they bring to the table. Everybody's got their own skills. Everybody's got their strengths and weaknesses. If one person's strengths are x and y then I'll make sure the other person has something else.

PATRICK TATOPOULOS

A very important step is your team. The people you work with. You have to give them space to bring something to the table. I've seen people who are so much in control of everything and so afraid to give away little bits and pieces. They control everything to the final stroke of a pen and I think this is a mistake. It's important to let people bring something to the table of whatever design you do. I have a tendency to design very roughly because if it can stay rough I can give my artists a chance to bring some of their own ideas to the project. At the end of the day I believe all of us have a specific style that we repeat all the time. I do, and I have to fight that. When you bring somebody else to the table and you give them a chance to bring something to your own designs, then every one of your works has a different flavor. That to me is the essence of the job.

MICHAEL NOVOTNY

In episodic that particular football team is running down the field and never stops. You have to shout as you run. So if someone's coming in to set-design I'm not going to sit there and look at a lot of drawings. I'm going to look at one drawing. I'm going to see immediately the way he thinks. I'm looking at the logic in the drawing and his communication to the carpenters. I will see immediately if he's an elegant designer. And if he doesn't show me that in the drawing I'll assume he doesn't have it.

The worst thing is when you go in and interview somebody like a set designer and they show you twenty-five drawings. By the end I'm like, *Throw some cold water on me.* I'm already falling asleep. And by then the phone's rung three times and I need to go do other things. That goes for assistant art directors, graphic designers, art department coordinators, anybody. They have to show me the essence of their job.

But can they do the job and can everybody be happy together doing the job? That's the second part of it and that's critical. That's where everybody typically loses the job. Because they're so egocentric that they're going to yap on and on–what this project was, what that project was, and so forth. As opposed to saying, *What are you working on?* You know, they don't plug themselves into the environment they're sitting in for the interview. Usually when I'm interviewing somebody I'm working. If that's the case then talk about what we're doing. You'll have a better chance of being more immediate and being perceived as invaluable. So I'm really looking for someone who can work well with others. Have a sense of humor, be light about it, be involved. But at the same time I would take a sourpuss who's a Leonardo Da Vinci–don't get me wrong. But you know I'd probably think long and hard about it before I did it.

LEE HA-JUN

While individual technique is important, I believe the basic mindset of collaboration is the most important characteristic for my crew to have. There is a separate division for 'Art Department', but the entire film crew collaborates: Directing, Producing, Photography, Lighting, Props, Costumes, Make-up, and so on. Many different teams need to think together and figure out what's best for one

CREW

film. There should be a lot of communication, collaboration, and compromising if needed. Within the overall team, we lead and follow each other to visualize the film as written.

EUGENIO CABALLERO

The most important thing for me in the first meeting is for them to fully understand what I'm trying to do. There are a lot of people with great technical skill and great organizational skills but if they can't grasp your creative ideas then it doesn't work. This is more important than them having a lot of experience.

DANTE FERRETTI

Resumes mean nothing. I need to meet somebody. It's what I feel when I look at somebody, I can say this is the right person, this is the right art director, this is the right construction coordinator, this is a good painter or sculptor. Of course I also have to see what they did but so far I haven't made any mistakes this way. Or maybe I did and I didn't know! So far what we did was not bad because we had really good people. This is very important because you can design a fantastic movie and then if you have the right people you can make this movie fantastic but if you don't have the right people it could be a piece of shit!

MARK FRIEDBERG

If I'm in New York I know who I'm hiring. The people I worked with on *Joker* I've been working with twenty years. There's a loyalty and an artistry and a trust and an economy and a kindness. They're my family. I spend more time with them than anybody else. But because I started as an untrained, inexperienced young guy and the youngest guy on my crews for the longest time, I hired old guys, or girls, to help me. As the movies got bigger I hired older crew to make sure that I was covered, to make sure that the stuff that I didn't know, somebody knew. And I found that I kept making the same movie that everyone else was making. That a lot of people who do this and do this and do this, certainly in art departments, reference other movies. Not so much the world that inspires the movies. And little by little I started relying more on the PAs and the young people for inspiration. And trusting my instincts about them.

As I became one of the old guys my point of reference started shifting to the young people who knew what was going on in the world and brought that energy in, and who were a little more visceral. I think that the thing I'm most proud of in my career is not the movies necessarily but the humans that I've worked with.

Nathan Crowley

Nathan Crowley brought Modernism and scale into Batman's formerly Gothic world, creating masterpieces of cinema with his friend, director Christopher Nolan. While he received an Academy Award nomination for Damian Chazelle's Neil Armstrong biopic *First Man,* the other five of his six Oscar nominations to date were with Nolan, including for the historic war film *Dunkirk.*

AS: When you were in art school did you have any idea you'd be a production designer?
NC: Not at all. I was thinking about continuing on with the School of Art and Design at Brighton. But I ended up getting hired after I got my art degree by a bunch of architects to draft. I did that for two years and it made me realize I didn't want to be an architect! No one was doing anything interesting. It was what I call "business architecture" and it was really uninspiring. I ended up thinking, *Shit, I don't want to do postgraduate architecture, even though I love architecture.* That was in the late 80's just as Thatcher destroyed England. It was time to leave.

I ended up coming to LA. I drove old sports cars across America for a while that were being shipped to Europe. I'd take the I-10 and drive them from LA to Jacksonville, Florida. My friend and I would buy old Porches and Spiders, I'd drive them across and ship them to him in England where he'd sell them. It was just enough money to live on in LA. And then that economic crash happened. We got left with a few sports cars and we couldn't sell them. I realized I had to get a job in LA somewhere!

And then I walked into Small's, a bar on Melrose, and bumped into a friend from art college who'd been working in Hollywood for a few years as a set designer. He said they needed set designers on *Hook*. There were none available because the Universal backlot had burned down, weirdly, and they'd hired everyone off the set designer's roster to redraw Universal. My friend said, *You can draw, can't you?* And Norman Garwood, the production designer on *Hook*, (and on *Brazil*) hired me as a junior set designer in the old MGM drafting room and he got me in the union. It was a couple of fortunate events.

AS: How did you make the jump from Set Designer to Art Director?

NC: Norman came in and said, *You don't know anyone in Hollywood, do you? How are you going to get a job?* I hadn't really thought that far. He said, *I know the designer on Bram Stoker's Dracula.* So he went next door and got me a job on *Bram Stoker's Dracula*. I didn't even know I wanted to do art direction. I was on it for eleven months as set designer and didn't get credit. Then they needed someone with Roman Coppola on second unit. I ended up doing all that puppeteering, the mirror work, matte projection, and hours and hours of cutouts for the opening sequence. That's where I really got into the magic of art direction. I'd always been interested in optical illusions. Even though I wasn't an art director and shouldn't have been on stage I basically got

assigned second unit and there I realized I wanted to be an art director. Then I went to work on *Star Trek* as a set designer again because I needed a job but it made me realize I didn't want to be a set designer anymore. I didn't want to draw, I wanted to be on stage. I quit that show and got hired as an art director on an independent Abel Ferrara film with Madonna, *Dangerous Game*.

> **THE MOST VALUABLE TOOL YOU HAVE IS BEING CREATIVE AND THERE ARE NOT THAT MANY PEOPLE WHO ARE. OUR JOB IS NEVER GOING AWAY BECAUSE PEOPLE WANT IDEAS. NO ONE IS GOING TO REPLACE THE IDEA.**

AS: How did Art Direction lead to Production Design?

NC: I was taken from LA to Ireland as an art director on *Braveheart* and it was there I realized I wanted to be production designer. But how do I do that? It's a hard jump to make. Very difficult in Hollywood. There were a couple of Irish producers on *Braveheart* who mentioned, *There are many small films coming here with Hollywood directors. They don't want to bring in people so they hire local designers but there aren't any local designers.*

I went back to LA and did some more Art Direction and then I thought, *You know I'm just going to move to Ireland.* I kind of went backwards. I started on big Hollywood films and ended up working on small BBC filmed-in-Ireland productions and low budget films. I also did a bunch of commercials. I trained myself as a designer. My first big break was when Barry Levinson hired me on *An Everlasting Piece*. The film did not get a big release but I met a few key L.A. producers.

> " I DEVELOPED A TECHNIQUE WHERE I TRY TO DETERMINE THE VISUAL PATH OF THE FILM. I FIND THE BIGGEST ROOM I CAN AND PUT THE ENTIRE FILM IN SCENE ORDER. I LOOK AT THE VISUAL PATHS OR PATTERNS OF THE FILM, TO TRY AND COME UP WITH SOME KIND OF THEME, AN OVERALL FEELING FOR THE FILM OR WHAT WE'RE TRYING TO SAY. *WHAT IS THE FILM ABOUT?*

AS: Was that in Ireland still?

NC: Yes, that was in Ireland. I moved to Dublin for three years. It seemed like a crazy plan but ended up being a successful plan to become a designer. I had to go back to those low-budget films. It wasn't a bad thing to start with big budget films and go backwards and do some training. I became an Irish designer even though I was English.

Then Mark Johnson, the producer of Barry's film, said, *What are you doing here? You're a good designer. I can help get you an agent in Hollywood.* Which he did. And the next film that came along was with an Irish director called John Moore and it was *Behind Enemy Lines*. John Moore was a good guy I knew from Dublin. We'd been doing commercials

together. It was an exhausting film and after the last week of filming I was sitting on the bow of the aircraft carrier USS Vinson with my feet hanging off, returning to San Diego harbor. The phone rings and it's my agent saying, *Hey, there's this English director called Chris Nolan. He just did his first film and he's got this other film called* Insomnia. *Can you get in a car and go meet him this afternoon?*

Yes, I can, because I'm just pulling into San Diego Harbor! And then I met Chris and the rest is history. We realized when I was a teenager I used to hang out on his street. My best friend lived a few doors down from him. He was quite a bit younger so I didn't know him then but we grew up in the same area. I met him and we became good friends.

AS: How do you exchange visual ideas with Christopher Nolan?

NC: In Ireland I developed a technique where I try to determine the visual path of the film. I find the biggest room I can and put the entire film in scene order. I look at the visual paths or patterns of the film, to try and come up with some kind of theme, an overall feeling for the film or what we're trying to say. *What is the film about?* On *Insomnia* we had a very short prep and I remember applying this to a big wall in Vancouver and Chris being very excited that he could actually walk and see the whole path of the film.

You can throw up anything really on the wall. It becomes a jumble of imagery. You throw up things that interest you–locations, ideas. You then find a path and patterns. It becomes like the lost and found wall at the school. It's like two hundred feet long because it's every scene in the film. It becomes a giant mass and a lot of people are like, *What the hell are you doing?* I'm trying to find themes of the film, *What are we trying to say? How are we telling this whole story visually?*

When we did *Insomnia* we did it in a hell of a hurry. The next film I worked for him on, *Batman Begins*, Chris said, *I should get you in earlier.* He does a first pass on the script with his brother and David Goyer. Then he calls me in and we start developing the visuals of the film. So when he writes he's writing scenes that are visually correct.

We started the whole process in Chris' old garage that had no heat or air conditioning and had a washing machine in it. Eventually we just grew out of it. It wasn't big enough.

Batman Begins had a clear design path to follow. But we were making an origin story with *The Dark Knight* which was different. We could take the design in a completely new direction. It took me a while to figure out the concepts of *The Dark Knight*. I'm sitting there in the garage thinking, *We can truly change this. But I don't know where to start!* And then weirdly I went to an exhibition in New York at the Dia Beacon about Minimalism. And it was just an eye-opener. *Let's modernize Gotham and take the Gothic out. Create a place where The Fountainhead had succeeded.* It was the utopia that anarchy came to destroy. The *Batman* films became about the

purity of Modernism. The Joker was about chaos, he was trying to disrupt it. So I said, *Let's be brave. Let's do big, empty spaces.* I realized I had become a Modernist!

> ❝ ONE OF THE MOST IMPORTANT THINGS FOR A DESIGNER AND ONE OF THE THINGS YOU DON'T OFTEN HAVE TIME TO DO IS PUT THE SCRIPT INTO YOUR HEAD. KNOW IT INSIDE OUT. KNOW SCENE ORDER AND STRUCTURE. YOU SHOULD KNOW THAT WHEN YOU'RE SCOUTING. YOU NEED TO BE PLAYING THE FILM IN YOUR HEAD.

When we started in the garage I didn't have a PA or any help. It was too early. We were in pre-pre-production and this meant I had to do everything myself. I was the PA. Chris used to say, *Hey, where you going?*

I'm going to buy some supplies at Home Depot. Chris says, *Oh, I'll come with you.* People didn't recognize him back then. *Okay Chris, if you really want to do something you can help me find some wheels for my model of the Batpod.* I think like most writers he would do anything to delay writing.

Even if the film wasn't in LA we'd go downtown and say, *Let's talk about it as if we could shoot it here.* We'd go out wandering. We'd spend the whole day. We'd have breakfast, wander, go back to the garage and then go out again. And when the films got bigger it was like, *Okay, let's go to India. Let's go wandering around India. Let's go to Iceland.*

> ❝ **THAT EARLY PRE-PREPRODUCTION IS REALLY ESSENTIAL. IT'S WHERE THE FILM IS DESIGNED. IT'S NOT DESIGNED IN PREPRODUCTION. IT'S DESIGNED IN CHRIS [NOLAN'S] GARAGE. WHEN WE LEAVE THAT GARAGE WE HAVE TO SUDDENLY INSTRUCT TWO HUNDRED PEOPLE WHAT THE ENTIRE FILM SHOULD LOOK LIKE.**

AS: You did research in foreign countries?

NC: Yes. In the beginning we went to Iceland and walked around Iceland. We'd go hiking up the glaciers and ravines all day long. We wanted the landscape in *Batman Begins* to mean something. To show Batman's journey. In the *Dark Knight Rises* we wanted to use landscapes again. Go somewhere remote. Bane would have come from somewhere remote. I'd been looking at stepwells in India. We flew to India and literally got in a car and drove from Dehli to Mumbai. Crazy few days. Then we flew to Romania and ended up in the giant salt mines wondering if we should change the Batcave.

You find the entire film scouting, but you know you have to give something up. You have to decide what you can and what you can't achieve. Find another version that's satisfactory. Compromise on some elements and hold fast on others.

It's brilliant having Chris there with me. We often walk all day discussing each scene. He's putting his version of each scene in my head. I'm sure he does it on purpose because he knows he'll get more out of me! One of the most important things for a designer and one of the things you don't often have time to do is put the script into your head. Know it inside out. Know scene order and structure. You should know that when you're scouting. You need to be playing the film in your head and hopefully it's the same film as the director's.

You might be scouting something specifically in the script, say, Japanese restaurants, and you might find a location and say, *My God, we gotta use this for this other scene one hundred pages earlier.* It becomes a giant jigsaw puzzle. Keeping the process loose you allow for the evolution of ideas. You don't necessarily have to scout for one thing you can scout with the whole film in mind. That early pre-preproduction is really essential. It's where the film is designed. It's not designed in preproduction. It's designed in Chris's garage. When we leave that garage we have to suddenly instruct two hundred people what the entire film should look like.

But all these things are gonna change. All these thousands of things come at you, the money, the visual effects, the actors' schedules, what you can do practically, what the problems are. But you're prepared for the bombardment. That's why you're doing the early work in the garage.

AS: Do you favor practical locations over building sets on a stage?

NC: Building a set is more about, Are we going to have this actor available on this date? Do we need to flood this or blow it up? Not like, Oh, we have to build this set. We don't have to build anything. You can build it on location. Like the Batcave. We were going to put it into a real cave to begin with. It should be a real cave. It must be believable. It's a hiding place. But then we decide we want to jump a real Batmobile into it and have a waterfall and river. So you end up building a set based on an existing cave you scouted. Design should be in the background. You shouldn't question whether it's a set. You shouldn't say at the end of the film, Oh, wow, that's a cool set. Then somehow you've failed.

AS: Sometimes I ask the question whether a set should be a character in the movie or if production design should be invisible...

NC: It depends on your film. I'd say it should always be in the background but then weirdly when I did the Bunker with its low, bright ceiling, everyone knows the Bunker set. The way I tried to make that set not stand alone was by using an enormous amount of Modernism across the film, like in the boardroom I had to play a low ceiling there to make the Batbunker not stand out as this isolated set. The only person who's ever gotten away with that in the past is Ken Adam. He defines his entire film with one set! Which I can really appreciate.

A set can be a character in a film if your story demands it. When I did *The Lake House* that set had to be a character in the film. I spent my entire budget on that one set. Which was a fight because I went to the producer and said, *I'm going to spend all my budget building this set because it's not something that exists, it's a memory of the past for the son and father. A forgotten time in their lives. The rest of the picture we're going to shoot in found locations. The Lake House* is not my favorite film but it's the kind of film where the set has to play a character. I oddly get many phone calls about the Lake House set. I have been asked by one architectural group to give a lecture on the design of the house.

> "DESIGN SHOULD BE IN THE BACKGROUND. YOU SHOULDN'T QUESTION WHETHER IT'S A SET. YOU SHOULDN'T SAY AT THE END OF THE FILM, *OH, WOW, THAT'S A COOL SET.* THEN SOMEHOW YOU'VE FAILED.

In *Batman* maybe the Batcave becomes a character. But you shouldn't lose the rest of the film, you have to make it fit into your world. A lot of logic went into it. If Gotham is New York then Wayne Manor could be in the Palisades. The Palisades have granite cliffs so the Batcave can have a waterfall. But your logic doesn't necessarily play to the audience. You're only playing in realism. You have to make it real because Batman is in a rubber suit running around the city! You have to believe that that could exist.

AS: You have a way of designing realism but with a bigness to it.

NC: I believe in scale. I think the audience going to the cinema deserves it. You're fighting against HBO, so cinematic scale is your advantage. James Bond did it very well with sliding walls, elevators that take you somewhere else. And Batman spends his time hiding so he needs elevators hidden in the floor or a secret wall. Chris said, *I want to access the Batbunker from a container.* Great, let's do that. You can get scale by opening a door to something vast. That's the beauty of cinema. Just take the door to location and shoot any background that you feel suits the scene.

> **I BELIEVE IN SCALE. I THINK THE AUDIENCE GOING TO THE CINEMA DESERVES IT. YOU'RE FIGHTING AGAINST HBO, SO CINEMATIC SCALE IS YOUR ADVANTAGE.**

In *Dark Knight Rises* the shaft built for Bane's prison was humongous but it's a simple shape. It's relatively inexpensive to build that and get scale. The thing about sets is sometimes detail is very expensive and it doesn't really play. You're much better off using something real to achieve detail and scale where possible. I like depth. I like rows of columns like when Bane fights Batman on the steps. If you actually look at the scale of those columns and the amount of them that's very intentional. That was a very intentional scout: *I want a big row of columns.*

That's the transfer point from one location in Wall Street to somewhere in Pittsburgh. That to me is how you get scale.

When I look back at films like *The Parallax View* they have great scale. You can have a man running through Madison Square Garden. You get huge scale very easily. Obviously the scene has to demand that. Scale is very lonely.

You often have to fight producers and ADs. *Oh we'll just pick up that scene while we're over here because they're just having a little conversation.* I call it throwing away a great opportunity. Producers and ADs will say, *Oh, well, it's an eighth of a page!* But some of the greatest visual scenes in film have no dialog.

Yeah, let's throw it away. Let's throw it away somewhere great! For me when I try to get scale in architecture I do it with real places. It's very hard to achieve scale by building a set. You'll never get the scale you get with real architecture. Combine the two.

AS: How do you feel about people trying to create scale by doing a small build and extending everything with CG?

NC: To me I rarely believe it. It doesn't feel right. There's no atmosphere in it. Like the bulbs in *The Prestige*. A lot of people would say you could do that digitally. We did that for real with hundreds of light bulbs in a field. And then we got fog that night. When they went on the camera operator was saying, *I can't see this!* But it was the most phenomenal shot in the film. The fog gave it emotion–something unexpected that you cannot plan digitally.

AS: Someone mentioned that the Bat vehicle in *The Dark Knight Rises* was really sixty floors up.
NC: You put it up on the real roof in New York so when they get out of it they're really sixty floors up. You have the conversation with Catwoman and Batman with the vehicle behind them with a real view of New York City and then you do the landing digitally. You do the taking off digitally. But you have the real thing in the real landscape with the real lighting. When you do greenscreen set extensions on a sound stage what are you matching? You're not matching anything but artificial light on a set and a plate reference.

When we're in the garage we just assume everything's real and there are no VFX. That's where we start and then we see what trouble we're in. Obviously there are plenty of VFX shots but we try not to start in that mind set.

AS: How involved are you with designing what the Bat looks like and the various other vehicles?
NC: They're the first things I work on. I usually design them in the garage using models. I designed all of them. It's a great way to start a process. It's just me and Chris. Again, he should be writing but he comes down to hover over my shoulder while I'm gluing this shit together. *Do you really want to put that there?* It's like, *Chris, leave me alone!* He just

doesn't want to sit down and write. Like every kid he wants to be playing with model kits in the workshop.

It usually takes me five concept models to get to the final design. Usually by then all the skin on my hands is gone because of the glue. The smell of glue is so strong I have to leave the garage and go out. I design them and then I give them to my 3D guy to draw up. I'm really proud of the Batmobile, the Pod and the Bat. The Pod was the hardest thing to come up with.

> " I THINK MY STRONG POINT IS SCALE. SARAH GREENWOOD'S STRONG POINT IS COLOR. WE ALL COME TO IT FROM A DIFFERENT PERSPECTIVE.

AS: What would you say are the ideal characteristics a production designer should have? Is being able to make models a requirement?
NC: I always believe you should be a jack of all trades. You have to have a love of design. The love of story. You have to love film. Films like David Lean's Great Expectations affected me. To me I get a lot of my inspiration from artists. Exhibitions. Museums. You have to be aware of the world. You should always be looking. It's about being adventurous. How can you describe something visually? Really engage someone *emotionally* through visuals? How can you do that? I think my strong point is scale. Sarah Greenwood's strong point is color. We all come to it from a different perspective.

I like being able to do things myself. I can get into a film before we start preproduction. I can explore it. I like not having to have a ton of people around to begin with. All the tools should just come naturally like a writer using a pen to write, you should just be able to access them. It helps you move faster.

AS: What advice would you have for someone just starting out in the business?

NC: If I was starting out with the knowledge I have now I'd be looking for young directors with great stories. I think those guys are usually writer/directors. You need to find people you want to work with and help them. Many directors starting out have no idea how a designer can help them. Young directors that have never had a production designer open their eyes. You have to make yourself be invaluable.

AS: What do you like about designing movies?

NC: I just get excited by stories. We were going to do a film on Alan Turing, a mathematician who lived during the Second World War and who came up with the idea around 1920 that machines think. What I love about film is that then you say, *Okay, let's explore math in film. How the brain thinks. Let's look at nature. Repetitive patterns. Patterns in snow,* *footsteps, rhythm.* We went down this road, this tangent that brings you back around into the story and you add that to the design.

You ask how people live. How does this character live? It's like being a detective. Then you tell a visual, emotional story with themes that underrun the characters.

AS: What do you think is the future of production design?

NC: I've worked on a lot of very digital films and I remember the art department being terrified we're all going to be out of work. I was like, *What are you guys talking about? The most valuable tool you have is being creative and there are not that many people who are.* Our job is never going away because people want ideas. No one is going to replace the idea. Design is about ideas and taste. You can't replace that. That is why you're valuable. Design will never change. The Art Directors Guild has nothing to worry about. Because people will always want someone who comes in with a different way of looking at things. Just keep retraining. Keep up with technology.

Eve Stewart

Eve Stewart has been nominated for four Oscars to date including for the tremendous historic epic *Les Misérables.* She's perfected a distinct British realism for Mike Leigh's films and an enhanced historic realism of Tom Hooper's. When I interviewed her she was extremely busy designing the worlds of *The Muppets* and *Victor Frankenstein.*

AS: What was it like making the transition from the emotional *Les Misérables* to your next film, the light-hearted *Muppets Most Wanted?*

ES: After *Les Mi*s I thought I would do the polar opposite and so I designed the *Muppets Most Wanted* film. A bit of light relief after the harrowing scenes of Fantine dying!

AS: Did you shoot that in America?

ES: The majority was in the UK but we shot a little bit in America.

AS: How was working with James Bobin on the *Muppets* different from the Tom Hooper and Mike Leigh films?

ES: Really interesting because I thought it would be very different but it was actually just as rigorous! James Bobin was really clever and really fast and really thorough. It was actually quite a similar experience!

AS: You've done many films with Tom Hooper– is he a really visual director?

ES: He is a visual director but more than that he's a

very good conductor of visuals. I'll always overdo it and just get loads of stuff together because I'm really enthusiastic. He's very good at filtering and kind of conducting it like a piece of music.

AS: Was everything built on stage for *Les Misérables*?

ES: Almost everything was a set on a stage, yes. With the exception of the outside where we did the funeral and the big elephant scene.

AS: Was the elephant based on something that actually existed?

ES: Yes, it was in the original novel. So I read the novel thoroughly and I found out that this elephant had been constructed by Napoleon to celebrate his successes in Egypt. It was made out of plaster and began to rot when he ran out of money. And in the novel Gavroche and all the other little urchins of Paris live in it.

AS: Was it a huge construction?

ES: It was a massive construction! It was forty-eight feet high and you could climb up inside it. We had one big enormous studio in Pinewood. It must have been about two hundred and fifty feet by one hundred thirty feet and by the end with all our sets we only had about ten foot left and all the monitors and stuff had to be snuck in around the back of one of the sheds.

AS: I remember you saying that you had read the full novel but not everyone in the crew had.

ES: Yes, I think it was only myself and Tom! It's got fourteen hundred and six pages of really tiny writing!

AS: Were you involved in the visual effects a lot?

ES: Yeah, we were involved in the visual effects a lot primarily because we had done all the research on all the buildings that would have been around that street in Paris. We made quite a lot of big 3D models of the buildings that they could photograph and use within their composites.

AS: Was that part of your previs?

ES: It was my version of a previs. [Producer] Cameron Mackintosh works in theater all the time. They're very used to seeing a big model of what the scenery would be. I made this giant, accurate model where the buildings were very realistic, and each about two foot high and all painted and colored like doll's houses so everybody was very clear about what they would get.

AS: A lot of production designers I talk to just do 3D models on computers. But there's something kind of magical about a physical model that people can look at.

ES: Yes, I agree, I think there is something magical. They're both very useful tools but I don't think you can completely just work with computer generated images because they never show the texture or the soul of the thing.

CG is very useful. It's a quick way of working. But in the end it's all about human beings and how they interact with the surfaces.

AS: With the sets in *Les Misérables* did you have to change a lot to accommodate the choreography as soon as they started singing and dancing?
ES: Only a little bit in the scene with all the prostitutes. When Tom saw the set he loved all the bits along the high walls so he began to want the ladies writhing around on them. We had to make a lot of them a lot stronger to take their weight.

AS: And the actors really experienced winter on set?
ES: Yeah, we were filming in the winter and it was really cold and I think they really began to experience the misery of life on the outside even though they were on a stage. There was no heating.

AS: How is Tom Hooper different from director Mike Leigh? Is Mike Leigh visual?
ES: They are both incredibly thorough about the understanding of the character and the time and place that they inhabit and nothing is taken for granted. With neither director would I ever get away with putting something on the set just because it looked nice. It has to be there for a reason. In that way they work in a similar way. With Tom you heighten it. You're very rigorous about making sure it's historically accurate but in the end we're making a musical. You're allowed to heighten it. That's the difference. Where Mike wouldn't do that. Although on *Topsy-Turvy* I often tweaked it a bit. But not to the degree anywhere near.

AS: Are you talking about realism versus being more stylized and theatrical?

ES: Not so much stylized and theatrical–just sort of raising the bar all the time. It's just exaggerating slightly. Not going into the world of the fantastical but if you've got a red room just making it more red than you would naturally have. Or extra cold or the wood slightly more decrepit. Just sort of pushing the limits up a bit.

AS: On The King's Speech you said a lot of it was locations. How was your role different?
ES: None of the locations were actually as you saw them. And we felt very strongly it would be good to work in the real places. We found his treatment room very near Harley Street in London. Plus the reality is that we didn't have as much money. I don't want to spend the money on building a wall if one exists and you can decorate it.

AS: Speaking of walls there was that one wall in *The King's Speech* that was so amazing.
ES: *The King's Speech* was quite a theatrical piece when I first read it. Tom and I though there would be a lot more of just looking at Lionel Logue and the King in one room. So we thought the room should be really, really interesting! The script developed as we went along but we kept that interest. We also thought it was really great to start painting it really theatrically–kind of a Shakespearean tan.

AS: Do you do a lot of sketching for every movie you work on?
ES: Yes, because I'm quite quick. I do tons. I did a whole sequence of watercolors and paintings for Les Mis. It gives you something to talk about with

directors. Even if something is wrong at least it's a starting point.

AS: Do you ever have set designers do sketches too?

ES: No. Although I sometimes get them to do a visual if it's a big street scene or something because studios like that sort of thing. But no, primarily with Tom he will happily work from my watercolors.

AS: Did you go to art school?

ES: Yes, I went to the Central Saint Martins in London. I did theater design in school and I worked in the theater for about eight years before I started doing films. I did the sets and the costumes when I did theater. I did design in theater for Mike Leigh and then he suddenly asked if I wanted to work on a film and I said yes because it sounded fun. I didn't realize it would be such hard work! But it is fun.

AS: Is the ability to work hard a characteristic you need to have as a production designer?

ES: You have to work all the time! You have to be so fascinated by everything because you're doing everything from what the wheels are like on a carriage to what they're eating. What the lighting is, controlling the colors, working with the cameraman, the director, the costume designer, and the makeup designer as well. I think it's very interesting that one minute you're drawing a picture and the next minute someone's throwing three million quid at you to hire carpenters and painters and ev-

erything. You've got to be a good politician as well. And good at adding up.

AS: In terms of how much money is being spent?

ES: Yes. You've got to stay all over it.

AS: When you are hiring all the craftspeople what kind of characteristics are you looking for?

ES: That they're really good-humored, mainly! That you can have a laugh. And that everybody gets on. The people that I tend to use also have a very theatrical background. They're very skilled. They've not only done film. They have an appreciation of real life and real characters.

AS: Jon Myhre told me if he ever walks on set and hears people complain about something he says, *Well, Goodness Gracious, we're working on a Movie! Isn't that fantastic?*

ES: Why make it work? And you're thrown into a really intense working relationship with people for a very long time and you're with them twelve, fourteen, sixteen hours a day. If you've got some misery stomping about, it disrupts everything.

AS: You said while doing *Les Mis* some of the tattooed crew members would sing the songs while building?

ES: Yes, they would start singing the songs while they were working! But then they did the same on *The Muppets!* They love it!

AS: Do you always work with the same crew?

ES: Yes.

AS: Have you mainly worked in England?

ES: I've worked a lot in Spain. The British do a lot of commercials in Spain because of the weather. And I've done an awful lot in Eastern Europe and Italy. And a little bit in the U.S., but not much.

AS: How would you say it's different working in England versus Italy or Spain.

ES: I would say the British are like the Germans. They're very ordered and meticulous about time-keeping and just have a general Protestant work ethic. A different approach. But then on the flip side some of the jobs I've done in Italy have had some of the most beautiful painting I've ever seen.

AS: Are you able to bring your crew with you to places like Italy and Spain?

ES: I'll bring the same core crew. But I've been very lucky for the past five years in that I've been working in and around London. My children are doing their final exams before they're grown up and I wanted to be around.

AS: When you were in school yourself were you planning on being a production designer on movies?

ES: No. I wanted to design operas! But there aren't many operas.

AS: And have you designed many operas?

ES: I've designed a lot of plays but nobody has ever asked me to do an opera!

AS: Dante Ferretti mentioned he's designed quite a few.

ES: Well, he's Italian–they do more in Italy!

AS: Would you recommend people go to art school?

ES: If they can afford it, yes, for sure. And if they can't afford it, still practice drawing. If you're sitting in a meeting and there are twelve people sitting around looking at you and you're all talking about a chair, unless you can draw the chair that you think is right, they'll all be thinking of something different. You've got to be very clear and communicate very well.

> **❝ I THINK IT'S VERY INTERESTING THAT ONE MINUTE YOU'RE DRAWING A PICTURE AND THE NEXT MINUTE SOMEONE'S THROWING THREE MILLION QUID AT YOU TO HIRE CARPENTERS AND PAINTERS AND EVERYTHING.**

AS: What is your relationship like with the DP?

ES: I'm really good at being friendly with everyone. You have to be. Being able to draw and make visuals look beautiful and being able to get your message across quickly has also been an enormous help with DoPs.

AS: Are you on set during shooting?

ES: I'm always on the set at the beginning of each new set to make sure it's all okay and has no teething problems and then I have to move onto the next one because they'll be eating up that scenery and then they'll be behind me. It's like having a supertanker up your arse! You have to really keep going.

> ## IF YOU'RE INVISIBLE EIGHTY PERCENT OF THE TIME AND TWENTY PERCENT OF THE TIME PEOPLE GO, *WHOA!* BECAUSE YOU'VE INTRODUCED THEM TO A NEW WORLD, I FEEL THAT'S A GOOD JOB.

AS: What would you say that you most like about production design?

ES: Probably the initial working-out period. The drawing and the research I really love.

AS: Is that part of it usually just yourself or do you have a small crew?

ES: It's usually just myself and the director. It's gotten quite more like that because my research ability and my resources have gotten quite great. I get called in earlier so I can work with the director to kind of show them, especially with a period piece, exactly what the world would have been.

AS: How do you go about that research? Is it a lot of internet searches?

ES: That's a big part of it but no, I'm very good at using the library resources in London and I have an enormous library myself. And I'll look at anything. I'll talk to anyone.

AS: Do you prefer period pieces?

ES: I love them and if you love research like I do that's a really big help. But I would love to do some science fiction, I just haven't gotten it yet.

AS: How do you feel about production design being invisible or visible in films?

ES: If you're invisible for the bulk of your time then you've done a really good job because it hasn't stuck in somebody's throat. If you're invisible eighty percent of the time and twenty percent of the time people go, *Whoa!* because you've introduced them to a new world, I feel that's a good job.

AS: Do you feel a set can be a character in a movie?

ES: Definitely. It's a massive illustration and it's a history-teller. It's a quicker story-teller than the script. Because people are so quick to assess the status, the history, the mood. They make a complete judgment on what they're seeing about the person who is involved there. It's an enormous resource.

AS: What do you think of the future of production design? More and more CG and green-screens?

ES: No, I think there's a sort of backlash if anything. I find that people are asking for more and more in-camera. Of course the really big movies are going to stick to doing green but I find that there's actually more being put in-camera and I think audiences get a bit tired of the kind of glossiness of the non-realism of CG. I think they like a bit of realism where they can connect. Definitely there's a backlash at the moment.

AS: Do you use a lot of painted backdrops?

ES: I love painted backdrops, yes. I use anything of the old craft. I think people love to see craft that other human beings have made with their own hands. It's something primal. People understand when another human being's telling a story visually. However they do it. With painted backdrops, sculpture, what they're wearing. If something's too perfect it feels cold, non-engaging.

AS: Have you ever worked on more than one project at a time?

ES: No. They sometimes overlap at the very end. But I like to try to give it my all. And I think a massive part of my job is to support the director all the way through it. You have to dedicate yourself.

AS: When you first worked with Mike Leigh you worked as art director. How was it different working with a production designer as an art director versus working as a production designer?

ES: I was a standby art director so I was on the floor. It was brilliant to fully understand you have to get everything ready and you can't take short cuts and leave the crew on the floor without extra stuff. It was all-in-all a good background before becoming a designer.

AS: In Mike Leigh films did you ever build sets?

ES: Not for films I art directed. But for *Topsy Turvy*

much of that was built because none of it existed how it would have been. But then with *Vera Drake* the majority was locations because Mike likes the history that you get from the real thing. It had ghosts in it and more lumps and bumps. It's been around the block and that's always good.

> **" I THINK AUDIENCES GET A BIT TIRED OF THE KIND OF GLOSSINESS OF THE NON-REALISM OF CG. I THINK THEY LIKE A BIT OF REALISM WHERE THEY CAN CONNECT . . . IF SOMETHING'S TOO PERFECT IT FEELS COLD.**

AS: Do you spend a lot of time with the location managers and scouts?

ES: Yes. But having grown up in London and done an awful lot in London I'm pretty good at knowing where stuff is now.

AS: Do you ever just go out on your own scouting?

ES: I don't go out on my own scouting but I'll certainly know where to suggest quite quickly. What would be a good area or what type of building would work.

AS: When you first get a movie what is one of the first things you do? What is your process at the outset?

ES: I'll always read it and start drawing all over the script. And I buy a new sketchbook and start drawing. I'll sit in a room with the director drawing and thinking. Looking at research and pulling out books and images.

AS: I hear you're on a *Frankenstein* movie now?

ES: Yes! I did *The Muppets Most Wanted* and then I did another *Call the Midwife* television series and now I'm doing *Victor Frankenstein*.

> " WITH *VERA DRAKE* THE MAJORITY WAS LOCATIONS BECAUSE MIKE [LEIGH] LIKES THE HISTORY THAT YOU GET FROM THE REAL THING. IT HAD GHOSTS IN IT AND MORE LUMPS AND BUMPS. IT'S BEEN AROUND THE BLOCK AND THAT'S ALWAYS GOOD.

AS: A historical period film?

ES: Yes. It's all set in the 1800's. It will be another big historical thing but given that I'm now doing the research I'm learning how to bring someone back to life. I should have it licked by the end of the year.

AS: Is that another attribute a production designer needs to have? The ability to bring people back to life?

ES: Yes, it's a useful extra skill!

AS: Say someone's starting out in the business. Any advice?

ES: Learn to smile all day! Be positive. And learn to draw. For God's sake learn to draw! It's the only way you'll ever get your own way.

Eugenio Caballero

Eugenio Caballero won an Academy Award for *Pan's Labyrinth,* the film many production designers cite as a benchmark of creative film design. Working with auteur filmmaker Guillermo Del Toro, he created both the hostile reality and the surreal dream-world of the movie. He's worked with Jim Jarmusch, Baz Luhrman, and designed the Oscar-winning masterpiece *Roma* for Alfonso Cuarón. When I caught up with Eugenio he was back home in Mexico after just finishing a movie in New York City with Sebastián Cordero.

AS: How was your experience filming in NY?

EC: My friend, Sebastián Cordero, the Ecuadorian director of *Chronicles* and *Rage,* was doing his first film in the United States and it was a small piece. Small projects are often more difficult to do than huge projects! You're there to make the best out of the resources that you have.

AS: Did you bring a crew into New York or did you work with local New York people?

EC: I worked with local New York people. Whether you hire a local crew depends on the project. On *Pan's Labyrinth*, I went to Spain alone and hired a local crew. I didn't know a single person in the art department before going. It was a fantastic crew and I've worked with several of them on other projects since then. For example, they worked with me on my previous film, *The Impossible,* which took a year and a half. We shot in Thailand and I took some of my old Spanish crew with me and also I brought a lead scenic painter from England. I took my two art directors, my propmaster, and my set decorator–the same one that worked on *Pan's Labyrinth* and *The Limits of Control*.

But it was a huge construction film and I worked with a Thai art director and he brought a fantastic local crew. I was especially impressed by the craftsmanship of the sculptors on everything that was custom-made and hand-crafted. You see all those skills in Thai culture as well as in Mexican culture. I try to work with local crews–there are always beautiful surprises.

> RECREATING NATURE IS ONE OF THE MOST DIFFICULT TASKS IN OUR CRAFT BUT IF YOU ARE ABLE TO DO IT, IT GIVES YOU A LOT OF FREEDOM TO DESIGN.

AS: Do you still do films in Mexico?
EC: It all depends on the project. The last film I did here was *Rudo y Cursi,* with Gael García Bernal and Diego Luna, which was very fun to do. After that I just went from project to project and it just so happened that the next projects were not here. And my previous film, *The Impossible,* went on for a very long time. It was a long process of research, scouting and shooting.

AS: How long did you shoot?
EC: We shot twenty-four weeks. But it was divided because we shot in Spain and in Thailand. We shot in Spain first, using the huge water tank in Alicante.

AS: Underwater shots?
EC: Mostly on the surface of the water. And then we shot our principal photography in Thailand. After that we had some more weeks of technical shooting back in the tank in Alicante which was very interesting, working with miniatures of a set that we had built in Thailand. We did a lot of tests with waves. The film is based on a real story that happened during the tsunami of 2004. It's a family story. It was very challenging.

AS: Was that a Spanish director?
EC: Yes, Juan Antonio Bayona, a very young, talented director. He did *The Orphanage*. But this film is completely in another register, it's more of a drama. We built a lot, we dressed a lot of locations, but for me the most beautiful piece of design was a tree that we had to build in the middle of a scene of devastation. I always love the challenge of recreating nature with our tools as designers. Sculptors are always involved. It's like making a Frankenstein out of different things: live plants, branches, a lot of sculpture, strong structure . . . Re-creating nature is one of the most difficult tasks in our craft but if you are able to do it, it gives you a lot of freedom to design. You can really push the boundaries.

AS: Was the tree in *Pan's Labyrinth* also a build?
EC: Everything in *Pan's Labyrinth* was a build. We always intended to build the tree because we wanted a very specific shape, reminiscent of the creature. The tree is shaped like the horns of Pan. The film is full of those connections between the real

world and the fantasy world. This suggests to the audience that the fantasy world is created by Ofelia's imagination, as an escape from reality.

The reality is a lot colder and more scary than the fantasy world, although the fantasy world is full of creatures. We wanted to be very clear with that. The color palette of the real world is all cold colors like green or grey or blue and the fantasy is full of warm color–it's red, it's golden, it's yellow. We did the same with shapes. We wanted the real world to be more hostile so we did a lot of straight lines and a lot of angles. We did oversized furniture and oversized beams and oversized fireplaces. In the fantasy you don't see a straight line. Everything is curved and organic. We played a lot with that . . .

Originally when we went location scouting, we were looking for some pre-existing construction to start with. But soon we realized that the visual concept for the film was so strong that if we wanted everything to work, we had to be very strict about our choices. In the end we decided that we needed a forest with two open areas where we could build the mill and the labyrinth.

When we were first scouting in the north of Spain, we went to this fantastic forest but we realized all of the trees were really organic–they were scary but in a warm way. We were not happy with that. Guillermo and I talked a lot about how the forest in the story belonged to the real world so it had to stay within our concept of straight lines and hostility.

Then we found a pine forest near Madrid. And the pines were really big and really straight, almost like spikes, really hostile. And we decided to shoot there.

> **MY PERSONAL TASTE CHANGES OVER THE YEARS– I DON'T HAVE THE SAME TASTE THAT I DID TWELVE YEARS AGO. BUT WHAT I CAN USE INSTEAD, TO UNDERSTAND IF A VISUAL DECISION WORKS OR NOT, IS I CAN ASK IF IT'S TRUTHFUL TO THE STORY AND TRUTHFUL TO THE CHARACTERS.**

When we were scouting it was February and everything was beautifully green and full of ferns, so we decided to start building at that location. But that year turned out to be one of the warmest summers in the last fifty years. Everything that was green started to turn yellow. All the ferns died. So suddenly we were half-built in a place that had been fantastic but was now changing and not really working anymore. What we ended up doing was creating fake grass and fake ferns too. We painted the grass that was yellow, but in the places near the construction there was no grass left. In the end we decided to create fake grass out of splinters of wood and mix different colors. So that's what I mean when I say that everything was a build or put there by the art department. The grass that's in the film is fake grass that was added by us, made of splinters of wood dyed different greens.

The script took place in the North of Spain and Guillermo and I always said that all the trees should be covered with moss. It was a very important thing in the film in terms of color and texture. It provides a lot of the greens that create a very cold environment for the girl. But when we decided to use a pine forest we didn't realize that pines never grow moss! So in the end we took the creative liberty of putting moss on the pines. So every single tree in the film is dressed by what "we called "The Moss Team".

All of these decisions are important in making the audience feel what the character is feeling. My personal taste changes over the years–I don't have the same taste that I did twelve years ago. But what I can use instead, to understand if a visual decision works or not, is I can ask if it's truthful to the story and truthful to the characters. What are they feeling? That's very important. As designers we have a lot of tools to transmit those feelings.

Color for me is also a very important thing. In *The Limits of Control*, the Jim Jarmusch movie that we shot in Spain some years ago, we started with this man who has been assigned to go and find certain people and accomplish a mission. In order to accomplish this mission he had to break into a heavily-guarded house. We decided that as that character starts his quest and meets these marvelous characters along the way and talks about all these strange subjects, he's gradually becoming a ghost. He's leaving all his baggage from the beginning behind so that he'll be so light, in a metaphorical way, that he'll be able to break into that house.

So we started with a very, very saturated palette. You can see in the beginning, when he starts in Madrid, the bars, the apartment, all the locations are all full of really saturated blues, oranges, reds. Then as he's walking this palette becomes less and less saturated. When he's in Seville there are warmer colors but less bright and less shiny and then when he gets to Almería, which is the place where this house is, everything is earth-tones with a lot of white. Desaturated colors. We lose the colors as he's walking in order to accomplish that mission. Then when he accomplishes his mission and he goes back to real life he reclaims his colors. There's a scene in which he changes clothes in a bathroom that has saturated colors again. He puts on a lime-green jacket and then takes some escalators, which are again blue and red and then he comes back to life. We worked closely with Christopher Doyle [the DP] on that palette so we could be completely coordinated.

AS: Do you always work very closely with the DP?

EC: I try to, yes. Normally I collaborate a lot with the DP. It's strange because most of the time the production designer starts before the DP. Since you have a longer preproduction, and you start making drawings, notes and concepts before that, you often start working directly with the director. When the DP comes into the project we discuss the things we've been working on. He adds his input and I'm very open to his contributions and very happy to discuss everything with him.

I'm a big believer in these creative discussions and the creation of concepts. If you create those concepts in the beginning with the director and the DP, when it's preproduction, then all of us are better suited to make decisions later and understand if those decisions are correct or not. Even if you have to answer seven hundred questions a day. It's very easy to give an incorrect answer when you're working at such an intense pace so for me the most important thing is to first create the frame of design for the film. That obviously also changes sometimes during the process.

I believe a lot in one's first intuition. I'm a Latin, I'm Mexican, so my approach is not on the cold side, it's very visceral.

AS: The *first intuition* you're talking about, does that come when you first read the script?
EC: When you first read the script and make notes. It's like a switch flips in your head. When you read a script you start that dream. You find answers to a lot of questions just by walking or by reading. You're looking for things and creating, but mainly you're just getting into a mood where you're more receptive to the things around you. I love that process. It's one of the things that I enjoy the most.

I feel a lot of joy in my job. One of the other things that I enjoy is the moment when you decide a set

is ready. You're not lacking anything and there's nothing there that shouldn't be. It's just an amazing moment. You've been working months, sometimes years, thinking about and creating a space. Suddenly it's there and it tells a story full of layers and complexity. This is very important for me in filmmaking, not just in design. A script that has many layers lets you as a designer put a lot of those layers into the final film.

> ❝ **THE MOST IMPORTANT THING IS TO FIRST CREATE THE FRAME OF DESIGN FOR THE FILM.**

AS: Do you find when you look at that final set that it's similar to your first intuition?
EC: It all depends. Logically sometimes it's different because there's a long process of construction and a lot of people involved. Normally the main ideas remain. The ones you had to defend with all of your heart. For me one of the things that experience brings is that during the process of creating a set I make sure not to lose a lot of the original concepts from the drawings that we first made. Even though all these practical issues come up when you're preproducing or building or scenicing or dressing or propping a set, you make sure that the original ideas do not get lost. That's very important. Sometimes practical things jeopardize that and it's something that we as designers really have to defend.

AS: What tools do you use to defend those original ideas? Sketches?

Do you also make physical models or use 3D software?

EC: Depends on the project. When I'm designing, the first thing I do is make a little book, a research book, and that book starts growing and growing and growing. The book reflects the spirit of the film.

Normally what I do in the beginning is put together these references and notes, even before we start making any sketches, in order to present and discuss ideas with everybody. With the director, with my own team. Then the second part is when we start scouting and have a better idea of what we want to do. Then you start sketching certain things. And those sketches evolve into concept art and from that concept art you start doing more technical drawings or models or 3D. It all depends on the complexity of the sets and the time and resources that you have. The most important thing is that you know the tools so you can adapt for specific cases. I still love to make physical models for construction. I love to see these miniatures and play with them with my hands. But I also really enjoy the digital tools.

When the studio era finished in America the biggest challenge to designers was to adapt their ideas to a less-controlled environment. To go on location. That gave a lot to a film–going on location is wonderful if it's well-chosen. When you go on location it's very important to understand why you're making that decision, why that location works or not. If the location is narrow, if it's tall, if it's hos-

tile, if it's full of windows. All this can increase the feeling of a character. If that character feels observed because there are a lot of windows, if it's a calming place or if it's an enigmatic place. All of those things are very important. So the production designers back at the end of the studio era had to learn to design with the idea of using locations. They needed to learn to use that new tool. It's the same for us with the digital tools.

It's very important for us to understand that our field is changing a lot with these new tools. The digital tools we have now are great if used correctly. We work with them on a daily basis and will be using them more and more–so we have to learn how to use them.

AS: Do you work closely with Visual Effects and the Visual Effects Supervisor on films?

EC: I try to work with them closely during the pre-production period. A lot of the elements that are generated later come from drawings and sketches and concept art that we created during preproduction. Then I try to work with VFX on the set too. And in post production I usually do some supervising. Normally you're on another project by then or you can't really be hired for that entire period of time. But I still supervise the progress of elements that are crucial to the visuals of the film.

AS: How do you see the future of production design? After seeing all the developments in the last ten years how do you see the field changing in the next ten years?

EC: It will be different in certain ways but not in the most important way. We, as designers, are meant to create visual concepts for films. The tools that we use to transmit them are evolving. We don't use the same tools that we did twenty years ago. Or even fifteen years ago. There are certain things that were not even imaginable ten years ago in the digital world. But the most important thing is that all of these developments have to support your visual concept for a film. And those visual concepts are what we as production designers must continue providing.

AS: Working with Guillermo on *Pan's Labyrinth*, it seems like he's less interested in relying on 3D visual effects than some other directors.

EC: That's true, he loves the textures of real things. Every film is different for him but *Pan's Labyrinth* was a very unusual project because we had total freedom. It was not really a studio film, it was done in Europe with Mexican and Spanish filmmakers. It was a very unique thing. We knew that in Spain there was a big tradition of construction that came from the days when a lot of American and English productions went to shoot in Almería during the Western period. A lot of films were shot in Spain in the 60s, 70s, and a good part of the 80s so there was a lot of craft in the construction field. The older generation has it. Nowadays construction in the Spanish film industry has changed and the films are not as construction-oriented. But we knew about this older generation–a lot of my crew was an average of sixty years old! They were really great–they were old maestros in scenic painting, in greens, in construction, in plaster.

So we used those old techniques in order to provide a certain texture for the film. The digital enhancements that we did were things that were not really possible to do physically. All of the sets were built physically except for the one in the end, the palace where the girl wakes up to meet the parents, which was a partially-built set. In this palace of the fantasy world certain built elements were enhanced with some digital set-extensions. But in the rest of the film we barely had any digital extensions on the sets. We even used some painted backdrops for the windows. We also did a physical miniature for the beginning of the film when there's a voice-over describing how the girl escaped from a fantasy world.

AS: What was it like working with Guillermo?

EC: He's an amazing filmmaker. He's very visual. He's one of those guys that has the ability to get the best out of everybody. He's very prepared. He has a very challenging visual culture. He has a lot of knowledge. It was very challenging for me to co-create a world with him. But he's a very, very warm person. He was very inclusive from the very beginning on how we should create those sets and especially on the visual concept of the film.

He asked me if I wanted to design the film before he even had the script written. We were at a screening of *Chronicles,* the film that I did in Ecuador, and he took me to a restaurant and asked,

Do you want to do this film–it's about this and this and that? And in two or three hours he described exactly what the film later would turn out to be. His initial ideas were so clear. It was amazing to know that he has all of these films in his head. And then he went back to write the script and I went back with my head spinning with all these things that I'd heard. I created my reference book and presented it to him when he gave me the script in Mexico some months later. That was the moment we bonded because he knew that a lot of these visual ideas that I was presenting were completing what he had in his mind. He also always referred to the book as "the serial killer book" because he said that it was so meticulous that if I wouldn't be a production designer I would be a serial killer! Guillermo also has the best sense of humor.

AS: How did you first meet him?
EC: In Mexico we're a very tiny film community. We cannot even call it an industry. We are a small film group. I knew him and then he produced a film that I did in Ecuador titled *Chronicles*. He produced it with Alfonso Cuarón. It was a very realistic film, a very tough film loosely based on two or three characters that were serial killers in the 80s. It's essentially about this guy and this group of journalists that come from Miami to this very poor community in Ecuador. They discover that there are some children missing and, touched by that, they try to help but for the wrong reasons. In the end the film had to look very realistic.

We ended up needing to recreate a lot of sets because it was not easy to shoot in that part of Ecuador. We recreated a feeling of this little town Babahoyo in a bigger city, Guayaquil. There was a lot of construction and dressing and scenic details because it was the tropics and the tropics are full of texture. As the producer, Guillermo saw how realistic our recreation was and he liked it a lot. And then Guillermo and Bertha Navarro, Guillermo's producing partner, talked about the possibility of inviting me to *Pan's Labyrinth*.

A lot of younger people come to me and say that there's not really a place where you can study to be a production designer. There are some schools but there are very few in the world and it's not easy for a vast majority of students from a lot of countries to find schools where they can learn their craft. A lot of people look for information in places like your blog or for master classes or workshops. But many of them come from countries where there's not much cinema and it's very hard to find anything.

In my case it was really natural. It was just nonstop working. I was always working and thinking about the next project. Soon I was doing things locally in Mexico, then I started working in Latin America but still very regionally. Then one thing led to another and then the next project opened a lot of doors. Now, some years later, I have access to better projects.

AS: Did you go to art school? How did you get into film in the first place?

EC: When I was seventeen I went to study art history in Florence, Italy. I was there for two years and when I went back home at nineteen everything had changed in my mind. But I still didn't know if I wanted to continue in an art school, or continue studying art history. I was also thinking of going to film school because I always loved film. While I was still deciding what to do I started doing a lot of shorts for my friends who were in film school. Everyone in film school wanted to be a director or producer or cinematographer or actor but nobody wanted to do the art direction, the production design. So I found a niche that I've felt very comfortable in. I did a lot of shorts with different directors, many of whom have become known directors in Mexico. And that led me to work with them more and also with different production designers as an assistant. Some years later I met the production designer Brigitte Broch and she became my mentor. I learned a lot about the craft from her, working with her for several years. I did a lot of things in her team–I was her set decorator, her art director on some films, I did props. She did *Babel* and *The Reader*, and we worked together on *Romeo + Juliette*, Baz Luhrman's film that was shot here in Mexico back in 1994.

I started very young. I was always learning on the set and I tried to complete my education with a lot of reading and watching films. I have always loved film and literature and music and I think all of those things contribute when you're designing a film.

AS: How was working with Jim Jarmusch different from these other directors?

EC: It was a fantastic experience. We have stayed very close friends. It was an experiment for everybody. We started preproduction with just thirty-five pages of a script. It was just ideas. And what's in the film later was informed by what we discovered in the preproduction phase, while we were looking for locations. There was a lot of liberty in a conceptual way. And Jim explored this with a lot of guts. It's not an easy thing to do. He wanted to do a film with that high level of risk. Being a part of that for me was a great experience that really opened my mind. And I still use that as another approach during preproduction when I design more normal films.

AS: It wasn't frustrating not to have everything set at the beginning?

EC: I started out thinking that way but then somehow because I was witnessing how he was doing it, my point of view changed. But there were definitely a lot of times when the pressure came on really, really strong and then you had to juggle your elements. It was a big learning experience for me.

AS: When you did prep for *Resident Evil: Extinction* did you play the video game a lot? Do you watch a lot of movies for reference?

EC: I think that the film *Resident Evil: Extinction* had a different visual feeling from the rest of the saga visually because I did not play the game very much. We had an expert on the game in Paul Anderson. He produced and also directed a small part of the film. For me it was a film about destruction. You know, a post-apocalyptic film. I viewed a lot of real war references, of a lot of abandoned places, a lot of earthquakes' aftermath.

And then obviously I had to see the films that came before and had to follow certain rules. So I knew those basic rules and I saw those films. Especially in order to understand the world of the Umbrella Corporation. Other than those references, I came very virgin to the design phase. The good thing was the exterior world was not really established in the films before. And the film was not really a direct reference to the video game. It's a creature by itself. I just had fun doing it. It's one of those shows where there is a lot of construction. All the sets are full builds. We worked in the desert which was a very good and very tough experience too. The temperatures were very high. This was before *Pan's Labyrinth* got released and I wanted to do one of those studio films in Mexico with a lot of the local departments and crew that we have here. Here in Mexico, we learned a lot of our craft during the 70s. Mexico had a big tradition of film before, back in the 50s and 60s. What they call the Golden Age of Mexican Cinema. But during the 70s and 80s it basically disappeared. A lot of people survived doing a lot of big Hollywood films that would come to Mexico. They would bring the departments heads from Hollywood and they would hire local people

that were then trained in the craft of construction, decoration, scenic painting, greens, production and special effects. I really wanted to make a film here as a Mexican and to work with a lot of these local crews. That was a very important reason I took that film.

AS: Did you work with Patrick Tatopoulos on that?

EC: In the very beginning. Patrick was designing the creatures. We had some contact over the basic concepts early on.

AS: I interviewed him as a production designer– he designed some big movies and then started directing. Do you ever have the desire to start directing yourself?

EC: No. I feel very comfortable with the tools of the production designer. I don't know if this will change–as creators everything always changes a lot! But I still have a lot of things to explore with these tools. A lot of stories to tell with these tools. Design can have a very subtle but profound influence on storytelling.

AS: Do you think design should be invisible or visible? Can it be a character in the movie?

EC: Again, it all depends which project. There are some projects which need spectacle and a big scope while there are others that really need the art department to walk side-by-side with the story-telling in a more subtle way. It all depends on the film. I tend to think that if a film has a solid concept, not just in design but in every single aspect: the cinematography, music, makeup, wardrobe, then it will always be a powerful film whether you notice the production design or not.

AS: What qualities do you think a production designer should have?

EC: First, the ability to work as part of a team. Second, to be able to lead a team. Your enthusiasm needs to be contagious. You have to inspire your crew to follow your dream. Each member of your team has to make a lot of decisions all the time. If they know why you need certain creative concepts defended they will make better decisions too.

AS: What are some qualities that you look for when you're hiring crew?

EC: The most important thing for me in the first meeting is for them to fully understand what I'm trying to do. There are a lot of people with great technical skill and great organizational skills but if they can't grasp your creative ideas then it doesn't work. This is more important than them having a lot of experience.

AS: What advice would you have for people just starting out? Say someone is in a place like Ecuador and they want to get into this business?

EC: I would say continuous work. That's the most important thing. And you have to do a lot of reading and watching films. With the internet you have access to a lot of materials. What you're doing with *Art Stars* is very cool. These interviews help a lot of people who are interested in the craft. In LA you can attend certain seminars and master classes but in a lot of places people interested in this career are all by themselves.

No matter where you are, it's important that your experiences feed into your production design. For example, when you go to an art exhibition, think about what visual decisions were made in order for the art pieces to work. Look at how they chose to do the framing, the lighting, the dressing. Every visual art piece has art direction, the artist decides which objects will live in the space that is shown. In film you're constantly making those same decisions.

> **DESIGN CAN HAVE A VERY SUBTLE BUT PROFOUND INFLUENCE ON STORYTELLING.**

But the most important thing is to work constantly. On small things, on big things, on things that are maybe not ideal, not necessarily the films that you aspire to do. But everything adds to your career and suddenly the addition of all those things gives you the tools, the opportunity, the knowledge, and the experience that you will use later. Doing short films, one of the things that is very easy to lose is the joy component. But you have to try to give the complexity that we were talking about to everything, even if it's something small–and you have to really enjoy what you're doing!

QUALITIES

What qualities should a production designer have?

A compilation of excerpts covering the subject of production designer qualities, taken from the interviews in this book

What do directors and producers need to look for when they are hiring you as a production designer? What characteristics do you need to cultivate to become more competitive in the field? Is it your passion that will get you the job? Your ability to sell ideas? Or is your artistic skill more important? Do you need to be more pragmatic than anyone else? How important is your ability to communicate across departments and get along with everyone? Or maybe you should start with the advice from Sarah Greenwood, John Myhre, and Dennis Gassner: *Know everything about everything...*

RICK CARTER

Being good collaborators both with the directors and the people they hire, production designers should maintain a certain amount of authorship that's not at the expense of someone else. I don't feel diminished by what other people have done on a movie that I have worked on. Usually it enhances what I do.

If you're going to be defensive about that then you've got a big problem. You're going to constantly be in friction with everybody about the size of the budget, the other people who are taking things away from you, the people who are taking credit for things that you think you deserve credit for, the people usurping your job, and you know, you've only got ten toes! So once they step on those ten toes . . . Some directors will step on all ten toes at once the first time you meet them!

For a production designer the most important thing is, if there is something there, enhance it. If there is nothing there, come up with something so that everyone else on the crew from construction to art department to cinematographers to set decorators to producers to location managers and visual effects people all have to have something to do. They have what Zemeckis used to call their "marching orders." Because if you don't, it just spins around and around and the production's just wasting money trying to get going.

JOHN MYHRE

You just need to be aware of everything and look at everything. Every life experience I've ever had has influenced my work. Even just us talking together, having this interview, maybe I'll use something of this in my job at some point. And I just feel I'm the luckiest person in the world. Because this is what I've always wanted to do. When I was a kid I didn't know if I wanted to be an architect or I wanted to be a director and now I found a way that I can be both. Because I get to design the visuals, the architecture, and tell stories with it the way a director tells stories with the actors. Being creative, being open, being excited about what you do, I think those are all great qualities.

SARAH GREENWOOD

You have to know everything about everything, you know what I mean? That's what astounds me. You know, you're standing on top of a mountain and you get asked, *Well, what does a badger hole look like, where do badgers live?* And you go, *I don't know.* You have to know or have a very strong idea of something, kind of an instinctive feel for something. You can't go wrong in whatever you do and wherever you go because it's all going to feed in. Life is always going to kind of feed into what we do.

It's interesting because you look at people coming through and wonder who are going to be the production designers of the next generation. You have ones that come through VFX, you have ones that have come through art directors, theater, set

QUALITIES

decorators. There's room for all sorts of talent. I think the most important thing is understanding the script and understanding the characterization. Really understanding why you're making this film. And then being sanguine enough that you can actually get on with people. And knowing when to shut up!

And it's gotta be fun. If it's not fun then there's no point in doing it. Because it takes so much of your life and energy over. You have to enjoy it. Good and bad you have to enjoy it.

JESS GONCHOR

[Being able to make something out of whatever you get] is the quality. Back in the days of the ancient Greeks or Romans they just had a rock in the sun, so I think that everything that we do is extra.

The more that you can do yourself, and the more that you can identify with the other people who are in your crew, the bigger advantage you're going to have. You're not just somebody walking around with a suit and a tie telling somebody what to do. I know what it's like to sweep the floor and I know what it's like to be on your knees banging nails and working twelve hours digging a ditch. All of those things prepared me for what I do now. *Okay, here's a sheet of plywood. Guess what: we're going to design*

this, that, and this, and we're going to cut off two feet of it and we're going to use those two feet over here to do this...

K.K. BARRETT

I'd say number one is curiosity. Number two is observation. Curiosity, observation, and decisiveness. That belongs, that doesn't belong. We don't need that, we need this. It's the same as being editorial. Making decisions quickly doesn't mean you can't change them. It means it unclutters the way so you can concentrate on things you haven't solved yet, that aren't so obvious to deduce. Setting aside all the quick, easy answers may inform the ones that aren't clear yet.

GRANT MAJOR

I try to stay fresh and stay young. It's a competitive business, it's a speculative business. Try to not pull out the same ideas over and over again. Try to be original and be your own person. Learn how to sell ideas. Ideas go nowhere if you can't get people to buy into them. A lot of it's how you frame ideas and how you pitch them to directors and producers. I've learned a bit of that along the way as well.

Over time I have been getting a lot more confident. I experimented a lot in the early days and learned a lot of lessons and made mistakes and had suc-

What qualities should a production designer have?

cesses. There's no equivalent to just doing it and getting better at it from a technical point of view. People get more confident in you. Your reputation grows so people now can come to you knowing that you can do a project of a size and that you can do it of a standard.

GUY HENDRIX DYAS

One of the most important goals of a production designer is to satisfy a story and a director's vision, so by definition this means that every film should be a completely new experience. Directors are really the ones guiding the way and our aim is to bring their visions to life. I hope my designs appear as different and varied as the films and stories being told. If there's a constant it's perhaps the fact that every film is a learning process and that for designers it's nice to be able to take those experiences, and the things you feel were the most successful, on to your next assignment. After a while you start assembling your own personal bag of tricks.

What I love about our job is that designers can rely on a variety of skills. There really is no one set of qualities that will either ensure you success or failure. If I speak for myself I tend to get excited by projects that are artistically challenging in some way or another. I've realized that for those films you're often asked to create an entire world so it's

good to have a strong vision, a good working ethic, good leadership skills as well as enthusiasm. I don't think people always realize how physical our jobs are, when we're preparing for a shoot there's rarely time to breathe. You have to enjoy that kind of pace.

PATRICK TATOPOULOS

The most important aspect a production designer should have is to first of all put in his mind that he doesn't own the design of the movie. The designer needs to do something very special. The job of the designer is not to bring his own vision to the table, it's to bring the director's vision and that should never be forgotten. Because you don't become a great production designer to a director if you're just trying to impose what you're doing. However, it's great to suggest. It's important to open doors to a director that maybe he hasn't seen. But you never, never forget that this is not your vision, it's the director's vision. I've worked with some very strong visionary directors. If *Dark City* was directed by somebody else it would not look like what it looks like now–and why is that? It's because the director Alex Projas was the man in charge. So I may have put ideas on the table, I may have created some direction for Alex, but ultimately the movie is his and the vision is his. That to me is the single most important thing for a designer to remember:

QUALITIES

that that vision is the vision of the director. And this means that you have to be able to communicate properly with this person.

NATHAN CROWLEY

I always believe you should be a jack of all trades. You have to have a love of design. The love of story. You have to love film. Films like David Lean's *Great Expectations* affected me. To me I get a lot of my inspiration from artists. Exhibitions. Museums. You have to be aware of the world. You should always be looking. It's about being adventurous. How can you describe something visually? Really engage someone *emotionally* through visuals? How can you do that? I think my strong point is scale. Sarah Greenwood's strong point is color. We all come to it from a different perspective.

I like being able to do things myself. I can get into a film before we start preproduction. I can explore it. I like not having to have a ton of people around to begin with. All the tools should just come naturally like a writer using a pen to write, you should just be able to access them. It helps you move faster.

DANIEL NOVOTNY

You gotta be able to draw. You have to be able to tell somebody how something will look on paper. However you want to do that. Drafting is a key, key, skill. You gotta know about lenses, lens sizes.

I think it's really important to know about the way that they're going to shoot something. If they're going to shoot it with a long lens or a wide lens. You gotta know a little bit about lighting. You gotta know how you're going to light your practicals, but also it's important to know how the DP is going to light it and where he's going to hide his lights.

Those are all things that you learn over time. But if a kid is just coming into the business, the important thing is you gotta know how to draw.

It's also really important to have a certain disconnect from what you think is right. A lot of production designers are artists before they're production designers. But you have to remember that this is a business above anything. And that's the only reason we have a job. It's not the business of selling fine art. You're getting paid to design sets that need to be shot by somebody, so it's really a business about creating environments that can be shot.

EUGENIO CABALLERO

First, the ability to work as part of a team. Second, to be able to lead a team. Your enthusiasm needs to be contagious. You have to inspire your crew to follow your dream. Each member of your team has to make a lot of decisions all the time. If they know why you need certain creative concepts defended they will make better decisions too.

What qualities should a production designer have?

JACK FISK

I would say passion. And I think if you have passion about what you're doing you may end up staying up all night. Once I hear about a film, my mind starts working and there's no way of shutting it off, even if I'm not physically up all night. Once I tune into a project I don't think about anything else.

PATRICE VERMETTE

You have to be curious. That's the main thing. You have to be a psychologist. You have to be hands-on. You never know when you have to jump in and roll up your sleeves and start moving things. You have to be a good leader of a team.

. . . Also, lazy people shouldn't go into production design. Lazy people shouldn't think about doing any job in the art department! . . .

Do it with your passion . . . It's the drive, it's the fuel. On days you feel tired that passion has to push you to try to go further, to go the extra mile. It's the passion that drives you. It's the motor of everything. If you're not passionate, even in life, you're wasting your time on earth!

DAVID WARREN

Tireless energy. And I think a designer needs a wide life experience. An appreciation of a lot of different things. You can bring very eclectic references to the table. You need imagination. There are certain personality traits that some designers use that get them through films easier than others. The ability to judge people really well–who's working for you and also who you're working with. Obviously situations arise when you've gotta fight your corner or you've gotta let it go.

The biggest one is always taste. Just good taste. And by that I mean, whether you're doing dragons flying through the air or just a salt and pepper pot on a table top, you still need to know that looks better than that! That's really what it boils down to.

KIM SINCLAIR

Everybody in the art department needs the same skill set: to be artistic and practical. Our role is to help the director tell a story. I'm amazed how many people I meet in the film industry who aren't driven by that narrative. Everything we do should be helping tell the story. What color is this curtain? If you're choosing a color at random or because it looks nice you're not doing your job as far as I'm concerned. What's the director doing in this scene, what's the set doing, what's the point of it? Is it a comedy? Is it a film noir? The decisions you make are narrative-driven. So I do think that needs to be part of your makeup to be successful in the art department. And you have to be able to

QUALITIES

think abstractly but also be practical and be able to deliver things on time and on budget. There are a lot of really talented artists out there but my God I wouldn't want them in the art department. You might employ them for the art department but you wouldn't want them in it!

EVE STEWART

You have to work all the time! You have to be so fascinated by everything because you're doing everything from what the wheels are like on a carriage to what they're eating. What the lighting is, controlling the colors, working with the camera-man, the director, the costume designer, and the makeup designer as well. I think it's very interesting that one minute you're drawing a picture and the next minute someone's throwing three million quid at you to hire carpenters and painters and everything. You've got to be a good politician as well. And good at adding up!

RICK HEINRICHS

The most important thing is communication. This also involves selecting people who can hear what you say. Having a good idea is also key . . . Tremendously hard work is also part of it. I work many hours at it in a day.

It's also about how you manage your fear about the trials you're going through. How far do you dare go down a path that might prove to be a dead-end? You play chicken with yourself a bit. There's a mind-game aspect to it that you've got to keep aware of and stay on top of. There's the art-intense focus that you're in the middle of and there's also the id and the ego–you've got to watch yourself too! Apart from that it's easy–anyone can do it!

RALPH EGGLESTON

The ability to make adjustments on the fly is one of a production designer's key attributes. And also, most of the folks I know that have done the job of production designer are interested in so many things. That's also really important. A lot of it comes from the joy of doing research. I love doing research. Doing the research for every film I've gotten to work on is like a four year graduate course in the subject matter of that film.

JOSEPH T. GARRITY

You've got to be a little crazy. And you've got to also realize that there's a deadline. You've got to be good with deadlines. You've got to be good with budgets. And you've got to be a good people person because you've got to get up there and sell an idea and do that well. 'Cause there's a lot of money that people are going to let you spend to do something. And you want to be clear and excited and be able to stand behind your idea and sell it well visually. You've got to be a problem-solver too. You

What qualities should a production designer have?

want to be the person who says, Okay, here's what we do. There are directors that need a lot more hand-holding and there are directors that are going to be very, very in-your-face. So you've got to be able to adapt. Some designers are very quiet and just do as they're told. The better designers have great ideas and solve problems and come up with great solutions.

ADAM STOCKHAUSEN

I think that communication is really important. My goal is to be making good scenery but also to be communicating the entire time what I'm doing so that when the day comes to shoot, the director and the cinematographer and everybody else comes to the set and looks around and says, *Great! This is exactly what I was expecting to see. Because I saw pictures of it yesterday. Because I had a discussion with you a few weeks ago and I've been totally on board with this direction.* To be a successful designer who

delivers that, you have to be good at having those ideas, communicating them, and pulling together a strong art department who can pull it off. Running your team in an efficient manner so that things are done in a timely way so that you can be showing these things before the last possible second when you have to shoot it and you don't have a choice anymore. Everything that it takes to get to that point is what it takes to do this successfully.

DENNIS GASSNER

Know everything. Take risks. Don't be conventional. Unless it's necessary. Develop a yoga practice too for strength and balance. It's all about strength. You have to be strong to be in this business. I train for every film. Physically train and mentally train for each film. My shoulders carry a lot of weight. And that's an important part of the business. And travel. Travel and learn from the world.

Dennis Gassner

Dennis Gassner's visionary work on *Bladerunner 2049* earned him one of seven Oscar nominations. Of those nominations, he took home an Oscar in '91 for his unique take on the 1940's gangster film *Bugsy*. Before he designed *Bladerunner 2049* or the innovative Sam Mendes war film *1917*, he had been the exclusive James Bond production designer–he created the look for *Quantum of Solace, Skyfall,* and *Spectre.* And before those big budget extravaganzas, he infused the Coen brothers' indie classics *Barton Fink* and *Miller's Crossing* with his unique vision...

AS: What drew you to the field of production design?

DG: My journey began in Vancouver, British Columbia and took me to Portland, Oregon; Eugene, Oregon; then on to Berkeley and Los Angeles. I've pretty much covered the West Coast. I was studying architecture at the University of Oregon when I went to see this technicolor film by David Lean, *Lawrence of Arabia.* It was my first Cinema-Scope film. The scale of it was so enormous and the power of the film was so awe-inspiring I said, *Who was the architect of that?* I wanted to know more and to investigate the field of production design so I took my van and my two-year-old daughter and my wife and we moved to LA. I went to the Art Center School of Design, the old school on Third and Highland, and I connected to that world of thinking. They'd just started the film program and I got to make short movies. There was also graphic design and fine arts, transportation design and advertising design. It was thinking beyond anything that I'd experienced before, in a multitude of facets.

AS: You were making short films on Super 8 or Super 16?

DG: Yes, Super 8. For the students with no money we did one-reelers. Three minutes of film every week. One-word subjects. The teacher was a French cinematographer. It was a very simple format because film can be so overwhelming. The point was, *How do you tell a story in three minutes?* You had to shoot three minutes, uncut, and tell a story.

AS: The teacher provided a one-word title?

DG: Correct. "Frenzy" was an interesting one. I thought, *How do I convey that?* I asked one of the local students if he knew of an orchard. He said his uncle had an orange farm. I asked, *Do you hap pen to know if he has a bee swarm there?* It turned out his uncle actually had one. *Would he mind if I came up and filmed it?* So I went out there with my camera. There were only a couple of cameras in the department. All fixed lenses. And I went up and met the owner and he said, *Well, there are two ways you can do this. You can either wear a bee-keepers's outfit or you can go in without the beekeeper's outfit.* I'd seen a swarm when I was a young boy. So I had a sense of it. He told me the bees aren't going to bother you because they're just circling the queen to make sure she's happy. That's what the movement is–to find a new nest. I said, *That's perfect.*

AS: No bee-keeper outfit?

DG: No. I walked all the way into the swarm and the bees came all over me. I walked into the center where it became totally black. Just bees all over me and the camera. And I slowly walked back out. So it was a track-in and a track-out. And that was my movie *Frenzy*.

> **PRODUCTION DESIGN IS ALL ABOUT THINKING. AND TO ME THE BOTTOM LINE IS STORY. WHAT IS THE STORY? . . . TELL THE STORY. HOW DO YOU TELL A STORY IN THE MOST BEAUTIFUL WAY YOU POSSIBLY CAN?**

So, what that school taught me to do was how to think. How to think about solving problems. I've been using this technique since. Production Design is all about thinking. And to me the bottom line is story. What is the story? What is the story in "Frenzy"? Tell the story. How do you tell a story in the most beautiful way you possibly can?

AS: Did you ever think of becoming a director?

DG: Being a production designer is being a director. I'm directing the visuals.

AS: What was your path from doing those three minute shorts to working on Hollywood movies?

DG: At Art Center I met a like-minded guy who had heard about a feature. He was at Art Center on the G.I. Bill. He'd been a helicopter gunner pilot in 'Nam. He came to me one day and said, *I heard* *about a film that's going to be starting soon and we're going to work on it.* And I said, *Great, fantastic. What is it?* He said it was called *Apocalypse Now.* And he figured out how to get on it. He took me along in his wake.

AS: Into the Art Department?

DG: He got in through the production side. He wanted to be a producer and I wanted to be a designer. Dean Tavoularis was the production designer and Dean became my mentor. They needed a dossier designed. Martin Sheen's character received a dossier with information from the CIA. I designed and manufactured all of it, all of Brando's character's history. Sheen's character needed to get bits and pieces of information as he went up the river. To get a sense of who Brando's character is before he meets him. So I designed a lot of different graphics throughout the course of the film and mailed them to the Philippines. Often they got lost in transit.

AS: They were shooting in the Philippines?

DG: Yes. And I was in LA sending them materials. I had family. But Doug went in. He rang them up and said, *If I fly my way to the Philippines will you give me a job as a PA?* And they said yes. He paid his own way to get out there. He ended up becoming the First Assistant Director.

AS: That's amazing he moved up so fast.

DG: That was the attrition on the film. People kept falling off. Because it was just too hard.

AS: I saw that *Hearts of Darkness* documentary about the making of Apocalypse Now...

DG: That was accurate. Doug stayed because of his tenacity and his willingness to tell the story. And the story was pretty amazing.

AS: You were hired based on some graphics experience you had?

DG: I had graphic design skills because of Art Center. The advertising department, graphic design. I'm a calligrapher, I'm a painter, I'm a potter, I've sculpted. Everything. Built a lot of things as well. I knew a production designer needed to do everything.

AS: Production design was your goal back then?

DG: The goal was to build big worlds. I didn't want to be stuck to one thing. I wanted to go into lots of different things. Being on *Apocalypse Now* with Dean and the art department was the catalyst. Angelo Graham. Jim Murakami. Alex Tavoularis, our illustrator, who was also Dean's brother. And then myself as the graphic designer. Subsequent to finishing the film someone said, *Well, we need a poster.* And everyone just turned to me. That was the first film poster I ever designed.

AS: You designed the poster for *Apocalypse Now?*

DG: Yes. Out of the fact that in the group I was the only one with graphic design skills.

AS: What did you learn from Dean Tavoularis?

DG: Well, Dean had worked at Disney before he

made *Bonnie and Clyde*. As a young man he was an in-betweener. The master animators would draw the keyframes and he would do all the in-between ones. What he learned was how to tell a story. Draw the story in between the two moments. So structurally he had storytelling in his DNA.

After we did *Apocalypse Now* we went to do a period film set in 1927 San Francisco. Wim Wenders came to the United States to do a film about Dashiell Hammett the writer. I remember starting the process with Dean. He put 3″ x 5″ hand-written cards on the wall, tracking the entire film from the first scene to the last scene. It was storytelling in words that we applied images to.

AS: Nathan Crowley also told me about creating a wall showing the arc of a film's story visually.

DG: Nathan had been Alex Tavoularis's art director! Alex had the same system. In fact, Nathan and I were at the Academy Awards one year and we talked about it and he said, *Of course, it all came from Dean*. It's the way that the movie company can see the film first. In a visual narrative form.

AS: Is the wall imagery culled from a myriad of sources?

DG: It starts out with research. It starts with the script and then you break the script down. You apply visuals from your research to the literal form. Like scene one of *Bladerunner 2049*: a flight from LA. The solar panels start to trickle off as they go into deeper desert. As you get away from LA you get a science fiction feeling graphically. Knowing

what it was specifically didn't matter because it had a feeling. Method design, where it has to resonate emotionally. That's what Dean had. Dean didn't really talk a lot about it. But what I saw was emotion start to hit the wall. Everyone in the art department had it because they'd done so many films with him. There was this kind of shorthand. I just sat there and listened. Dean always had exquisite taste. Emotional taste.

EVERYTHING IS ARCHITECTURE TO ME.

AS: Emotion was a big part of it?

DG: The emotion was most of it. A film can look like a dystopian world but there's always an emotional context behind it. The emotion applies itself in a structure. And then from structure comes the color. The set decorator's input into the emotional side is a synchronistic thing too. You find someone who is like-minded and has a great sense of style.

AS: Some people talk about cracking the code of a movie. They do a lot of research and at some point they "crack the code." Do you ever feel there is a certain "a-ha moment?"

DG: I do that before I even start. When I'm meeting with the director. The first thing after we have our chit-chat. I said to Denis [Villeneuve, *Bladerunner 2049* director], *If you can imagine one word that would describe the film what would that be?*

And Denis kind of paused and he said, *Brutality.* What are we going to do with that word? We're going to take it and start with the Spinner from the original film. We spent a lot of time developing the new Spinner. Ryan was in it more than any other set. We wanted to honor the first film but the original Syd Mead Spinner had a softness to it. We needed to make it much harder and more robust. It's got to be a tough-looking piece of equipment with enough strength to combat not only the rain but the snow and other elements. Extremely functional and also very beautiful at the same time. When you look at the film it actually is really beautiful but in a brutal way. Finding that balance is what I'm always looking for.

But "cracking the code" sounds like a safe thing. I call it *Pattern Language*. *Pattern Language* is an architectural term. There's an amazing book titled *A Pattern Language* on creating the language of architecture. Everything is architecture to me. Any time you start to organize something that's going to be functional that's an architectural element. Furniture or a house. The book *A Pattern Language* defines creating your own visual language. When we talk, a lot of people don't understand what we're talking about because it's our own language. It's not a privileged language. It's just a learned language. A language of details.

AS: Do you use the same process on every project?
DG: Every time. But the first time I ever used this process it was kind of a spontaneous thing. It was when I was doing *Miller's Crossing,* my first Coen Brothers' film. Joel and Ethan are Minneapolis

boys. T-Shirts and jeans, big hair. We were in this strange little hotel room. I'd read their screenplay the first time and shut the script and said, *That's amazing but I have to read it again.* It was the language of the 1927 gangster world with dark humor woven into it. I read it a second time and I said, *I have to do this film.* And so I met with them and we talked a little bit about my history and so on. And they said, *What do you think of the script?* I told them, *I'd really like to do this movie but I have a question. I've come up with one word that could be a touchstone. When we get in the fray we can always go back to that one word. And if we can agree on that, it would be fantastic. The word is "Columns."*

Ethan looked at me. He was quitting smoking so he had a toothpick in his mouth. He looked at me and then they both came and sat down. They kind of looked at each other and then he said, *Yes!*

I said, *Good! Now we can start!*

The word "Columns" came from a question to myself, What was *Miller's Crossing?* And of course it was the forest.

AS: Like the trees are columns?
DG: And it's also a big dick movie. It's all about men. Gangsters. "My dick's bigger than your dick." So I put columns in every set. Some form of column in every set. Some small, like candlesticks.

AS: This was all inspired by the script?
DG: Yes. But when I first read the script it was like

an arcane, foreign language to me. Arcane gangster phrases like, *What's the rumpus?* It takes you a while to get tuned to it. The Coen brothers wove the layers of dialogue together to make this beautiful language almost like Shakespeare. Normally I'm going to be a certain percentage behind the actors and the dialogue, but I have to push even further back now because if one little nuance of language is missed you miss so much. So I'm going to push back even further. To give more room for the dialogue to be accepted. If I push too far forward then I could disturb that. I really, really muted the pallet back. Which also set the tone for the period.

AS: Do you remember the very first moment you decided to become a designer?

DG: It was when I was five. My father and his twin brother were building our family home in Oregon. I had so much energy and it was so exciting seeing saws and lumber going up. I said, *Daddy I need a job!* And he gave me a little tin cup. He said, *If there's a nail that drops down in the dirt go down and get it.* And ping! there was a nail. So I stood there with my little tin cup full of nails and he said, *Well, give me one.* I handed one to him and he said, *It's bent. Here's a hammer–go straighten it out.* So bang, bang, bang, bang and I showed it to him and he said, *It's not straight yet.* Bang, bang, bang, and he said, *Well, it's straighter but it's not straight.* Bang, bang, bang and he took it and said, *Good.* He took it and banged it into the wood. And that's the first time I ever built anything.

My father taught me a few things. It's gotta be a straight nail. It's got to be structurally sound. Even though it's damaged it doesn't matter, you can always get things back. In that one moment so much of who I am became part of me.

AS: When you're hiring your crew what do you look for?

DG: How a person feels.

> **TO BE A DESIGNER YOU HAVE TO BE A TEACHER. I TEACH EVERY DAY.**

AS: You know right away?

DG: Yeah, I'm good at reading things. I've been doing this a long time. Elon Musk says when someone walks in a room he knows almost before they start talking what it's going to be like. It's a people business and you have to learn how to read people really well in order to understand first of all what their problems are. And what they can do for you and how you can help them. And to me, to be a designer you have to be a teacher. I teach every day.

AS: When you're doing a movie with a huge budget are there people from the studio who voice opinions or do you mainly just engage with the director?

DG: The director. Although on the Bond films I deal with the producers whom I adore. Barbara Broccoli, Michael Wilson. They are integral to the team. They have the most knowledge because they were born into the franchise. But to me the designer, the director and the cinematographer make this incredible triangle. Like on *Skyfall* with Sam Mendes and DP Roger Deakins. The nice thing about a triangle is that if there's a question that has to be resolved between three people you can resolve it easier than with two. Because there's strength in that triangle.

AS: I talked to Sarah Greenwood and she described how when she did the *Sherlock Holmes* movies the actor Robert Downey Jr. saw her set and said, *It's great but I'd have swords on the wall and weapons all around.*

DG: If you have a really good set decorator and a really good propmaster, the actors will be invited to come look and have the choices of that. It's part of my job as well to make sure they understand the game that we're playing and they can make those choices. Don't wait until the last minute. Don't wait until they come on set and say, *I want to change this and that.*

But things always change along the way. They change because the narrative changes. Countries change. When I was doing *Skyfall* we'd set up a production company in Shanghai, China. We were going to Shanghai to do a whole sequence there. We had already planned and scouted it. We're back in London months after the scout and the budget came in from Shanghai. It was way over what we had. Barbara and Michael came into my office and said, *What are we going to do?* I said, *That's okay let's just build it here.* So we built all of that at Pinewood.

I did invite fourteen Chinese artists to come build. And it was a beautiful scene. That was going to be done in a temple just outside of Shanghai. There's always another way of cutting it.

The same thing happened again on the same film with India. We planned a whole sequence in India and they came back with a similar number. And Barbara said, *What are we going to do?* And I said, *Let's go to Istanbul.* It was the rooftop sequence in the opening of *Skyfall*. Bond crashes down into the Grande Bazaar. All that was done in Istanbul and the Turks were amazing. They just opened up their doors to us and it changed a big part of their culture. That's why I love doing film.

I did the same thing in Mexico City when we created the Day of the Dead for *Spectre*. You can take a big name franchise like Bond and come in and really help the community. And I said to the ministry of tourism in Mexico City, *I want to help you guys change the way the world sees Mexico. Let's do it through the arts. Through the art of your culture. I'm going to design it but you're the experts. You build this.* I sent them all the plans and they built all of it and it was an amazing sequence. And I said, *After filming I'm going to give you everything to store and bring back next year for your own Day of the Dead.* The following year someone said, *You should see this YouTube clip.* It was the Minister of Tourism on the Day of the Dead the following year saying, *We thank the Bond crew! We've had hundreds of thousands of people come in to Mexico City to celebrate.*

AS: That's an amazing way to give to a community.

DG: That's always been my approach to filmmaking. Enrich the people in whatever community you're in. Leave it the same or better. Hopefully better, and let them have an experience. They're our audience. They are the people that are going to be telling their family and their extended family to go see the film. They all worked so hard and here's the end result.

AS: In contrast to most film work, in episodic one often has to do a big design presentation to the network. On these big tentpole movies like the Bonds are you ever asked to do a big presentation to the producers?

DG: No, I don't do that. The presentation is the wall.

AS: And your wall is the concept art showing the story in chronological order almost like storyboards or a graphic novel?

DG: Yes. Concept art. Some set design pieces, some 3D modeling and so on.

AS: How about the research, say for the 1920s? Or other references you use for inspiration?

DG: That's in a different place. My researcher does that. I have a wonderful assistant. She has good intuition. I tell her, *I'm thinking about this and this and this today* and bang: ten to twelve images arrive on my computer. And I look at them and then maybe out of five or six images I get a piece of something.

AS: Something sparks . . .

DG: That's all you need. Because there's always so much information you're dealing with throughout your day. You need time to generate the ideas. And I'll do little teeny sketches. I don't draw elaborately anymore. There are people who do that so well. I do a two minute sketch and give it to a concept artist and have him work on it for three days. It comes back and it's amazing. So you keep circulating that information within the concept department and the 3D department and allow it to nurture itself. Then I just follow up, *Adjust this, and this, and this*. And eventually it gets there.

AS: Does your team do physical models?

DG: Sure. White cards.

> **KNOW EVERYTHING. TAKE RISKS. DON'T BE CONVENTIONAL. DEVELOP A YOGA PRACTICE FOR STRENGTH AND BALANCE. IT'S ALL ABOUT STRENGTH. YOU HAVE TO BE STRONG TO BE IN THIS BUSINESS. I TRAIN FOR EVERY FILM.**

AS: You're talking about foam core models?

DG: Yes. I call them white cards. That's just to get volume up. You do 3D models and the concept artists take them and paint them and that gives you some volume. My staff will do all of them as white cards. So the director can actually get down into it. Lipstick cams for the fly-throughs. So they can feel what it's like. Of course as we start to build I always invite them to come down and get a sense of it and see the process. And then the day before shooting I invite them. Everything is done and dressed and that's where the magic begins.

AS: So the director and the producers will come and see it as you're working on it?

DG: Always. There's no reason not to have them come. They're paying for it and it's their movie ultimately. Everybody should be involved with the process. The director sees where it's going and they get excited about it. When they come in I want to hear one word, *Wow.*

AS: That's the goal.

DG: I say it to myself when I come in once everything's decorated! We finally walk away from it and then come back in. Of course the thing that we don't usually have at that moment is the lighting. However, what I like about working with Roger Deakins is that with Roger we're integrating the lighting as we go.

AS: He comes to the set as you're building it...

DG: That's part of why *Bladerunner 2049* looked the way it did. We integrated all the lighting. Roger Deakins saw our work and his lighting scheme was in concert with what we were doing. This is the luxury of having a big production. That's why films are so powerful when you have the time and the finances to support them.

We built eighty-five percent of *Bladerunner 2049* as physical, scale models. WETA also did massive model work. I like that technique because it gives volume, especially for lighting, The lighting is the trickiest side and it sets the reality. You can extend off of that and the digi guys can come in and sweeten it. They have all the perfect references. But the lighting always gives it away. Our book, *The Art and Soul of Bladerunner 2049* tells the whole story.

AS: That's an amazing book! Speaking of concept art, what was your interaction with the futurist from the original *Bladerunner* movie, Syd Mead? Aside from revamping his Spinner design . . .

DG: Syd did concepts for us for the Vegas environment. Denny wanted him to be involved. He did Syd Mead stuff and we reorganized it. It was great to have him involved.

AS: Do you ever have the fear that when you leave your film in the hands of VFX artists in post production that they might alter your vision?

DG: I give everybody a document. *Just follow the document.* That's their foundation. It's digital–a PDF of all the concept art, scene by scene by scene.

AS: How do you see the field of production design changing in the future? Do you see films becoming all virtual reality?

DG: Something will come out of virtual reality but I don't think anyone knows what it is yet.

AS: What about a situation where you're watching a scene take place in front of you in virtual reality and you hear a noise behind you so you turn your head and you can see another movie sequence unfolding in the world behind you?

DG: It's a gimmick. It's a great piece of technology but the future is still just telling good stories. Finding good stories and styling them in the proper way so that the environments and the lighting and performances all tell the story. That's all.

AS: Any thoughts you have for someone trying to get into the field of production design?

DG: Having the strength of a strong mentor is important. In my case it was Dean Tavoularis. Production designer Rick Carter and I are good mates and we talk about this a lot. His mentor was Dick Sybert. Dick and Dean were the two top guys when I was coming in. *The Godfather, Chinatown* and so on. Both interesting minds. And bravo to you for doing the *Art Stars* blog because it's also like a great mentorship.

AS: Thank you! Is there a difference in your process between working on big tentpole movies versus more independent Coen Brothers films?

DG: You take the advantage of your circumstances. The budget you're allowed. You can't build a lot if you don't have any money. Everything to me is a logical presentation. You have to justify it. Because the justification says, *You spend this amount of money.* You have to spend money to make money. The producers are just looking at the back-end bottom line.

AS: And they're looking to spend as little money as possible.

DG: Exactly. But if we, the art department, the director, the cinematographer, are united in what

our wishes are then that's a force. And that force has to be unified to find the path.

AS: What characteristics would you say are good to have as a production designer?

DG: Know everything. Take risks. Don't be conventional. Unless it's necessary. Develop a yoga practice too for strength and balance. It's all about strength. You have to be strong to be in this business. I train for every film.

WHEN THEY COME IN I WANT TO HEAR ONE WORD, *WOW.*

AS: Physically train?

DG: Physically train and mentally train for each film. My shoulders carry a lot of weight. And that's an important part of the business. And travel. Travel and learn from the world.

AS: Any advice to avoid the mistakes and pitfalls?

DG: Do all the things I just told you and you won't make any mistakes.

AS: What do you love about production design?

DG: I love the whole process. This comes from way back. From listening to Dean Tavoularis talk about the Godfathers and about The Conversation and about other classic films and how they were all put together. The uniqueness of the filmmaking process. You work so hard but then you sit in the cinema and there it is. It's an extraordinary thing. It's one of the most amazing art forms we have.

Sarah Greenwood

Production design doesn't get any better than Sarah Greenwood's interpretation of London for Guy Ritchie's *Sherlock Holmes* films. She gave us a lived-in, layered city full of texture and grit with a perfect meld of style and realism. Her work with director Joe Wright on period movies such as *Atonement* and *Pride and Prejudice* is stunning. Then, in a dramatic show of range, she created the unforgettable candy-colored world of Greta Gerwig's *Barbie.* When we talked, she had been scouting in Russia for Joe Wright's *Anna Karenina,* for which she has since received one of her six Oscar nominations to date.

AS: You just got back from Switzerland for *Sherlock Holmes: A Game of Shadows* and Russia for *Anna Karenina*. Do you ever find locations yourself or does the location department always provide you a selection to pick from?

SG: It depends on the show. I work very closely with a location manager called Adam Richards. I've worked with him on *Pride and Prejudice*, *Atonement*, *Sherlock*, and we work really well together. When

you're looking for something that's off the beaten track that you can't find in books I very much like to go out early days and just get a sense of it. Then Adam will carry on with his scouts and look further.

On *Atonement* the big house that we shot in for six weeks we found by going through the archives of *Country Life* with my set decorator. We were looking at old photos of 1930's houses–the things that you won't find in books. We found this article about this house, and then we went to have a look at it. We ended up using it and it was fantastic.

AS: There was a stark contrast in *Atonement* between the country house and wartime Dunkirk. You went from a colorful to a desaturated palette and then there was red associated with Cecilia and green in the house. Is color-design a big part of your work on a film?

SG: It is, actually. And you use it many different ways. Interestingly, green is a color I tend to stay clear of, and to use the amount of green we used in the house in *Atonement* was not what I would normally do. But it's a decision that we made. Like the green of the corridor and that kind of arsenic green of the servants' area. We referenced a fantastic house called Tyntesfield where the walls were painted that arsenic green. It's like you wouldn't have dared to use it had you not seen it with your own eyes. So yes, that green was a very specific color in the house and in that whole first part, the garden and the lake and Keira's dress. Joe wanted a dress that was what he called "paddy green." It was a very vibrant kind of Irish green. The dress was incredible. Very bold and very much a statement on Joe's and [costume designer] Jacqueline Durran's part as well.

And that house was a listed house but it wasn't National Trust–it was empty. The woman who had inherited it had to sell off all the furniture to pay for the roof and other renovations so it really was a blank canvas. There was no furniture in it and there was no wallpaper, there was nothing. It wasn't derelict but it was empty. Which was just brilliant for us and we just moved in.

> **" THE MOST IMPORTANT THING IS UNDERSTANDING THE SCRIPT AND UNDERSTANDING THE CHARACTERIZATION. REALLY UNDERSTANDING WHY YOU'RE MAKING THIS FILM. AND THEN BEING SANGUINE ENOUGH THAT YOU CAN ACTUALLY GET ON WITH PEOPLE.**

AS: You always wonder how many locations were like that and how much was brought in.

SG: It varies. On *Pride and Prejudice* we did this whole thing to the Bennett House that was a listed house so you couldn't touch the walls. What we ended up doing was kind of cladding the hall and some of the stairs and then building within the room. We rebuilt all the paneling, within the room, so we could paint it. Which was quite extreme. Ordinarily you might have built that on a stage because the interior was quite small, but Joe wanted the interior and the exterior to work together. That was just such a fantastic house. And again, it wasn't lived in so we were given kind of carte blanche as long as we didn't affect the actual fabric of the building.

AS: In *Sherlock Holmes*, his amazing office doesn't feel like a set–it feels like an actual place.

SG: What was interesting there was the set had to say so much about *Sherlock*. Every single thing had to have a reason and a rationale. So we dressed it and we showed it to Robert and he just said, I want more. The philosophy was that he would have rented those rooms and that the wall-coverings and the key pieces of furniture would all be in there from Mrs. Hudson. And then it's what Sherlock did to the room. Which is deconstruct it in a way and then layer it up with all the things that he would have done: past cases, rationales, disguises, you just build on and on and on. Frankly what we've done on *Sherlock 2* [*Sherlock Holmes: A Game of Shadows*] is even more extreme! I looked at that set and I didn't know how they could shoot it. Because you couldn't walk in it, let alone take a camera in there. They did. And also Philippe Rousselot is an amazing DP. The way he works with the set and the way he lights really brings it to life.

AS: Is the second *Sherlock* in a similar color palette, with a similar feel?

SG: What we're not doing is we don't stay in London quite so much. We move to Europe. And as opposed to the first *Sherlock* where we stayed in London and we kept coming back to Baker Street, on this next one we are constantly moving forward. You know, we go to Paris, then we go to Germany, and we end up in the Alps, and so down and dirty industrial London doesn't feature as much. You obviously get a sense of it but it's not part of the story as much. As far as the feel goes, in some parts we go quite light in colors. We end up in the

Alps at the top of a mountain at a fortress which we had to build. We shot in Strasbourg about three days but the rest of it we shot in the UK. The rest of the journey across Europe, I'm not joking, we shot within twenty-five miles of London. In fact this weekend they're up in Wales. It worries me extremely that they're up in Wales shooting a sequence that's supposed to take them from Paris to Germany! You've got to keep off the hill because otherwise it will look like Wales.

AS: Nowadays, because of tax incentives in the U.S., states like Georgia and Louisiana are doubling for many other locations that look nothing like Georgia and Louisiana.

SG: When I was over in LA working on *The Soloist* with Joe I remember I was having an argument with an accountant about how we have to go to Cleveland to shoot a small sequence in Cleveland. I was saying, *We have to go to Cleveland because it's so different from LA,* and they were arguing with me saying, *Well, you'll go where we tell you to shoot.*

And I go, *Well, hang on a minute, since when has that happened?* On *Sherlock* we could have afforded to go to Paris and Germany and everything but the whole thing was we only had Robert for a very limited amount of time and we didn't have the time in the schedule to be doing him traveling. And the risks of traveling in the snow–either having no snow or getting snowed in. So you really have to think hard about how you can make it work doing it in London. I'm really interested to see how it turns out.

AS: How is it to work in London compared to other places you've worked like Prague and Finland and Morocco and now Russia?

SG: From my point of view London is fantastic because it's home. It still has a very strong kind of film structure here. At the moment we are swamped with too much work. And last year was the same. You know, finding studio space, fighting for crew. When you go to all the prop-houses, you know, you're constantly doing deals with colleagues working on other films. *If you get that back in time we'll give you this if you give us that.* It is like a kind of bartering system. London is fantastic for filmmaking. England as a whole is very good for filmmaking–there's an incredible variety of landscapes and architecture.

AS: When you go abroad do you bring crews or use local people?

SG: We brought British crews to Morocco and to Finland as well. We used German crews in Berlin. We were out of Babelsberg Studios, which, between you and I, was not a marriage made in heaven for me.

AS: Working with Guy Ritchie and Joe Wright–are those guys very visual?

SG: Do you know something–they're polar opposites. They both have a fantastic kind of vision. I would say Joe is very visual and working with him is a real treat. But equally Guy is very visual and very appreciative of what you give him.

Guy had never done period. You say to him, *Don't worry about that, let's do the story. The actual practicalities of the visual will come.* The authenticity had to be absolutely as spot-on as we could make it to allow that madness to come within it.

On this *Sherlock* we've done a ball like in an old Hollywood movie of the 40's. A ball with a hundred and fifty extras and amazing ball gowns and uniforms. Then you put in Holmes and Watson dancing together and that's what makes it funny. It wouldn't be funny if the ball was comic in any other way. So as mad as launching the ship in the first one was when you read it on the page, (you just felt, *Well, that will get cut!* and of course it didn't!)–as mad as that was, it had to be completely real and potentially believable. We didn't want to do the Jules Verne version, it had to not be fantasy. The story was fantastic but it couldn't be fantasy. So in that sense it was great, the very extreme, contrasting environments that you have with *Sherlock.* Whereas working with Joe is much more cerebral and atmospheric and intellectual I suppose. So I love working with both.

AS: Did you work closely with visual effects? Like with the bridge sequence on *Sherlock Holmes*?

SG: Yes, that was very interesting for me because I hadn't done big CG movies before and didn't know a whole lot about it. Chas Jarrett was the effects supervisor and he was fantastic to work with. He demystifies it, for a start. What I particularly liked about the first *Sherlock* was your set extensions. It means the camera can move much more fluidly within a period location. So we do as much as we can and as the camera moves across it you sort of glimpse London beyond. All of that works amazingly.

Where I don't think it works fantastically is where some of the camera moves became not possible, you know what I mean? There's one shot from the bridge where Rachel McAdams comes to the top of the bridge and it's a helicopter shot basically–it just distances you from what you're seeing. I just wonder if there weren't other ways of taking you less out of the process.

But that said, it was a fantastic way of working. We created a library for him of buildings and research and did lots of visuals of what old London should look like. And then they went out and photographed it and put it together. There's always places where you think, *That's too extreme, you don't need to go that big and wide,* but that's just my personal taste. And Joel Silver and Guy want it really big and that's what they got. But interestingly for a lot of the critics that was one comment they had, that some CGI went a bit too extreme. That is what the producers wanted as opposed to what Chas and I necessarily would have said. But it's very exciting to have that technology and not be scared of it.

AS: Are you ever involved with visual effects after the end of principal photography?

SG: I can keep an eye on it. I do go in and have a look. For *Sherlock,* we did four weeks work with my illustrator and art director, setting them off into post. In an ideal world I should be on for the whole time with the team. In reality that's the last thing I want. That's not what I do.

The geography of the factories in *Sherlock 2* was as involved as I got, really. We found locations in Germany that we photographed and did visuals for, sort of overall concepts. We've given them potential layouts.

AS: Do you ever build foamcore models or use 3D programs like SketchUp?

SG: Both. I've always made models to different scales and for every set we build we make a model. Even for sets that are going to be digital we sometimes make a model. But interestingly, for the first time we just had this amazing guy Nick Henderson who's a 3D modeler with SketchUp. And having him do the fortress models for various shots was incredibly useful. 3D imaging has been there before but it's never been so easy to use. It's always been such a pain in the ass. It's always taken so long that we've almost built the set by the time they've worked it out.

But this time what he could do was incredible and very fast. Like to position the fortress in the valley. It was literally a kind of wire-frame and you can push it and make that mountain further in. That kind of technology was incredible and worked really well. I mean I'm all for technology when it works. Personally I'm crap with it but I can see what it can do. When somebody knows what they're doing and can do it with ease I think it's great.

Now I know that much more about CGI and how it can work. It's great to be able to get it to Joe with more confidence and to use it more subtly and use it in a way that it will give us more scope. And also it's getting cheaper as well. In the old days you couldn't afford it.

AS: Do you yourself get to do any sketches when you're working on a film?

SG: I scribble. It's called "The Art of Sarah Greenwood." It's basically crap. They photocopy my sketchbook with scrappy plans and ideas. So no, I very much rely on the artistry of my team! I have an amazing illustrator that I work with called Eva Kuntz. She's German and she is brilliant and I've worked with her on the last three or four films. The illustrations we do, they're slightly more "montagey"–do you know what I mean? They're not polished. I really don't like polished, finished illustrations. They're atmospheric, they give the mood of the scene. They're not detailed as such. Maybe they're slightly disproportioned or the perspective is slightly off but you know I quite like that. They're atmospheric, to give a feel. They're not these perfect, glossy, finished pieces. They're done from my initial location photographs, from references, they're the juxtaposition of all sorts. You play with the color and the texture of things. That's a strong tool.

AS: Did you go to art school or to film school?

SG: I went to art school and did theater design. And I worked in theater for three years and then I went to the BBC which was a fantastic training ground. To come up through television is great because you get a real hands-on knowledge of everything. And I've been freelance maybe fifteen years. I actually got my first feature film through a director that I worked with at the BBC doing dramas. And the BBC drama department was and is amazing. You can't want for better training area than that.

> "IF YOU WANT TO BE AN ART DIRECTOR AND YOU'RE STARTING AS AN ART DIRECTOR ASSISTANT THEN BE INTERESTED IN WHAT SET DECS ARE DOING, BE INTERESTED IN CONSTRUCTION, BE INTERESTED IN THE WHOLE PROCESS. GET OUT ONTO THE FLOOR. SEE HOW FILMS ARE MADE. IT'S SUCH AN AMAZING BUSINESS. AGAIN, WHY DO IT IF YOU'RE NOT INTERESTED?

AS: Do you feel production design should be visible or invisible when you're watching a movie?

SG: I think it depends on the film completely. You know I think something like *Sherlock*, that's really in-your-face. Something like *Atonement*, you know the green is very strong but it's atmospheric, it's helping to tell the story. It shouldn't be overriding. But I love films that are so laid-back like Mike

Leigh's where it's all about performance. I don't tend to do that kind of degree of naturalism. In my films it's always pushed slightly.

AS: To have some style . . .

SG: Yes, I think it would be very difficult for me to do something that is just so untouched. A Lars von Trier film is probably not for me to work on. Not that I don't enjoy them. I think as long as it's appropriate to the piece it's great. You know there are films that I won't mention that it's just in there to make a big statement and I think that's gross.

> " YOU HAVE AN ART DEPART-
> MENT OF FIFTY ON *SHERLOCK
> HOLMES* BUT I EXPECT EVERYBODY
> TO HAVE READ THE SCRIPT AND TO
> KNOW WHAT'S GOING ON IN THE
> SCRIPT. AND TO GO OUT AND SEE
> EVERYBODY ELSE'S SETS.

AS: If it takes you out of the story...

SG: Yes, too extreme is too much. You have to be very careful. We often have to pull ourselves back and just say, *Well, that's just a bit much.* Sometimes we fail but I think it's very important to try and get the balance right.

AS: What are some good characteristics of a production designer? Knowing when to pull back in those stylistic choices? What are other characteristics?

SG: You have to know everything about everything, you know what I mean? That's what astounds me.

You know, you're standing on top of a mountain and you get asked, *Well, what does a badger hole look like, where do badgers live?* And you go, *I don't know.* You have to know or have a very strong idea of something, kind of an instinctive feel for something. You can't go wrong in whatever you do and wherever you go because it's all going to feed in. Life is always going to kind of feed into what we do.

It's interesting because you look at people coming through and wonder who are going to be the production designers of the next generation. You have ones that come through VFX, you have ones that have come through art directors, theater, set decorators. There's room for all sorts of talent. I think the most important thing is understanding the script and understanding the characterization. Really understanding why you're making this film. And then being sanguine enough that you can actually get on with people. And knowing when to shut up!

AS: Would you say those are similar requirements for the crew that you hire?

SG: Yes, I think so. I have an amazing crew that I work with. You know some people drop off and we pick out new but generally I have a core team that I always work with and that's brilliant because as prep times get shorter and shorter you need that shorthand with them to get things fast and moving.

It's very much a meritocracy. If you're good at something, then do it. I'm not one for saying, *Oh, they're only an art department assistant, they can't do that.* If they're a fantastic propmaker, or they're fantastic at something, then do it. I'm not hierarchical. Interestingly, my team all tend to come through one particular woman called Moira Tate who used to run Kingston and then she was running a course at the National Film School. I think she's been at the Royal College. I've had loads of people who'd been through her hands. Those were the ones that I really liked working with. Also I really like working with people who have come through TV because it does give them a more egalitarian approach to filmmaking which is the way I like to work.

AS: Would you say it's good to learn from eposidic work because the pace is faster and there are smaller budgets and you have to come up with things quickly?

SG: Yes, absolutely. And also on a TV drama you maybe have got a production designer, an art director and a standby art director and one set decorator and you do everything and you know about everything. It's very important that people do know about everything. How the whole film goes together. You have an art department of fifty on *Sherlock Holmes,* but I expect everybody to have read the script and to know what's going on in the script. And to go out and see everybody else's sets. Don't just work on your tiny little bit and not ever leave the drawing board. Why do what you're doing if that's where you'll be? Be interested in the whole process and the failures and the solutions that we come up with. It's funny because sometimes you'll have people who've worked on the film and they'll go, *My God, I didn't realize it was going to be like that!*

And you go, *Well, hang on a minute, why? You were there with us, you should know everything!*

And it's gotta be fun. If it's not fun then there's no point in doing it. Because it takes so much of your life and energy over. You have to enjoy it. Good and bad you have to enjoy it.

AS: When you get a project and get a script what's one of the first things you do when you're starting in on it?

SG: Which is what I'm doing at the moment, actually. Well, if there's a book that goes with it like *Anna Karenina,* you read the book. I'm reading another fantastic book which is by Orlando Figes called *Natasha's Dance* which is all about Russian society from the 1600s. Why they built St. Petersberg, what Moscow was like, what society was like at the time. Frankly, if you don't know that I don't see how you can understand how Anna Karenina in worked Tolstoy's mind. You have to know that. Whether you choose to use it, to apply it, is up to Joe and myself. But you have to know as much as you can know about the subject. That's even before we start.

And then for me I just get as many visual references as I can. When we came back from Russia we had to buy another suitcase. It was way overweight: forty-two kilos of books I bought in Russia. I can't read any of it because it's all in Russian–they're all visual, pictorial, photographic. So then you go through that and then you start trying to figure it out.

You know at the moment I'm trying to figure out how we can make the UK look like Russia in the snow, which is incredibly difficult.

AS: Are you doing fake snow?

SG: We will be I would imagine. The thing is we did a lot of fake snow on *Hanna* which was a disaster. Not that it was anybody's fault, it's just that fake snow is not as good as real snow. And that's one of the reasons we ended up having to go to Finland on *Hanna*. The snow in Russia is just so exceptional. When we were in St. Petersberg it was packed up ten foot high with more snow on top. And so beautiful and the light is so different. So we will be doing the majority of the snow scenes in Russia.

AS: Do you anticipate bringing your crew to Russia or hiring a local Russian crew?

SG: We'll try not to build too much out there but we will be taking core crew out without a doubt. I've heard it's very corrupt and really expensive. It's more expensive than London, the hotels and everything.

AS: Say someone's starting out in business–any advice to avoid pitfalls?

SG: You just have to be really persistent. Particularly when I'm just starting this project and everyone gets a sniff of it and I have twenty emails a day, or phone calls or texts. Somebody might have texted me three months ago and I go, *I'm not doing anything.* You need to be at the right time, at the right moment.

And just be open-minded and interested. If you want to be an art director and you're starting as an art director assistant then be interested in what set decs are doing, be interested in construction, be interested in the whole process. Get out onto the floor. See how films are made. It's such an amazing business. Again, why do it if you're not interested?

AS: What attracts you first about a project, what would make one more interesting than another?

SG: There are a lot of considerations. There's the practical consideration–I do like to be based out of London. I don't mind filming abroad but I don't want to be based abroad again. I've done enough, I want to be home with my family and friends. So that counts quite a lot at the moment. Although never say never! And then obviously, the director and the script. I do like doing contemporary. I know I do a lot of period but I do like doing contemporary sometimes. And I quite like to do different genres. I'd love to do a Western, like *True Grit*, which was just amazing, I'd love to have done that. You know, *There Will Be Blood*–fantastic. The Coen Brothers are brilliant. I'd love to work with them. But you know Jess Gonchor's got that tied up! He's great and I think his work is fantastic.

So you know we'll see what comes in. I quite like small budgets as well. I'm reading another script at the moment which is very low budget. It's set in one house and I was saying, *What could be nicer?* Rather than doing these massive, multiple-location, very difficult films, you think, *Actually, wouldn't it be nice to do a film that was just set in one place?*

AS: How closely do you work with the DP?

SG: Very closely. You do as much as you can and it's almost like handing over your baby when it's done. They just make it better and better. And the way they use space, I love the way things come to life. Both Seamus McGarvey and Philippe Rousselot, they appear to be very effortless in the way that they light. It just happens, which is just fantastic. It doesn't appear to be a struggle to achieve what they achieve. Seamus in particular works so closely with Joe and he's so bright, and clever and articulate. That's another layer when you're talking about characterization and feel and atmosphere. They're great. They're the third part of the triangle.

AS: How do you feel about the future of production design and movie making? There seem to be more and more greenscreens and visual effects. How do you think that will affect what you do?

SG: Well, personally I'm glad I'm doing it at the time I'm doing it because I think it might go further that way. I don't know that I'd be interested in doing any more greenscreen than I am doing. It's almost too much, what I have been doing! I think that there's going to be horses for courses, really. I think there's a place for all sorts of movie-making. The bottom line for me is good scripts. But I do think it's very important that we embrace the whole digital side of things and that we are involved in post production.

The concept that when it's done in post, in the CG world, that it doesn't need designing, that's just ignorance beyond belief. I think it's great that films like *Avatar* and *Alice in Wonderland* have won because it just shows actually that these are production designed, these films. Whether it's fair to put them against films that are made differently I don't know. I don't know whether that means there should be another category.

> **THE CONCEPT THAT WHEN IT'S DONE IN POST, IN THE CG WORLD, THAT IT DOESN'T NEED DESIGNING, THAT'S JUST IGNORANCE BEYOND BELIEF.**

It's important that you don't have some techie in some basement doing the visualization of something. I've heard of directors saying, *Give me a hundred versions of this.* And that's wrong to my mind. They're not the right people to be doing it. If you want it designed, then get it designed. It'll be interesting to see how it pans out. It's a good time to be working in the industry.

AS: Have you always wanted to be involved in films or is it just something you fell into through the theater?

SG: I wouldn't say that I set out to be a production designer, no. When I started out I didn't know that you could go and study theater design. I went from theater to television because the creativity in theater was not what it could be and I thought, *Well, if it's not overly creative then I might as well* go to television and make loads of money and not be overly creative. TV is amazing–I just love the speed with which you turn things around. In theater you spend three months designing and building one set that's on stage for three months. Whereas in film and TV you might have six weeks to design ten sets and get them in and out. It was like a total revelation. A completely different approach to designing.

AS: One thing I noticed in the first *Sherlock Holmes* was how many sets there were!

SG: There are even more in *Sherlock 2!* It's just absolutely crazy. The mad things that you get to design! It's a good game to be in. I love it, really.

Rick Heinrichs

Rick Heinrichs designed arguably two of the greatest films ever made, the Coen Brothers' *Fargo* and *The Big Lebowski.* He also designed two of the mega-budget *Pirates of the Caribbean* films, the *Star Wars* film *The Last Jedi,* and multiple Tim Burton films including the awesome *Sleepy Hollow* for which he won an Academy Award. We caught up with him at the next-generation entertainment studio Fourth Wall, where he was helping to envision the future of entertainment.

AS: What are you working on right now?

RH: When I finished *Dark Shadows* and *Frankenweenie* in London about a year ago I met up with the guys who run Fourth Wall Studios. The future of our industry has always been a big question in my mind. Are we going to continue to be able to be making the big feature films that we've been making in the kind of numbers that we've been making them in? And there's the brave new world of distribution over the internet. What are the sort of economies we are going to look at now if indeed we're going to be producing and designing films that are going to end up on a small computer screen?

As a production designer I love to build sets but when you're in a structure that doesn't allow you to build sets what are you doing? We're using a lot more digital and virtual sets. But it's life-sucking to work on a greenscreen set. The challenge is, *How do we make it a usable tool that is actually cool to work with?*

AS: When designing films like the *Pirates of the Caribbean* series do you spend a lot of time on these greenscreen stages or do you go out on location?

RH: For the *Pirates* movies I was all over the Caribbean and the Bahamas and Hawaii. And I think I saw every bit of Hawaii from a helicopter, every bit of every shore of every island. Which is not a bad thing to do. We'd take boats around islands with the director Gore Verbinski and swim in to shore because it was too rough to dock the boat. And then we'd discover that the beach we're scouting is called Tiger Shark beach! If we'd swum in a couple hours later there would definitely have been tiger sharks! Or we'd be led out on goat trails on cliffs where you can fall two-hundred feet to your death. You're walking through jungles where people get killed all the time from falling coconuts. It was life-threatening and physically taxing but an incredibly stimulating adventure at the same time. You're going to these really remote, beautiful places that nobody gets a chance to go to and imagining how you're going to use it in a movie. It's really an unusual thing to get to do and I love that aspect of it.

AS: You've also worked with the Coen Brothers.

RH: Yes, being able to work with those guys was a wonderful, early career milestone for me. Of all the movies that I've done over the years *Fargo* and *The Big Lebowski* are two of my favorite movies. And it's just one hundred percent those two guys and their ear for dialog and their head for creating characters and cobbling together these different elements. No one else would make those connections. You get a sense with their movies that they've created these characters and wound them up and they're just watching them bump into each other. Then they'll throw in another story element and see what happens with that. It gives you an amazing sense that anything can happen with their movies–and it does.

AS: The design in those movies is stylized but it's grounded. It feels like it could actually happen.

RH: Right. People have asked me what I actually did on *Fargo* because there were a lot of practical locations and environments. A lot of it was the selection of the environments. One of the greatest compliments I ever got on *Fargo* is that people claim they've seen that Paul Bunyan statue somewhere right outside of Brainerd! We made that statue! We took the two pieces up to the Canadian border where there was the last bit of snow of that season to shoot that scene where it was standing next to the highway.

Part of the research for that was that sensibility of monumental sculpture that you'll see in the flyover states. I like to call it *America's idea of having fun.* Taking an idea and making it big. Whenever you take road trips you see a lot of that around. I think it's one of the really wonderful, cool, kitschy aspects of our culture.

And then *Big Lebowski* had a different look to it. Interestingly both of those films were set in the recent past. They weren't contemporary. Even though they were in the recent past you could already feel it was this period that had this very distinctive quality to it. In *Fargo* that tan Sierra car had sort of already had its day; the very 80s way that Mary Zophres designed the wardrobe was definitely over and done with.

AS: Jess Gonchor described working with the Coen brothers as almost like working with two production designers.

RH: They're very sophisticated visually, no question about it. A lot of the process of arriving at the look of those films was to pare and select, and pare and select, in a constant process of, *this doesn't work, this doesn't work,–this works.* And then starting to make these really interesting connections between visual elements. You start to see the pattern behind it all that works for them.

AS: Have you ever been to the Lebowski Fest?

RH: I've been to Lebowski Fest one time. Anonymously. I didn't want to have my body ripped apart and my clothing taken! And once was enough actually. It's interesting how beloved the film is.

AS: In contrast, your design on the *Pirates* movies has such a cinematic scale. Did you think about that when you were working on them?

RH: Yes. Mythic, epic, all the other ic's you can think of! And Gore himself is epic. He was definitely a take-no-prisoners director. I loved working with him because he was such a motivator and so enthusiastic in a really cool way. When I first met Gore he was drawing pirate ships with tentacles all over them. He tries to come up with ideas visually at the same time as he's coming up with character and story elements.

AS: Did you go to art school?

RH: Yes, I went to Boston University School of Fine Arts. And then I was at Visual Arts in New York taking cartooning classes with some of my heroes: Harvey Kurtzman and Will Eisner and people like that. I was really interested in animation so I came out to California. The one year I was at CalArts just happened to be the year that Tim Burton and John Lasseter were there. The year before was Brad Bird and Henry Selleck and these other directors. Really amazingly talented people who worked across both live action and animation were there at the same time.

AS: Is that where you first met Tim Burton?

RH: I saw his films and knew who he was but I didn't meet him then. It wasn't until we were at Disney Studios together and I started doing in-betweens of his drawings for *The Fox and the Hound*. Then we were thrown together developing concepts for *The Black Cauldron*, which was their next film. The studio was not sure what to make of Tim and his work. They knew it was cool but they didn't know if they could make use of it because it was so un-Disney. So they said it was too flat. My background was sculpture at college so I did sculptures of some of his work. I told them, *See, it's not flat!* And that was really the beginning of working with Tim.

AS: What was collaboration like with Tim? David Warren said he was always sketching.

RH: He's always sketching. You're not going to find him doing Photoshop painting with a tablet. He's very much a hands-on artist. He does these very sketchy, very elegant, very economical line drawings of things and throws color on it. He can say so much with such economy. You know exactly what he's talking about. And you can then flesh it out and create a world around it.

AS: So it's true he prefers working in the physical world as opposed to CG?

RH: Tim is very much about seeing and feeling and is much less interested in the technology that is required. He loves stop-motion because it is very much a see-feel thing. You can see the object in real life. It's amazing what we can do digitally with visual effects and it's changed everything we do. It has become an absolutely essential part of the art department and all the other departments. But there is something inherently mechanical or computational about it.

I remember having these discussions a lot with Gore Verbinski on *Pirates of the Caribbean*. Gore is also a huge believer of getting as much as possible in camera. Rango not withstanding, which is a completely CG film. But for those things that involved live-action characters it was incredibly important that we capture the immediacy of something spontaneous and alive. Your great visual effects artists and supervisors would agree they are only as good

as the information they are given. And while it may be true that you can do anything in CG, nobody has that kind of time and money. There are always going to be decisions and compromises that get made along the way. So if you can give them real objects in real light to work with they are always very grateful.

AS: Nathan Crowley described how Christopher Nolan will film actual bats flying around in a space and give that to visual effects as opposed to creating CG bats.

RH: We did bats also for *Batman Returns*, CG bats, and it was one of the first uses of CG bats that I'd seen in a movie and I remember thinking at the time, *What a perfect subject matter for CG because their movement is so erratic and strobey and bizarre!* It was actually perfect for the technology of the time.

AS: With the *Pirates* movies are you involved after principal photography?

RH: I do try to stay involved to a degree. As the process of making films collapses and the whole prep, production, and post fuses into one huge movie-making period you are going to see a lot more elasticity in the involvement of the designer. It is becoming more clear to studios and producers that it is a continuous process that needs the continuity of a designer. One vision going all the way through.

AS: After doing *The Lord of the Rings*, Grant Major told me that he prefers to be there the whole time and not just to leave and say, *Okay, you guys take it from here.*

RH: Doing two movies back to back with *Pirates*, I got to be on for all of post production for *Dead Man's Chest* while we were shooting the following movie. It was great to be able to be the advocate both of the director's and of my own vision.

AS: Do you deliberately work with very visual directors?

RH: It's more fun that way. You'll see that's a thread running through a lot of the directors I've worked with.

AS: Brad Silberling?

RH: Even Brad. There are a few directors I've worked with that draw stick figures. Spike Jonze. Brad. But when you look at their work they are also extremely visual. Brad knows his art. He loves photography and he knows how to talk my language using images.

Lemony Snicket actually started with Barry Sonnenfeld in New York and then when he dropped out of the picture it came back to LA with Brad. He just sort of picked up the whole idea of the parallel universe with all these different periods layered on top of each other. We weren't trying to say, *This is history.* We were trying to tell a story. Once you're on that road you start seeing all these connections between things that you wouldn't have thought. It felt like we were inventing a new era that had an Edwardian feel to some of the clothing, layered with the Art Deco we had going on in there. We had the modern technology of cell phones and tape recorders but taken way back in time and reinvented

for that period. Which was really cool. Every day became a kind of an adventure to figure out how we are going to propagate that feel throughout the world we were creating.

> **" WHILE IT MAY BE TRUE THAT YOU CAN DO ANYTHING IN CG NOBODY HAS THAT KIND OF TIME AND MONEY.**

AS: *Sleepy Hollow* was another film where you created a fantasy world from another time.

RH: The adventure of doing *Sleepy Hollow* with Tim was the opportunity to really experiment. The original idea was to create Hammer horror movie-style exteriors on stage. We'll throw some atmosphere in there and light it theatrically and stylistically. We thought, *It's okay if it's a little theatrical.* But we were combining that with real locations. We hit upon this sort of naturalism that we brought onto stage with us and left the Hammer horror thing behind. The DP, Chivo Lubezki, was incredibly talented at lighting exteriors on stage.

AS: Beautiful movie...

RH: It was also exciting to not depend so much on visual effects and to be in a stylized and theatrical world. It had a heightened naturalism to it. I ended up calling it "Colonial Expressionism" at the time. But that's when I was combining Expressionism with almost any other word! And it kind of works! The idea was to come up with these very emotive images in almost a painterly way. When you're not just going to locations and selecting them but you're actually building everything from the ground up you can concentrate on the metaphors, like a village where the houses are crowded together fearfully. There's a herd of sheep that you can hear the bleating of and when you get Danny Elfman's music and Johnny Depp and Chivo's lighting and Tim's direction then you get a feeling from all those elements that transcends and creates that heightened naturalism. That is why I love working in the industry and why I love going to movies.

AS: Were you always drawing pictures as a kid?

RH: I was always drawing but I hadn't the faintest idea what an art director was–unlike today where almost every film school has a course in production design or art direction for film. I worked for a bit in New York pursuing cartooning and animation and then came out to CalArts to study animation and ended up at Disney Studios.

How did I get to be an art director from that? A lot of it was working with Tim. I could make models and sculptures and draw and provide the world for this guy. Doing that I realized, *Oh, this is actually a job that somebody does. You make the world for what they're trying to do and it's called art direction.* I remember in an old cinematographer's magazine I saw a photograph of a chart at one of the old MGM Studios titled, *What Does an Art Director Do?* It was broken up into maybe sixteen panels showing an art director, a man wearing a coat and tie, and all the various things that he does on his day. It showed him drafting, working with set designers, and working with visual effects, which was called

special effects in those days. At that point in time special effects included everything from hanging miniatures to glass-shot matte paintings. It made me realize, *That dude does everything! That guy is making the world happen in every possible way. That's really cool! That's what I want to do!*

AS: How did doing those models and sculptures with Tim Burton at Disney lead to actual production design?

RH: There was a transition from working at Disney Studios with Tim to working with Tim independently. We got a studio together in Pasadena and we started working on *Frankenweenie,* the original live-action short film for Disney. On *Frankenweenie* I couldn't get the title of art director because that was a union position so I'm listed as associated producer. The head of Disney, Tom Wilhite, liked Tim and me. We were kind of a mini-team. And the head of the art department at Disney, the old gentleman John Mansbridge, acted as a mentor. He hired one set designer to work with us on *Frankenweenie* and while I was making illustrations and models this guy was breaking all these things up into construction drawings. I watched the whole process happen before my eyes just like in that chart that I saw.

I continued to make models and do stop-motion animation and special effects on *Peewee's Big Adventure,* and on *Beetlejuice* I was the art director of visual effects. It was then I got to know Bo Welch who was an excellent production designer who took me under his wing. I let him know I wanted to be a production designer and when he had the opportunity to bring me on a picture that was going to start non-union and go union he hired me in his art department and put me to work. That was *Ghostbusters 2*.

It took me a number of years to work my way from model-maker/set designer to art director and finally to production designer. But I really am glad I went through that process because it's a very professional world in the motion picture industry and I wanted people to feel that I had the authority to make the kind of comments that I would make about the work they were doing for me. If you haven't really been there and set designed and had to do the whole slog through art direction then it's hard to understand what it really is people are doing.

AS: What do you think are the required characteristics of a production designer?

RH: The most important thing is communication. This also involves selecting people who can hear what you say. Having a good idea is also key. Bo Welch calls the process "Breaking the Code" of a movie. It's immersing yourself in it and not thinking you've got a quick and easy answer. Starting with the very basic building blocks and building from there. That preliminary period is incredibly scary and yet really a kick in the butt. It's the most important period and what everything else leads from. That's what separates the men from the boys or the women from the girls!

AS: How do you crack the code? Do you put up a whole bunch of images on a wall?

RH: That's part of it. I just need some alone time where I'm parsing through that stuff, collecting it. It's this very important period of research where you're trying to come up with something that is not the go-to, cliché answer. You arrive at it by doing the hard work of thought and study and research. Then you also start working with people who share a take on things and have a shared ethic of work. Most movies I've done are with John Dexter as supervising art director, he's fantastic. He's actually working with Nigel Phelps right now on *Invertigo*.

> "BO WELCH CALLS THE PROCESS "BREAKING THE CODE" OF A MOVIE . . . IT'S THIS VERY IMPORTANT PERIOD OF RESEARCH WHERE YOU'RE TRYING TO COME UP WITH SOMETHING THAT IS NOT THE GO-TO, CLICHÉ ANSWER. YOU ARRIVE AT IT BY DOING THE HARD WORK OF THOUGHT AND STUDY AND RESEARCH.

And it's really important to be able to draw. To do some of the work yourself whether it's drawing a plan or an illustration. I do a very rough version of most of the illustrations I want people to work on. They're shitty, they're not rendered, but they say everything I want them to say and it gives the illustrators enough to get going. Excellent illustrators help because what you want to do is communicate to the director both the fundamental spirit as well as the particulars of a given set.

Tremendously hard work is also part of it. I work many hours at it in a day. It's an exhausting amount of taxing on your resources but this prep time, which seems to get shorter and shorter every time that we do it, is just so critical to the work that gets produced afterwards.

It's also about how you manage your fear about the trials you're going through. How far do you dare go down a path that might prove to be a dead-end? You play chicken with yourself a bit. There's a mind-game aspect to it that you've got to keep aware of and stay on top of. There's the art-intense focus that you're in the middle of and there's also the id and the ego–you've got to watch yourself too! Apart from that it's easy–anyone can do it!

AS: How does playing chicken with yourself contribute to the process?
RH: You're trying to come up with something fresh by following your intuition down a new path. But you've got to always stay above it slightly in order to manage the resources available to you, both your own and the other resources. You need to see if this is really going somewhere. Do I have enough to put this across to the director or is this something I need to abandon right now? Or should I have another option going?

AS: Do you see the movie industry leaving LA?
RH: Yes, and it's just such a shame the industry is moving away. Because we have the best home for an industry. We've got the best facilities, we have the best trained craftspeople here. I do love working in London. They have excellent art department people there. They do have Pinewood and Shepperton and Leavesden and they have this wonderful tax break for the studios. However it's not my home. It's just a shame that we don't have the same thing happening here. It probably would be considered corporate welfare here in California.

It's a different world than the one I was coming up in. Much more international. We're being asked not simply to design a film but literally being asked to design a production. A production footprint. You've got to solve all of these problems that are very economic-based problems. In the go-go 80s and 90s you didn't have to think as heavily about that.

AS: When you're traveling to these various places are you able to bring people or do you have to hire a new crew in every place?
RH: I would always try to bring my supervising art director with me. For instance on *Captain America* we were starting here on Manhattan Beach. It was to be done here in the studio. The more we got into it the more we asked, *How do you do London in LA? Where do you find 1940's army barrack-looking places? And the more important thing these days is where do you get the tax break?* It can get you an extra twenty million dollars worth of production value on the screen. Within the first couple of months we were looking all over the world. We were looking in

Budapest, Czechoslovakia, Germany, Italy, London, Montreal, and we briefly thought of New York. All these are places that offer tax incentives. We finally ended up in London. And I did insist on bringing John with me. I did the same thing with John on *Sleepy Hollow* ten years earlier. Typically I don't get to bring anybody else.

AS: Any advice for people just starting out in the business?

RH: You need to set yourself apart from everyone else. It comes from what you were interested in as a kid or what you were interested in as a young adult. The travels that you did in life. The things that made you curious growing up. You want to be considered a professional who can do the job but at the same time all of these things help distinguish you as a designer.

I would also tell anyone to learn SketchUp because it's such a great, easy program. If they feel that they are going to be a set designer and draftsman they should probably get into Rhino. But for an art director or even a production designer it's good to be able to really study the scale of things in three dimensions.

AS: What do you like most about production design?

RH: This is where my explorations into the greenscreen are going to leave me dry. I like walking onto a set I built that was living in my mind for a really long time. In particular something with forced perspective and some theatrical elements to it. I like to just sit there and enjoy the environment. Like in the back portion of the Van Tassel estate in *Sleepy Hollow*. It was this back porch where you look down on a driveway to the stage at Leavesden. We only had thirty feet but we had a coach and horses and we had this apple orchard where we had shrunk all these trees in the background for forced perspective. And we had this mountain-scape that we'd sculpted so it took light. And a small windmill and painted skies. And some of the stars, Michael Gambon and Ian McDiarmid, would sit back there smoking cigarettes and relaxing like they were enjoying the afternoon out on the back porch. The level of deep satisfaction that I got out of that has been with me ever since.

CHARACTER

Can a set be a character?

A compilation of excerpts covering the subject of sets being characters, taken from the interviews in this book

By asking the same question of multiple designers it was possible to deconstruct certain conceits about production design. One of these conceits was whether a set can be a character in a film. The companion question was whether production design should remain invisible. Both are focused on how aware of the production design an audience should be. Some sets reinforce the realism of a film by remaining subliminal while others demand the attention of the audience. All of them tell the story by communicating what the written descriptions in the script only allude to...

JACK FISK

Sets are characters. The house in Days of Heaven was a character. One of the producers and I had a disagreement because he thought it should have been a ranch house. You know, a Texas ranch house. But Terry [Malick, director] wanted a belvedere. He had shown me a picture of a Victorian house and then I looked at the Edward Hopper picture of *The House by the Tracks*–it's just so pleasantly bizarre to put a belvedere out in that environment. It was so big that you could see it for miles away. I think that house became a character.

K.K. BARRETT

I suppose in Hitchcock's *Psycho* the hotel was a character in the movie. Because it embodied the past. Usually it's a character support rather than a character itself. It's more like a coat, you know? Sometimes it's like when an actor can't really find themselves until they put on the character's clothes.

NATHAN CROWLEY

A set can be a character in a film if your story demands it. When I did *The Lake House* that set had to be a character in the film. I spent my entire budget on that one set. Which was a fight because I went to the producer and said, *I'm going to spend all my budget building this set because it's not something that exists, it's a memory of the past for the son and father. A forgotten time in their lives. The rest of the picture we're going to shoot in found locations.*

The Lake House is not my favorite film but it's the kind of film where the set has to play a character. I oddly get many phone calls about the Lake House set. I have been asked by one architectural group to give a lecture on the design of the house.

In *Batman* maybe the Batcave becomes a character. But you shouldn't lose the rest of the film, you have to make it fit into your world. A lot of logic went into it. If Gotham is New York then Wayne Manor could be in the Palisades. The Palisades have granite cliffs so the Batcave can have a waterfall. But your logic doesn't necessarily play to the audience. You're only playing in realism. You have to make it real because Batman is in a rubber suit running around the city! You have to believe that that could exist.

JOHN MUTO

I think that's a very glib, bullshit thing that people say because they think it sounds clever. Characters are characters. A character is an entity. Generally it's like a human being that walks around on two feet, talks and stuff. Maybe it's a ghost. Godzilla's a character, but for Christ's sake a set's a set. A set's a setting. It's someplace something happens. Maybe if it's the house in the *Haunting* that's a character because it does things and it talks to you.

MICHAEL NOVOTNY

You know I've been told that we're in charge of everything that's out of focus behind the actors. Which to a large extent is true. But there are moments when we break out of that and we establish

CHARACTER

clearly a visual character in the script that's distinct. I had a great moment watching *K-19* when I first saw that submarine out at sea–because I saw that's a character that I made. And it really was a character. It was about that boat.

MARK FRIEDBERG

I don't have a rule about that stuff. You could say that of anything, "That's a character in the story". I don't know what that means. In the case of *Joker,* our Gotham is either an extension of Arthur– something that literally came out of him, or it is the thing that is bearing down on him and causing him on some level to act the way he acts.

RICK CARTER

It's never binary. In the question is the answer. Sometimes it's more this and sometimes it's more that. Sometimes it's more of a character. You know the Gump house in *Forrest Gump* or the Tara house in *Gone with the Wind.* Where literally you can't imagine the movie without the place because the place orients you to what your emotions are. So it functions like a character.

But sometimes it helps when you prioritize the importance of a set, to not go too crazy with architecture and details if you're only trying to get across something in relationship to what came before and what will come afterwards. This can help you on the budget because you might first think, *Well, this is a very important scene because it's a palace with a million details.* Then you realize, because of its impact on the movie, it really should be something that instead you work out with the cinematographer to do a long lens shot and have it be out of focus or see just one part of it. Those decisions are happening intuitively all the time in budgeting, the decisions of what to make, how to shoot it, and how to edit it.

EVE STEWART

[A set is] a quicker story-teller than the script. Because people are so quick to assess the status, the history, the mood. They make a complete judgment on what they're seeing about the person who is involved there. It's an enormous resource.

GUY HENDRIX DYAS

This is something that's dictated by the script. While some sets are meant to be more inconspicuous, every once in a while the opportunity arises to be a bit more experimental and exuberant and let a set become its own character, one which demands its own attention.

Can a set be a character?

ADAM STOCKHAUSEN

Other people have said that [a set can be a character]. I don't focus on it. You just try to make sure that the set is the best that it can be as a background for the story and to support the story and to support the actors and to be as real and rich and full as you can possibly make it be. But I don't think about it beyond that. To me it's always the thing that's there in the background to be supportive rather than to be aggressive.

RALPH EGGLESTON

It changes depending on what the storytelling needs are. I do believe a set can be a character and needs to be a character for the film, but it should also be invisible! It's a character in the film but that doesn't mean that it needs to "show off" or be precious.

DAVID WASCO

I think any set that you're in for a long period of time can become a character. Traditionally the rule of thumb is we really are trying to do something that's going to support what the actors are doing and help the director tell a story. Plain and simple. Quentin specifically requested [The Jack Rabbit Slims set in *Pulp Fiction*] to be over-the-top and when that's a director's request it's your opportunity to do something interesting.

Kim Sinclair

Kim Sinclair won an Academy Award as Set Decorator/Supervising Art Director on the record-breaking blockbuster *Avatar* and has also production designed numerous films, all from his home base in New Zealand. He lives on the cutting edge where virtual and practical sets come together, as exemplified in his work as visual effects art director on films like *The Adventures of Tintin* with Steven Spielberg, and as supervising art director in *Avatar 2* for James Cameron.

AS: On *Avatar* your primary involvement was the physical sets?

KS: We shot all the live-action in *Avatar* here in New Zealand. If at any time, in any frame, there were humans either in the foreground or the background, any humans at all, they were shot in Wellington. We provided a lot of large sets. The vehicles, the weapons, the props, the dressing. It was all pretty straightforward but the trick was the integration into the digital world. There were shots that were purely digital and there were shots that were purely live action. However, a large percentage of the movie featured digital characters in real environments or real people in digital environments. And that was really the challenge.

AS: What was your process collaborating with Rick Carter and Robert Stromberg?

KS: Rob Stromberg headed up what we used to call the virtual art department, in LA. He had a team of designers and they designed the look of the planet, the look of the vegetation, and they headed up the creature designs. They did some 3D modeling but basically that went to Weta Digital in New Zealand. That became the virtual world, the digital world. Meanwhile Rick Carter headed up a design art department in LA and designed the sets and the vehicles. There was overlap and integration between these departments but basically they designed the traditional, built environments. That information then all came down to me in New Zealand. I had one meeting with Jim [Cameron] in LA during pre-production but for the most part Rick dealt with him in preproduction because they were both in LA. Rick used to come down to New Zealand about once every three weeks for about two or three days at a time.

While we were building the sets we used to do video conferences with Jim. I would actually walk around the sets with a video camera plugged into my laptop and then Jim would give us his comments. Some time before the shoot Jim came down and we had him full time in New Zealand. It was a two-way process with Jim but basically he said, *Okay here's the idea, make it work.* We were really getting it out of his head and onto the screen.

Some of the sets, particularly the aircraft, were quite challenging. They were quite lucky in LA in that they had "blue sky design". They could design something and not worry about how to build it! So we'd get it and go, *Holy cow, how are we going to build this?* We couldn't change it because in many cases it had become motion capture assets. And we'd have performance parameters. If a door was a door it had to be a door. It could look like anything but it had to be that exact size, that shape, that place in space. The pivot points couldn't be changed or the spatial volume. So that was quite "challenging. We pulled out hair out over that one.

"PEOPLE WILL SAY [AVATAR] WAS THE MOST EXPENSIVE FILM EVER MADE BUT EVERY DAY WE DIDN'T DO SOMETHING THAT WE WANTED TO DO BECAUSE WE COULDN'T AFFORD IT.

It was also challenging because we were working to a budget. People will say it was the most expensive film ever made but every day we didn't do something that we wanted to do because we couldn't afford it. We often had to find cheaper ways of doing things. Jim is very practical. Giving him two choices he would sometimes say, *Which one is cheaper?* Or, *Which has the best production value?* You would say, *Well, this looks slightly better but it's gonna cost a lot more* and he would say, *Look, I don't think the value is going to be on screen. Go with the cheaper option.* It was quite fulfilling to work with a producer/director–someone who was wearing a director's hat but who was also conscious of cost.

AS: Was it overall a good experience to work with James Cameron?

KS: He was very good in New Zealand. He might have been "good Jim." He was very good to work with because it was his world we were building. He was very good at communicating what he wanted.

And very practical. I got on really well with him. In fifteen months I got shouted at twice and apologized to once. So that's pretty good! Jim would seek me out, pat me on the back and say, *This is a great set, I'm loving it. I couldn't ask for anything better, good work.* I don't know how many years I've been doing this but it's quite unusual for a director to publicly seek the designer or art director on set. They might think of it but not say it. Jim would often say it on set in front of crew, which is nice.

AS: Working on *Tintin* now do you also collaborate closely with Spielberg?

KS: No, not at all. The difference is that Jim was on the job probably 24/7 for four years. The thing about *Tintin* is that Steven Spielberg is in LA or often around the world. We have poly-conferences with the directors. Polycons are part of the slightly more virtual process where you don't actually sit down with the director and bring out all the drawings. It's a much more filtered approach to filmmaking.

I've been working on *Tintin* since April last year. It's not being released until December. That's the nature of these performance-captured, animated, 3D features–they go on and on! They're using the same camera and technology that was used on *Avatar*. As soon as *Avatar* finished I jumped onto *Tintin*. What we're doing is designing the look of the movie after it's been shot, which is a tricky one. It's the way of the future but it's not terribly satisfying.

AS: Not satisfying because it's not physically happening?

KS: Yes, I like to get my bloody boots on in the snow and the mud. Worry about the weather and employ people to build the sets and get all the props. Now it's just five-hundred people sitting in front of computers. Although it's ultimately satisfying when you see it on the screen, the process is not as visceral and engaging as what I've been used to.

AS: Your background is designing practical sets . . .

KS: I was an architect and after a couple years I became a builder and made a living building things that I'd designed. People came to me wanting a new house and I'd design it and I'd build it. I'd be the contractor. It's quite hard to make a living though.

My wife was an architect and she answered an advertisement in the paper in 1982. *Wanted: People to work on feature film.* Paramount was making a large pirate film based in the South Pacific called *Nate and Hayes.* It was the start of the film industry in New Zealand. There were three or four films that had been made but they were very do-it-yourself. This was the first Hollywood studio production made in New Zealand. These experienced guys came in and they kind of went, *Where's the film crew?* And the answer was, *There is no film crew.* So they were just advertising in the classified ads in the paper. I was an unemployed architect/builder at the time. They were advertising for draftsmen and set designers and I got the job, along with my wife.

We worked on this film and we had a great time, traveling around the country. I've been working on films ever since.

Neil Kirkland, who later became construction supervisor on *Avatar*, was also on that job. He designed this set which was the interior of this German First World War battleship and then he actually built the set. He was the foreman of the carpenters. Then all the painters got called off to paint something else so he painted the set and then when they filmed it he actually acted in it–he was the sailor that loaded the gun. For him, it was a very Kiwi process.

That's pretty much what happened to me on the next job I did. I was the art director of the job after that, then I was the production designer. There were not very many film crews in New Zealand so it was very easy to rise through the ranks.

We have a very big commercial industry in New Zealand because of the locations. Particularly from Europe and Asia. TV commercials are a bigger economic unit than feature films here–it's a lot more money. They'll fly in and go to scenic spots and make an advertisement for Chinese butter or German milk or American turkey. I've never really got involved in commercials but the point I'm making is that the film industry has always been location-driven in New Zealand. It's a long way from anywhere and the reason to come to New Zealand is the destinations, the variety of land- scapes in New Zealand. We've done TV movies set in Los Angeles, Florida, Pennsylvania, Tennessee, North Carolina. About fifty percent of the United States you could shoot in New Zealand if you went to the right place. The problem of course is that the cars drive on the wrong side of the road here. The film industry would probably be twice as big in New Zealand if we drove on the right hand side of the road!

> **I LIKE TO GET MY BLOODY BOOTS ON IN THE SNOW AND THE MUD. WORRY ABOUT THE WEATHER AND EMPLOY PEOPLE TO BUILD THE SETS AND GET ALL THE PROPS. NOW IT'S JUST FIVE-HUNDRED PEOPLE SITTING IN FRONT OF COMPUTERS. ALTHOUGH IT'S ULTIMATELY SATISFYING WHEN YOU SEE IT ON THE SCREEN, THE PROCESS IS NOT AS VISCERAL AND ENGAGING.**

My background is doing location work. I've carved out a career doing difficult locations. I've worked in Mexico and South Pacific Fiji on *Castaway*. *Legend of Zorro* was Mexico. Thailand on *Beyond Borders*. The Southern Alps on a film called *Vertical Limit*. Basically looking after art departments in places that are a bit inhospitable. Islands, tops of mountains. I've done loads of films where you have to fly around by helicopter. And get materials in by helicopter. We shot *The Last Samurai* in New

Plymouth, which is quite a remote part of New Zealand. We built the village there. There was no road access. We actually choppered in all the materials. The point is that *Avatar* was quite interesting in that it was the first time that a major American feature film has come to New Zealand not for any location shooting at all but totally because of the human resources, the facilities, and now also the modest tax break.

> **" THE DIGITAL WORLD ALLOWS YOU TO DO THINGS YOU CAN'T OTHERWISE DO. AND IF IT ALLOWS YOU TO DO THINGS YOU CAN'T AFFORD TO DO, THAT'S WELL AND GOOD. BUT FOR THE VAST MAJORITY OF DRAMAS YOU'RE GOING TO WANT PEOPLE AND YOU'RE GOING TO WANT A SET.**

AS: From when you first started would you say the film industry in New Zealand has transformed radically?

KS: Yeah. We had almost nine hundred people working for Weta Digital on *Avatar,* just the month before it was turned over. That's all human resources, that's all brainpower. The largest percentage of people on the crew were New Zealanders. The second biggest group were Americans but there were a lot of Germans, Italians, French. They had people from forty-four different countries working at Weta while they were finishing off *Avatar.*

AS: Do you work on a lot of New Zealand productions as well?

KS: There's a reasonable feature industry here. They tend to be small scale. The average budget for a New Zealand film is between three to ten million dollars. A big one will be ten million. A lot of them are at the three million dollar mark. We're pretty lean and mean. A lot of the time you're challenging the art department. *They don't really have enough money for what we want to do, so what do you reckon we can do?* We're very used to coming from that end on New Zealand productions. There's a viable film industry here. *Whale Rider* was a good film that springs to mind.

AS: How did you first get connected to the *Avatar* team?

KS: I'd worked with Rick Carter on the *Lost World* which was the sequel to *Jurassic Park.* It was shot in Hawaii but the original plan had been to shoot it in New Zealand. We had started six weeks pre-production. We actually found all the locations, did a lot of work and quite late in the gameplan they decided not to come to New Zealand. Steven decided to go to Hawaii for reasons that weren't totally clear. But I met Rick and got on with him really well.

When he was shooting *Cast Away* for Bob Zemeckis we eventually found this island in Fiji called Monuriki, about thirty miles off the shore of the main island of Fiji. And they needed somebody to explore the island and map it and work out where they could shoot on the island. Through a complete random set of circumstances I got the job. And once I got the job I said, *Well, who is the designer?* And they said, *Rick Carter.* I thought, *God, I know Rick.* I kind of went from map guy to art director overnight. And so that was my original tie-in to *Avatar.* As soon as I heard Rick was designing it I rang him up and I went up to meet with them. They hadn't yet made the decision to shoot in New Zealand but then all the wheels clicked into place. And I came back and started crewing.

AS: When you go to the remote locations like Fiji do you bring crew with you?

KS: Yeah, absolutely. We always try. The producers always want you to use locals, for obvious reasons. And case in point in Thailand, we basically crewed up out of Bangkok and then what I did was identify where there were gaps in the local skill base. I used a New Zealand construction manager because we were filming in the North of Thailand and also in the South–so we needed a split team. I needed someone who was used to coordinating a split construction department. And that was that initially but then we discovered that they didn't really have a proper, professional greensman so I used a New Zealand greensman. And we ended up getting a bit stuck for scenic artists. They actually had some really talented scenic artists but they couldn't quite adjust to the style of the job. We needed guys who could use an airless spray gun and spray buildings quickly. Age them and so on. They were more small scale. We ended up with a couple scenic artists but other than that I used a mostly Thai crew.

Similarly in Mexico they've got a pretty big film industry. On *Zorro* we basically crewed in Mexico. Funny enough, they had the same shortcomings. We ended up using a construction manager and a New Zealand greensman. In Thailand I found amazing sculptors and similarly in Mexico we found very good sculptors and fiberglass workers and metal workers. Very skilled people, very low maintenance. I've never done a job where you just go out and bring a film crew from overseas. Fiji is a bit of an exception. There are not really very many Fijians who are full-time film workers. There's a really good gaffer but in the art department it's slim pickings.

AS: How do you see things changing in the film industry with CG replacing practical sets?

KS: About ten years ago people started to say, *You guys'll be out of a job soon. It's all going to be digital.* And we were like, *Yeah right.* It's kind of gratifying that *Avatar,* which has the most digital content of any film ever made, also had the biggest art department I've ever put together. The live action part was eighty-eight days. With Jim the average day is a fifteen hour shooting day. That's quite a lot of shooting on practical sets. If you've got an actor it's a lot better if you can put a real background behind them. It's better for the actor, it's better for the director. Secondly, this process is pretty expensive. It's kind of wanton to say you can do away with the sets with digital ones or just greenscreens. That's a device on 300, it's been done to give the film a look but I think it's a stylistic thing and I don't think it'll ever replace sets. The digital world allows you to do things you can't otherwise do. And if it allows you to do things you can't afford to do, that's well and good. But for the vast majority of dramas you're going to want people and you're going to want a set.

> **EVERYTHING WE DO SHOULD BE HELPING TELL THE STORY. WHAT COLOR IS THIS CURTAIN? IF YOU'RE CHOOSING A COLOR AT RANDOM OR BECAUSE IT LOOKS NICE YOU'RE NOT DOING YOUR JOB AS FAR AS I'M CONCERNED.**

AS: What are the characteristics that are needed to be a great production designer?

KS: Everybody in the art department needs the same skill set: to be artistic and practical. Our role is to help the director tell a story. I'm amazed how many people I meet in the film industry who aren't driven by that narrative. Everything we do should be helping tell the story. What color is this curtain? If you're choosing a color at random or because it looks nice you're not doing your job as far as I'm concerned. What's the director doing in this scene, what's the set doing, what's the point of it? Is it a comedy? Is it a film noir? The decisions you make are narrative-driven. So I do think that needs to be part of your makeup to be successful in the art department. And you have to be able to think abstractly but also be practical and be able to deliver things on time and on budget. There are a lot of really talented artists out there but my God

I wouldn't want them in the art department. You might employ them for the art department but you wouldn't want them in it!

AS: Do you still do any sketching yourself when you're working on a project?

KS: No. We joke that nobody in my New Zealand art department can draw! There are so many talented conceptual artists and illustrators whom I employ. A little sketch on the back of a napkin is about as far as I get these days, if you're lucky!

AS: What do you say to people who are just getting into the industry? Any advice for them?

KS: These days I have to say that it's essential that you have computer skills–but don't get seduced into thinking that's the be-all and the end-all. You can learn Maya but then maybe you're going to sit behind a computer the rest of your life doing modeling when you could actually be a really good art director. Computers are just tools, you need to know how to use them and be familiar with the applications. But I still think it's much better to get a bit of life education. Get out there and watch movies and do things. Travel. Get experience.

AS: Is there any one set that you worked on or decorated that you're particularly proud of?

KS: Well, from a set decoration point of view a set that was deceptively simple was the commissary in *Avatar*. It was quite a big practical set with no real greenscreen or digital work. We put a lot of work into that, which may not have been on the screen. We designed and fabricated vending machines. We designed the food packaging that was inside the vending machines. We pretty much designed the food. They eat a lot of refried beans in Pandora apparently! A lot of work went into that set. We designed the tables; we designed the chairs. Everything got made. It works really well in the movie and it's not a big, "Look at me, I'm an amazing set" set. It's a nice background for the action. We got a lot of pleasure from that.

The laboratory had literally millions of dollars of dressing. We had real electron microscopes and loads of medical and imaging equipment. That came out really well. The ships too came out really well because we only got the design for them ten weeks before they were due to be shot. They were the first thing that got shot and the last thing that got designed. They were satisfying in that we got the things finished and they looked pretty amazing.

The set that we had the most fun with was the aircraft. Apart from the engines and the rotors it was pretty much a real aircraft, inside and out. With all the working avionics. Lots of input from helicopter pilots and aviation specialists and electronic guys. You sit in it and it smells like an aircraft. And feels like an aircraft. Jim was really delighted with it. When we got that they were like, *Hey these guys know what they're doing.* Quite surprising to us too!

AS: Would you say your life has changed after winning an Oscar?

KS: Not yet! I feel tireder!

AS: Do you feel like your roles will change?

KS: From my point of view I have to support my wife and daughter and I do anything. It's a real New Zealand thing actually that we move around between roles. It makes me mad when people send me their resumes and they say they can do anything. *How can I employ you? Just say what you want to do! I'll give you a job.* When I get CVs from New Zealanders they say, *I can build, paint, I production designed this TV commercial, I did some props work.* It's like, *I can't employ you! Say what you want to do!* Unfortunately I'm as guilty as they are. If someone offers me a job as a set dresser I'll probably take it.

> **"WHAT I HATE IS SETS THAT ARE OVERLY FLASHY AND COMPLICATED AND TOO IMPORTANT FOR THEIR OWN GOOD. *LOOK AT ME! LOOK AT ME! I'M AN AMAZING SET.***

AS: Do you feel design needs to be *invisible* or *visible*?

KS: It depends on the film and it depends on the director. I find there are two sorts of directors. There's the director with a very clear vision of the film, including the look of the film and the design. And there are other directors who will write a script set at a house and when you start talking to them you find they have no idea about the relationships between the rooms or even how the scene plays out. But there are other directors, like Jim, who are just completely visual. They're building it in their minds. I'm not saying one form of direction is better than the other.

But I favor the subliminal thing. Your job is not to distract from the story. However, sometimes the set or the prop is the story and in that case it becomes the forefront. It may become more important than the actors. But it's really story-driven. What I hate is sets that are overly flashy and complicated and too important for their own good. *Look at me! Look at me! I'm an amazing set.* It's silly. It would be like a film where people just drive a car, and the car itself is not another story point. You find some amazing Ferrari or something. Then everybody watching the movie is going, *Oh wow, look at the Ferrari!* It takes you out of the story. The same thing goes for sets. It really depends on the story. I favor the background thing, I'm more of a background guy.

AS: Are you involved with previs a lot?

KS: No. When previs started it was a good idea but what happens now is that the movie becomes de facto designed during the previs stage and then the art department becomes involved later. You're reverse engineering things and it's very unsatisfactory. So the answer is no, on *Avatar* we weren't involved in the previs at all. A lot of the sets got delivered to us as MotionBuilder files. MotionBuilder is a plugin for Maya. It's like a video game–you get an environment that you can walk-through or fly-over with your mouse. We got sets delivered to us that were from the previs that they used for motion capture. We would actually walk around the set virtually, taking screen captures and saying, *What do those steps do? They go down. How may are there?* Re-

ally just like you were visiting a location and doing a location survey. In *Tintin* a similar thing is happening but we're finding that during previs they'd made design decisions that really would have been better made by a production designer or art director. You do reverse engineering and you get these performance parameters where, for example, the table is a certain height, a door is in a certain place and so on. It's a constraint on the look of the film. I would really make a plea that people doing previsualization in film employ a production designer earlier in the process.

AS: The director gets the 3D model version stuck in his mind?

KS: The director gets used to seeing it. The previs guys always say apologetically, *Oh, it's just a place holder.* Well, it's a placeholder that gets into the director's psyche. The problem with *Tintin* is that in the previs they didn't care about what year the movie was set. It's set post war in Europe and we have to come up with that sense of time and place. It's an important part of your role to give it that sense of authenticity. Sometimes we can't change what's been established in the previs. And we have to do workarounds which can be pretty unsatisfying.

AS: You're forced to change the design to accommodate the previs...

KS: Yeah, absolutely. The role of the art department in the digital production of films is still being fleshed out. It's the same for director of photography. The lighting, how digital films are lit, is still being thrashed out. As is the role of camera-people in digital production. You know they'll have big challenges too.

But nothing beats the adrenaline rush of a film. You design for twelve weeks and then it's shot for twelve weeks and everyone's around and working on the same movie at the same time. The DP and the designer see each other every day, they discuss things over lunch. You know that's the proven way of getting a good result.

When the process takes three years and the departments don't overlap, the processes don't overlap, how do you get the same result? I definitely know you lack that energy, you lack that rush of everybody working on a common goal. In those visual effects houses you've got people working on different projects at the same time. The guy doing the work might not even know what project he's working on. He's just given something to model or to texture or to extend the set of. And it's like everything has equal weight. He doesn't have that drive that you've got when you're working on a film production. It's challenging.

AS: You mean the guy at the visual effects company often just works nine to five . . .

KS: The guy could be working on one project one day another project the next day. The delight for me working on films is really the energy that comes from working on a team, all working toward a common goal. And as much as everyone complains and bitches all the time you actually are loving it. And you've got the satisfaction of making a movie–that's why it's called making a movie! It's not a nine-to-five job. It's about that energy and we have to find a way of putting it back into the process.

Jess Gonchor

Jess Gonchor knocked it out of the park with his first movie as production designer: *Capote.* Since then he's had his hands full delivering realism with style on the Coen brothers' movies such as *No Country for Old Men, True Grit,* and *Hail, Caesar,* the last two earning him a pair of Academy Award nominations. Demonstrating he was not locked into the world of poetic violence, he also designed Greta Gerwig's classic historic romance, *Little Women.*

AS: You live in New York City but do you do all of your work out of New York?

JG: No, I've probably designed three movies here but no, I just like it better here. I think every director that I've worked with lives in New York. Maybe it's just coincidence but it's worked out that way. I like LA too but this is where I call home.

AS: You get hired out there and then come to LA to do movies or travel to various places?

JG: Various places. Most of the movies begin in Los Angeles. They evolve from a studio or independent. I can only think of one movie that didn't get packaged up and born in Los Angeles. Sometimes I have to go out there. The majority of the time it's somewhere else. Nowadays they seem to be making movies somewhere else besides Los Angeles. They make a lot of them in New York. But you tend to have to travel to some of the other places for some of the cooler scripts.

AS: It seems that's happening more and more these days with all the tax incentives in other states.

JG: Yeah, that makes it very attractive to shoot a movie in Louisiana or New Mexico or any of those places. I've been fortunate enough to go to those places and have a good shot at using them for what they are. I haven't been asked to go to New Mexico and shoot a movie about Ireland yet–which, believe me, they do! Really, I think the most talented people are in Los Angeles. And it's hard to get something off the ground there these days but hopefully soon.

AS: You've worked with the Coen brothers a lot– how much input do they have on the visual side of things?

JG: They have a tremendous amount of input. I always say it's like a team effort. It's like having two other really talented production designers on the job. They're very close to the story. If they haven't written something that's original they've adapted it. I truly believe they have something in mind as they're putting it down on the page. So they're very involved with the look of the movie. Usually we'll talk about it, they'll hand me the material and we'll talk about it some more. Then they'll sort of let me go on my own and I'll gather up some photos or generate some drawings or take some of my own photos. Do an exploratory view of what I think this thing is going to look like. Then I'll come back and lay it all out on the table and we'll decide, *This is good. This over here is good,* and then sometimes those things trigger other ideas. So it's really a back-and-forth thing between myself and them.

Obviously the first movie we did together was about getting to know each other and each other's style. It's gotten a little bit easier as the movies have gone on. They really have an amazing vision not only for the writing but for the look of the movie. I feel really fortunate to be working with them versus somebody who just leaves the entire thing in my lap. That's fine too, but it's just nice that we push each other.

> "A CLOTHESPIN, A CAR, A PIECE OF GRASS, A BUILDING. IT'S ALL A VERY CAREFULLY CALCULATED SCHEME. YOU NEED TO BE INVOLVED IN EVERYTHING.

AS: *No Country for Old Men* won four Oscars and happens to be one of my favorite movies. One thing I love about it is that very distinct color palette. It has that whole sepia-tone feel.

JG: That's definitely what we were going for. You know it seems like half of my job is praying for good weather or bad weather. In the summer that location traditionally should have been quite green but they were in a drought so here I am cheering for the drought to continue while the rest of the state is worried about their water consumption. It wasn't until the very last day of shooting that it opened up to really rain buckets so I was happy about that.

I tried to give the sense of West Texas and Mexico and tried to keep it in those tones. The palette of the earth. You take a shovel of the ground–that's what's going to come out down in those parts of the States. Between Roger [Deakins'] amazing work and costume designer Mary [Zophres] we managed to keep it mainly in that strike zone.

That was the first thing I came up with. I made a sheet, a knock-off Rothko of the colors that I thought should be in the movie. It was the very first thing I presented to Joel and Ethan and I was like, *What do you think about this as a general tone for the movie?* And they said, *Yeah, that's great!* So those five colors were what we stuck with the whole movie. And I think we did a good job with that.

> " I MADE A SHEET, A KNOCK-OFF ROTHKO OF THE COLORS THAT I THOUGHT SHOULD BE IN THE MOVIE. IT WAS THE VERY FIRST THING I PRESENTED TO JOEL AND ETHAN AND I WAS LIKE, *WHAT DO YOU THINK ABOUT THIS AS A GENERAL TONE FOR THE MOVIE? AND THEY SAID, YEAH, THAT'S GREAT!* SO THOSE FIVE COLORS WERE WHAT WE STUCK WITH THE WHOLE MOVIE.

AS: Did you go out to West Texas before you started shooting?
JG: No, I didn't. I did some research. I'd been to the Midland/Odessa area before so I knew what it was all about. You know these movies did not have a tremendous budget. I really had to just start work-

ing. Start figuring out how to tie the whole movie together–you know, the exteriors to the interiors. It's just so much to figure out.

So I didn't really have any time to go. I've done it on other movies. On *Capote* there was no way I was going to Winnepeg [the shooting location] before I saw where this crime, the four murders, took place. I had to go see that [in Kansas] because I didn't know what it was. But West Texas I had a pretty good idea about.

AS: *No Country for Old Men* feels like it's very realistic on one hand but it's also very stylized, like the writing is. How do you get that balance between the realism and style?
JG: The first thing is to keep it real. It's gotta be believable. Especially on *No Country for Old Men*, it first of all has to be believable, otherwise it's going to take away from the story. My job is just to facilitate. To pull the audience through the movie visually and not to go too far with the craft. William Eggleston's photographs were very influential and if you look at that guy's photographs they're stylized but they're real. I sort of adopted that mantra in the look of *No Country*.

It was a three-way chase: Moss was running from Chigurh, and Chigurh was running from the law. So how could I keep the amazing pace of this movie without up-staging all the great things? You make it real but push it to the mark just before it starts teetering on the edge and becoming unbelievable. This took place in 1980 and really 1980 in that part of the country could be the 1970's. So I had the luxury of really making it dated without, obviously, paisley patterns and things like that. Just that real, sun-drenched, oak veneer William Eggleston, desert dirt look.

AS: You mention not upstaging the story. I often ask the question whether production design should be visible or invisible...

JG: It's not completely invisible. I try to pay attention to detail. I try to get a couple of great things in the shot that also help tell the story about the character or the place. The things that you get into the frame are not an accident. It takes a lot of time to figure out what are you going to put in there. That's why I keep working on those Coen brothers movies–they're very well planned out. This is what we're going to shoot on this day, it's going to be shot in this direction and the sun's going to be over here. You're able to take the time to figure out what the best thing for that scene is–supporting the character and supporting the page that's written and the location that it's in. It's really very important.

AS: In those Coen brothers movies how much do you build on a stage and how much is shot practically?

JG: Well, it's very rare that you get something all-in-one, there's always some restrictions on whatever it is. In *True Grit* the boarding house that Mattie slept in was broken up into three different elements. We built the exterior of it as part of this town that we built. It was basically three sides of the boarding house and a porch. Once Mattie opened up the door we shot at a practical location. Which was a couple of miles away from that town. It was an old Victorian house that we completely redid. And then also on stage we built the bedroom because we had to have some camerawork and some special lighting and it needed to be controlled. The actual room in the Victorian was too small to do it all practically.

> **" YOU MAKE IT REAL BUT PUSH IT TO THE MARK JUST BEFORE IT STARTS TEETERING ON THE EDGE AND BECOMING UNBELIEVABLE.**

So the two scenes at the boarding house were broken up into three different locations and shot over six days in three different parts of Texas. It all depends on how much you can shoot practically and how much you control. A lot has to do with the confinements of filming, and the angles. On *No Country* we used a couple of exteriors of hotels but we didn't really shoot any motel rooms on location. We built all of the motel rooms. There was all the interaction with the air-shaft. Four or five motel rooms were all built on stage. For a couple of them we shot the exteriors of existing motels.

The Coen brothers edit their movies. That's another amazing thing. They can visualize how the movie is going to fit together. And I say, *Is it okay if we do this here and that there?* And they look at each other and say, *Okay, we can make it work. That's going to be the best way to carve it up.* But sometimes it's not. Sometimes you have to look out a door and see something across the street–you can't just cut to something else. How much you shoot practically and how much you shoot on a stage also really depends on if you're shooting at night or if you're shooting during the day. Personally I love to shoot things practically, I think the things look more real. But there are reasons to do things on stage like for the sheer factor of all those motel rooms having so much gunfire going off. We have to put squibs in all the walls and there's all the blood, so you have to build those.

AS: For those built sets do you create scale models and do a lot of sketches?

JG: Yeah, we draw them. I find that the practical, quick model is the easiest way. You can pick it up and look at it and handle it. Stick it up to your eye and look through a door, look through a window. I don't have all the money in the world so I'm going to say that it's a little antiquated what we do. There's a lot of stuff on the computer, yes, but there's also a lot of stuff that's done the way it's been done forever. It's cutting up cardboard and putting the pieces together and holding them up to the sky and seeing how they react to the light and seeing how you can stage the action. So I use a combination. I'm pretty old-school with some of that stuff. I still like to do it the old-fashioned way, building some models even if they're not to the greatest detail. It helps the conversation. Get everybody in front of that and really just poke it

with a pencil and push it one way and shove it another way. It's like reading *The New York Times* in newspaper form instead of on-line.

AS: I was just talking to John Myhre and he described how on *Wanted*, the director Timur Bekmambetov was a big Russian visual effects guy and at first he laughed at John's foam-core models but then he was won over and ended up asking him to do one for every set.

JG: I can see that. I mean in this day and age everything is just pre-visualization and that's fine, I love it, it's cool. I'm into it. But on *No Country* and *True Grit* we didn't have all the money in the world and we didn't have all the support in the world with lots of sophisticated gear, so we did it the old-fashioned way and quite frankly I prefer that.

AS: Do you have a certain set crew that you always work with?

JG: I'd like to, but people are not always available. I certainly have my favorite people. I've worked with the same people two, and three, and four movies. But you can't always hire right when people are available. If I could I would. I have two different teams of people that I work with and they're both extraordinary.

AS: When you go on a location like New Mexico do you end up having to crew up with local people or do you bring a lot of people out?

JG: With these movies you're encouraged to hire local people because they're much cheaper. For *True Grit* out of maybe ten people in the art department, including art director, assistant art director, draftspeople and model-makers and things like that, three of them were from LA and seven of them were from New Mexico or Texas.

AS: I noticed that you did some work as a construction foreman before going on to become an art director and then production designer. How did that transition happen?

JG: I got a job building sets one day and I enjoyed it and they were giving me more and more responsibility and it just sort of came naturally. I was having a really amazing time doing it but always in the back of my mind I knew I wanted to be the guy that was in charge of this whole thing. So it was a little bit of hard work and lots of luck. I slipped into a couple of jobs where people gave me a shot at being an assistant art director or set designer. I took advantage of that and there was a lot of luck involved. You know somebody drops out of something and you take their slot. Then when the time was right I got my own movie and fortunately for me it worked out really well and I didn't have to spend a lot of years doing things that I didn't like. I was fortunate that the first thing out of the gate was really very successful. I've only designed nine movies now and I'm proud of them all. I may have had to design nineteen movies to get to this point if that first one wasn't good, so I'm just real fortunate with that.

AS: Did you go to art school or to film school before that?

JG: I worked in the theater and that's where I get my frugalness from. There's no money in the theater. You have a couple of tin cans and string to tie them together. Somebody gives you a hundred dollars you're like, *Wow, let's do something.* I really credit working in the backstage crew at Mamaroneck high school for really giving me my chops. To not be afraid to do what you want to do even if you don't have the money to do it.

> ❝ THE WHOLE THING IS CONTAGIOUS . . . IT IS PEOPLE PUSHING EACH OTHER. PEOPLE STIMULATING EACH OTHER. NOBODY'S BETTER THAN ANYBODY ELSE AND I REALLY THINK THAT'S WHY SOME OF THE THINGS THAT I'VE WORKED ON HAVE COME OUT SO WELL–THERE ARE NO EGOS.

AS: Would you say that would be one of the qualities that you think a good production designer should have–being able to make something out of whatever you get?

JG: I think that's *the* quality, I really do. Back in the days of the ancient Greeks or Romans they just had a rock in the sun, so I think that everything that we do is extra.

The more that you can do yourself, and the more that you can identify with the other people who are in your crew, the bigger advantage you're going to have. You're not just somebody walking around with a suit and a tie telling somebody what to do. I know what it's like to sweep the floor and I know what it's like to be on your knees banging nails and working twelve hours digging a ditch. All of those things prepared me for what I do now. *Okay, here's a sheet of plywood. Guess what: we're going to design this, that, and this, and we're going to cut off two feet of it and we're going to use those two feet over here to do this.*

That's my style, that's who I am and I don't think that's ever going to change. And I think that's why I stick with these types of movies. I don't know if I'm going to be the guy that does the *Batmans* and the huge comic-book things. I'm not saying no, but right now I don't know that that's me. I think it's an amazing tool to understand what everybody's doing out there. It's nice if you're familiar with what's happening in your world.

> " I'M NOT GOING TO DESIGN A WHOLE MOVIE AND THEN TURN IT OVER TO SOME VISUAL EFFECTS COMPANY. THEY NEED TO BE RESPECTFUL AND UNDERSTAND WHAT IT IS THAT EVERYBODY'S WORKED SO HARD ON.

AS: Are those similar qualities that you look for in your crew-members?
JG: No, not at all. When putting together a team everybody should have their strong-points and my strong-point is what I've been talking about. People hire me because I can go to a town with three buildings in it and say, *Okay, guess what: we're going*

to put up twenty more buildings. You have to make a decision because you're up against some kind of schedule, some sort of start date and some sort of end date and you have to back into that. But I tend to hire people that have different strengths than me and together it becomes a cohesive department and everybody pushes each other. I don't care where the ideas come from–it could be a drawing left out on the table. The cleaning crew came in and left a note on the table, *Hey, I think you should paint this this color.* I don't really care as long as it's a good idea. That's how I like to operate.

AS: Say someone was just starting out in the business and wanted to avoid any pitfalls along the way?
JG: You just gotta do it. You gotta work. You can only learn so much and then you just have to start doing something and making mistakes. The cliché is so true: *How do you get to Carnegie Hall? Practice, practice, practice.* You have to get out there and do something. If you're in school you should also be doing something at night or on the weekends. If you want to be a DP just start shooting stuff. For everything you do there's a lesson learned, whether it's good or bad. It's every single thing that you do. You know to be in this business you have to be out there and aware and absorbing information all the time. I just keep my ears and my eyes open, seeing what's out there.

AS: Is it really different to shoot movies in New York City?

JG: The difference is it's not a business here, it's not as formal as it is in LA. You can't really compare both places. In Los Angeles they have the most incredible craftspeople around. I think they do in New York too, it's just a little deeper in LA cause they just do a lot more there. They've been doing it for a hundred and something years over there. Usually people shoot here for locations and some cool city exteriors but at the same time there's more and more stage work now. They're building more and more sound stages here too now.

It's a little more challenging here which is what I like about it. I think that's the big difference. Shooting a movie in LA is more a way of life. Shooting a movie in New York is more of just bringing a new challenge every day to your job. They don't make it easy for you here, I have to say. You go and do a movie in LA and it's so easy and you wonder why you don't do that all the time.

AS: Do you have one particular set in a movie that stands out as your favorite?

JG: *A Serious Man* probably has all of my favorites in it. That's the best-looking thing I've ever done. I think the rabbi's office at the end is amazing. We transformed an entire neighborhood back to 1967 and that was an amazing transformation. It just blew my mind what we did over there. I could single out a couple of things but I think that entire movie is my best work and I don't even know if it's going to get better than that! I just love everything about that movie. I mean I know a lot about the 60s, I know a lot about the music that was in that

movie, I went through that whole bar mitzvah routine myself. So I would say that that's my favorite so far.

AS: Are you usually really involved with the locations department?

JG: I'm very involved. I've been fortunate to work with some good location managers. But really, it all starts in the art department. They'll go out and photograph and then come back and I'll choose some things. It makes your life a lot easier when you have a great location manager and some great scouts that have some good eyes and are really on to what your vision of the movie is. And I've worked with a couple of the same people more than once and that's great. I like to gather the whole locations team up and I'll make a book, a sort of reference book of photos that have something to do with the look of the movie. If it's not the exact thing that I want to find it's the color of something or it's the rhythm of something or it's the feel of something. So I'll usually take the whole location department through the book and through all the photographs and I think they like that. They like to be involved. They have an assignment then. A photo assignment to go and seek this thing out and bring their own game to it. They go, *Hey Jess, I know you wanted this, but I found this, what about this?* I'm like, *Man that's great. Let's go see it. Let's see what we can do about it.*

The whole thing is contagious. I really think a film crew is contagious. It is people pushing each other. People stimulating each other. Nobody's better than anybody else and I really think that's why some of the things that I've worked on have come out so well–there are no egos. People push each other's buttons in a good way and it's a contagious reaction around the whole community to make something great. It starts with the directors. Because dissension amongst the ranks starts at the top. If you have a good leader, the rest is going to happen. It's going to translate onto that screen.

AS: Do you get involved closely with other departments like, for example, picture cars, and show them your book?

JG: Yeah, everything that goes on the screen has to fit into the movie. You can't have something show up that doesn't fit. A clothespin, a car, a piece of grass, a building. It's all a very carefully calculated scheme. You need to be involved in everything, you need to be involved with what wardrobe is doing, you just need to be involved with everything.

AS: I hear you recently completed another Bennett Miller movie?

JG: Yes, it's called *Moneyball* and it's about this eccentric general manager of the Oakland A's, Billy Beane. We completed that and now I just signed on to do *The Lone Ranger*. It's a little ironic because it is a big Bruckheimer action adventure, which is outside my norm, but at the end of the day it's still a dusty old Western. No computers, no spaceships, no super powers. Just a gun-slinging Western. I'm going to apply my same old approach to the whole thing and see what happens.

AS: How did working with Bennett Miller on *Moneyball* and *Capote* compare to working with the Coen brothers?

JG: Well the Coen brothers have made fifteen movies. Bennett's amazing: he's a super-intelligent director and he also has an amazing vision and an amazing eye for what's right and what's wrong and the level he plays at is really, really high, maybe higher than anybody I've worked with. So he also pushes you. The difference, and I think he would admit it too, is just experience. If you have fifteen movies under your belt you're different than if you have two movies. But I love working with him. I think *Capote* was amazing and I think he killed it. He killed it in so many ways. And I think this *Moneyball* thing is going to be amazing too. He's a tremendous guy.

AS: Any other sources of inspiration for your design work?

JG: I think my inspiration has always been hanging around with my father. He's an architect and the most creative person I know. The apple didn't fall far from the tree. Ever since building stuff in the basement and making sculpture he always encouraged me and the encouragement was unbelievable. That's really my inspiration, where I draw from. What are you made up of? There's somebody in your life that really said something to you, that encouraged you, that taught you. And for me that's my dad.

AS: Are you very involved with visual effects on movies?

JG: On *A Serious Man* and on some of the Coen brothers stuff you do, there are some visual effects. It's mainly a matter of erasing bad elements that have been captured in the frame. But I'll put my two-cents in. I'm not going to design a whole movie and then turn it over to some visual effects company. They need to be respectful and understand what it is that everybody's worked so hard on. I'm involved not to the point where I'm reporting and going to work with the visual effects company every day. But when production's over and we see what we need then I'm going to generate some comps of what I think it should look like. And react to what has been done and put my two cents in.

AS: It looks like the future of production design may involve a lot of greenscreens and a lot more visual effects . . .

JG: With everything being shot digitally it's just so easy to change things so it's not just happening, it's here. You can still find the odd movie that doesn't have a lot of visual effects but it's getting harder and harder. Times are changing. They've already changed and you've got to get on board with it, you have to change with the times. I'm totally fine with that. They're never going to stop making period movies so you're always going to have a shot at that. Then you gotta go the other way and get involved with all the new technology that's out there. And that makes it exciting.

David Warren

David Warren was nominated for an Academy Award for his work on Terry Gilliam's *Imaginarium of Dr. Parnassus,* a film that effortlessly bridges the practical with visual effects. Over the years he's risen from art director to production designer, learning along the way from the best: legends Dante Ferretti, Roy Walker, and John Box.

AS: What was it like working with Terry Gilliam?
DW: There is a certain amount of chaos. There's quite a lot of creativity and imagination. I think to a certain extent that part of the job is understanding where he's coming from and getting on his wavelength. That's common to a lot of directors. What's interesting with Terry is that in the opening stages of preparation he's all about giving. It's all about getting it from Terry. Some directors want to be pitched. But Terry is very forthcoming and he puts a lot of information down on paper because I think the design of the film is something he's particularly interested in doing.

I could see a circumstance arising where if you're a designer who doesn't have a lot of graphic skills but instead is a very good organizer and a good interpreter then I could see Terry simply feeding you all the information.

AS: He does sketches himself as well?
DW: Yeah, he does. He uses Photoshop really well and he does it really quick. And I think the task is to kind of fill in the bits that he doesn't do and also to challenge the ideas that you might not think have gone far enough. He does provide a lot of information up front but you're always thinking, *There's*

no way you can run off and build that! or *There's no way you can do that as a matte painting.* That means another circuit of sketches and drawings and improvements.

So in a way he raises the bar very high in terms of art department work but the trouble is it's all that much higher to jump over! People ask what was the most difficult aspect of the film. Well, in the opening stages it was just sheer quantity. I know there were two designers but it felt like we were doing two movies in a way. We were doing a physical one with normal set decoration, props, art direction, the wagon, and all that kind of shmutter, and then we were doing a visual effects movie through the mirror, six hundred and fifty shots. I know a lot of people talk about *Avatar* being the world that was explored to the nth degree, which was fantastic, but every time we went through the Imaginarium mirror Terry wanted to see something different. It was a very labor-happy film from that point of view.

AS: You yourself do a lot of the sketches?

DW: I do, yeah, because that's my background. I come from a background of illustration so the first thing I reach for in any situation is a pencil. And in the early stages we were hammering out drawings on the drawing board. When Terry likes it he comes over and puts his fingers all over it and it gets messy. Then he grabs a pencil and he starts scribbling on your drawing. That's the language that we used to make decisions. Because the trouble with Terry is that ideas, when they are writ-

ten in the script by him and Charles, read very esoteric. I mean, when I first read the script with some of the landscapes I didn't know what the hell they were talking about. You've got to see the image and as soon as you see the image you go, *Oh, that's the shape of the mountain. Oh, that's what you mean by the balloon . . .*

> **NO MATTER WHAT WE DO IN THE FUTURE, FILMS WILL ALWAYS BE MADE BY PEOPLE, NOT COMPUTERS. THE WAY THAT IT IS THRASHED OUT IS BY PEOPLE TALKING OVER ENDLESS NIGHTS AND CUPS OF COFFEE!**

AS: It was you and Anastasia Masaro working together at all times?

DW: No, because in the history of the film I came on earlier than she did. When I came on I hit the ground running and I started sketching and drawing. She came on the set six weeks or so later and then she had to get up to speed very quickly in England. So we prepped it together in the UK and the plan was always that she would run the Canadian half of the shoot. That was the sets that went on blue-screen stages and some locations and also anything we didn't complete in and around the wagon. So that's more or less how we divided the work.

AS: Did you enjoy working with Peerless and with visual effects in general as a designer?

DW: I get a huge kick out of it. The effects work in

a visual effects film is integral to the design which is why Robert Stromberg's work became so integral to Rick Carter's on *Avatar*.

You break it down around a big table. You go through the sequences at length, talk through the line between physicality, miniature, and CG. That's always a negotiation around a table–you don't go and decide on that in a closed room. You've got to sit together and say, *What if we build that? You sure you need that? Well, hang on a minute, that's grass so we do need that because it's a hell of a thing to do digitally*. No matter what we do in the future, films will always be made by people, not computers. The way that it is thrashed out is by people talking over endless nights and cups of coffee!

I worked very closely with Peerless. I like them a lot. I still go in there if I'm in town. I'll just drop in and say hello. They're a really good bunch of people.

AS: Do there end up being a lot of visual effects meetings throughout the process?

DW: Yeah, I'm pretty sure actually that we must have gone through every sequence at least twice in those early stages. You know, sitting around a big conference table in Peerless just going though it scene number by scene number, storyboard by storyboard. That's the only way to do it.

Terry had done an immense amount of prep work because the onus was on his shoulders to make the film work financially. In the early stages he loves to come to the table and say, *I've thought about this film and I've got a solution to make it.* I thought it was fantastic that Terry took the time to sit around the table with us and say, *Why the hell are we building that? We don't need it.* Or vice versa: *You know I think I need that physically there. Can I get it lit? I want to see the reflections in it.* I've never spent so much time with a director face-to-face on a film.

AS: Would you say that previs is pretty indispensable?

DW: Yes, I think it is, with key sequences. But there's a lot of conversation about it being eye candy. When it comes to shooting, the director wants to shoot what he wants to shoot anyway. With Terry it was a little bit different. I think in the early stages of the film it was a very, very useful tool for calibrating certain sequences. Because storyboards are great but obviously what previs gives you is it gives you motion and you can see exactly where the camera's gonna go. Yeah, I think it was really valuable. I've still got the original previs from *Parnassus* on my computer.

AS: I noticed that you've worked with a lot of the old-school production designers like John Box and Roy Walker. Is their kind of design fading away or is it basically the same thing with different tools?

DW: I think it is the same thing with different tools because it's always a matter of taste at the end of the day. And I think that the problem with digital films these days is that we have the ability to do anything with a computer but that doesn't mean we should do anything with a computer. And you have to be aware that visual effects films really are genre pictures because they fit into a certain box.

The thing about working with John [Box] years ago is that he was a much more sanguine and a much more paced art director or production designer. You know he used to quote *Lawrence of Arabia* and *Dr. Zhivago* in meetings. He'd bring it up and say, *Well on that we did this*, and fuck, you can't argue with that! He won four Oscars! I think he would have been bemused by the modern way of filmmaking.

AS: What would you say are some attributes that production designers need to have?

DW: Tireless energy. And I think a designer needs a wide life experience. An appreciation of a lot of different things. You can bring very eclectic references to the table. You need imagination. There are certain personality traits that some designers use that get them through films easier than others. The ability to judge people really well–who's working for you and also who you're working with. Obviously situations arise when you've gotta fight your corner or you've gotta let it go. You know I just think that's a matter of personal judgment.

The biggest one is always taste. Just good taste. And by that I mean, whether you're doing dragons flying through the air or just a salt and pep-per pot on a table top, you still need to know that looks better than that! That's really what it boils down to.

Production designers are all human beings– they're all different. Some of them draw, some of them don't. Some of them have got tireless energy and excitement. Some of them are much more quiet. I don't think you can write this on a piece of paper and say, *Well, that guy can draw so he'll be a great designer.* I know that John Myhre for instance doesn't draw a lot but he still has two Academy Awards. He's obviously got a fantastic eye for references and he knows exactly what looks good when it's built. He knows how to dress a set.

> " THE BIGGEST ONE IS ALWAYS TASTE. JUST GOOD TASTE. AND BY THAT I MEAN, WHETHER YOU'RE DOING DRAGONS FLYING THROUGH THE AIR OR JUST A SALT AND PEPPER POT ON A TABLE TOP, YOU STILL NEED TO KNOW THAT LOOKS BETTER THAN THAT! THAT'S REALLY WHAT IT BOILS DOWN TO.

AS: You worked with Tim Burton and Dante Ferretti on *Sweeney Todd* and Dante on *Interview with a Vampire*. What was it like working with those guys?

DW: Working with Dante is great because he's a very kind, generous fellow and he's a really nice guy. When I was coming up in the film industry he was the first guy I worked with. And before I started I didn't really know what a production designer did. Do a first film with Dante and then you walk away from that film thinking, *Well that's what a designer does.* And then after that you have fifteen years of disappointment!

He was fantastic, he really was. He does draw and he does it in the Italian way. Doing these big, charcoal sketches of the sets. Lots of color, lots of lighting. He does them very quick. He just gets out his colored paper and draws these beautiful visuals from his imagination. He uses reference obviously but then he commits it to paper himself. He will say very early on, *I want everything to be linear, I want it as real as possible.* He likes stuff to be quite rigid and there's often symmetry. It's just very, very interesting to work with him.

AS: On *Sweeney Todd* did Tim Burton do a lot of sketches himself or was it all Dante?
DW: The triangular room with the huge window was something Tim sketched with Dante, they sat at a table together. Tim had seen this huge, skylight window somewhere before so he was absolutely convinced that was what he wanted. But most of it was completely Dante. Tim was in on certain icons. But Dante did the big street, the cellar, the great big room in the bad judge's house–all of those were his ideas and his solutions.

Tim was very interested in seeing what the big oven looked like underground, what sort of door that Mrs. Lovett gets pushed into in the end. Tim was like, *I want it to be this big, I want the door to be that shape.* He's interested in certain things and then other things he's like, *Just make it like the city of London–that will be fine!*

AS: What was your background? Did you go to art school?
DW: Yeah, I went to art school like I suppose everybody does. In my third year at college I did a course in illustration and I had to do a thesis, a written dialogue. I knew Terry Gilliam from *Baron Munchausen* and *The Fisher King* so I based it on Terry. In the back of your mind you're sort of thinking, *I wonder what it would be like to have a chat with him.* I went to my thesis teacher and he said, *Well you haven't got a cat in hell's chance. But don't worry about that just write your thesis you'll be fine.* A guy I was working with said, *No, no, you've got to interview him. Of course you have.*

So I did write him a letter and eventually he got a hold of me and said, *Yeah, yeah, I can spare you an hour.* In the interview, which I still have a tape of somewhere, he said, *Well, what are you doing?* And I said, *Trying to be an illustrator.*

He said, *I'd love to see your stuff.* So I went and visited him, I brought my work to his place in Highgate and it was like nothing more came of it. *Great, really interesting stuff. Well, a friend of mine's putting together a film. We might need storyboards–we'll bear you in mind.*

It all kind of went dead and I went back to my day job. I was working in North London doing odd jobs just to keep some money coming in. Then eventually out of the blue he called up and said, *I'm doing preproduction on a film called* Defective Detective. *I've got a designer obviously but I need somebody in here to help make some models and things like that.*

So I went and worked for him in Camden Town for four weeks. The designer he had was Dante Ferretti. Dante had already started working for him doing sketches. Lovely to just spend four weeks working with Dante, just watching him draw. At the end of that Dante looked at me and said, *This film's never going to happen.* Although he loved Terry he knew how difficult it was and he said, *I'm going to go do something with Neil Jordan, maybe I'll call you.* And two weeks later he did.

I got on my first feature film as an art department assistant or as you call them in LA, PA's. You're running around printing drawings and making tea. But on that first movie you learn more than you can learn at college. You learn how a film gets made. I did three movies back to back like that.

After Dante I did four or six weeks with Roy Walker who was doing *The Scarlet Letter.* I was making tea for him and also making little models and bits and pieces. At the end of that he said, *Right, I'm off to Nova Scotia but John Box is coming in here. I'll have a word with John.* The next week John comes in and he says, *Right, you're coming with me.* And that was

that. That's how I worked with those three guys at the beginning.

It was luck. I was packing up the archive boxes for *Interview with the Vampire*, everyone else had left the movie, and I was literally putting the lid on the last box when Roy came in the door and said, *Hello, my name's Roy what do you do? I'll talk to my producer. You can stay on. I need somebody running around for me.* If I'd literally packed that last box off and gone to my car I'd never have met Roy. And then I'd never have met John. It's as strange as that.

> **IT'S LIKE EVERY SIX MONTHS A DEVIL COMES AND TAKES A SIX MONTH BITE OUT OF MY LIFE THAT I NEVER SEE AGAIN! AND THEN A YEAR GOES BY AND YOU SIT IN A CINEMA WITH A LOAD OF STRANGE PEOPLE WATCHING YOUR WORK COME UP ON THE SCREEN.**

AS: Any advice for people just coming into the industry?

DW: It's interesting because the industry's going through a sort of minor technological revolution and at certain points in the film industry's history, especially in Britain, people have been able to capitalize on that and move up very quickly. At the moment there's a big question about the amalgamation of visual effects and the art department.

My advice to anybody coming in would be, *Be creative, be imaginative. Learn the current tech-*

nology to the highest level you can because you'll move a lot faster. Old guys like me look at people that are twenty-five who are very, very fluid in current software and say, *I need that guy with me on the next job because I haven't got a clue how that works.* You know it is as simple as that.

> ❝ DESIGNER STEVE SCOTT WHO DESIGNED *HELLBOY* ONCE TOLD ME, *NEVER BE GOOD AT ANYTHING YOU DON'T WANT TO DO THE REST OF YOUR LIFE.*

The art department still has so many different pathways within it. I think designer's obviously what everyone wants to be but still you can make a good career out of being a good sketch artist or a visualizer. You can make a career out of being a set decorator. You can make a good career out of being an art director. You have to make that decision at some point.

Because the trouble is any one film only needs one production designer or possibly two, like we had. But you'll always need more art directors and you'll need a lot of set designers and you'll possibly need two set decorators. You know, the further down the pile the more possibility you've got of getting a job in the beginning days.

AS: So get in there with one of those jobs and then make your choice . . .
DW: Sometimes it's by a process of natural selection. Designer Steve Scott who designed *Hellboy*

once told me, *Never be good at anything you don't want to do the rest of your life.* If you're good at designing you'll be a production designer for the rest of your life but it is true there are people that are phenomenal sketch artists and they get very well paid for it, but they end up on those rails. And a few, like Robert Stromberg or Rick Heinrichs, they break out and do other things.

AS: Do you plan on doing more jobs as production designer or as an art director?
DW: I'm art directing this film for Dante but I thought to myself, *Well, Dante's a very, very good designer and Martin Scorsese's a very, very good director. Martin's probably never going to use another designer again apart from Dante.* So I thought that this was actually a good thing to do. Dante said to me, *You should be designing. Please do my movie but after that I never want to see you again!* It's been written on the wall for me now. I'm going to do this film and then I'm going to see what happens afterwards.

AS: Has the Oscar nomination changed your life in any way or is it pretty much the same?
DW: It was really weird because everybody on this movie knew I was going to the nominations. That always has an effect on what happens in meetings because people are making jokes about it. *Well, because of your Oscar nomination I suppose we have to do that.* Great, thanks a lot guys!

I just had an email from someone this morning saying, *Can we check on your availability? We're looking for a production designer.* I said, *Well I'm here with*

Dante so I'm pretty fucked! I'll just have to see what happens really.

AS: Would you say the future of production design belongs to be the people who are going to effortlessly combine the visual effects with the practical?

DW: I think so. Although we should never get away from the fact that there are films being made every year that are normal films. That aren't great visual effects extravaganzas. Out of the movies that were nominated this year, the one that Patrice [Vermette] did, *Young Victoria*, probably had like ten visual effects shots in it–matte paintings and a little bit of augmentation. That was a film all shot on location. *Avatar* has two thousand visual effects shots yet both films were still nominated. So it's interesting that it's still just about taste and what looks good to the eye.

What Robert Stromberg did on *Avatar* is symbolic of the way that film design may go in the future. This bridge between visual effects and the art department is a very strong thing. Doug Chiang was the production designer on *Beowulf* and he was the visual effects design director for the first two Star Wars movies. But then Gabriella Pescucci did costume design for *Beowulf* and she's a real old hat. You have a very young, modern team designing the sets–these were guys that bridged with visual effects–but then for costume they brought in somebody who worked on movies in Italy. It's about how costumes flow, how stuff is cut, and how stuff holds onto the body.

But I think as time goes on people like Bob Stromberg bridging visual effects will become more and more common.

AS: What do you see as the difference between designing for film and other forms of design?

DW: In the public sector you probably design a big building project over three to ten years. But we say, *Right, we're going to do all that in fifteen weeks.* And your feet don't touch the ground. They really don't. It's like every six months a devil comes and takes a six month bite out of my life that I never see again! And then a year goes by and you sit in a cinema with a load of strange people watching your work come up on the screen. That's how I describe it. It's the weirdest thing, it really is!

Ralph Eggleston

Pixar production designer Ralph Eggleston explains that while the production process is different with animated films, the design thinking is the same. An Academy Award winner, Eggleston has contributed his artistic vision to features at Pixar since *Toy Story.* Over the years he's production designed a series of beloved, animated blockbusters including *Incredibles 2, Inside Out, Finding Nemo,* and more, all adding up to a worldwide gross close to 4 billion.

AS: Normally live action production designers go from one project to the next, not knowing what, when, or where the next one will be. What is it like being a production designer with the security of going into an office every day?

RE: It's akin to to the old studio system in a way. I start before we have much of a script at all, and I'm there all the way through helping out with marketing and merchandise. The longest show I've ever worked on was five and a half years and that was

Inside Out, the shortest was *Incredibles 2*, which was two and a half years.

AS: When you went to school was your goal from the outset to be an animator in feature films?

RE: Originally, yes. I'm an okay animator. And after school I ended up doing a lot of moving titles. I designed and boarded and animated a bunch of titles with Bill and Sue Kroyer for Kroyer Films. They did titles for *Honey, I Shrunk the Kids, Troop Bever-*

ly Hills, National Lampoon's Christmas Vacation and also animation for rides at the Disney parks.

AS: That intro to *Christmas Vacation* is classic.
RE: We had a good time. I was never quite good enough to animate for Disney. And I was interested in more than just animating. I started to get interested in design and how you put the whole thing together, the visual part of the storytelling. Because of that I found myself, over the course of a few years, pretty well-equipped to do art direction and then production design. I knew enough about the various roles in production, and how to start at the end of production and work my way backwards towards the beginning. How to think about planning a film. What does something mean to the following departments in the pipeline?

And for some reason when I read a script or someone's telling me a story I'm able to really just see it unfolding in my head. Sure, I do lots of research, but I really am able to see it and I'm able to put it down with a drawing or a painting to communicate with the director. Or to get a dialog going about how we ought to be thinking about telling the story.

AS: You end up drawing throughout the process?
RE: I do draw a lot. When inspiration hits me, I'll draw it–and sometimes paint an idea up. But what I have taken to more recently is getting 3″ x 5″ index cards and outlining each character and each set. Just writing a series of words to describe the "character" or "personality" of each character and set, with a thesaurus handy. I write them out, pin them up on a large board, change them, move them around, refine them and simplify them, so there are not five hundred but only like, ten words that communicate the idea of a character, or the world, or this set, this moment of the film. I try to limit it so that it's not overwhelming to myself or to the director or anyone else that might be involved.

I start with the general framework of the story. But I also try to identify how the characters interrelate in terms of what I want to draw, before I start drawing it. So I put a list of words together and talk about it with the director. They'll throw some stuff away and put new stuff up and we'll refine it and while we're doing that, I'm starting to gather reference materials. I categorize them with either those specific words or those specific ideas, bigger buckets and then smaller buckets for each one. And then I really start thinking about drawing, and ideas for shapes, and framing. Cinematography and composition. I try to distill all of it into a handful of visuals that can be the major themes and then find ways to do variations on those themes through the course of a scene or a sequence or a character. Designing the characters is also a big part of what we do within the Art Department on an animated film.

I tend to have three art directors, sometimes four, depending. I have a character art director and their primary job is to supervise the design of the characters. Then I'll have an environment art director, or the sets art director, and a texture art director. What they design in terms of textures is what the virtual lights pick up on and what the audience will see in the final film. It's a really important job. And then, depending on the complexity of needs on a film, a graphics art director. *Incredibles 2* had a lot of graphics versus a film like *Brave* or *Good Dinosaur*, which had graphics too but they were fairly limited. So depending on the level or amount of graphics I might have that fourth art director.

AS: Does your job start when you get a script as with live action production designers? Or are you involved before that?

RE: Most often before that. For example, right now I'm doing nothing but development work for upcoming features at Pixar, working on the next six or seven projects. They'll pitch me an idea they're just beginning and ask for some visuals to support it.

I've rarely started on a film where I had a finished screenplay or even a finished story. In the case of *Incredibles 2* we had three distinct, vastly different versions of the story and as it progressed Brad Bird would come and bounce ideas around and we'd evolve the visual aspects of the story that way. It was great because I got to evolve the visuals with the story, and they became well-integrated. But every film is different and every director is different.

AS: Bo Welch talked about getting to a point where he would "crack the code" of a film. It sounds like you're cracking the code before you even have a finished script?

RE: It happens earlier during the development process–sometimes with just a simple pitch. It's funny, because I hate reading scripts. I find the format difficult to read. I would rather have the director tell me the story. And I have them tell me the story every few weeks. And as they tell it, it's evolving and changing and growing and hopefully getting better. The things that they repeat tend to be the things they are really excited about. And I make mental notes and literal notes on what is starting to stick and where their mind is going as they're telling the story. I would rather have them tell me the story because it's a door into the director's mind.

The production designer Richard Sylbert was a huge inspiration for me on how to think about all of that. You whittle it down to those basic character-driven conceits or "cracking the code," as they say. We had a PA, now a barber in Oakland, who was dating one of Dick Sylbert's daughters. When she came to visit the PA at Pixar she brought Dick Sylbert. I showed him around and asked him to come back and give a talk. So he came back and I spent a few days with him. He gave his talk about designing *Chinatown*–which is basically in the Vincent LoBrutto book, *By Design*. He was so happy to see how much real drawing and painting we were doing–some of it on the computer, but a lot with pencil, pen, paint and pastel. In the introduction of his autobiography he said if he and his mentor William Cameron Menzies started out now they would be working at Pixar, which was a huge compliment! Sam Wasson's book *The Big Goodbye*, about the making of *Chinatown*, also has a lot about Dick Sylbert and his approach. It's one of the best books ever written about the making of the film.

AS: Dick Sylbert was on the same page with discovering a film's visual theme.

RE: I started calling it building corrals of visual information. But when I started at Pixar, when we did *Toy Story* in 1995, we would have to be very specific about every little thing. There were very tight blueprint drawings of everything we did, characters, sets, textures, everything. I come from traditional animation where it's a much more "freeform interactive" process. But when we started on *Toy Story,* people were writing the software and building the hardware as we made the film. They were brilliant, but most of them were computer scientists that didn't have great visual skills. Over the first few of the Pixar features we had to make tight blueprints but we had to do it less and less as A, the software and hardware got better, and B, the people got better, and C, two or three generations later, many art schools have computer graphics programs–so our newer staff show up at Pixar already with great visual skills.

Incredibles 2 was the first film where I turned off my concerns about how we were going to get things on screen. That's something I'm happy I don't feel the need to do anymore. Instead I focus on the design, the corrals of visual information, and I fight to find those central conceits. I crack the code so that I can present that to every department and they find what they can bring to the table. And I don't have to explain to them that this needs to be softened here, or this needs to be more straight there. Instead it's, *What is the character of this scene about?* And of course the technology has gotten better

so we're able to see literally everything as we're making the film, whereas on the first ten movies we were lucky to be able to see three things in a room as it's going through animation. Details and set dressing were often done at a later phase–as the computing power wasn't available to render entire sets at the time. It's evolved, it's so much more collaborative now.

AS: Designing a live-action movie you're always up against budgetary constraints, but in feature animation can you, for example, add an unlimited amount of airplanes to an airfield?

RE: There are still budgetary limitations. Here's an example. On *Finding Nemo* there was originally a sequence where these seagulls chase a pelican through downtown Sydney, Australia. I was the only one who went to Sydney to do research and the producers were upset with me for spending the money I needed to gather the research I felt we needed. I got in a water taxi and went around the entire harbor all day long, getting off wherever I wanted to, to take pictures. I got back to California and was doing my job when they wrote this sequence with a dentist office set in downtown Sydney, Australia. The producers were rubbing their temples like, *We can't afford to build down town Sydney, Australia! It's a huge city!*

So I said, *Well, why don't we set it across the bay?* Most people have not been to Sydney, Australia and if you're downtown you don't know it's Sydney. In closeups it just looks like any other city. If it was Tokyo or Hong Kong it could have the signage to communicate the differences. I said by putting it across the bay, number one, you always have the picture-perfect view of the bridge, the opera house, and the tower, so the audience gets right away where we are, and two, we can put the chase in a small dock down the hill–but still across the bay.

> **IF IT ISN'T SUPPORTING THE STORY AND THE CHARACTERS IT'S NOT WORTH IT. I HAVE NEVER BEEN ONE OF THOSE PEOPLE WHO WATCHES A FILM AND SAYS,** *GOD, THAT WAS A TERRIBLE MOVIE BUT I LOVED THE WAY IT LOOKED!*

The producers asked me if I thought I could convince the director to do that. And I said, *I can try!* He loved it. The little extra money spent scouting the Sydney Harbor saved the producers a lot more in the end.

You over-prepare, at least mentally. Know what the options are for the director or for changes on the fly, on the day. You've thought of fifteen options already. This is what you want, but it's not going to work, so I'm going to try and sell this other idea instead. And sometimes it works!

AS: Does previs help a lot on animated features?
RE: Pixar was really slow to use previs. I would ask, *Why aren't we using previs more?* And the producers would say, *Why would we want to make the film twice?*

I said, *We're already making it seven times, I don't see what the problem is!* Previs was always just to solve a specific problem here or there. It wasn't to help design the production. Early on, there were valid reasons for not using it, as most of our software was developed in house and wasn't compatible with most mainstream computer software today. Or it didn't exist! The original software we used was too big and slow to do previs. The first film we utilized previs from the get-go to actually design the film and get the story department and director on board, was *Incredibles 2!*

I worked directly with the head of story, the director, our supervising technical director Rick Sayre, and our previs artist Philip Metschan on *Incredibles 2,* to design that process. The only reason I was able to get it that far was that it came out of my budget. Rick Sayre designed a game controller where the director and story artists could put VR goggles on to look at the set we were designing and plan shots. They could use it either literally, or as inspiration, where they'd print out images to hang up and look at.

The trick was to be very disciplined and not overbuild it. And the great thing was that we were able to get our layout/camera DP on seven months earlier than normal, to come in at least twice a week and test-drive the sets.

Our DPs are split into two roles, one for camera and one for lighting. Our lighting DP was also able to get in there and start testing out lighting ideas earlier. It was the first time at Pixar that we were able to work that collaboratively, that early on. It was the best experience I've ever had on a show because of that. We wouldn't have been able to do that if it hadn't been for the director, Brad Bird, allowing us to utilize previs. We built twice as many sets that ended up in the film and still brought it in under time and under budget. It was really about discipline, not overdoing it. And I was in sync with Brad in that if I thought that something would get cut I would shelve it.

I told our set designers, I want you to design it exactly as we need to see it. Then when they were done I would ask them to take another pass and break it into "Lego pieces." I said, *Break it down into as many reusable components as possible but don't compromise your original design.* That way, we gain a library of things that A, save us time and money, and B, start building a kind of a consistent visual language for our world.

AS: What kind of components would they break it down into?

RE: Things like shelving or desks, or chairs, even the room itself. Then they change the colors, the textures, the scale, redress it, shoot it from a different angle. It's not a new idea but it's amazing how little we have done that as an "up-front" plan.

AS: Do you see the style of animation changing at Pixar?

RE: What's funny is that now, as we finally get to the point of real-time rendering with robust lighting tools and our skills are better and the technology's better, many want to go non-photorealistic with the imagery!

> ❝ I WANT TO BE TAKEN AWAY WHILE WATCHING A FILM. I DON'T WANT THE DESIGN TO DISTRACT ME.

The computer has always known how to do realistic–or at least try. Getting the rendering power and the computing power to catch up took a decade or so, but it's doable now. I mean look at the movies that are made. Now going and doing something that is stylized and not photorealistic is gonna be a huge challenge. It's a lot of what I've been working on and thinking about with these future films. If you want something to look different that means throwing out our old pipeline and reimagining it. Are we, as a studio, willing to do that? Are we ready to do that? Do we really want to do that? There are no guarantees.

One of my anchors has always been, if it's distracting from the story and the characters, it's gotta go. If this isn't supporting the story and the characters it's not worth it. I have never been one of those people who watches a film and says, *God, that was a terrible movie but I loved the way it looked!* Not that I don't appreciate the craft of it. But I find that I want to be taken away while watching a film. I don't want the design to distract me. It's like my own definition of the difference between a look and a style. A "look" to me is like a watercolor where it shimmies, the whole frame is moving and it's beautiful, and in my opinion more appropriate for a short film or maybe a commercial. Not appropriate when an audience has to identify with a character and really fall in love with a character. It becomes a barrier for them to get attached to the character and it's gotta go. The movie *A Monster Calls* has some terrific animation sequences that work well within the context of the movie, but probably couldn't have carried an entire film. "Style" to me is what we want to lean more towards. Just think of what David Hockney did on some of his theater sets, it's wildly stylized and yet very clear and understandable.

AS: Should production design be invisible? Should a set be a character or just fade into the background?

RE: It's both and it changes depending on what the storytelling needs are. I do believe a set can be a character and needs to be a character for the film, but it should also be invisible! It's a character in the film but that doesn't mean that it needs to "show off" or be precious.

AS: How many people are on your team for a given feature? Do you always work with the same team?

RE: Every film has different needs for staffing–and we often have several films in various phases of development, production, and post at any given time. I would say ten percent, maybe twenty percent,

could be the same people that move from film to film to film. But they want to advance their careers and become supervisors or move from animation into story and art into story or story into art. But the art department alone on a given film is probably on average twelve people, total. Production Designer, Art Directors, and then we have Set designers, Texturers, Illustrators, Previs artists, Graphic artists. It varies, depending on the scope and needs of a film.

AS: And the rest of the team?

RE: It depends on the film and the complexity of the film but on a given film it's usually about two hundred and fifty people total. And they're overlapping because we often have a few films in development, one film pre-production, one film in full production, and then one film at least in post production.

AS: Are all of those people in-house at Pixar?

RE: All of them are in-house, except for music and sound mixing. With COVID it's a little different, but it's the same people, they're just working at home.

AS: You start with the director and your art department team, but then at one point does it shift over to all the animators and you oversee them?

RE: I want to clarify something if I may–animators have a very specific role. They are the actors. We have a modeling department, a texturing department, a lighting department, a tools department that develops new technology for us, lighting and camera, layout, editorial. And then we have sculptors who sculpt both in clay and Z-Brush. A lot of folks call anyone who works at Disney or Pixar or Dreamworks an "animator." These are all very different roles.

For all these departments to know what the goal is, you need a good, clean, clear design plan. They can push the walls and break the parameters of that plan if they have a better idea. I keep calling it corrals of visual information. They can see where the corral is and they can contribute to the ideas within it, and the director or producer know at the very least they're going to get these ideas in the film. And if they break a fence down because there's a better idea, let's go for it. We'll make the fence bigger. But you can't just throw people in a room and expect it to just happen. You need a clear plan up front. The story doesn't necessarily need to be completely detailed or written or storyboarded or edited in the beginning stages. You start by just focusing on the big elements and planning.

AS: And if you don't have a plan?
RE: Well, there was a sequence in the original *Incredibles* where Bob is going down this lava pit, fighting this zombie droid, and then he races over into a waterfall, leaps over it, drops a bomb blowing the water out, and then swims through a cave. That whole scene was so technically messed up it was horrifying. I told them, *You can't render any of this!* The producer, (who was new to CG animation), didn't understand why.

The reason was that it was put together with low resolution models. It wouldn't hold together on the big screen! *Where are the set designs?* There were none! They just used the storyboards (which were fantastic) for the basic designs. And that's great but it's not high enough resolution for production. So I suggested we could save eleven weeks on the next two sets if they could give me one extra week on this one set. We just had to re-plan it. We redesigned everything, with all reusable elements (rocks, trees, plants). It became the rocks down to the lava pit, the lava pit, the waterfall, the water hole he jumps into, and the cave. These were all the same set, just redressed. If you watch the film you can't tell it's the same thing over and over!

> **DOING THE RESEARCH FOR EVERY FILM I'VE GOTTEN TO WORK ON IS LIKE A FOUR YEAR GRADUATE COURSE IN THE SUBJECT MATTER OF THAT FILM.**

Brad was willing to play ball at that point because he started understanding the weirdness of the virtual world. He was great on *Incredibles 2*. I always said, *Brad, we can cheat every single shot if you want. But there's no reason to do it!*

AS: In your talks you sometimes discuss what defines film design that doesn't work . . .
RE: Yes, I used several films in one of my talks to show bad film design. I avoided naming names. I worked hard to avoid mentioning anything recent because I was afraid one of the production design-

ers might see the talk! But it was harder to find older films that I thought were distracting–because back then when they said "Action!" time was literally money! The lights, the film running, everything was money.

Now, they can run a computer twenty-four hours a day! A computer is a great tool but it can become a crutch really fast. It was more difficult to find "bad design" in some of the older movies, but one of my highlights, which offended a few people, was *Night of the Hunter,* which is beautiful but that's the problem! There's no modulation to it– every shot is equally beautiful. And *Camelot.* Wow, that's a lot of brown! I'm not a "color hater" but that's too much of a great color! Then I had to utilize the *Transformers* movies! I even used the film, *Toys.* That movie is really weird; the art direction is telling one story, the actors are telling another, and the filmmaker's telling another. Originally I had even included what I call the "nipple *Batman* movies!" But of course Barbara Ling also did *Once Upon a Time... In Hollywood* which is brilliant. Let's just say she did exactly what the director asked for on the *Batman* movies . . .

AS: What are some of the characteristics a good production designer has, besides having a good visual aesthetic? Would they include thinking on your feet?

RE: That's one of them. One big thing happened on *The Incredibles 2.* One set was completely finished, their 2,300 square foot house. In the original film it was a 1,500 square foot Eichler-style house that was destroyed at the end of the film. But in the sequel Brad wanted a bigger house. And so we built a bigger, 2,300 square foot house. It was all finished and they were animating an entire sequence in the bedroom. Everything was done and we were already moving on to other sets.

And then one day the head of story came to me and said, *We've got a problem. Brad has to consolidate some story elements. He has to get to this one point faster so he's got to consolidate five sequences into one.* I said, *Too bad he didn't go with my original idea, this bigger house, like this rough idea I had.* And I showed him an old, rough sketch.

And he grabbed my hand and said, *You have to tell Brad that now!* And so we went into Brad's office and Brad said, *Yes, do that!* And our boss at the time, John Lasseter, came in and said, *Yes!*

So I went home that night and wrote this Ted Kaczynski-style, single-spaced letter, *If we want to do a new house, here's what I'd do and here's how I would do it, and here are the sketches for it.* And I walked in on Monday and sure enough they said, *Let's do it.* So we went from a 2,300 square foot home to a 20,000 square foot home! And whereas we had six months to design the first home, interacting with the layout and camera and animation and lighting departments to make sure it was all going to work, now we had three weeks.

I got everyone in the art department and we just jammed for the first week. We showed Brad rough sketches and then took the stuff down he didn't like and separated out the stuff he liked. I started working with Phil Metschan in previs and a couple of our artists to really zero in and focus. We started delivering sets the day before they were coming into animation and layout. Our crew was really well-oiled at that point and they did such great work. It was crazy but it resolved a lot of story issues.

One of the tricks we did was with an animated sequence in the bedroom. Bob and Ellen were talking, it was almost finished in animation. And then we had to lift the animation, and the bed, and the nightstand, and move it to the hotel. We couldn't change the scale or the distance or any of that because it was already animated. So we actually moved the entire animated scene from the house to the hotel. That's the kind of thing you can do in the computer but that you'd have to reshoot in live action.

So yes, the ability to make adjustments on the fly is one of a production designer's key attributes. And also, most of the folks I know that have done the job of production designer are interested in so many things. That's also really important. A lot of it comes from the joy of doing research. I love doing research. Doing the research for every film I've gotten to work on is like a four year graduate course in the subject matter of that film.

AS: Does the research start with a lot of Google searches?

RE: The internet is a great tool but I tend to work hard not to only use the internet as visual reference for material because it becomes somewhat homogenized. A friend of mine called it a "Google storm of bullshit." I love that phrase because if five different people are doing the same film and don't talk to each other but use Google to do research most of it's going to be about the same. So I value seeing the real thing, talking to experts, thumbing through my books, watching old movies, a little bit of anything and everything. You have to be interested in it all. All kinds of music, and theater, and dance and just going out in nature, bike riding, hiking, talking to people, just all of it!

> " IF YOU'RE THROWING A NEW VISUAL IDEA AT AN AUDIENCE AND THEY DON'T UNDERSTAND WHAT YOU'RE TRYING TO DO WITH IT RIGHT AWAY, THEY'RE GOING TO SPEND THE NEXT FEW SECONDS ASKING, *WHAT IS THIS?* AND THEN THEY'RE NOT PAYING ATTENTION TO THE CHARACTERS AND YOU MIGHT LOSE THEM. YOU'VE GOTTA MAKE IT HYPER-CLEAR.

With *Finding Nemo* we had a wonderful research guy, Adam Summers. We called him "our fabulous fish guy." He knew everything about the ocean and fish. He studied sharks six months out of the year. He talked about wave structure and fish scale structure. Really enthusiastic. Same with *Wall-E—*

we had a guy from NASA come in and talk to us. Dr. Keltner, a neuroscientist, for *Inside Out*, where we were designing the mind, not the brain. What does the mind look like?

> **I REALIZED EARLY IN MY CAREER I COULD EITHER DEDICATE MYSELF TO LEARNING ALL THE TOOLS OR DEDICATE MYSELF TO DESIGN. I CHOSE THE DESIGN ASPECT.**

AS: Did the visual depiction of the mind in *Inside Out* first develop out of discussions with you and the director?

RE: Yes, Pete Docter, and our head of story, Josh Cooley, and our co-director Ronnie Del Carmen. It was a world that literally didn't exist so we had to start setting boundaries. Number one, because we've got to produce it, and two, because the audience wants to understand it. You can throw some crazy visual ideas at the audience but you have to set them up first. You have to prime them. The audience matters.

AS: Some logic has to be in there.

RE: "A" logic. It can be made up, so long as you're willing to spend the effort making it clear and consistent for the audience. If you're throwing a new visual idea at an audience and they don't understand what you're trying to do with it right away, they're going to spend the next few seconds asking, "What is this?" and then they're not paying attention to the characters and you might lose them.

You've gotta make it hyper-clear. You're building a hermetically-sealed world that this entire film takes place in. So there is a lot of inter-departmental interaction. A lot of map drawing. A lot of conceptual work. More conceptual artwork done on *Inside Out* than on any Pixar film ever, times three. We did hundreds of designs of one of the set pieces. We were able to utilize confocal microscopic photography of brain images for inspiration. That's where they inject different dyes into cellular structures and photograph them to see what's going on. While we were designing the "mind" and not the "brain," certain concepts of how the brain worked were just more clear to the audience—and we utilized them. As a production designer, finding a way to make yourself interested in all of it, even if it doesn't seem that interesting to begin with, is really important.

AS: Finding your own way into the subject matter.

RE: Finding your own way into it, absolutely. And aside from this love of research, I also found that some of the best production designers that work in animation have made at least a film or two themselves. Even if it's a student film. Understanding the element of screen time in putting an idea across is really, really important. It affects the contrast, the colors that you use and how you compose an image! It's one of the most important things. People always ask, *What should I put in my portfolio?* You'll need the normal stuff–some life drawings, some fast sketches, some color work, some paintings, but if you really want to get their attention make a short film. And by short, I mean two minutes. One or two characters. Not some twenty minute epic trying to solve your problems with your parents.

AS: And what do you look for in the crew you hire?

RE: Communication skills are really important. And while it's really important to have a certain level of art skill, I think it's really important that people broaden their interests besides just doing artwork. I'm not really trained as a painter but I've done lot of artwork. I look at a lot of portfolios of students and the skill level's out of this world! And they'll sit and explain a painting to me that they've done and they'll tell me the whole story behind it and I listen, and when they're done I say, *Why isn't it in the painting? You told me this whole story and it's beautiful but shouldn't I understand it just by looking at it?*

AS: Did you start out by going to art school?

RE: Yes, CalArts. I moved to California from Louisiana to study animation. Less out of a love for drawing, although I did draw a lot, but more for a love of filmmaking. I wanted to figure out everything as a kid. A great way to get out of class is to make little animated shorts and go show them around to the local schools! After CalArts I did a lot of commercial work and some television work. Brad Bird gave me my first job.

AS: Brad Bird, future director of the *Incredibles* movies, *Ratatouille*, *Mission:Impossible-Ghost Protocol*, *The Iron Giant*...

RE: Yes. Brad Bird was at CalArts the first year they opened the character animation program. They had an animation program before that but it was more experimental animation. CalArts is a very liberal school and when they started the character animation program it was kind of poo-poo'ed and seen as a Disney training program. Which others at CalArts looked down upon. Lo and behold, because of the structure provided in the character animation department, with its focus on basics, and story, and design, and life drawing, and visualizing, and making a film every year, the character animation program is now one of the diamonds in the CalArts school curriculum. Right after CalArts I moved to Hollywood.

AS: Were you at CalArts at the same time as Tim Burton or Rick Heinrichs?

RE: They were just before me. My class included the great animators Tony Fucile, Doug Frankel, and Sue Nichols. Right after me were Andrew Stanton and Brenda Chapman and after that was Pete Docter, in the early to mid 80s.

After CalArts I ended up working on a film at AFI because they needed a set designer for a project that actually never happened. So I was just working at AFI as a set designer when I got a call from Brad Bird to work on an episode for the second season of *Amazing Stories*. It was an animated episode called *Family Dog* which he wrote and directed. My CalArts classmate Tony Fucile was hired by Brad to animate on Family Dog and they were looking for one more person to work freelance so he hired me.

Originally I was working at home in Hollywood, freelance, but I was hungry and I had to pay rent and so I would drive back and forth to this place in downtown LA. They had a desk there that was for assistant animators to do cleanup drawings and I kind of appropriated that desk. If someone needed the desk I would get up from animating and go eat or walk around the block or explore the neighborhood. That was my first real job and it was great. *Family Dog* was later turned into a series that was horrible but Brad was no longer involved. He was busy helping on *The Simpsons*.

> " PRETTY PICTURES ARE NICE HANGING ON A WALL BUT IF YOU START THINKING ABOUT DESIGNING A FILM FROM A PURELY DESIGN POINT OF VIEW, OR A PICTURE POINT OF VIEW, YOU'RE GOING TO PAINT YOURSELF INTO A CORNER. START BY THINKING CHARACTER FIRST.

AS: How did you first start working at Pixar?

RE: I was working with Joel Silver on a couple projects and then my friend, the writer/director Andrew Stanton, called me up and asked if I was available to talk about working on a film they were doing at Pixar. I went and showed them my portfolio, and was hired on the spot.

I had been working on a film that had fourteen producers and they would pontificate about every little thing for hours. I'd be thinking, *Oh my God, can somebody make a decision?* So I started doing these little pastel drawings and they would say, *Yeah, kinda like that!* So having a visual to look at really helped them a lot. And suddenly I was art director. So I had a ton of that artwork in my portfolio and John Lasseter had an affinity for pastel drawings because he also works in pastel. John saw them and looked at me and said, You're hired. *Can you drive us to the airport?*

I said, *Sure!* I thought that it would be a few months before I had to go up but I got a call from Bonnie Arnold, one of our producers, and she said, *No, we want you up next week!* I'd just signed a year lease and movers showed up the next morning and they packed me up, moved me up to the Bay Area from LA. And then I worked my tail off.

AS: And then there was no turning back.

RE: Kind of no turning back. But right after *Toy Story* finished I moved back down to LA for another ten months, trying to get another project going, but it didn't work out. I'd sold a screen story to Warner Brothers that I tried to get off the ground. But little did I know they didn't want to make an animated comedy about a serial killer! Then I got a call from Steve Jobs to work on *Monsters Inc* and I've been back at Pixar ever since. What I learned about Pixar is once they decide to make a movie, they're going to make that movie. It's not like traditional Hollywood production companies with twenty projects in development that they're not sure they're going to make next.

AS: Working at Pixar do you spend a lot of time learning all the latest tools?

RE: I realized early in my career I could either dedicate myself to learning all the tools or dedicate myself to design. I chose the design aspect. I gave a talk with [Hitchcock production designer] Robert Boyle at The Academy of Motion Picture Arts and Sciences a few years back. It was a talk about the digital tools of production design now. Robert Boyle got up and gave his talk about design and how he'd get to work in the morning and get his coffee, read his paper, make notes, do some drawing, make rounds to his department, and then go to the set. That was old-school, right? Some other folks got up and talked about the digital tools, and they're great people–but that frankly, that aspect of it bores me to tears!

When I got up on stage they asked me, *Well, what's your day like?* I said, *I get to the office and drink my coffee, read my paper, sit and draw for a couple hours and at nine am people are filtering in and I go and make my rounds, visiting the departments.* It was just like Bob! It was exactly the same thing! It was just in a computer, that was the only difference!

AS: Does that fact that it's all in a computer affect how you interact with the cinematographer?

RE: *Incredibles 2* was the first Pixar film I worked on using virtual physically-based lights. I would do a painting of a shot and our DP would come in and say, *In order to achieve that, I need the set to do x, y, and z.* And so we would make that adjustment.

Before physically-based lighting, if you had a white floor and a character with a green jacket on, if you wanted to bounce light from the jacket you would actually have to put green lights in the jacket to give the impression of bounced light. This would lead to five thousand lights in every shot. Very difficult to keep track of. The cool thing about the physically-based lights now is it's more like live action. And then the irony of course is that now that we're able to do that, people want to do *nonphotorealistic!* They can make it look realistic out the box really fast, but in order to stylize the lighting, more effort is involved. We still have a lot to learn so it doesn't just come across like we're only trying to imitate live action.

> "I LOVE PRODUCTION DESIGN. I'VE HAD A FRONT ROW SEAT TO THE CREATION OF SOME OF THE MOST WONDERFUL FILMS OF THE LAST TWO DECADES, BY WORKING ON THEM.

AS: With *Monsters Inc* I noticed you're credited as one of the writers too.

RE: Yeah, very early story work. Then I was able to make a short film called *For the Birds* and I got to win the Oscar for that.

AS: Great film! What was the Oscar experience like?

RE: Thank you. It was an awesome experience. I was knee-deep into working on *Finding Nemo* when the Awards happened–so it was quite a flurry of activity for a time! Afterwards, having become a member of the Academy, I was asked to go from the short film branch of the Academy to the design branch by Jim Bissell. Harley Jessup and I moved over. We took this very seriously. We helped educate the design branch about what production designers for animation do. The production process is very different, but the design thinking is the same. Many live action production designers are really interested in maintaining the design intent from the early days of design through the shoot, and then through post production. That's something that as production designers in animation we have always done. It's something that's just part of our process.

> ❝ ONE OF MY FAVORITE QUOTES ABOUT THE HARD WORK THAT GOES INTO FILM DESIGN IS FROM ONE OF OUR ART DIRECTORS, NOW A PRODUCTION DESIGNER, JASON DEAMER: *PAIN IS TEMPORARY. SUCK IS FOREVER.*

They asked me at an Academy thing what was my favorite production designed movie of all time and they thought I was going to say *Pinocchio* or *Bambi* but I said *Little Foxes* by William Wyler. He's my favorite director. Steven Goosson designed the sets and Gregg Toland shot them. Everything's about pricks, all the clothes have polkadots and everything is needlepoint. They expand on the world by keeping the camera centered and they start ro-

tating and expanding the house and by the end of the film the house is huge, you just didn't know it in the beginning. And yet it feels more confining at the same time. All this brilliant stuff that Wyler crammed in there visually. It's brilliant.

I also go back to Richard Sylbert's comments all the time. He told me a great story about working on *Who's Afraid of Virginia Woolf?* with Mike Nichols. He'd hired Dean Tavoularis as art director. Tavoularis had built the house bathroom, painted it, dressed it, and it was beautiful. Richard Sylbert came in, looked at it and said, *This is good.* Then he kicked over the magazines, he grabbed some toothpaste, water, spewed it everywhere, started rubbing his hands everywhere and Dean Tavoularis said, *What are you doing?* And he looked at him and said, *These characters are alcoholics!*

His thinking behind all that was character-based. Pretty pictures are nice hanging on a wall but if you start thinking about designing a film from a purely design point of view, or a picture point of view, you're going to paint yourself into a corner. Start by thinking character first. It seeps into the film in ways you can't anticipate.

For example, in the film *Paper Moon*, it's brilliant how they tracked the characters' success and their relationships through the hotel rooms in the film. In the first hotel room, there is one bed and he sleeps on the floor. The next hotel room is two beds, then the next one is two beds and a bathroom, and the next one after that is two rooms connected with a bathroom. They finally get two individual hotel rooms and then, the very last time, at the very end of the movie, they're back in one room. It has two beds but the entire scene is shot in the mirror, in reflection. It's a simple idea that helps the audience pay attention to the characters and yet understand the building of their relationship. It's so brilliant. Listen to the *You Must Remember This* podcast on the *Paper Moon* production designer Polly Platt.

But I've seen some animated films that are better designed than many live action films, no disrespect to anyone. The day *Ratatouille* came out I didn't see any live action film better designed than that film. Harley Jessup should have been more recognized for his work on that film than he already was.

AS: Do you want to write and direct more films yourself?

RE: I would love to direct some day, but when I see what some directors go through, I'm more happy to be their support than to be in that particular hot seat. I love production design. I've had a front row seat to the creation of some of the most wonderful films of the last two decades, by working on them. Some production designers feel the need to put their own thumbprint on a movie. I'm of the mind that the best you could hope for is it gets up, walks away, and takes on a life of its own. One of my favorite quotes about the hard work that goes into film design is from one of our art directors, now a production designer, Jason Deamer: *Pain is temporary. Suck is forever.*

INVISIBLE

Should design be invisible?

*A compilation of excerpts covering
the subject of invisible design,
taken from the interviews in this book*

A film is a delicate balance of many elements and a designer needs to know when to pull back and when to step forward, based on the story being told. Kim Sinclair advises against being too flashy, avoiding the design that screams, *Look at me, I'm an amazing set!* But how invisible does your work need to be? The same question can be asked of other departments: the costume design, the acting, the score, the cinematography. Should you keep it as invisible as possible by default? Or do you go all out?

DANIEL NOVOTNY

It depends on the movie. I think a film like *Harry Potter* or *Lemony Snicket*–I don't know how the production design on that film can be invisible. It really depends on the project. I mean take a film like *Dog Day Afternoon*. That production design was invisible, you couldn't tell that those were sets. Or a show like *American Beauty*–it was well shot but I think the production design was kind of invisible. Then a show like *Napoleon Dynamite* I don't think that that show was meant for the production design to be invisible. It was intended for you to really notice that everything was wacky and quirky, right? So I think it really depends on what the concept is, going into the project. I mean you have some science fiction films like *Star Wars* where the production design was much more invisible than it was on some *Star Trek* films, you know what I mean? The original *Star Wars* was so realistic–you looked at it and you couldn't even comprehend that those were sets, they looked real, they made sense. *Godfather* was invisible but *Pan's Labyrinth* was obviously not.

KIM SINCLAIR

I favor the subliminal thing. Your job is not to distract from the story. However, sometimes the set or the prop is the story and in that case it becomes the forefront. It may become more important than the actors. But it's really story-driven. What I hate is sets that are overly flashy and complicated and too important for their own good. *Look at me! Look at me! I'm an amazing set.* It's silly. It would be like a film where people just drive a car, and the car itself is not another story point. You find some amazing

Ferrari or something. Then everybody watching the movie is going, *Oh wow, look at the Ferrari!* It takes you out of the story. The same thing goes for sets. It really depends on the story. I favor the background thing, I'm more of a background guy.

JOHN MYHRE

I don't think you'd ever want to feel like you're being hit in the face with any element of the movie. You try to make it a very cohesive whole. For me it's about story-telling. We're not architects, we're visual storytellers. And when I read the script for the first time I see the movie in my mind. What can you do to help define the characters? I often try thinking of it like it's a silent movie. And if you don't have any dialog how do you tell the story? It's gonna be the visual setting you see. It's gonna be the lens, how wide are you, how tight are you? The lighting, the clothes, the architecture, the set-dressing, the colors. That's how we look at it.

SARAH GREENWOOD

I think it depends on the film completely. You know I think something like *Sherlock*, that's really in-your-face. Something like *Atonement*, you know the green is very strong but it's atmospheric, it's helping to tell the story. It shouldn't be overriding. But I love films that are so laid-back like Mike Leigh's where it's all about performance. I don't tend to do that kind of degree of naturalism. In my films it's always pushed slightly . . . I think it would be very difficult for me to do something that is just so untouched. A Lars von Trier film is probably not for me to work on. Not that I don't enjoy them. I think

INVISIBLE

as long as it's appropriate to the piece it's great. You know there are films that I won't mention that it's just in there to make a big statement and I think that's gross . . . Too extreme is too much. You have to be very careful. We often have to pull ourselves back and just say, *Well, that's just a bit much.* Sometimes we fail but I think it's very important to try and get the balance right.

NATHAN CROWLEY

It depends on your film. I'd say it should always be in the background but then weirdly when I did [Batman's] Bunker with its low, bright ceiling, everyone knows the Bunker set. The way I tried to make that set not stand alone was by using an enormous amount of Modernism across the film, like in the boardroom I had to play a low ceiling there to make the Batbunker not stand out as this isolated set. The only person who's ever gotten away with that in the past is Ken Adam. He defines his entire film with one set! Which I can really appreciate.

GRANT MAJOR

[Visible or invisible?] Neither one of them. Where it needs to tell a story it's got to be seen for what it is. For example, the great big underground laboratory in *Green Lantern* has to be seen because it's very much described in the script. Other ones, like people's offices, rooms, bedrooms and so on, they want to play a support role to the drama that's be-

ing played out by the actors. So it really depends on the brief in a way, on the script. At the end of the day people are really taking in a lot by osmosis. For the osmosis to be readable it still needs to impress itself on people's imagination even if it's indirectly.

JOHN MUTO

I mean, is the design of this restaurant invisible? We like this restaurant because we like the way it looks, not because it's invisible. If you're on the beach is the beach invisible? The beach is sand and spray. If you're in the desert is the desert invisible? I think it's another way of trying to sound clever. Life is full of sights and sounds and smells. Nothing's invisible really.

EVE STEWART

If you're invisible for the bulk of your time then you've done a really good job because it hasn't stuck in somebody's throat. If you're invisible eighty percent of the time and twenty percent of the time people go, *Whoa!* because you've introduced them to a new world, I feel that's a good job.

LAURENCE BENNETT

Hopefully it doesn't take you out of the story . . . We don't want to be anything but the setting, for the most part! But there are exceptions. In setting the tone of a scene, in reinforcing something that's going on dramatically in a scene, sometimes you can play against it. The obvious temptation in a scene that is emotionally very hot would be to do an environment that's very alive and very warm. Sometimes the right decision is to do something that's counter-intuitive. Do something that's cool and removed. Let the emotion of the scene contrast with the setting. Those are some emotional tricks that you can play with color.

ADAM STOCKHAUSEN

You never want to be pulled out of the story for any reason. You never want to be pulled out of the story to say, *Look at the clothes they're wearing!* You never want to be pulled out of the story to say, *Look*

at that visual effect! But it depends piece by piece on how quiet or how bold it can go.

GUY HENDRIX DYAS

Our work is about treading that fine line between invisible and visible production design and knowing what's best for the story. It should be invisible unless the story calls for more ostentatious visuals. This is what differentiates production designers from other designers. Personally I love both expressions of what we do, the invisible work as well as the more stylized and mannered aspect of production design.

Adam Stockhausen

Adam Stockhausen brought his artistic style to the Wes Anderson masterpiece *The Grand Budapest Hotel* and brutal southern plantation realism to Steve McQueen's *12 Years a Slave*. He received two of his four Oscar-nominations for these classics and won for *The Grand Budapest Hotel.* Since then, he's continued to design Wes Anderson movies and has also become Steven Spielberg's production designer of choice, for whom he designed the classic *West Side Story,* among others. But before all this, he was inventing ways to keep blood off hardwood floors for horror maestro Wes Craven.

AS: I hear you just wrapped your job as production designer on Steven Spielberg's *Bridge of Spies*...

AS: Yes, we just finished. It's a true story. We shot half in New York City and half in Berlin with a brief side trip into Poland. It was a wonderful experience for me. I had a blast.

AS: How was Spielberg to work with?

AS: Fantastic! We did a lot of sketching. We'd work things up and then go to see him and show our materials and it was a wonderful collaboration.

AS: How was working with Spielberg's DP Janusz Kaminski? Is he really involved in the production design?

AS: Absolutely. He's a fun guy and a wonderful artist and it was just great. We looked at every location together. He looked at all the drawings of what I was planning to do. How we were going to light the scenes is always a critical part of the discussion. In a way it's the most important part. If you can't see what's going on it doesn't matter what the set is. It was a fundamental part of the discussion at every location and every set and he was right there at the center of it.

AS: In terms of practical lighting fixtures and windows?

AS: Coming up with an answer to the question, *What's the light for this scene? Are we in a box with no windows?* Which might be okay if that's right for the scene. Or, *How does the lighting for this piece of the story compare to the lighting needs for the other parts of the story?* This movie goes from New York to Berlin and the feeling of the light is different in the different parts of the story. And so we were trying to make sure that the scenery allows for that.

AS: In contrast, what was it like working with Wes Anderson's DP Robert Yeoman?

AS: Bob is just the sweetest, greatest, most laid-back, awesome DP. What we do a lot of on Wes's movies is we plan these choreographed, intricate camera moves and the lighting is central to that plan. It's not the kind of thing where you can think it up on the day. Quite often we're moving and spinning and seeing a lot of territory so the lighting has to be either integrated into the scene or delicately placed where it's going to work. Like for instance in the lobby of the Grand Budapest Hotel. We worked together for a long time trying to plan all these practicals [lighting elements seen

on camera]. There are thousands of practicals in that hotel! In the introduction scene when we're walking through the hotel and Zero's being interviewed by Monsieur Gustave we quickly see that entire lobby. Bob and I sat and worked out the plan for the practicals and how much light do we need out of them and how many of them do we need and where do they need to go.

> **"HOW WE WERE GOING TO LIGHT THE SCENES IS ALWAYS A CRITICAL PART OF THE DISCUSSION. IN A WAY IT'S THE MOST IMPORTANT PART. IF YOU CAN'T SEE WHAT'S GOING ON, IT DOESN'T MATTER WHAT THE SET IS.**

AS: I noticed that the lobby changed for different time periods and that at one point there were a bunch of fluorescents on the ceiling.

AS: For the 60s we had this idea that the Brutalist architecture of the Soviet period had a way of roughly plastering over the delicate elements of what had been underneath. You'll take a beautiful building and slap wood paneling over it. The location where we shot the dining room scene had this balcony with a beautiful rail frieze of angels. At one point it was renovated and the angel's heads stuck out too far because they were going to plaster over it with some kind of panel. So they just knocked all the heads off the angels, because they were in the way. You can actually see that balcony rail in the movie for a split second in a scene when Zero and

Agatha are on a date at the movies. In scouting we had seen a building that had taken what I'm sure was a beautiful ceiling and put a bank of fluorescents over it. Not just a couple fluorescents, a sea of egg crate. We saw this detail and wanted to pull it in. So for our 60s lobby the hotel has this beautiful, five-story atrium and at the first level we just banked it with fluorescents. So there's this fluorescent egg-crate that's ten meters by twenty-five meters across. So it gave a very different lighting style to the 60s hotel from the 30s hotel.

AS: How did you end up transforming a department store into the hotel lobby?

AS: Wes had done some very early scouting when he was finishing the script and going around the area of Central Europe where this takes place. He was looking for a needle in a haystack. What you can find a lot of is beautiful old hotels that are still working. But you can't shoot a movie like our movie there because you can't shut down a major hotel. So you can find those but you can't use them. And you can find a lot of really derelict places where the ceilings have fallen in, bats are flying around and the paint is all peeling off the plaster. Those are great but it would cost a fortune and take forever to rehabilitate them. It would almost be easier to build the thing from scratch. So the needle in the haystack was this beautiful Art Nouveau department store in Görlitz, Germany. The shell of what we made it into was there and in perfect condition. The doors had just been shut.

AS: It was just sitting there empty?

AS: There was one little perfume shop in one tiny little corner of the front but the rest of it was just standing empty. It was unbelievable. And so that motivated Wes to take the entire film to Görlitz. We based out of there and ran the whole operation from Görlitz. We went to a couple of little locations nearby but essentially the whole film was done there.

AS: How many months were you in Görlitz?

AS: I moved out to Görlitz in mid November and I was there until we finished in late March. A cold, snowy run!

AS: Did you build sets there as well?

AS: We did a lot of location building where we take a location and modify it significantly. And then we had some standing sets as well. After we shot the dining room we cleared away the tables and that became our sound stage and we built all the train interiors there and several other sets.

AS: How involved is Wes Anderson in the design?

AS: It's a total collaboration. He's a total partner in every aspect and every detail. We talk through every piece. It's not just, *Let me know when it's done.* We're talking though step by step by step the whole way.

AS: Does he get to the point where he's like, *This is not the right mauve?*

AS: He's extremely involved in every detail of it. We'd discuss the exact shade of pink for a very long time. And then there are other elements that we'll have just one discussion about. Other things we'll have fifty discussions about.

AS: The production jumped back and forth with the miniatures on that one. How involved were you with the miniature builds?

AS: We had a separate miniatures construction team led by Simon Weisse and Frank Schlegel. Jeremy Dawson, one of the producers on the film, oversaw the whole operation. My guys in the art department would draw it up and do draftings and then we'd hand it off to the miniature shop who would build it just like the full-size shop would build the full-size scenery.

AS: Do you ever do any sketches yourself? Do you have an art background?

AS: I do have an art background. When I have time I'm extremely happy to get on a drawing board and be sketching. Reality being what it is I end up not doing as much as I would like to. I was a set designer for theater and worked for a while in New York as a freelance set designer for regional theater and opera and that was great fun. In theater you're doing all your own sketches! And all your own drafting. It was because I was drafting that I came into the movie business. I started working in the art departments just doing a couple days here and there drafting.

AS: Dante Ferretti designs a lot of operas and has always gone back and forth.

AS: I haven't quite figured out the back and forth part yet! But that would be a lot of fun.

> ❝ THE BUDGETS ARE A BIG PART OF THIS . . . BEING ABLE TO SMARTLY SPEND THE MONEY IS A HUGE PART OF THIS JOB.

AS: So after starting to do movies you've never gone back and done any theater set design?

AS: Well, there was an incredibly difficult year and a half or so of overlap when I unexpectedly started working full-time in movies. I was working on the movies during the day and then I'd go to my office and work on my theater shows at night. I still had this full calendar of set design work to do. That was a rough year–but I survived it!

It's very difficult because the theater projects book so far in advance. They say, *Hey, we'd love you to do this set a year from now.* And it's difficult because you want to say, *I would love to!* . . . but a year from now I could be in who knows what country and it's going to be a little hard to get to the technical rehearsals. I've done that a couple times and it works out but it's very difficult.

AS: How did you first get into the film side of it?

AS: I was living in New York and I had some friends who I'd gone to school with who were working half in films and half in theater and I called them up. In particular Suttirat Larlarb, who designs now for Danny Boyle. She and I were pals and she brought me in.

AS: Just to do some drafting?

AS: Yes and then it rolled from that. I was doing a couple days here and a couple days there and then I met Mark Friedberg who had just designed *The Life Aquatic with Steve Zissou* for Wes. We hit it off and he said, *Hey why don't you come and be with us more full time?* Four years later it was still going really well.

> " COMMUNICATION IS REALLY IMPORTANT. MY GOAL IS TO BE MAKING GOOD SCENERY BUT ALSO TO BE COMMUNICATING THE ENTIRE TIME WHAT I'M DOING SO THAT WHEN THE DAY COMES TO SHOOT, THE DIRECTOR AND THE CINEMATOGRAPHER AND EVERYBODY ELSE COMES TO THE SET AND LOOKS AROUND AND SAYS, *GREAT! THIS IS EXACTLY WHAT I WAS EXPECTING TO SEE.*

AS: What did you learn from him?

AS: An immeasurable amount of knowledge about production design and about the business and how it works. And he introduced me to the crews in New York. It was just an amazing education.

AS: Is starting as an Art Director a good route to becoming a Production Designer?

AS: There are so many different ways in. There's my path through theater. I'm not by any means the only person to have done that. Some people come from architecture. Some people come from film school. Some people come from fine arts and being painters or sculptors. But I think the art directing path is a great one. You learn all about budgeting and about the crews and working with a construction shop. You learn the nuts and bolts from the inside out. The budgets are a big part of this. It's really key to say, *Here's what we have to work with now. How can you get the most on screen for that money?* And being able to tightly control that budget allows you to answer that question really well. To say, *I think I can get you this, I worry about being able to get you that. But if we make this decision and that decision, that will open up a little more to get us this thing we really need.* Being able to smartly spend the money is a huge part of this job. You can get good at that from art directing.

AS: Is New York your home base?

AS: Yes. It was really nice this last year that half of the Spielberg film was in New York. And before that I made Noah Baumbach's *While We're Young* and that was entirely New York. Before that I don't think I'd done a film in New York since 2009. You go where the work is. I've shot in Rhode Island, Michigan, Connecticut, Germany, all over the place.

AS: Do you always work with the same crew?

AS: No. You can't say, *Here's my whole crew and we're all going to travel together.* It's just not always possible financially. And then people aren't always available. So you try to patch it together and meet new people and start over each time. I've met wonderful folks working away from home.

AS: What do you look for in a crew?

AS: You look at what they've done. It depends on the skill-set of the individual job. With some it's easier than others. For somebody who's going to be doing drafting or sketching you can look at the drawings or the sketches. It's a very clear, simple conversation. With other people like a set dressing leadman it's a little bit trickier. You're trying to assess somebody's style of managing other people and communication. You do your best and try to get a sense of that from discussion and check their recommendations. Then you take a gulp and dive in.

AS: How about as a Production Designer? What characteristics are good to have in this job?

AS: I think that communication is really important. My goal is to be making good scenery but also to be communicating the entire time what I'm doing so that when the day comes to shoot, the director and the cinematographer and everybody else comes to the set and looks around and says, *Great! This is exactly what I was expecting to see. Because I saw pictures of it yesterday. Because I had a discussion with you a few weeks ago and I've been totally on board with this direction.* To be a successful designer who delivers that, you have to be good at having those ideas, communicating them, and pulling together a strong art department who can pull it off. Running your team in an efficient manner so that things are done in a timely way so that you can be showing these things before the last possible second when you have to shoot it and you don't have a choice

anymore. Everything that it takes to get to that point is what it takes to do this successfully.

AS: When you were studying at Yale did you ever think of getting into movies?

AS: No, not really. Not because I didn't want to but only because it didn't seem to be on the table. I wasn't aware of how to make that happen.

AS: Do you think a set can be a character in a movie? Is the Grand Budapest Hotel one?

AS: Other people have said that. I don't focus on it. You just try to make sure that the set is the best that it can be as a background for the story and to support the story and to support the actors and to be as real and rich and full as you can possibly make it be. But I don't think about it beyond that. To me it's always the thing that's there in the background to be supportive rather than to be aggressive.

AS: Some people say that design needs to be invisible.

AS: Not always. You never want to be pulled out of the story for any reason. You never want to be pulled out of the story to say, *Look at the clothes they're wearing!* You never want to be pulled out of the story to say, *Look at that visual effect!* But it depends piece by piece on how quiet or how bold it can go.

AS: What do you do when you first get a script? Do you start making sketches?

AS: No. Sketches come much, much later. I start with imagery. I start pulling references for things.

AS: You go online and find reference images?

AS: A lot of it starts online now because there's so much there and every year there's more. But then you start watching films as reference and you start looking into books. And stuff that isn't always online. And then you start going places and looking at the real thing. So it grows.

AS: Does Wes Anderson suggest a lot of references like books and movies?

AS: Yes, absolutely. For *Grand Budapest* he had a whole list of things that we watched and discussed together.

AS: Out of curiosity what were a few of those?

AS: *The Shop Around the Corner,* Bergman's *The Silence, The Earrings of Madame de . . ., The Life and Death of Colonel Blimp.*

AS: How about Spielberg?

AS: Yes, we had a few that we were watching for sure. *The Spy Who Came in From the Cold* was one that we were looking at quite a bit.

AS: How was Wes Craven different?

AS: I adore Wes Craven. He's really great to work with. We made two movies. *My Soul to Take* and *Scream 4.* He hired me for my first design job on *My Soul to Take.* The big difference with his movies is that you have to figure out how to deal with the blood!

AS: Like needing special paint so that the fake blood comes off easily?

AS: Exactly. Which is fine when you're on a set. It's a little trickier when you're on location at somebody's house. But we got a system down. We had to add a certain amount of sheen to the paint on the walls and we had a clear film that we would put down on hardwood floors. It was like vehicle wrap that doesn't have anything printed on it and we'd cover the whole floor. Because the blood gets in the cracks!

AS: On *12 Years a Slave* was Steve McQueen as involved in the details as Wes Anderson?

AS: We didn't talk as much about a specific color, but we did talk just as much about the specifics of the details of the story. The research was pretty intense and we did our best to get it right. Solomon's is such an important story and the last thing in the world I wanted was to have to have some detail blow it. For instance I remember us discussing a whip that was used on Solomon, a cat o'nine tails. What is that exactly and why is it called that? And you start looking into the damage that this thing was designed to inflict on the human body. It's terribly upsetting. But it's important. It's not just a random whip. Steve wanted to find those real details.

So it was a process of digging and trying to find as many of these specific details as we could to bring them into the story. And that was a piece where, back to your earlier question, we wanted to be totally invisible because Steve wanted to be in the past. He wanted these plantations to not feel like Hollywood stage sets. He wanted to be on working farms in the 19th century. The great houses of these plantations are still standing but everything else is gone, so we rebuilt the farms in the back. And we'd build as much of it as fully as we could so that you could walk into all of those different buildings and they would be finished and dressed on the inside. There weren't jacks and big lights just off camera because the process of making the film was one of total intimacy for Steven and his wonderful DP Sean Bobbitt and the actors.

AS: Watching the film you feel like you're a witness to something real that wasn't just fabricated.

AS: Like in the scene where Solomon is being hanged from the tree outside that plantation we knew that we were going to go three-hundred-sixty degrees around him and so that entire world was planned out. As you're looking this way these things don't stack up on each other, they're stagger-set so that we can see the entire farm not helping him. And the trick was to get all that to happen without feeling the design of it.

AS: Are you on the set as you're making a movie?

AS: I'm on the set every day. I start in the morning with the shooting company and I'm on set for the first few shots to make sure that everything is going well. Then at some point in the morning I jump forward and go to the set for the next day and I work on dressing that or finishing the paint-work or whatever it is. Then I'll move forward again to the shops and look at how the construction is going for something that is going to shoot a week later . . . all the time taking pictures. Then I loop back to the set some time in the afternoon. Sometimes you're bouncing back and forth three or four times. I generally try to end the day with the shooting company so that during lighting set-ups we can be looking at photos of what's coming and discuss the work moving forward.

AS: Are you ever involved in the VFX side of things?

AS: When that work actually happens is in post production when I'm no longer with the film. However, from the very beginning I try to design the full thing, complete with the extensions or whatever it's going to be so we all know what the road map is. That creates a coherent look and helps with an efficient workflow. We'll use sketches and 3D models. If you're in an interior and you're building the first twenty feet of it but the room's meant to be seventy-five feet tall with all this architectural detail you'll try to build the full thing into the 3D model, not just the first twenty feet. It helps when you're framing up a shot on set to know what you're going to be looking at.

AS: John Myhre talked about flying little cameras through physical models. Do you do those?

AS: Totally. A physical model is a really great tool. Physical space is not that easy to understand sometimes when you're just representing it in two dimensions. Any way of pulling it into 3D helps the communication.

AS: Did you do scale models for *Grand Budapest?*

AS: We didn't need to because the hotel was the big set and we were in the space. Our offices were upstairs. We'd just go downstairs and look at it! We'd bring samples downstairs and stand them up. We were doing it live.

We did the same kind of thing on *Moonrise Kingdom*. We'd done all the maps of the Bishop house interior and then built a 3D model of it and did little animatic mockups of the camera moves through the digital model. But then we were there together in Rhode Island and we would walk those stages together when they were in very rough shape. We'd stand up rough plywood walls with no paint and Bob would bring lenses and Wes would come and we'd march through the shots. We'd push a wall a little bit here and there and we actually ended up bringing the ceilings down. We had planned the ceilings at eight and a half feet and we actually brought them down to seven and a half feet.

AS: The interior Bishop house was all construction?

AS: Yes, although we didn't have a stage at all–we had a Linens 'n Things! We were in a strip mall at a defunct Linens 'n Things. We had a Barnes & Noble on one side of us and a PetCo on the other side. The exterior was a lighthouse in Jamestown, Rhode Island but the interior was all set. And the set wasn't one set, it was five different sets. Each built to cut through a different way.

AS: How was shooting *The Darjeeling Limited* in India?

AS: Really amazing. Overwhelming and magical. It sounds corny and cliché but everything people say about the place is absolutely true. It's awe-inspiring.

AS: India has a huge film industry of its own.

AS: It was incredible. Such an amazing crew. I art directed that film and Mark Friedberg production designed it. I stayed mostly in Jodhpur trying to get the train set finished while Mark ran ahead and sorted out all the location sets.

AS: Was any of the train built on a stage?

AS: It was an actual Indian Railways train that one of the producers on the film, Lydia Dean Pilcher, convinced the Indian Railway to loan us. We got this train and stripped it down to the bare steel. We built the entire thing inside of it and the movie was all shot on the real train while it was moving on the tracks.

Because we were moving we had other cars that you don't see. We had a dining car for the crew where people ate lunch and we had a car full of cast greenrooms, and we had a production car that had offices set up. It was such a fun set to work on.

On a slightly terrifying day in prep we figured out that we weren't going to go in a circle, instead the train was going to go out in the morning and come back in the afternoon. So you're going out in the morning and the background's going left to right outside the cabin window but in the afternoon on the way back you don't want the background going like that! So we had to make two!

AS: Wow. That reminds me of Jack Fisk making two matching sets of the boy's bedroom in *Tree of Life* to get the most out of the natural light. They would actually move set dressing from one to the other depending on time of day that they were shooting it! So you did the same thing, with one train car set facing one way, one facing the other?

AS: Yes! And in the morning we'd shoot one and in the afternoon we'd shoot the other.

AS: Any advice for someone just starting out in this business?

AS: The big thing I would say is if you think that you're going to design this set all on your own and come up with this brilliant thing and never need to talk to anyone about it and that they're just going to show up at the end and it's going to be amazing, you're making quite a large mistake. Involve your collaborators in the process early and often.

AS: How do you envision the future of film production design?

AS: The technology is certainly a growing part of the process but it's just another tool. I don't see it as fundamentally changing what we do. Computers are much more involved now but it's not changing anything. We're still doing exactly the same thing, trying to communicate and tell these stories.

> " IF YOU THINK THAT YOU'RE GOING TO DESIGN THIS SET ALL ON YOUR OWN AND COME UP WITH THIS BRILLIANT THING AND NEVER NEED TO TALK TO ANYONE ABOUT IT AND THAT THEY'RE JUST GOING TO SHOW UP AT THE END AND IT'S GOING TO BE AMAZING, YOU'RE MAKING QUITE A LARGE MISTAKE.

AS: What do you like about designing movies?

AS: On a basic level, getting paid to play make-believe is pretty great! It's fun and really challenging that each movie is a whole new experience that you have to dive in and figure out, to become fluent in a new language for each new project. For *The Grand Budapest Hotel* it happened to be Art Nouveau and Jugendstil architecture from Central Europe at the beginning of the Twentieth Century. This is the fun of being a production designer—you never know what the next thing is going to be.

Laurence Bennett

Laurence Bennett designed *The Artist,* a black and white, silent film that won five Oscars, including Best Picture. His beautiful, meticulous, Oscar-nominated design transports the audience to an artful portrayal of 1920-30's Hollywood. I spoke with Bennett after he returned from Canada where he had just designed his next film, *The Company You Keep,* directed by and starring Robert Redford.

AS: Some production designers try to avoid using other movies as reference when designing their films but it seems *The Artist* is full of homages to other movies. What did you look at for inspiration?

LB: We watched a ton of movies. Trying to pay tribute to, and build, this world of Hollywood of the late 20's and early 30's we really needed to look at how filmmakers then portrayed it. I'd long been a silent film fan but my exposure since I'd been a

kid had mostly been Chaplin and Keaton. Michel Hazanavicius, our director, opened up the world of that era to me. Murnau was probably the biggest single influence in the design of the picture and the mood of the piece. His films *Sunrise* and *City Girl* in particular. But we watched Lang, Von Sternberg, King Vidor. Three pictures by King Vidor really impressed me–*Show People,* which is about the studios at the time, *The Crowd,* and *The Big Parade,* which is just devastatingly good. Research about the period in general was key in trying to get into the heads of these people. They were inventing the language and business of filmmaking.

People think of the technique and technical aspects of film at the time as being fairly crude. That's not at all true. There were beautiful, artful, and very sophisticated techniques being used. There are tracking shots and crane shots that are absolutely beautiful. There is a crane shot on a boat coming into dock that just blows me away. There's a tracking shot through a village that's incredibly artful in its reveal and its contribution to the mood of the scene.

AS: The movie is about the transition from silents to talkies, and some have compared that change to our transition today into visual effects-heavy movies. How do you feel about that as a production designer? Did you use a lot of visual effects in *The Artist*?

LB: One of the themes of *The Artist* is the fear-inducing capability of change in peoples' lives. George closed himself off, shut down, and became less than he might have been when he so firmly rejected the new technology. I think there are obviously parallels in what we're seeing today in our industry. When we were making the picture Michel used to joke that everybody else was hot on 3D and we were making a 1D picture! While it's not strictly true it's indicative of how against-the-grain we were in doing this.

All the same, we knew that we would need to use whatever technologies were available to us. Pencils and computers work side-by-side in the art department. I work in pencil, the set designers worked in pencil and in computer modeling. All these things are tools. Aside from the one-sheets and the newspapers that are montaged into scenes, the visual effects are some set-extensions and a little bit of digital replacement for some of the street scenes and one interior on location. Phillipe Aubry was the vis effects supervisor and he came over from France and worked with us for much of the shoot. He was absolutely a delight. One of the most fun, easy, workable people I've ever encountered. He just made it really simple. We showed him research for how we thought city backgrounds might be extended and he did a great, great job of it. Made it look seamless.

PENCILS AND COMPUTERS WORK SIDE-BY-SIDE IN THE ART DEPARTMENT.

AS: I noticed how you also used some painted backdrops from the old days . . .

LB: Yes, onstage we only used painted drops. There's really nothing that I could find still in existence from the 20s or 30s but we used the oldest primarily black and white drops we could find. When I came across a couple of drops from *Casablanca* in black and white down at JC Backings I had to figure out how to put one of them to good use! Michel responded immediately and we decided to make one of Peppy's films set in Morocco. It was like unrolling a holy relic.

AS: Did you paint the sets in black and white?

LB: The sets that were shot as film sets within the picture were rendered in black and white. And the stage sets that we built that were meant to be portraying real life in the picture were rendered in naturalistic colors.

AS: You did tests to see what they would look like in black and white?

LB: Yes, we tested all the wallpapers and fabrics and paint samples before we committed. My department and [costume designer] Mark Bridges' department continued testing things in black and white during the shoot as questions arose.

AS: How was working with Michel Hazanavicius as a director? Is he very visual?

LB: He's tremendously visual. Not only did he write a beautiful, inspiring gem of a script, he basically storyboarded the entire picture. He had a very shot-specific idea about how to approach each scene. And while he was open to change and input, he was very good at communicating what it is he felt he needed to get out of each scene and how he wanted to approach it. His enthusiasm and his vision were really infectious.

AS: You worked with director Paul Haggis on a few films, how was he different to work with?

LB: Paul and I go back a long way. Paul says that I can always tell what it is he wants, that I can tell what he's thinking. Which is a frightening thought! We just have a way of discussing the visual elements of an entire piece or of individual scenes

in a very oblique manner. For example when we were prepping *In The Valley Of Elah* we were in different parts of the country and we spoke on the phone briefly just to get going. He asked me what I thought and I said, *I think it's a Western. I've been watching a lot of John Ford because I think it's about individual in landscape and individual in society. The strength of morals and ethics and conviction.* And Paul said, *Yup, that's great. That's right along the lines of what I was thinking.* And that was pretty much the entirety of the discussion that he and I had to set the tone for the design. Paul is remarkably visual. It's just that the way that we discuss it is less direct and more oblique.

AS: You've done a lot of episodic work as well– how do you feel working on movies is different from working on episodic?

LB: Television is wonderful, engaging, hard work. For me it was just a great grounding in telling stories through film. The process was absolutely the same. It's not tremendously different other than budgetary and schedule differences.

Whether it's a television show or a film I try to sit with the director for one very focused session after we've had some time to prep for a while. Just do a scene-by-scene quick skim through the script and discuss tonality and imagery. Bounce ideas off the director of what I might bring to complement what's going on in the script dramatically. Also to find out from the director if there's anything that I might have missed or that they can add.

AS: I noticed some of your sketches in *Perspective* magazine, do you do a lot of sketching when working on a movie?

LB: I do. I don't publish many of them! But I'm constantly scribbling and for a lot of sets that's the easiest way for me to puzzle through layout and determine how complex or how simple it need be.

AS: Did you go to art school?

LB: I studied art at a fine arts college. I went to Occidental in Los Angeles and Waseda University, Tokyo. I studied at Otis years later and I actually taught art for four years in Dublin. Visual arts have always been a part of my life. When I was about seventeen one of my first jobs, summers before I went to college, was working for a very small design firm in West Hollywood. The focus of the firm was interiors and the principal had been a part of the Eames group down in Venice. He'd left to go off on his own. It was from him, Chuck Kratka, that I got a great background in space planning, layout, presentation and a disciplined work ethic.

AS: I loved all the vintage graphic design that your team did in *The Artist*.

LB: Martin Charles was the graphic designer on the show. He's incredible. In prep we worked at trying to establish a level of realism and really get the flavor of the graphics of the time. The graphics in the picture not only enrich the movie but were also incredibly helpful in informing everyone in the entire crew, as well as the cast, about the feeling of the time.

AS: How did you go from traditional design to production design?

LB: I lived in Ireland for a long time and although I had a design practice with a friend and showed my paintings at a gallery there in Dublin, I also worked in fringe theater. I think it was working in theater that inspired me to work in a collaborative form with other people. The power of a collaborative artistic effort has a kind of resonance and strength that very often individual efforts can't match. And so, in the 80s I went back to Los Angeles and started working on the fringes of film design. I assisted an art director for a while and shortly after, possibly too soon, was designing projects on my own.

> **FOR ME IT BEGINS NOT WITH BLOCKING OR THE PHYSICAL NEEDS OF THE SET AS MUCH AS WITH LIGHTING. LIGHTING IS ALWAYS AT THE FRONT OF MY MIND WHEN I BEGIN DESIGNING A SCENE.**

AS: What is your process when you first read a script for a movie you're about to design?

LB: When I read a script for the first time I see a version of the movie in my head. I visualize it. The first movie I see may not be the one that we make. It's important not to get too attached to your first conceptions. Everything's always in flux. Sometimes they are the right intuition and sometimes that can take you off in the wrong direction. I try to stay open to what the world out there might tell me, and open to the people I meet, the other creatives, the co-creators on the show. The collaboration can only enrich it. Because I am only one person.

AS: Do you always work very closely with the DP?

LB: Absolutely. Probably the most serious education I got in how I needed to approach design from film was not from a designer but from cinematographers. I was fortunate enough to do a lot of commercials even before I began doing television. And it was a time where the rage was for agencies to get the world's best cinematographers to direct their commercials. I worked with Allen Daviau, Vilmos Zsigmond, and László Kovács. Jordan Cronenweth was a great mentor to me, he had a lot of patience and was very giving of his time and his talent. From Jordan I learned the most about how to approach what I built for the DP to shoot, in really simple terms. For me it begins not with blocking or the physical needs of the set as much as with lighting. Lighting is always at the front of my mind when I begin designing a scene.

AS: One set that stood out for me in _The Artist_ was the stairwell where both literally and symbolically he's going down and she's going up. For location scouting, do you spend a lot of time going out on your own?

LB: What I try to do, depending on the project and the time-frame and what part of the world we're in, is to both get out by myself and with the location manager as quickly as possible. To just get a feeling for the region we're working in. Usually the first weekend I'm in a new city I get in a car with no maps and just get lost. That's the way you learn a place.

The project that for me best illustrates how I approach locations and how they fit into all the visuals would be _Traitor_. Although we shot two days in Chicago much later on, principal photography was in Canada, England, France and Morocco. Having separate art departments in Canada, France and Morocco and bouncing back and forth repeatedly between all those locations while at the same time staying in touch with the locations people and the art departments in each of them, and keeping them all moving forward, was probably one of the most exciting exercises in contrast that I can imagine.

AS: In those locations you hired local art departments?

LB: In Toronto I had a Canadian crew. In Marseilles I had a French crew with an art director and construction coordinator that came down from Paris. And then in Marrakech I had a Moroccan crew led by a French art director that I had met in Paris. So I had two French and one Canadian art director on the show. I'm very proud of the work we did. It was not a large budget; I think the picture cost less than twenty-three million in the end. And considering that we shot in three countries and portrayed about twelve countries in those locations it was a pretty remarkable achievement.

AS: When you're going to these locations what characteristics are you looking for in the art department crew that you're hiring?

LB: When you're hiring a department you're looking for skills that complement your own. But every project is so different. The needs are always different from any other one you've done before. This is exciting to me. Throw in additionally the challenges of language and significant cultural differences and you've got the potential for some really interesting stuff to happen. Staying open to the contributions that people might bring you is vital. Hire people whose judgment and skills you trust and then let them do their jobs and bring you things that will excite you.

AS: And what qualities should a production designer have?

LB: In life and in art it's important to stay open and curious and excited about what you encounter.

AS: Any advice to somebody trying to get started in the field of production design?

LB: I usually advise people to first watch as many movies as they can. We have now a hundred year history of film from all over the world. When I'm not working I spend a lot of time watching movies, trying to continue my education about film. And it's an exciting thing for me. A lot of great stories have been told on film in the space of that hundred years. And being familiar with it and learning from it is really key.

I would also advise people to find designers whose work they admire and pick their brains. Find someone who you respect to work with if possible. If you're studying in film school, I can't imagine there's much substitute for actually making films. In addition to being a student, sign up and design small projects for people for free or whatever you need to do to get as involved as possible in the process because that's where you really learn your craft.

> "IN REINFORCING SOMETHING THAT'S GOING ON DRAMATICALLY IN A SCENE, SOMETIMES YOU CAN PLAY AGAINST IT. THE OBVIOUS TEMPTATION IN A SCENE THAT IS EMOTIONALLY VERY HOT WOULD BE TO DO AN ENVIRONMENT THAT'S VERY ALIVE AND VERY WARM. SOMETIMES THE RIGHT DECISION IS TO DO SOMETHING THAT'S COUNTERINTUITIVE. DO SOMETHING THAT'S COOL AND REMOVED. LET THE EMOTION OF THE SCENE CONTRAST WITH THE SETTING.

AS: Where do you see production design headed? Do you see a lot more greenscreens?

LB: As technologies develop, the right tools for any given story will be employed to make those pictures. On a piece like *The Artist* it wouldn't have made sense to rely too much on digital technology. In the case of *The Artist* it made more sense for us to look closely at how the artists and craftspeople of that era had approached design and to try to emulate that. Having a chance to work in a version of their world was really exciting and incredibly informative. I have enormous respect.

AS: How do you feel about production design being visible or invisible when you're watching a movie? In *The Artist* there are some great homages to other films.

LB: Hopefully it doesn't take you out of the story. Its funny, the people who are not in the business ask me if the way that I watch movies is affected by what I do. I have to say for the most part, No. I want to be entertained. I want to be told a story. I want to be taken someplace. As designers we make believable, living environments for the story and the characters. We don't want to be anything but the setting, for the most part! But there are exceptions.

In setting the tone of a scene, in reinforcing something that's going on dramatically in a scene, sometimes you can play against it. The obvious temptation in a scene that is emotionally very hot would be to do an environment that's very alive and very warm. Sometimes the right decision is to do something that's counter-intuitive. Do something that's cool and removed. Let the emotion of the scene contrast with the setting. Those are some emotional tricks that you can play with color–but it's really not the point when you're talking about a black and white movie!

AS: Do you find yourself doing more with shapes and textures when working in black and white?

LB: Texture and pattern. Absolutely. And also luster. You know, having sheens or flat surfaces to contrast is another way to get separation.

AS: Do you ever find yourself involved on movies after principal photography ends?

LB: Not as much as I'd sometimes like to be. But I'm always in touch with the producer and director through post. I often drop in to editorial if I'm in the same part of the world. But we do need to look at how the designer can be more involved in post, as is necessary. You've talked to a lot of designers in the past while–this must be something that comes up.

AS: People like Sarah Greenwood, who did the *Sherlock Holmes* movies, said she finds it interesting but that she really has no desire to be involved after principal photography. Meanwhile Grant Major, *The Lord of the Rings* designer, is hoping to craft his future contracts so that they include him remaining on during post.

LB: For certain kinds of pictures that might really make sense. I think there's a balance to be struck. Certainly I want to be as available as necessary throughout the process if I can help make the picture better.

AS: When you're shooting, are you on set during principal photography?

LB: Yes, but not nearly as much as I'd like to be. I open every set and try to steal as much time as possible to watch performance and be involved in how the set is shot but frankly with aggressive schedules on small or medium-sized pictures, you never really finish prepping. Prep continues through the shoot so it's a matter of chasing between the mill, the stages, the locations, and back to set.

I just got back from doing a picture with Robert Redford directing. And it was just incredible to watch. Just an honor working with Redford. He's incredibly collaborative. The cast in this picture was so phenomenal that I couldn't resist the temptation to keep popping back to set whenever I could, day or night, to watch some masterful acting.

AS: Was that *The Company You Keep* with Robert Redford directing and starring?

LB: Yes, along with Shia LaBeouf, Julie Christie, Anna Kendrick, Sam Elliot, Stanley Tucci, Chris Cooper, Susan Sarandon. It's a contemporary piece. Bob plays a former member of the Weather Underground who goes on the run when he's about to be exposed by a young reporter, after living under another identity for thirty years.

AS: Is Robert Redford visual? Is he involved in the production design?

LB: Yeah, incredibly. He studied painting. He thought he was going to paint. That really informs the way he sees and the way he communicates. He

was very involved. For one set in particular that had great emotional significance to the characters and story, Bob and I traded sketches with one another about how it might be oriented and laid out. And we poured through a lot of imagery for tone, specifically paintings. Andrew Wyeth's work was a touchstone of mood for me for that sequence.

AS: I've asked a few people about whether they like being on set during the shoot and Jack Fisk, who did the Terrence Malick movies, said that he likes being on set as much as humanly possible. After putting that much work into the sets he wants to shepherd them into existence.

LB: I love Jack's work. I have enormous respect for him. He's doing something right. Maybe I should be spending more time on set!

AS: What do you like about production design?

LB: We are so blessed to do what we do. I make my living by helping tell stories. Entertaining people. Maybe challenging them, maybe teaching them a little something now and again. Maybe inspiring them. I travel to fascinating places and go backstage into people's lives and jobs. See things that most people never get a chance to see. While that's a responsibility it's also just a huge, huge blessing. I'm very fortunate–I get paid to play.

Patrice Vermette

Patrice Vermette rose from the world of Canadian music videos and commercials to become one of our leading film production designers, winning numerous awards and Oscar nominations for his work on movies like *The Young Victoria, Arrival, Sicario* and *Dune,* for which he took home his first Academy Award.

AS: You met the director of *The Young Victoria*, Jean-Marc Valée on a short film?

PV: We met on a short film in 1995. It was called Magical Words. And then we went on to do lots of TV commercials together. In 2002 he came to me and said, *Do you want to do a feature film with me?* And I said, *Well, yes, sure.* And he said, *I'll give you a script and you tell me what you think.* And I fell in love with it. It was called *C.R.A.Z.Y.*

AS: That film won numerous awards.

PV: Good writing by Jean-Marc. And then he

brought his close collaborators with him for the adventure in England.

AS: When you shot *The Young Victoria* in England did you bring your crew from Montreal or hire a local British crew?

PV: I hired a local crew. Because I felt they have a great expertise over there for period films. To bring my own crew from Montreal on that endeavor, on that adventure, would have asked too much from them. Because they would have had to start from scratch. I read for four months to try to acquire as much knowledge as I could about that period in time and about all the characters that were real, the characters in history. I went a bit mental, just to acquire the knowledge. But people in England have done period films before and they already have an expertise so it becomes just about bringing my approach to their art.

AS: In addition to the reference books for *The Young Victoria*, were there also movies?
PV: You know the film that really inspired me was *The Leopard* by Visconti for the richness of the look. That's the film that I really devoured aesthetically. Which had nothing to do with what we were shooting except that it was a period film. I like the richness of it. I like the colors of it.

My approach to art direction is not to try to overshadow the story but to accompany it and give little clues on the characters. The Duchess of Kent, she's nouveau riche, she wants to become the Queen of England but she will never be. So in art direction you give cues in her environment and in the rooms that belong to her. You give the cue that there's too much gold, you know, it's overdone. Nowadays people who want to show off their money overdo it.

Every room has got to tell a story, a strong story. It's the backbeat of the real story, like the bass line on a piece of music.

AS: Almost subliminal . . .
PV: It has to be invisible but in a certain way tell a subliminal story. I like to play with symbolism a lot as well. For example with Queen Victoria when she's sharing her room with her mother in Kensington. The color of the paint is incandescent green–my painters had to work hard to get it. It was a very difficult color to attain because of the incandescence of it. During that period some people were using arsenic paint. So basically the room was poisoning her while her life was being poisoned by the people who surrounded her.

> " EVERY ROOM HAS GOT TO TELL A STORY, A STRONG STORY. IT'S THE BACKBEAT OF THE REAL STORY, LIKE THE BASS LINE ON A PIECE OF MUSIC.

I'm just going into the details but there's a broader philosophy within the production design of that film. For another example let's take the last room where we see King Edward in Windsor. I chose to do that room on location, but in a small chapel in a castle that we found. Because it's just before he dies–you know, he's in the chapel. He's ready to leave, you know. So it's religious symbolism.

Each room plays a role like that. I treat each room as characters in the film but then within the room you can add extra details. In the corridor which links all these rooms in Buckingham Palace the colors are bright because she's free. Victoria is now queen, she's blossoming as a young woman. But at the end where she meets with Conroy and she asks him to exit we had a big painting of Christ pointing outside.

Remember when Melbourne, the prime minister, picks up a letter underneath Victoria's desk, the blue letter from Albert? In that scene we put a door holder, a brass door holder which has the figure of a fox.

> **I OFTEN COMPARE PRODUCTION DESIGN WITH SOUND DESIGN BECAUSE BOTH CREATE MOODS.**

AS: So as he's reaching down to the ground—

PV: In the shot you see a fox. That's my approach in every film. I like the subliminal symbolism in films. In the movie *C.R.A.Z.Y.*, we hung a specific painting in Zach, the main character's bedroom when he's a teenager. Zach turns out to be gay. The painting is one he made of the Pink Floyd album cover from *Dark Side of the Moon*. The prism, the triangle. I picked that album because the prism projects the rainbow, the colors of the rainbow. So it's like seeing into the future.

AS: How do you accomplish creating that symbolism in practical locations?

PV: Bring set dressing or find the rooms that suit the vision. It's not just finding any room that looks great. It's about finding a room that looks great but also follows the vision.

AS: Tells the story.

PV: Yes, tells the story. We shot the Duchess of Kent's drawing room at a castle where there was a great regency style room that was just totally, totally over the top. That room was peacock-themed which I thought was perfect for her.

AS: Before you did the short with Jean-Marc that lead to *The Young Victoria*, you studied at university?

PV: Yes. I started very young actually. I studied sound design at Concordia in Montreal. That's why I often compare production design with sound design because both create moods. Just as music creates moods, production design should create moods. Good music in a film puts you in a mood but you don't hear the music–it simply puts you right where you have to be.

AS: Did your background in sound lead to doing any audio work in films?

PV: Yes, the last year at Concordia I did a multitude of soundtracks to student films. I wrote the music for the scores and played the music and recorded it. My friends for whom I'd done the soundtracks started working as production assistants for commercials so I started doing that too. They hired me when they needed an extra production assistant. And I looked at the people who were doing the set construction–they seemed to be the ones having the most fun! Little did I know they were the ones working the hardest!

Because it was good fun you know–they were passionate people and I wanted to be with those guys. So I did a couple of gigs as gopher, an art department runner, and then I became assistant to a guy who was production designer. Shortly after that I was working on a music video as a PA and the woman who was supposed to do the art direction on the gig was not able to do her job and I was asked the day before the shoot if I could help with the art direction. It was something that I'd never done before and I looked at the director and I said, *I think I could have fun but I've never done that in my life.* He looked at me and he said, *You know what, I'm kind of screwed so I can use whatever you can provide me with.* So I did four different sets overnight and from then on that director gave me all his music videos. That guy became very, very popular doing music videos. So he helped me build a name for myself. After that I started working with other guys and in 1995 I met Mr. Valée.

AS: Designing these projects did you tend to do sketches beforehand?

PV: Yeah, I did sketches. But it depends on each project you know. It's like right now I'm doing a Bud Light commercial. I did a sketch for the time machine we're making. We're having fun right now in a workshop–the time machine is like a sculpture. I'm actually doing it with a friend of mine. I know most production designers rarely touch the tools and materials themselves but I still like to do that once in a while. You keep close to where you came from.

AS: What do you do when you first receive a script?

PV: When I read a script I don't necessarily think about the production design aspect of it, like whether I will have a lot of sets to build. Instead, I tend to read it and just ask myself, *Would I be interested in seeing this film?* And then, *How can my approach make that film even more interesting? Do I have something to give, to add to the script?*

> ❝ WHEN I READ A SCRIPT I DON'T NECESSARILY THINK ABOUT THE PRODUCTION DESIGN ASPECT OF IT, LIKE WHETHER I WILL HAVE A LOT OF SETS TO BUILD. INSTEAD, I TEND TO READ IT AND JUST ASK MYSELF, *WOULD I BE INTERESTED IN SEEING THIS FILM?* AND THEN, *HOW CAN MY APPROACH MAKE THAT FILM EVEN MORE INTERESTING? DO I HAVE SOMETHING TO GIVE, TO ADD TO THE SCRIPT?*

AS: What would you say are good characteristics of a production designer?

PV: You have to be curious. That's the main thing. You have to be a psychologist. You have to be hands-on. You never know when you have to jump in and roll up your sleeves and start moving things. You have to be a good leader of a team.

Picking your crew is also very important because you're only as good as your crew. The people you interview want to please you because they all want the job. But you have to see through that because you know you're going to have to live with those people for seven or eight months. And within those eight months you're going to go through all these different stages of human behavior. You're gonna be scared, you're gonna be angry, you're gonna be happy. All these emotions will go through the entire crew so you have to find a team that will stick together and be strong together. Through the good and the bad. It's like being married I guess.

> ❝ **LAZY PEOPLE SHOULDN'T GO INTO PRODUCTION DESIGN. LAZY PEOPLE SHOULDN'T THINK ABOUT DOING ANY JOB IN THE ART DEPARTMENT! YOU HAVE TO BE A BIT CRAZY TO DO IT. YOU NEED A BIT OF INSANITY AS WELL!**

AS: Is that where the psychology comes in?
PV: Yes, psychology is useful there. But psychology is also needed with the producers and the directors obviously.

Also, lazy people shouldn't go into production design. Lazy people shouldn't think about doing any job in the art department! You have to be a bit crazy to do it. You need a bit of insanity as well!

AS: What do you do when you disagree with the director or producers?
PV: Well in the end of the day the director is always the one that you're working for. If he doesn't agree you have to remember he's the captain of the ship. But the director has to choose you the same way you choose your own team. He chooses people who will be able to be in line with his vision and also to bring their own vision to help his vision grow.

But you know, I'm pretty skilled at convincing. I learned that doing TV commercials, because there you have to convince people all the time. You need to just be passionate about your ideas. If they're good the director or the producer will go for them.

You also have to be able to say, *Okay, I was wrong.* And at the end of the day it's the director's film. Good producers are also intelligent and have some ideas. They will bring another dimension to the film, they are people who will listen as well. Good discussion in preproduction solves so many things. You can never emphasize that enough.

AS: What was it like working with set decorator Maggie Gray on *The Young Victoria*?
PV: She's got a great sense of humor. We're a great team because we're both intuitive. She knows when it's time to push for an idea and when to retreat. We're a good team because in discussion with production we'd always be on the same page. It was just wonderful. Maggie has so much experience and I was lucky to have someone like that willing to work with me. She's done all sorts of films. Obviously she did the set decoration on Brazil but she also did a smaller film called *The Life and Death of Peter Sellers*. And when I saw that film I just related a lot to the design and the set decoration in it. Hopefully Maggie and I have many years together in the future.

AS: You mentioned on the ADG Production Design panel that one of your earliest design inspirations was *Star Wars*.

PV: My dad took me to see *Star Wars* when I was seven years old. His dream was for me to become a lawyer like him, just to follow in his footsteps like every dad, but his mistake was to take me to see that film! From that moment on I knew what I wanted to do!

Remember the *Star Wars* figures? My parents had an unfinished basement and a bit more than a third of the basement was my *Star Wars* world. My parents said, *The basement is unfinished and you can do whatever you want with it.* I had a lot of cardboard and scale models. Whenever my parents had their friends over for supper they took them downstairs to show them my *Star Wars* world!

During the same period I was very influenced by KISS as well, that theatrical rock. My parents took me to see them in 1979 when I was nine years old. That was production design from a kid's perspective.

AS: How is working in Canada different from the States or the U.K.?

PV: It's very different because our films are a much smaller budget. You have to wear many hats when you do a film in Canada. What I really enjoyed about England is you can concentrate on your real job. Because in Canada most of the time you're your own set decorator and your own art director. Sometimes you have to do a bit of painting and carpentry. You have to because otherwise the job won't get done. You can sit on your ass and say, *I like the location as it is,* or you can go the extra mile. *You don't have time to do that? Okay, give me the tools, let's start rocking.* It's good. The industry is a lot more artisan. So you touch a lot of things as opposed to the big business where you only do the vision and simply oversee every department under you to make sure that they follow the vision. You do that as well in Canada but sometimes you have to go the extra mile.

> **" PASSION HAS TO PUSH YOU TO TRY TO GO FURTHER, TO GO THE EXTRA MILE. IT'S THE PASSION THAT DRIVES YOU. IT'S THE MOTOR OF EVERYTHING. IF YOU'RE NOT PASSIONATE, EVEN IN LIFE, YOU'RE WASTING YOUR TIME ON EARTH!**

AS: How have things changed since you were nominated for an Oscar?

PV: My life is not really different so far but I hope to have access to good stories.

I'd like to be able to do more films in the budget range of *The Young Victoria*. More like *There Will Be Blood*, *Crazy Heart*, *Boogie Nights*. James Gray material. Good stories, good films, great film makers. Those are my heroes as opposed to the Michael Bays. Those are the types of films that I really want to do.

AS: What are your thoughts about working with visual effects?

PV: It's a great tool. For instance at Lancaster House where we shot the ballroom scene after the coronation in *The Young Victoria*, the room was pretty darn big. We had a lot of extras but we needed to make it more impressive. So that's when visual effects comes in. Let's double the size of that room. Let's triple it. You bring references. Let's hang that picture on that wall there. There's good teamwork with visual effects. For *Westminster Abbey* it was impossible to shoot a real coronation so we did it on greenscreen.

Visual effects is an essential tool in moviemaking right now. Another good example is what Sarah Greenwood did on *Sherlock Holmes,* with set extensions. I saw the latest Tim Burton film over the weekend, *Alice in Wonderland.* I consider it really amazing production design. I think all types of film will still exist but with visual effects you can go the extra mile. Instead of showing just a quarter of the street because you only have enough money to dress that much well, you can shoot a bit wider and say, *Hey, let's have the rest.*

For example, it would have been impossible for the production to shoot the exterior we needed in Bavaria where you see mountains with a bit of snow on them so we added those mountains in post production.

There was also a scene that was supposed to be taking place on the Isle of Wight and I looked at Jean-Marc and said none of the locations we have are next to water. But when we were walking in the parking lot of a castle we realized we could actually shoot that scene right there. There were flatlands and a bit of mountains so we kept the mountains but we replaced the flatlands with water, in post.

So that's why I can't stress enough what a great tool it is.

AS: What advice would you have for production designers starting out?

PV: There are two ways. You can start out being the apprentice and production assistant and go the feature film route. Or you could go into music videos. That route goes faster because you shoot different projects and you meet different directors. And every director in music videos and commercials has a hidden script somewhere that they want to write eventually. They all wish that eventually they'll be recognized as feature film directors as opposed to commercial directors. They all dream of that. And by meeting these people on commercials and music videos eventually you're going to make a good connection. You're going to meet a guy like I did with Jean-Marc Valée. Someone that you click with and you have basically the same philosophy with about filmmaking. And that person will take you onto their feature film project. It might take four, five, or six years to write it and to finance it but eventually they will finance it. One of the directors that you work with will get their project on the road. Might not be a great budget but you just do it. Do it with your passion.

AS: Would you say passion is important as a production designer?

PV: Yeah of course, it's the drive, it's the fuel. On days you feel tired that passion has to push you to try to go further, to go the extra mile. It's the passion that drives you. It's the motor of everything. If you're not passionate, even in life, you're wasting your time on earth!

You have to be passionate with food, you have to be passionate with music. People who say food is just to feed yourself–that's boring! Come on, have fun! Having fun is also a key thing. When you're passionate you have fun because you don't count the hours.

We're lucky enough to have the best job in the world so you might as well enjoy it, right?

APPEAL

What do you like about production design?

*A compilation of excerpts covering
the subject of production design's appeal,
taken from the interviews in this book*

Despite the long hours, despite the intense pressure, despite those last minute panics when everything changes, despite the challenges, every single production designer I've interviewed loves their job. To an outsider it may appear to be an insanely demanding profession, so why do all these working production designers love it so much? What makes them stay up all night, every night, obsessing? Is it the closely-bonded team collaborating towards a common goal? Is it the world of illusion they create? Or is it stories that must get told?

MARK FRIEDBERG

The collaboration is the part I love. The thing that is the opposite of being a painter is that as a painter I sit in a room arbitrarily experiencing my bad childhood over and over again. There's no other point of reference but me. And no particular challenge except to keep going. But when you step into campaign mode in cinema it feels a lot of times like it's life or death. It's terrifying. You know if your set's one minute late you're done. And if it's not awesome you're done. It's got to be awesome, and on time and cheap and brilliant. It's terrifying! So you join forces with a team and that's the coolest part. The working together part. The fact is that the efforts of two people who work apart from one another is much less than the efforts of two people who join forces. In the collaboration world one plus one can equal four.

RICK CARTER

I can't believe that there's a job in which I've gotten to do what I've been able to do, not knowing from the beginning what it was I even wanted to do, and yet I've had an almost fifty year career doing it. And that there's an actual title for it. And it's called production design. What is the metaphor for this process that you've been hearing from all of these production designers? Obviously "magician" has a lot to do with it because there's a suspension of disbelief. There's the magician's point of view but there's also a bit of the fool, there's a bit of the visionary, there's a bit of the best friend. It's eclectic and it shape-shifts for every movie. It's something that I didn't understand in the beginning nor do I think that it's fully comprehendible to me now. But I think that to have a career in something that's both as abstract and as concrete as this is, has been kind of a miracle.

The movies that I've worked on have all been journeys with a sense of catharsis and even some enlightenment along the way. They reflect things that I care about. Spiritual moments and certainly human values and the value of heroes in various contexts. That all fits very well with what I would have imagined, what I would have liked for my life. And now going forward I look for what I can do to help other people do more of it.

GRANT MAJOR

The whole thing is pretty amazing. But in terms of a phase, the phase I like best is the "blue-sky thinking" phase at the beginning of a project where the film can be anything. The middle part of it you've just got your head down dealing with the day-to-day making of the thing. But those first ideas that come out go full-circle, sometimes taking years. Then you're sitting in the cinema and you're looking at the film and here it is on the screen. It's taken this long to get there. I like how where we begin influences where we end.

JACK FISK

The thing I like about production design is the idea of illusion. The magic of it. We're creating worlds that don't exist. When I was a kid I saw a *Little Rascals* show on television. They'd built a fort and when you were outside the fort and looked across the fence you saw people marching by with guns. You go inside the fort and it's these two little kids marching with a broken ladder. One rail was missing and the rungs of the ladder were sticking up so you thought it was a platoon of kids marching with guns. That image just stayed with me. I thought, *That's magical.*

DAVID WASCO & SANDY REYNOLDS-WASCO

DW: It's probably the most unstructured job that you can ask for now. And we get to work together. Sandy gets asked to work on movies all the time independent from me and it's a choice that I ask her to wait for my next movie, to be working with me, and she honors that. We get to travel together and get paid to do that and we get to meet and be friendly with some very interesting people.

SRW: Every story is different but most importantly every director is different. What they pull out of you is different every time and what you learn in that process is really wonderful. The more demanding they are, the more you learn and grow and go the extra mile. And do things you've never done before.

NATHAN CROWLEY

I just get excited by stories. We were going to do a film on Alan Turing, a mathematician who lived during the Second World War and who came up with the idea around 1920 that machines think. What I love about film is that then you say, *Okay, let's explore math in film. How the brain thinks. Let's look at nature. Repetitive patterns. Patterns in snow, footsteps, rhythm.* We went down this road, this tangent that brings you back around into the story and you add that to the design.

You ask how people live. How does this character live? It's like being a detective. Then you tell a visual, emotional story with themes that underrun the characters.

RICK HEINRICHS

This is where my explorations into the greenscreen are going to leave me dry. I like walking onto a set I built that was living in my mind for a really long time. In particular something with forced perspective and some theatrical elements to it. I like to just sit there and enjoy the environment. Like in the back portion of the Van Tassel estate in *Sleepy Hollow*. It was this back porch where you look down on a driveway to the stage at Leavesden. We only had thirty feet but we had a coach and horses and we had this apple orchard where we had shrunk all these trees in the background for forced perspective. And we had this mountain-scape that we'd sculpted so it took light. And a small windmill and painted skies. And some of the stars, Michael

What do you like about production design?

Gambon and Ian McDiarmid, would sit back there smoking cigarettes and relaxing like they were enjoying the afternoon out on the back porch. The level of deep satisfaction that I got out of that has been with me ever since.

HANNAH BEACHLER

I'm very lucky in that I get to travel for the films that I work on . . . Those experiences inform my design. Meeting people and hearing their stories informs my ability to create a world. Whether I like it or I don't like it, whether I'm in a situation that makes me nervous or not. You cannot create any world if all you know is the bubble that you're in.

I'm a traveler. I'm an adventurer, although maybe sometimes a reluctant one! You cannot be a designer if you do not open your world to those types of experiences.

COLIN GIBSON

[What I like most is] the chance to think about something. Sometimes we just don't think about stuff enough. What I love is you get to look at a script and you get to go into it as deeply as you allow yourself. And that gives you the chance to break it down and to start to understand how the component parts work and how they affect other people. I think it's a fantastic way to look at how we communicate and how we think, how we feel. And if you think about it enough and you have enough good people around you they can turn what could have been the bad poetry in your bedroom into something the whole world can share.

DENNIS GASSNER

I love the whole process. This comes from way back. From listening to Dean Tavoularis talk about *The Godfathers* and about *The Conversation* and about other classic films and how they were all put together. The uniqueness of the filmmaking process. You work so hard but then you sit in the cinema and there it is. It's an extraordinary thing. It's one of the most amazing art forms we have.

Rick Carter

Rick Carter is a legend in the field of production design. With *Avatar* and *Star Wars VII: The Force Awakens,* he designed two films that have to date each made over two billion in the box office. He's spent a career teaming up with three of the greatest filmmaking visionaries who ever lived–Steven Spielberg, James Cameron and Robert Zemeckis, to create such classic films as *Jurassic Park, Forrest Gump, Back to the Future II* and *III.* To date he's won two Academy awards, one for *Avatar* and one for *Lincoln, and been nominated for a total of five.* Most recently he designed *Star Wars IX: The Rise of Skywalker.* I connected with Rick in the middle of the worldwide pandemic, with our industry on hold.

AS: Is all production and prep shut down for you because of the COVID-19 virus?

RC: It really is. There's some prep going on but for the most part it's shut down. Keeping people safe is the first and foremost thing. Secondarily, what kind of art can we create in this environment? It will have a profound impact on what movies are and how they're made.

The job of production design is not going to be dependent on what we've had in this last epoch. Production design is not a static thing. Just the advent of computer imagery into the process caused a development that we've all had to adjust to, those of us who've been around for a while. And here comes another change and this one's going to be very, very trying but I think it will lead to great solutions.

Designers will have to really help design the production, not just what it looks like. Designing the future will be a part of the production designer's role. We'll look up and in five years from now there will be a group of people who will have shown the way. And some of them will have been production designers that have helped fundamentally to shape how movies get made.

Some of it will become more virtual. Some of it will become more divided up into groups, bringing aspects of the movie together both in realtime and later. But how much of a "collage" can the movie sustain, so that it still feels like it's of a whole? It's like when they first thought about going on location and they discussed how to integrate that with stage sets or back lots and still make it look whole. My mentor Richard Sylbert looked at me at one point and said, *It looks like you're going into the digital realm. And whatever it's becoming now, it's going to be different.* It has to evolve and the design challenges will evolve and I'm interested to see where it goes.

AS: Several films you've co-designed with another production designer. How do you feel about sharing the job?

RC: I love it. Collaborating is the way I've been able to maintain a career and progress and prosper in these last twenty years. Because if I drew lines around what I thought was "mine" I wouldn't be helping the production. On *The Polar Express* we were all digital and that's why I brought in Doug Chiang, who could go from conceptualization all the way through to the end of the visual effects process. There was a period of time where the idea existed of a territorial battle between production and post production, from the time of the *Star Wars* prequels all the way through 'til maybe eight years ago. But I will always engage the visual effects people as though they are co-designing with me, as the directors are. That's why Robert Stromberg said there were really three of us designing *Avatar*. And there were. There were many, many more people on that team that were contributing mightily to what you see before you.

> " DESIGNING THE FUTURE WILL BE A PART OF THE PRODUCTION DESIGNER'S ROLE. WE'LL LOOK UP AND IN FIVE YEARS FROM NOW THERE WILL BE A GROUP OF PEOPLE WHO WILL HAVE SHOWN THE WAY. AND SOME OF THEM WILL HAVE BEEN PRODUCTION DESIGNERS THAT HAVE HELPED FUNDAMENTALLY TO SHAPE HOW MOVIES GET MADE.

I've certainly been involved in post production but sometimes I work for free to do that. And I don't blame a producer for saying, *We don't have the money to have you around for this.* I just want to be involved if I can to help the process. But generally, the narrative of the movie and the characters and what their motivations are, and why something should be the way it is, is embedded strongly enough in the production that's shot, that in post it simply carries through. Not to say you just relinquish everything, but I think these territorial battles or non-battles have been irrelevant to my process. Any time a production designer feels like they have to be territorial they're missing the point of their job. Because their territory is the movie. And what's best for the movie.

No one's ever going to "step on my toes." I've always maintained that you're never going to find my toes. That's not possible. I don't care who the person is. It could be Jim Cameron who knows how to art direct a movie and can come in and production design, while he's directing, any movie. It's just that his process is enhanced when he has collaborators who are also production designers such as Rob and I were with him on *Avatar*. We brought so much to the feeling, the process, of what was accomplished.

There are egos everywhere and everybody can move into the zone of just trying to have their own vision accomplished. But really what you see in most of the people that you've interviewed is that the production designer is trying to enhance, and get to the essence of the director's vision. Maybe along with the producer and along with the writer. For me it's always been director-centric. And I've gotten to work with such good directors and powerful visionaries. They always make my work look much better than I could on my own. That doesn't mean that I don't have opinions. It just means that I don't put those opinions over theirs and then fight with them about it. Instead I try to really listen to what it is they want.

I hear what they want metaphorically and then go out ahead of them, and beyond. It's my interpretation but then it becomes our interpretation. It becomes bigger than the sum of the parts of the conversation. And setting the stage is not just the literal, physical stage, or even the digital stage or the mo-cap stage, it's the stage for good ideas and a process that leads to real collaboration. For me, that's the only reason I've gotten invited to do the movies that I've done and to last as long as I have. It's because I like that part of it.

You can look at the group of people you've interviewed and see how we are actually similar even if it's somebody who says they draw everything or somebody else who says they don't draw anything. Nobody in that group says, *I just come in and do it all on my own and nobody helps me, and I don't have to create a great team around me.*

Especially now when we go somewhere and we're just dropped in. We don't necessarily have people there that we knew beforehand that we're going to be working with. We have to size the local crew up. I thought Dante Ferretti said it really well in one of your interviews. About having good instincts in picking people. He said, *I don't think I've made a mistake yet, or maybe I have I just don't know it!*

Everybody finds a way to be a really good collaborator. I know Dennis Gassner and I talk about that, Jim Bissell [*E.T.* production designer] and I talk about it, Guy Dyas, Nathan Crowley, Sarah Greenwood. We all talk about this all the time. Because even the directors themselves, no matter who they are, no matter what their vision is, they have to work through other people. Otherwise even Jim Cameron would just have one movie and he'd probably still be working on it by himself. That is, if he didn't know how to engage large groups of people and get them to understand his vision.

That's not always simple because the director may be right on the edge of technology or on a concept that's not easy to see at first. What is Eywa? That's a spiritual force that's at the center of *Avatar*. And it informs everything that you see. You need to understand how real that is to Jim. Or the Force which George [Lucas] brought into being. We had to interpret it for another generation and hand off the latest *Star Wars* movies.

Nathan Crowley's been with Chris [Nolan, *Dark Knight* director] forever. Working out of their garage to do these incredible movies. Such expanse and yet it always starts just with a language of "intuitive understanding and collaboration.

AS: How did you first get into the business?
RC: I'd grown up around the business because my father [Dick Carter] had been the publicist and partner with Jack Lemmon. So I knew a lot about Hollywood culturally. I didn't think I wanted to have anything to do with it necessarily. After I dropped out of college and traveled for a year and a half around the world, I went to New York and got into painting. Most of my paintings are portraits, they're people. I have a sort of split vision, I have

a left eye that's far-sighted and a right eye that's nearsighted. So I tend to look differently with each eye, never at the same time with both eyes. I'm not actually seeing 3D in the way most people see 3D, even if I'm working on Avatar! I've had to make up for that. So I was painting but found that lifestyle too solitary for me. I asked my father what an art director did because it had the word "art" in it. He knew [production designer] Richard Sylbert and said, *If you end up back in LA I'll introduce you to someone who can give you a point of view about what an art director does*. Because at the time I thought it was just placing a painting on a wall.

> **" ANY TIME A PRODUCTION DESIGNER FEELS LIKE THEY HAVE TO BE TERRITORIAL THEY'RE MISSING THE POINT OF THEIR JOB. BECAUSE THEIR TERRITORY IS THE MOVIE.**

AS: Up until that point had you been seriously considering a career in fine art? Had you gone to art school with the goal of becoming a fine artist?
RC: Well I was at Berkeley for the first two years and a sociology major during what seemed to be such socially tumultuous times. I'd always been an artist but I didn't see any of what we at that time called "relevance" in being just an artist. But after I traveled and came back, I went to the University of California at Santa Cruz and graduated with an art major. I tried to be a fine artist but I found that the gallery scene in New York was not easy. Painting

had been declared dead. Conceptual art was "in." And so I started looking elsewhere to see where I might be able to pull together a career. And fortunately when I did come back to LA I met Richard Sylbert and he invited me to come for lunch. He was working on a movie called *The Fortune* that Mike Nichols was directing. I went there for that one lunch but it turned into a whole summer of just going back every day. He would just talk to me about what he was doing. He would use metaphors–he would say if it was music he was interested in the writing of the songs, he was interested in all the instruments, he was interested in the conducting and even the selling of the music.

> **BEING GOOD COLLABORATORS BOTH WITH THE DIRECTORS AND THE PEOPLE THEY HIRE, PRODUCTION DESIGNERS SHOULD MAINTAIN A CERTAIN AMOUNT OF AUTHORSHIP THAT'S NOT AT THE EXPENSE OF SOMEONE ELSE. I DON'T FEEL DIMINISHED BY WHAT OTHER PEOPLE HAVE DONE ON A MOVIE THAT I HAVE WORKED ON. USUALLY IT ENHANCES WHAT I DO.**

He also once told me, *If you're looking to come into a profession where you think anybody's ever going to understand what you do, you're in the wrong place. They will never understand.* And I can tell you forty-five years later people still don't understand. You can do all these interviews and have all the behind-the-scenes shoots but I think you have to actually do it to understand it. Because there's no rule book.

After Richard Sylbert I met the production designer Michael Riva as well as Michael Haller who both had less formal ways of doing their jobs. Once I was with Michael Riva we got to do *Goonies* together and that was like being two kids paid to be swashbucklers. And that's where I met Steven Spielberg and Kathy Kennedy [producer]. We'd done a big pirate ship and all these cave sets and I took them through those and that's when Steven offered me *Amazing Stories.*

Amazing Stories was two years of television with a very eclectic group of stories. That led to the relationship with Steven and then with Bob Zemeckis. The next twenty years was just the two of them so I never got beaten up by going out into the world to have multiple directors have different interpretations of what I could do or not do. Instead I could hone my point of view and they seemed to appreciate it.

I made lots of mistakes but I kept the thing going and that was the beginning. I was a very good assistant. I took lots of notes. I was very good at communicating. I've always needed the people around me, the set designers, set decorators, illustrators, and people who were so good at doing their specific jobs. It's a little like learning how to conduct before you know how to actually play the instruments. I see that communication as an integral part of the job for me, that leads to results, so that then the directors like having me around because I'm delivering for them. But I'm also imbuing it with something that they might not have thought of.

With Robert Zemeckis often I would start off and say something I thought was important and he would kind of have his eyes bulge out and say, *Well, what I thought you were going to say was . . .* and then he'd go into something that was a full-blown idea that would go right into the movie. And then I would ask, *Were you thinking about that before I started talking?* And he said, *No, just while you were talking this came to me.* He was using the energy I was providing as a reconnoiterer of concepts and then picking that energy out and making it his own.

And sometimes with Steven we'll be talking and I can just tell by the way the conversation's going that he's about to circle back and have a really good idea, so I'll try to set the stage for that.

AS: Would you say that spirit of collaboration is the most important attribute a production designer should have?

RC: I certainly advocate it from my own experience and you've heard that through many of your interviews. Being good collaborators both with the directors and the people they hire, production designers should maintain a certain amount of authorship that's not at the expense of someone else. I don't feel diminished by what other people have done on a movie that I have worked on. Usually it enhances what I do.

If you're going to be defensive about that then you've got a big problem. You're going to constantly be in friction with everybody about the size of the budget, the other people who are taking things away from you, the people who are taking credit for things that you think you deserve credit for, the people usurping your job, and you know, you've only got ten toes! So once they step on those ten toes . . . Some directors will step on all ten toes at once the first time you meet them!

For a production designer the most important thing is, if there is something there, enhance it. If there is nothing there, come up with something so that everyone else on the crew from construction to art department to cinematographers to set decorators to producers to location managers and visual effects people all have to have something to do. They have what Zemeckis used to call their "marching orders." Because if you don't, it just spins around and around and the production's just wasting money trying to get going. With each one of these directors I've been involved with, I learned that there was a language that they needed to have as a primary launching place to go from. Then you have to solve issues that come up. And sometimes they're not rational issues. With Martin Scorsese on *Amazing Stories*, the whole show was about these mirrors and in particular the breaking of a mirror, and he said, *I can't break a mirror on set. That's just bad luck.* I had to come up with a way to help him break a mirror in the scene without ever breaking a mirror on a stage that he was a part of. So we had a plexiglass mirror with shelves of glass in front. They threw something at it, the glass broke, and then we cut away to the thrower, then when we came back and the mirror was broken. The mirror had been done off stage somewhere and brought in.

Thirty years later I was at the Art Directors Guild getting an award for lifetime achievement and Marty Scorsese was there getting an award and I couldn't help referencing that event even while I was getting my award. I noted that we were talking thirty years later while both getting life-time achievement awards so obviously we didn't have bad luck!

> [RICHARD SYLBERT] ONCE TOLD ME, *IF YOU'RE LOOKING TO COME INTO A PROFESSION WHERE YOU THINK ANYBODY'S EVER GOING TO UNDERSTAND WHAT YOU DO, YOU'RE IN THE WRONG PLACE.* THEY WILL NEVER UNDERSTAND. AND I CAN TELL YOU FORTY-FIVE YEARS LATER PEOPLE STILL DON'T UNDERSTAND. YOU CAN DO ALL THESE INTERVIEWS AND HAVE ALL THE BEHIND-THE-SCENES SHOOTS BUT I THINK YOU HAVE TO ACTUALLY DO IT TO UNDERSTAND IT. BECAUSE THERE'S NO RULE BOOK.

AS: What is your process when you first get a script?

RC: The first thing I do is to let it wash over me so I can just experience the first reading, which will be the freshest I'll ever have. Just experience what the movie means to me and what comes out to me.

In your interview with Guy Dyas he talked about sketching what he saw along the way, but however one does that, whether one makes notes or doesn't make notes, sketches or doesn't sketch, one gets a feeling from the script.

Now let's just say, as it's been numerous times for me, and as it was on the *Star Wars* movies, there's no script when I'm starting. Concepts are just being developed. *Polar Express* was that way, there was just the children's book. And *Avatar* was only partially developed. I'm looking for the feeling and what flickers and the little glimpses and associations I make. I try to note what they are without interrupting the flow because I'm not only looking at it moment to moment as though it's a series of stills, I'm looking at it cinematically, in motion. Then I see what aspects of characters or scenes I associate with something else in a script. They are either connected literally or are not connected but should be.

For instance, on *Avatar* I could tell that I was on a journey that seemed like *The Wizard of Oz* as it would meet *Apocalypse Now.* Those are both journeys, and one goes one place and one goes another. And then for *Avatar* it's even portrayed as mystical and there's a connectedness that is invoked. There was this connection between the "Kansas" human world and the "Oz" world. On many of the things I've gotten to work on, it's about digesting it and then coming back with an honest, direct, emotional response to what the script is and what the director wants to accomplish. I'm the first believer or one of the first believers. I'll say, *I can believe this,* and then help to make this as believable for an audience as possible, so that the suspension of disbelief is not a negative idea, it's an invitation to believe. And then I get something to believe in for the next however long I'm on that movie. It becomes like a dream that you'd want to help come true.

When it works out at the other end where you look at it and you really like it, that's fantastic. And then if other people like it, even better. And then if it takes off into being something that lots of people like, it's fantastic but it also becomes something that you have to let go of. Because everybody has it as their own version. That's what we've seen of course with *Star Wars.* It's no longer just the movie that the movie makers were making, even if it's George Lucas. It's no longer just the movie that the people who worked on it were designing. It's in that space between where the audience is and where the movie is on screen. That's this hybrid gap where cinema explodes and becomes something you all experience as different.

Any script that you're looking at could go to that place but first has to be broken down into many, many pragmatic jobs that people need to do. The job of production design is to see the alchemy that's right in front of you and yet you still have to film something that can actually be accomplished, and in the time frame and in the budgets.

AS: You make it into something concrete . . .
RC: It's only concrete at the end. And even then it's

not concrete. Even at the point when it's a digital series of zeros and ones it only comes alive when it's not concrete. You go out of yourself and you meet it half way. How concrete is that?

> **WITH MARTIN SCORSESE ON *AMAZING STORIES,* THE WHOLE SHOW WAS ABOUT THESE MIRRORS AND IN PARTICULAR THE BREAKING OF A MIRROR, AND HE SAID, *I CAN'T BREAK A MIRROR ON SET. THAT'S JUST BAD LUCK.* I HAD TO COME UP WITH A WAY TO HELP HIM BREAK A MIRROR IN THE SCENE WITHOUT EVER BREAKING A MIRROR ON A STAGE THAT HE WAS A PART OF.**

AS: It's like you're selling something that doesn't physically exist. You're transferring that dream to somebody.
RC: That's right. And when you have that as a communal experience with a lot of people in the theater it's fantastic. And even if you have it in a more individual experience on your iPhone or at home on a screen, it can take you to a place that doesn't just take you out of your head and life, it puts you into your life on some other level. It invokes the dream state. That's why I think that most of the production designers, certainly all the ones that you've interviewed and have on your site, they're dreamers. But they want, as Richard Sylbert said, to have their dreams come true. And they're result freaks. You know, they don't just talk about it, they do it.

AS: Nathan Crowley puts the whole movie on a long wall that includes every single scene in the movie, represented with imagery. Do you ever do anything like that?

RC: Always. I don't know anybody who doesn't. I call it the movie-scape. I used to call it the film-scape before film went away. You can traverse it by looking at all the images and feel like you're looking at the movie. On *Avatar* not only did I lay out all the scenes linearly across but I also put them at three different levels. Like an EKG, I had yarn taking us up and down, moving left to right through all the imagery of the movie so that you were at the Kansas level then you had the Pandora level, the Na'vi level, then you had the phantasmagoric level which was the Eywa level. It progressed with the images that we were working on plus research, literally the *Wizard of Oz* and *Apocalypse Now*. It ended up having some impact on the movie. That's why Col. Quaritch says, *You're not in Kansas anymore.* He references that.

AS: Should production design be visible or invisible? Should a set become a character in the movie?

RC: It's never binary. In the question is the answer. Sometimes it's more this and sometimes it's more that. Sometimes it's more of a character. You know the Gump house in *Forrest Gump* or the Tara house in *Gone with the Wind*. Where literally you can't imagine the movie without the place because the place orients you to what your emotions are. So it functions like a character.

But sometimes it helps when you prioritize the importance of a set, to not go too crazy with architecture and details if you're only trying to get across something in relationship to what came before and what will come afterwards. This can help you on the budget because you might first think, Well, this is a very important scene because it's a palace with a million details. Then you realize, because of its impact on the movie, it really should be something that instead you work out with the cinematographer to do a long lens shot and have it be out of focus or see just one part of it. Those decisions are happening intuitively all the time in budgeting, the decisions of what to make, how to shoot it, and how to edit it.

AS: Speaking of budget and resources, what advice would you give to someone going from a small or medium budget movie to a two hundred million dollar movie? Is it the same job or are there specific things to watch out for?

RC: Well, again, it's both. Ask Hannah Beachler about that one! I'd spoken with her before *Black Panther* came out and I could see the determination that she had to bring that vision to the screen. She might not yet have had all the technical chops to do all those things, but nobody does. Nobody has all the chops to do everything all the time. And so you have to bring people together and find a way to get the director to believe that what you're doing can lead to what they need. The main thing you say is just, *Yes*. And you try to make it the best way you possibly can. Hannah had the relationship with [*Black Panther* director] Ryan Coogler and he knew that she would take whatever directions that he could give. She knew how to keep it cohesive and then reach out to all the people that she needed to help support her on technical levels. It comes across so well because you feel the intuitive nature. Only certain types of people are capable of doing that.

You need to surround yourself with people who know things. And be very open to listening. Don't be arrogant and egotistical about it to the point that you don't listen to peoples' input. Don't try to make all the decisions yourself. Actually try to elicit help. That's how you can get to those bigger budgets.

What I've done is I've taken on a partner to share the load as I've gotten older. I pick really, really ambitious people and very talented people. I don't look at it as an ego thing where I have to be the one that gets all the credit for the design of the movie. It allows someone else to take on real responsibilities with me.

AS: Dennis Gassner advised doing yoga and meditation to be physically and mentally ready for the job. Do you ever think about that side of it?
RC: All the time. As you get older you have to pay attention to that, otherwise you just won't be able to get up in the morning and do it at all.

The work has not been local in the last twenty years so there's a lot of flying around, whether it's London or New Zealand or New York or Richmond, Virginia. Since I have a family I like to come back as much as I can. That has worn on me quite a bit. Especially this last year when I was on the production part of *Star Wars IX*.

> ❝ MOST OF THE PRODUCTION DESIGNERS, CERTAINLY ALL THE ONES THAT YOU'VE INTERVIEWED AND HAVE ON YOUR SITE, THEY'RE DREAMERS. BUT THEY WANT, AS RICHARD SYLBERT SAID, TO HAVE THEIR DREAMS COME TRUE. AND THEY'RE RESULT FREAKS. YOU KNOW, THEY DON'T JUST TALK ABOUT IT, THEY DO IT.

But I try to be mindful of it. I try to get enough sleep. And walk and get some exercise. Being ready for the production and how much it takes out of you is a big part of it. You've encountered it in many of your interviews, like talking with Jack Fisk and all those places that he's been and how physical it is when he makes movies. Even if you're doing it more digitally like Robert Stromberg, it's still going to be very stressful.

So how you manage stress is important, whether you have some form of a meditation practice or something that you do on your own, whether it's your family or your own art. I paint on my own as an artist. I still do all the faces that I've done my entire life. While I'm doing my left eye production design, the more external, I'll call it pop art, I'll also do the more personal, right eye, introspective painting on my own in my own studio.

I also try to bring that deeper level to the movies that I work on, especially in my collaborations with the directors. I try to go as deep as I can in understanding what it is they're after. Not just emotionally but even spiritually. I don't mean only a specific religion like Eywa in *Avatar*, but usually there's a core "something" there, like the Force in *Star Wars*. Steven looks at the Force as being, literally, intuition. So he draws very much upon his intuition in any given moment as something he can trust, rather than to overintellectualize choices. And Bob Zemeckis is so expansive in his thinking that he just delights in where the brain can go. It becomes a kind of a mental play. That helps me stay healthy mentally through the arduous journey that every movie is.

AS: I once had a basement set on a movie I was designing and my initial sketch was windowless and bare and pretty unshootable. The DP said, *Look what Rick Carter did here for the basement set in* War of the Worlds *with the textures and midground elements and the light coming in the high cellar windows.* Your basement set became a great inspiration to me and actually changed my whole paradigm about production design! Was there was a set like that, that inspired you in the beginning of your career?
RC: First of all, regarding that basement–and there were actually two basements in *War of the Worlds*,

there's one near the plane crash and there's one at the end of the movie with Ogilvy, the Tim Robbins character. I tried to make those two basements seemingly of the same design, with a stairway right in the middle. That allowed you to be able to shoot it in a variety of ways whenever someone went up or down the stairs. That central point of reference is something that Steven always likes, as with the central visitor's center in *Jurassic Park*. When you have something in the center you can move around it and you can use it as a foreground. That was one of the ideas.

Of course, with the lighting you're always trying to have some place the DP can light from. *In Back to the Future III*, Bob Zemeckis asked, *You know the cave entrance is over here, but we've got a cave down here so where's the light coming from?* And the DP Dean Cundey said, *Well I think it's coming from the same place as the music!*

AS: That story is legendary! I heard it from someone a long time ago but I never knew the original source!
RC: Well maybe Dean had heard it from somewhere before that but I was there when he said it and I just cracked up.

But in terms of sets that I saw, in *Gone with the Wind* that image with the Tara house in the background framed by the oak tree became the iconic image that I wanted to have for *Forrest Gump*. So we put the house right where it would be framed by the oak tree at the end of the oak alley. When we dug the foundation for the front steps of that house we actually ended up finding the foundation of steps in exactly the same place where a house had been built one hundred years before.

Forrest Gump was also a southern story about a war that comes and damages so much around Forrest's life, even thought the house itself never gets taken. It felt to me like I was going to a place that I was resurrecting from an old set. An old story that was about grieving about the loss of a way of life but in an entirely different context. That resonated for me in a specific way. There are many environments that I'm in that I find myself associating to previous movies but that's the one that comes to mind as a specific set that had a place in the movie I was working on.

AS: Speaking of *Forrest Gump*, I remember you built a simple structure to show Robert Zemeckis the scale of the Gump house before it was built. John Myhre also told me how he mocks up sets either out of plywood for the dancers to practice on, or out of refrigerator boxes to give the director a sense of the space. Do you often mock up a set, to scale?

RC: I've done that a lot. It's very helpful. On this last movie, *The Rise of Skywalker*, what we did, before we even knew what the scenes were, was to create the cave set based on the idea the co-designer Kevin Jenkins had of putting the Blockade Runner ship in the middle of the cave. We made it as a model that he could get down and look at, as though he was a kid. But we also showed him how

big it would be on a stage, mocking it up in very rough ways. We did the same thing with the snowy city Kijimi set. We first made a model of what we wanted to build and then, with scaffolding, we put it up in the parking lot to give J.J. [Abrams, director] a feel for how big it would be. That's how we got the go-ahead to build the sets even before J.J. knew what all the scenes were. We had to get a head start to be shooting in five months.

Sometimes you have to come up with ways of showing your ideas that are inspiring, so the director can grasp what it is and particularly so they get the scale of it. And with the Gump house, for instance, we were able to show Bob what the light would be like where it would be situated. We did the same thing on *What Lies Beneath* with Bob. But when I saw what we had planned and I put it up with scaffolding I could see immediately that it was too big. We had a whole scout coming out that weekend to look at it. I called Bob up and said, *I can't show it to you like this because all you'll do is look at it and say it's wrong.* He said, *Well, good, I'm glad you're not wasting our time. We'll reschedule it for next week.* Sometimes you bite the bullet and say, *That's not what I thought it was going to be.* You don't try to talk yourself into the idea that it's really okay when you know it's not.

AS: People get so attached to their own idea and then try to convince themselves it's great.

RC: You don't want to be out there thinking it's so great and then have everyone else come and say, *It's not so great. And not only that, it's not what we* *want.* It's fine if it's in the preliminary stage, up to a point. Although that's a lot of money to have everybody fly across the country just to look at something you know is wrong. Worse, of course, is to not have everybody come to see it in some way ahead of time, so that instead they're doing that the morning of. And then that's a real problem. You've created this situation where now a lot of work has to go into fixing something that earlier could have been much less of a problem.

AS: Do you have any advice on navigating conflict on set if someone doesn't like your idea but you have a strong feeling about it?

RC: You have to work it out. You don't have a choice. You can get fired if you want to make a big deal out of it and put everyone else on a defensive level. Or you can figure out what's the solution. What's the problem and how can we get around that problem.

I can give you an example from *Lost World* where there's a scene of a dinosaur T-Rex coming to the kids' bedroom. The T-Rex will first be seen from a side angle and then it has to crash into the window. Well, the huge mechanical T-Rex puppet was on tracks so it couldn't be seen sideways and then be made to turn and bash the window. It had to have the ability to be seen in two different ways. And then we had a third scene that was in the script with the kid running to the parent's bedroom. But that part was left out of the storyboards that Steven did. I was also working on *Amistad* at the same time and splitting my time between the two. So I

was away when they did the walk-though of the set and nobody picked up on the fact that there was no parents' bedroom. Nobody knew there was supposed to be a parents' bedroom. So that morning I came in from the East Coast where I was scouting on *Amistad* with Kathy Kennedy and I get a call from the set saying, *Please come to set, Steven wants to know where the parent's bedroom is.* And they'd all walked the set on that Friday before.

I come in and Steven looks at me and says, *Well, where's the parent's bedroom?* And I said, *Well, it's not in the storyboards.* Everybody sort of steps back and I'm kind of looking, *So I'm the fool here?* And he said, *Well, it's in the script.* Since we didn't have a parents' bedroom to shoot that day, I said, *What if you do this? We have two bedroom sets, one for the T-Rex going sideways and one for the bashing into the window, so what if we shoot the sideways version first, then you go down and you start shooting the bashing in of the window. While you're doing that we'll take all the dressing out of the first bedroom set and we'll get dressing from the scene dock of a parents' bedroom and we'll put it in the first room. Then you come back and just shoot that bedroom as the parents'.* Now, it just happened that that could be a solution. Everybody said, *Oh, good,* and went on with their daily schedules.

So this can happen and does happen. I've had various times where I've had to switch the dressing because an actor coming in that day doesn't like what they see or there's not enough of some element they think is important to their character. And you just have to scramble. You do what's best for the movie at that point and have a good attitude about it. You see the bigger picture. It's part of the process. You don't come up with some problem that's really your own ego acting in opposition to what's good for the movie.

AS: What do you love about production design?
RC: I can't believe that there's a job in which I've gotten to do what I've been able to do, not knowing from the beginning what it was I even wanted to do, and yet I've had an almost fifty year career doing it. And that there's an actual title for it. And it's called production design. What is the metaphor for this process that you've been hearing from all of these production designers? Obviously "magician" has a lot to do with it because there's a suspension of disbelief. There's the magician's point of view but there's also a bit of the fool, there's a bit of the visionary, there's a bit of the best friend. It's eclectic and it shape-shifts for every movie. It's something that I didn't understand in the beginning nor do I think that it's fully comprehendible to me now. But I think that to have a career in something that's both as abstract and as concrete as this is, has been kind of a miracle.

The movies that I've worked on have all been journeys with a sense of catharsis and even some enlightenment along the way. They reflect things that I care about. Spiritual moments and certainly human values and the value of heroes in various contexts. That all fits very well with what I would have imagined, what I would have liked for my life. And now going forward I look for what I can do to help other people do more of it.

Patrick Tatopoulos

Patrick Tatopoulos production designed the blockbusters *Independence Day, I, Robot,* and *Live Free or Die Hard.* He is also famous for creating incredible creature effects for films such as *Silent Hill, The Ruins,* and the *Underworld* series, the last installment of which he directed. I ran into Patrick on the slopes of Big Bear and he agreed to share some of his wisdom.

AS: You went from effects to production designer and now to director–how did you first start out?
PT: I left Europe and came to the States to be a sculptor or designer for creature effects. The thing that actually appealed to me the most about movie making was special makeup effects. That was my first big target. After seeing the movie *The Thing* I said, *This is what I want to do.* So in a few weeks I sculpted a bunch of creatures–I was in Greece at the time–then I took pictures and came to the States. I had a few meetings but the one that became really, really important was with a compa-

ny called Makeup Effects Laboratories. Those guys ended up hiring me and getting me my Green Card so I could work as a creature sculptor. I spent a year or so sculpting, making molds, and designing creatures for them on a few small movies that came to the shop. I built a couple of creature effects for *Star Trek: Next Generation* and then a company came and we had to do *Beastmaster 2*. They saw my drawing and said, *Hey Patrick we have a great production designer on board but he doesn't draw. We would like someone like you to be the art director.*

On that small project I started to discover the world of the art department and production design. I worked with Alan Jones who was a very cool designer, very open minded. I still wasn't really calling myself an art director per se but I had a bit of experience. I went back to concept art and worked on *Bram Stoker's Dracula* and a few movies where we got into the world of concept design.

My big, big break was my meeting with [producer] Roland Emmerich. Roland saw some of my concept work for *Bram Stoker's Dracula* and said, *Hey, we're doing a movie called* Stargate *and we need a concept artist on board.* I jumped in and started to work in the art department again–designing the whole city of Stargate. Then Roland said, *Hey, we need quick designs of warrior Egyptian creatures.* He liked the drawings very much and said, *Patrick, I love your design. Now who's going to build it?* I said, *You know what? Let me build it for you.* I was a bit ballsy but Roland was a very open-minded person. He liked the design so much that he said, *You know, you should do it.*

So that's when I created my creature effects company. From that point on I did a lot of makeup effects and creature work but at the same time I wanted to keep moving on into the production design aspect of things. What quickly became obvious to me was that I wanted to do both. To be the designer and also to bring the creature to life that belonged in the world that I designed.

I became very, very interested in the way they do movies in Europe. In Italy the designers are usually people who do sets, costume, hair, and so on: a much broader range of design. In Hollywood people have a tendency to label you a makeup effects artist or this or that. The combination of the two became a bit of my trademark. Not that I'm the only person on this planet who can do both but it really became my identity in Hollywood. *There's a guy who does creatures and design.* For a while people didn't understand what I was. Some people said, *Well, he's a creature designer,* and other people say, *No, he's a production designer.*

PASSION IN THIS INDUSTRY IS THE SINGLE MOST IMPORTANT THING.

On Stargate, the creature helmets I designed really inspired Roland Emmerich and he said, *You know, I'm doing* Independence Day *next, you should production design the movie for me.* I was lucky enough to be in the right spot at the right time for him to give me a chance to design a movie of that scale. We had no idea how this movie would turn out in the end.

AS: Were there other factors that helped in your getting hired as a production designer on *Independence Day*?

PT: When I was in France before I came to the States I went to the Ecole des Arts Décoratifs which is one of the great schools of Paris for art and multimedia. (I was born in France, then moved to Greece–but I was in France for a while.) At the Ecole des Arts Décoratifs I really took an interest in architecture. Although I did like creature effects I'd been very much attracted to architecture so the leap for me from creature effects to production design was natural. At the end of the day it is about creating worlds. People don't hire me to make a romantic comedy–I've always been someone you call for Sci-Fi or fantasy because that's kind of my thing. And in that kind of work it's very important to be very loose and very open-minded. You need to bring something to the table which is different from what you see every day.

AS: How does your background in creature effects and production design inform your directing?

PT: It's interesting–directing is such a different job. The more you have knowledge of those other departments the better suited you are to direct.

Directing is about bringing a vision and a concept to a screen. More than that, it's being able to tell a story that people can understand and relate to. That's not something that was taught in any of my jobs before. So this is the area I really focused on when I became lucky enough to do my first directing job. I said, *You know what Patrick? You know the design stuff. But this time just concentrate on your actors, concentrate on your story, make sure you're telling it the right way, as clearly as possible.*

The jump from designer to director was interesting to me because there are different types of directors just as there are different types of designers. You know some designers are very much just coordinators of the art department–very strong at making things happen but maybe creatively speaking not the people who are going to take a pencil or even a computer and create images. And that's okay, that's one type of designing. But there are also designers who are concept artists.

Directors are the same. Some directors are storytellers and can work on the screenplay. Writers who come and direct may not have a practical vision of something but they have the concept. I come from the other side. Look at people like Ridley Scott and James Cameron, they're people who actually draw their movies before they even start preproduction. For me it's about putting visuals together and starting to design my world in preproduction, even as a director.

But when the movie starts really gearing up, just let go of all that so you can meet the production designer and say, *This is where I want to go, this is the direction,* and just be clear that you don't want to step onto that person's work. Just show him a direction that's interesting for you and then you step out. Don't forget that you're not the designer this time–somebody else is. That's a part that I really like–saying, *Hey, this is where I want to go with this, and seeing them work from that.* It's phenomenal.

AS: As a director, do you still feel like you design your movies?

PT: I do design all the time. And I also haven't

dropped the world of creature design. Right now I'm working with Len Wiseman on his next project. While my own movie is getting green-lit and moving forward, I have a little time. So when a friend says let's work together, I still work in the capacity of creature designer or production designer, helping to develop movies before they really gear up.

But when my own movie starts I stop everything. I concentrate on the vision for my movie. I put together a vision so that quickly my art department, my costume department, and my camera department know what I want.

AS: What are the attributes that you think a production designer should have?

PT: I think the most important aspect a production designer should have is to first of all put in his mind that he doesn't own the design of the movie. The designer needs to do something very special. The job of the designer is not to bring his own vision to the table, it's to bring the director's vision and that should never be forgotten. Because you don't become a great production designer to a director if you're just trying to impose what you're doing. However, it's great to suggest. It's important to open doors to a director that maybe he hasn't seen. But you never, never forget that this is not your vision, it's the director's vision. I've worked with some very strong visionary directors. If *Dark City* was directed by somebody else it would not look like what it looks like now–and why is that? It's because the director Alex Projas was the man in charge. So I may have put ideas on the table, I may

have created some direction for Alex, but ultimately the movie is his and the vision is his. That to me is the single most important thing for a designer to remember: that that vision is the vision of the director. And this means that you have to be able to communicate properly with this person.

> ❝ THE JOB OF THE DESIGNER IS NOT TO BRING HIS OWN VISION TO THE TABLE IT'S TO BRING THE DIRECTOR'S VISION AND THAT SHOULD NEVER BE FORGOTTEN.

And then the next very important step is your team. The people you work with. You have to give them space to bring something to the table. I've seen people who are so much in control of everything and so afraid to give away little bits and pieces. They control everything to the final stroke of a pen and I think this is a mistake. It's important to let people bring something to the table of whatever design you do. I have a tendency to design very roughly because if it can stay rough I can give my artists a chance to bring some of their own ideas to the project. At the end of the day I believe all of us have a specific style that we repeat all the time. I do, and I have to fight that. When you bring somebody else to the table and you give them a chance to bring something to your own designs, then every one of your works has a different flavor. That to me is the essence of the job.

AS: What happens if there is a disagreement between the director and the production designer?

PT: That's a very personal question. You have to create an explanation for the director to understand why yours may be a great idea. It happens very often that the director's going to turn around and say, *You know what, actually that's a great idea,* or, *You know what, I really don't want to go there Patrick.* And you have to know when to stop.

> AT THE END OF THE DAY I BELIEVE ALL OF US HAVE A SPECIFIC STYLE THAT WE REPEAT ALL THE TIME. I DO, AND I HAVE TO FIGHT THAT. WHEN YOU BRING SOMEBODY ELSE TO THE TABLE AND YOU GIVE THEM A CHANCE TO BRING SOMETHING TO YOUR OWN DESIGNS AND THEN EVERY ONE OF YOUR WORKS HAS A DIFFERENT FLAVOR.

With your team it's the same thing. When you're working with your team give them a chance to tell you why. And maybe it will become really clear why this could be a better idea. You know you're not working in a factory with a bunch of machines. You're working with people who are all here to bring more to the table. Take it, work with them and I think you're going to grow for the rest of your career. If you get stuck in your own little vision this is very limiting and not fulfilling.

AS: There were a lot of visual effects in *I, Robot*– how do you feel about working with the visual effects department?

PT: Working with visual effects is the same thing. It's teamwork. If you design everything and you don't collaborate with them in the early stages of creation you're going to drop things on them that they could have helped you make better. So it's the same story. Today a production designer has to know visual effects, especially in that style of movie. I love to work with visual effects, I've done that for years and I respect them a lot. I don't consider them to be the next step after the designs are done and built. They need to be there at the very early stages with you. Once you have an image you bring them on and say, *How can I make this happen?* And they say, *Well, Patrick, you could do it that way or that way or that way,* and you make your decision from there. Sometimes production may be hesitant about hiring visual effects too early. But at the end of the day the secret of everything is everybody sitting together early and giving all their proposals and issues about how this thing may go. So you have an understanding and there's no crash and everything moves smoothly. You need to listen to people who have a better idea of what to do in specialty work, you know? You need to really be open-minded to that.

AS: Is it true that it's a good idea to do sketches on spec to get a job as a production designer or as a creature effects artist?

PT: It's beyond true. My competition is fierce. You need to attract a client in some way. When a client comes and visits you and you've read the script before and you show a couple of images it's a big, big, big deal, even if they don't go with you.

I've gotten movies in the early stages of my career as both a designer and creature person by just showing my excitement for the project, showing my passion for the concept. People come and sit down with you and you drop three drawings on the table that you've done yourself–you didn't hire a concept artist, you've done them yourself–and they look at that and they can tell right away that you care about the project. So they see that and they go with you.

But I can't tell you how many times I've worked with a director in the early stages of design and then the director turns to the studio and the studio says, *Well, sorry, we have a relationship with this other group*, like Stan Winston or Rick Baker, you know big names like that. So out of ten times you're gonna lose five or six times. But those four times you're going to gain a new relationship with people who think, *Well, this guy's into it, he's interested, he's passionate*. This is how you sell the set the most. People meet you and they see the passion in your eyes and they believe that and they react to that. As a director if I meet a couple of costume designers and two of them are a little cold and intellectual and then I see someone who's living it I'm going to go for that person. That's how I function. That means a lot to me. Passion in this industry is the single most important thing.

PT 2

UPDATE: A lot has happened since the preceding interview, both in our industry and in Patrick's career, not to mention a global pandemic that shut down most US productions. I had the opportunity to talk with Patrick again in between his big-budget design jobs, the most recent being *Maleficent: Mistress of Evil.* Our latest conversation follows . . .

AS: Knowing what you know now, where do you see the field of production design heading?

PT: More and more, a designer on a big project needs to know visual effects very, very well and needs to know how to work with the visual effects team. When you budget you need to know what needs to be done in CG. And you'll be creating 3D models that will be handed to the visual effects department. For example, with *Maleficent: Mistress of Evil*, the whole castle was designed by the art department all the way to the last little tower. People didn't necessarily know that we designed the castle because in the movie it's visual effects. But you need to make sure when you build the balcony for the facade of a building that the architecture and scale of the balcony fits the architecture of the rest of that building. So what do you do? You design the whole thing in 3D first.

I used to say the production designer is the person that designs the look of the movie and that VFX creates the effects. We have to be careful when we say that today because it's teamwork. Ultimately both visual effects and the art department create the look of the movie now. But if you give them enough tools, in the end it's still going to be the movie you designed.

The best way to do this right is to have a great relationship with the visual effects supervisor and their team early on. Don't look at it like, *Well, those guys are just going to do their own stuff.* No, those guys are working with you to make the best looking movie ever. So you work with them. The closer you work with them the more chances you have to make sure the vision carries across.

Often in post production the look changes not because the visual effects supervisor wants to change it or the director decides to change it. Sometimes it's simply because they don't have enough elements. And at the end they ask, *Should we call the designer to come back?* The studio says, *Well, we don't want to pay for the designer now.* But the visual effects supervisor will still call you directly if you're a collaborative person, and I've always been cool about this because I care too much. I tell them I'll even sketch something if they need it.

But sometimes they just do it on their own because they don't have time to look for you. That's why you need to design everything and model as much as possible. There's no way you design just what's to be built on stage. You have to do more than just the concept art today. Years ago when we did *Bram Stoker's Dracula* it was sketches first, then the production designer took all those elements and they drafted the sets. Then the matte painter and model makers would come look at what extensions were needed. Today, the art department requires 3D upfront. And sometimes we do outputs because the director wants to see them outside of the computer. We'll create an output in 3D of the castle to scale and the director can look at it and say, *Wow, I can fly the creatures in this way.* We'll add this to the base of the whole village tabletop model. For directors to be able to see that to scale and walk around and take pictures with their own camera is great. But to do that you have to design the whole castle, not just what you'll be building.

AS: With all the up-front visualization that we're seeing on a show like *Mandalorian*, do you think the industry will shift and they will start bringing on a visual effects supervisor before they bring on the production designer?

PT: We're not there yet but we're starting to get to a place where the two of them are hired at the same time. For that very reason you have to clearly establish the look and design of your project. If you have a good relationship with your director and you also work collaboratively with your visual effects supervisor, you're gonna come on strong. They know you're the designer. But it's not a new concept that production designer and visual effects supervisor could become one job.

> " I USED TO SAY THE PRODUCTION DESIGNER IS THE PERSON THAT DESIGNS THE LOOK OF THE MOVIE AND THAT VFX CREATES THE EFFECTS. WE HAVE TO BE CAREFUL WHEN WE SAY THAT TODAY BECAUSE IT'S TEAMWORK.

The problem the studios have to resolve is visual effects, not construction so much. Visual effects are like three, four, ten times the budget of construction sometimes. So from that perspective, the studios are going to look closer at visual effects. They are going to start talking to those guys up front, not because they think the visual effects house should design the movie but only because they better figure out how to make that stuff work. So they talk to them. For example, on this Netflix movie they started developing one character because they wanted to make sure it was going to work. But when you scatter the design project between ten, fifteen concept artists in multiple visual effects houses, nobody's really designing, and that's a pity.

The reason I like designing everything at the beginning, is that I take pride in it. This is why

I'm here, why I went into this business! And you work with teams of artists who are going to make whatever you do ten times better than what you created. My gut feeling is that in the end art and visual effects are going to melt down into one department.

> **" IT'S NOT A NEW CONCEPT THAT PRODUCTION DESIGNER AND VISUAL EFFECTS SUPERVISOR COULD BECOME ONE JOB.**

AS: What advice would you have for someone going from low budget to big budget movies?
PT: Ask yourself what kind of production designer you are. Are you a great coordinator-type that likes to assemble visuals to bring out your vision, but is not necessarily a hands-on conceptual guy that can draw? If so, I would say start by framing yourself with great concept artists.

So let's say I'm going into a movie like this, I just got the call, I got the job. First, I'd do my homework. I'll do the research based on my idea of the movie, do my own kick-ass visuals, with great moodboards, to impress the director with something like that. Next I'd hire some top-of-the-line concept artists. And obviously a top-of-the-line art director who has worked on big movies. That person will look at two things, they'll look at their next salary and also how to keep working at the level they're currently working at. They want to work on the next big movie. If you are someone that's enjoyable

to work with, and someone who knows what they want, you don't have to be an incredible illustrator or a concept artist.

You might say, *Well, I want to bring some of my team from the smaller films*. If you want to do that, you can do that, but they should also frame themselves with people who have worked on big movies. Big movies are not necessarily more difficult than small movies but it's a different way of thinking. You need many more people to make those projects work.

And lastly, don't be afraid to be humble. Don't be afraid to say, *Hey guys, I've done this in the past but I haven't done it to this level, what do you guys think?* When I did my first movie as a director I had no directing experience whatsoever. Len Wiseman [*Underworld* series creator/director/producer] came to me and said, *At the beginning of my career I had no idea about lighting, I barely knew what kind of light a 10K was. So I took my little sketch pad and sketched my idea and said, "I would like this, I just don't know the term for it."*

I've done the same thing for my movies and people reacted in a very positive way. You have a vision and they respect that. You don't try to make believe you know everything. When I designed *Independence Day* with Oliver Scholl we both started as concept artists. We both came from nowhere and then suddenly we're production designing a movie of that scale together.

What we did was, we hired James Teegarden, who was one of the top art directors at the time. He's one of the best I've ever met. The director knew Jim was the backbone of the art department. He knew that the set would happen because that art director knew what he was doing. We never tried to make people believe we were in charge out there, you know what I mean? We designed, Jim made sure it happened. Stay humble, people will respect you for that.

AS: On those bigger films with ten or more art directors do you ever get a producer coming up and asking, *What are all these art directors doing?*

PT: First of all, those discussions happen pretty early on. If the movie is big enough you're going to need people. Your supervising art director becomes the person that oversees everything, not just technically, but artistically as well. He or she can only spend so much time on each individual set every day. It then becomes clear that you'll need to have somebody else be the next person in line that's going to be specifically dedicated to those two big-scale sets or that one big-scale set. If it's really, really big then the studio understands that you need someone who's just going to work on that one set. If it's one of the key sets, it's huge and it needs to have 24/7 dedication to it. They expect that because of the scale of the movie.

Maleficent: Mistress of Evil, I was told, was the biggest, most expensive construction art department ever for a Disney film. Not that I'm proud of that!

Joachim [Rønning], the director, is simply a man who loves big sets. We built more than we would with another director. But Joachim has made a lot of great movies that way. You realize if you have that many sets you'll need an art director that's going to take care of the locations. Maybe some locations are really far from each other and there's no way one guy can travel ten hours a day to go from one location to another.

> ❝ MY GUT FEELING IS THAT IN THE END ART AND VISUAL EFFECTS ARE GOING TO MELT DOWN INTO ONE DEPARTMENT.

The other thing you do is you bring on two or three assistant art directors and as you work with them you discover their talent. You discover how invested they are in a project. And then those people can be called art directors by the end of the project because of dedication and the quality of their work. That happens on every project. My supervising art director and I will go back to the producer at the studio and say, *Hey, he's been doing great work.* The producer loves the set and helps them get to the next level for their next film. So at the end of the movie you see more art directors than you had at the beginning. It's understood because of the scale of these projects. Studios are aware of this.

However, you still need to feel it out, because nobody wants to spend money just to have a bunch of people hanging out. So you've got to really be sure all those people are necessary for the process. The studio will battle with you a bit and say, *What, do you really need that guy and that guy?* And then we debate and sometimes we lose because maybe they're right, we could do it in a different way. But I don't remember the last time there was a producer I couldn't work with. Everybody's been great the last few years. They make it work as much as possible for you. The job becomes about having a great relationship with the people around you, the producers, directors, everybody. It's teamwork. Everyone wants it to work, not to make you comfortable per se, but to make sure you can achieve what you were meant to do.

AS: Is Zack Snyder really visual as a director?
PT: Absolutely he is. He's very much that kind of guy. When you look at his movies it's always Zack's vision.

Zack does his own storyboards and they're minimalistic but powerful. They just tell exactly what he wants. He rarely shoots something different from his storyboards and in his storyboards you barely see décor. Because more important for him is the story and the characters. What you need to give him are all the tools to do something great. And then he's going to enhance it.

Sometimes we end up constructing more than what's written. I always refer back to my Batcave [in *Batman v Superman*]. The Batcave was a huge set, with thousands of possibilities of shooting.

From one room you could see through three of four other rooms because they were made of glass. But the movie is not about the Batcave. It's not about trying to sell "Great Design", it's about trying to tell the story of Batman. As a designer, you're going to try to do a great design but at the end of the day maybe a third of that's going to be used. Because the story doesn't require more than that. But you still have to build it. And if you build it and don't see it, this is where the little ego of the designer says, *Oh my God I wish we'd seen this! I wish we'd seen that!* Every designer will tell you the same story. *I wish they'd shot it this way or that way.* But you look back at it later and the movie's amazing. Are we making a documentary on the Batcave? No, you have to tell the story. So you step back and you realize that this is what you were here for, to help make *this story* work.

The other thing that sometimes happens is that it will go the other way around, where suddenly another set you didn't think much about ends up getting featured by the director. Ultimately you need to really understand that this is not your movie, it is the director's movie. You do the best work you can and just let it go.

AS: What do you think about the recent use of the *Unreal* video game engine and volume stages for in-camera visual effects that require very little post production work?
PT: It's insane. We're all trying to get into that now. But it's not a cheap way to do things. If you do this you have to design the whole movie upfront,

in 3D, rendered with textures. A lot of movies are going to start considering this. It's a great way of working but you have to be aware of how to handle it. You have to create sets based on that concept. The studios have to agree to a huge upfront design phase. But the thing that's amazing is the quality of it. It's stunning! It's definitely the way of the future.

AS: Are you still directing?

PT: I'm directing all the time. But I'm not directing all the time. I've got three projects I'm directing and I'm not even talking about my personal project in development. *New Pennsylvania* is the closest one. It's a sci-fi thing based on a best-seller called *Pennsylvania* by Michael Bunker.

When I directed *Underworld: Rise of the Lycans* it did quite well for a small movie. It made close to a hundred million dollars and it was my first film. It was well received, with good critical reviews and the audience liked it. To me it's far from being a masterpiece, I was thrown into it with little time to prep, but I had the best time. And after that I began to get directing offers. But as a director you start a project and you can be working on it forever and the thing still might not happen. It's a much harder world to be in. It's a lot of commitment that could potentially lead to nothing. So I've been developing the things I believe in and still doing my production design and having a blast of a life.

Michael Novotny

Michael Novotny worked with James Cameron on *True Lies* and *Terminator 2* and production designed *K-19: The Widowmaker* for Kathryn Bigelow. With these hundred million dollar features under his belt, he moved on to designing episodic series including *Better Call Saul* and seven seasons of the hit CBS crime drama *The Mentalist*.

AS: What first got you into the field?

MN: Probably painting. I always painted, starting around fourteen. And then in our small town of three thousand I was able to get a free pass to the movies for six months at a time by doing very bizarre, outrageous cartoons. The cartoons depicted what happened on the balconies and in the main seating area when a bunch of animal-like teenagers came in. The manager liked them so much he would put them up in his office and I could get in for nothing. So that was my first commercial art deal. I was a kid–you're just trying to be cool. That's when I found out that art was cool!

And then I was fortunate enough to move to a town near Pittsburg that had a high school where they could offer advanced art. We did subjects like intaglio etching. We had very high-pressure presses, kilns, we did stained glass. From there I went to Goddard College in Vermont, which was a very experimental college with a very small campus of maybe two hundred people. David Mamet was my dorm-mate. There were no grades, you designed your own courses. I studied the bushmen and Kalahari by producing large sand paintings, eight by sixteen feet. When I left Goddard I went to the University of Pittsburgh and I went into premedical studies. I did a lot of physics and chemistry and that sort of thing. But soon I'd had enough and I left and went to England. I started a communal theater company, Footsbarn Theater, with a group of friends from Goddard College. It's still going in France.

AS: Were you involved in set-building there?

MN: Totally. I was painting, we did a lot of sculpting. We wrote all our own pieces. They were folk tales of rural England–tales and legends of the giants, the formations of St. Michael's mount, King Arthur's castle, Camelot. Everybody had to do everything and I was really much better at painting than at performing. But everyone had to have their time on stage. I did that for about four years in England and then we did six years based out of Amsterdam. We did almost every Western European city. From North Africa all the way through to Scandinavia.

AS: You would travel to different cities?

MN: Constantly. We did probably close to three hundred shows a year and we performed in farmers' fields, we performed in statehouses. The World Theater Festival invited us back three times. We had a train in Nancy, France, that we redid as multiple theaters. The train traveled through Alsace-Lorraine near Strasbourg. You'd buy a ticket and get onto the car and go to a train station and there'd be a show greeting you. We had a show that was about one hundred people in silver jumpsuits all with saxophones and they would greet you at the train station, playing one note when the train

came in. And we often would be leaning out the windows with blank revolvers in Wild West garb firing at them as we came in. We played forty to fifty different festivals all over.

Friends Roadshow International was our touring company that was very sacrilegious and surreal. Anything that was happening in the news that day was game. So we would do big opening numbers with dancing nuns and the curtains would open up and there would be Jesus on a foam cross and he'd break out with a microphone and do a Frank Sinatra number. It was very Marx Brothers-esque. We traveled with a full band.

> ❝ **THE EPISODIC PROCESS IS THE MOST FLY-BY-THE-SEAT-OF-YOUR-PANTS AND RUN-'TIL-YOU-DROP-DEAD PROCESS THAT THERE IS IN FILM MAKING–WHICH IS WHY I LIKE IT SO MUCH.**

We also had an inflatable theater we built that seated about fifteen hundred people and it could blow up around the crowd. We'd pull several vehicles into position and then these large, several meter high doughnut-like rings would blow up around them. The stage would fold out from the back of a truck and then these decorative buttresses would go about three stories high up behind the audience.

We did shows right in the Piazza della Senorita in Florence and got arrested because we were busking. The crowd loved the show so much that when the police took everyone to the police station right there on the square, they went crazy. My son Daniel was about two and a half years old at the time and the crowd in Italy loved kids. When they saw the cops taking the kid into the police station they went nuts. The crowd made such a racket that the police gave up and said, Everybody just get out of here. So they threw us out. And the next year the city brought us back and paid us an enormous amount of money.

AS: Would you bring other set pieces?

MN: The set concept always had to conform itself to fit in the truck. So unless you were doing a special show you had to get everything in the truck. And so that limits you severely. An exotic piece would be a big neon but it was a pain in the ass to pack it and then move it. When I left that theater company after all those years I was so glad to get off the road. I wound up in Los Angeles because it was basically the last stop before you got wet.

The gig that I was going to in the Coconut Grove was going to be very promising. But that thing blew up because it was a veterans' fundraiser and some veteran had driven his jeep through the glass doors of the Federal Building during preproduction. It shifted the focus entirely from Los Angeles to Washington. So the gig evaporated and I was stuck here. But it seemed like a good place to work from and then I started sculpting for restaurants and doing their logos and stuff like that.

Through friends I met Bob Skotak. John Muto was art directing for his effects group. I rolled in and I said, *I want a job.* They said, *What can you do?*

I said, *What do you want me to do?* And they said, *We need to sculpt this underwater mountain range and all these whales and sharks.*

Great, I'll do that. And they were like, *Are you a specialist in that area?*

No, I've never done it before but I'll have a go at it. So I just took big billets of foam and just started sculpting and they said, *You're on. You can stay.*

AS: Was that for *Jaws 3D*?

MN: That was *Jaws 3D*. We worked on *Jaws* and that company folded. Then we did dog movies like *Creature* with Klaus Kinski, total *Alien* rip-offs. Get a warehouse in Burbank and violate every fire law there is. Get a chainsaw and sculpt extraterrestrial landscapes. Unbelievable the stuff that we did for nothing. And we would literally cruise with a truck down the alleys of the aeronautics areas in Burbank and look for odd shapes. If we saw water tanks or we saw an old jet cowling that wasn't being used for something we'd take it.

AS: And it becomes a spaceship . . .

MN: Well, we made a junk pile in a warehouse. Bob Skotak would come and look at this junk and he'd start to sketch. *Well, let's make this–here's the airlock door, we'll put this over that. Oh, you didn't finish that* *lunch? Let's take that little package.* He used everything. Once you stand back and take an airless and spray everything grey it looks like it's on purpose. So functionality starts to come into the design element and it all seemed to work.

AS: And from there you gradually made your way to art director . . .

MN: Well, I was art directing on that show. They brought me in as a construction coordinator but the art director candidate they had got drunk and left or something. Nobody predicted anything that could happen on those kinds of shows. Usually it was like, *Well, you're going to have to be the art director now, okay?*

Okay, alright, I'm going to be the art director. And then to all your friends that were working with you, *Hey, I'm the art director now.* So it was a very informal, very shoot-from-the-hip process but it got the job done. And actors would commonly come in the next day and they'd be dealing with wet paint because you had to work all night. It was the only way–they couldn't afford to spend money on anything.

Then I left that show and did a lot of commercials and music videos and met Bill Creber. Somehow he heard of me through some of the effects circles. He summoned me to a meeting at MGM and when I came in he asked how would I build this spaceship he was conceiving. I told him how I would build it and he seemed to think that was different from what anybody else had told him. So he hired me.

And that was *Flight of the Navigator* with Disney. That was a very interesting project because it went from LA to Ft. Lauderdale and then I got a phone call to take the spaceship and pack it up to Norway. We shot all the interiors in Norway because they were doing a sharing production deal. We shot there for months. That to me was like everything I'd been doing for ten years. Everybody else thought that was sort of exotic but it didn't seem very exotic to me.

> **"TAKE A LOOK AT THE SCRIPT. IT'S GOT CERTAIN STORY BEATS IN IT–HOW ARE YOU GOING TO PUSH THAT ALONG? THE CLOSER YOU CAN GET TO TELLING THAT STORY, THE CLOSER YOU CAN GET TO YOUR PRODUCTION DESIGN MAKING SOME REAL, PERTINENT STATEMENT.**

AS: What are a couple of the steps that you go through from the point of getting the script to shooting the movie? Do you sit down with a sketchbook?

MN: It varies script to script. Some scripts require a lot of very specific sketching, some scripts require none. A lot of it's just conceptual. I read the script once, very briefly, just to get an overview. That's mostly to send an emergency message to the location manager saying, *Here's the big one this time.* Then we tackle that part together first. This is for episodic–features are very different. The episodic process is the most fly-by-the-seat-of-your-pants and run-'til-you-drop-dead process that there is in filmmaking–which is why I like it so much. And it's a question of reading the script and then pulling out the elements, making the break-down. The breakdown sort of gives you a sense of the quantity. Once the quantity's assessed you allocate areas of responsibility. And this is where you're close to being a scientist because you really have to quickly assess what the ingredients are. Once you do that you can start to allocate areas of development to other people. When you do that, and you have good people, you have a good project. So I think half the battle is to let those good people do their job. And I have been working with my team for years. They're like an extension of me. I can sketch on the phone, talking about past creations that we've done together, and I will know that we're all talking about the same thing.

It's very different when you're dealing with someone who's entirely new to you and it's a new team. I went off to do a series in Canada and I was able to bring nobody. So I approached it very differently. I did a lot more very specific sketching and so forth. It depends on the show.

AS: You said you prefer episodic over features because of . . .
MN: The spontaneity. I like the spontaneity. You know I've done features where we spent a year developing things. When we started *True Lies*, Jim [Cameron] had already done effects boards and the effects boards were done beautifully, as you may well imagine. So there are images of what the show is going to be. I was art directing, Peter Lamont was

production designing. So it was already defined by the time preproduction started.

And when preproduction started there were no limits on what you would do. It was only driven by story. If you wanted to land the Harrier Jet at Pigeon Key it wasn't a question of could you afford the Harrier Jet. It wasn't a question of could you get it there, because you knew you could make a phone call to the president of the United States and get the Harrier Jet. It's a whole other process. So now you're looking at your calendar. It's not the money and it's not the influence. It's not the availability. It's the time. So now you have to figure out when do I have to get it because this is going to shoot . . . next year. There's a process right there that makes it different!

AS: Instead of next week . . .
MN: Yes, the calendar is more extended. And the fact that somebody might come to you and say–and they did–*You can't land a Harrier Jet there because it's a tarmac road.* So we'll get cement mixers and we'll pour a new concrete road. Eighteen inches deep. Fine. Well, let's get a map. We'll see how big that road really is. Okay, get somebody down there and measure it. What's for lunch?

So that process keeps going on and on and it's very exciting for Jim because I'm sure he has all sorts of wheels and gears spinning. But if you're a functionary it's not so exciting. Whereas here [on *The Mentalist*] I'll say to somebody, *You'd better give me that viral lab retinal scanner,* because I've got to build that thing tomorrow. *Give me your best juice–go for it.* And they start drawing and they hand you something by four o'clock. You look at it and say, *You just got to pull the monitor up here, the shot's at this height.* We're going to do this change or that change. And that's pretty much it. You'll find that they're going to give you their best stuff.

Whereas in a well-funded movie you'll have several illustrators give you several permutations of the drawing. Many of which will show that they are skilled draftsmen and skilled illustrators but they have nothing to do with the story. Yet they certainly justified that week of illustration. And I'm already asleep.

Episodic is far more fun. But then again maybe I was just the victim of doing extended, big builds. *K19: The Widowmaker*–I never want to do a show again where you have to wear steel-toed shoes and a helmet!

AS: That submarine was a huge build . . .
MN: Build an exterior submarine four hundred feet long that goes to sea. We better rush it because we have an impending strike. It's winter, the snow is blowing horizontally in Halifax. Extended, long preproduction . . .

But it can be wonderful. It can be great. There are shows obviously that are delicious that way. And there are other shows where it's that many more headaches that you're going to have. So I would honestly say that big is not necessarily better.

AS: How do you feel about communicating ideas that are different from what the director and DP have in mind?
MN: Well, there are a couple of different ways people have varying opinions from you. One is that they have a better idea. And if they have a better idea then it helps to have a state of mind that lets you see better ideas. So that's something you have to caution yourself about. In other words, not being so egotistical that you always assume that yours is the best idea.

So once you get that under control–and I would say most new production designers have a bit of a problem with that–then that brings you to the other point. And that is, *How do you collaborate? How do you take that new idea and make it work?* Or you may know from experience he's making the mistake that you made five years ago, ten years ago, twenty years ago. And you honestly know that that's going to be a bad direction. Now you have to diplomatically get in there in such a way that, even though you disagree, everyone's still going to give you their best ideas and not shut off to you. The best way to do that is by example. Pull something out that you've done in the past and show them. Or sometimes even show them a scene and call their attention to something in the scene that has nothing to do with what you want them to see . . . And maybe they'll see the other thing.

A lot of it's smoke and mirrors but I think that that goes on in human interaction in general. That's not unique to the film industry. So it's just a question of being open-minded, I think. A good idea can come from anybody. And particularly from people who have the mental space, who are not so engrossed in the film that they don't see what's right in front of them.

I often have people who are sweeping up on the stage come up and talk to me about what looks good. I think it's a good idea to talk to them. They're the people watching the show. There's a lady here at Warner Brothers, Sally, she's the cashier at the commissary. I talk to Sally every day when I go to the commissary and I ask her what she thought of the show and she tells me. I've taken her over to stage fourteen and shown her the main set. *What works for you? What didn't work for you?* She loves Simon Baker. *He's really cute, Sally, but how'd you like that scene?*

AS: What kind of attributes do you look for when you hire crew for episodic?

MN: In episodic that particular football team is running down the field and never stops. You have to shout as you run. So if someone's coming in to set-design I'm not going to sit there and look at a lot of drawings. I'm going to look at one drawing. I'm going to see immediately the way he thinks. I'm looking at the logic in the drawing and his communication to the carpenters. I will see immediately if he's an elegant designer. And if he doesn't show me that in the drawing I'll assume he doesn't have it. The worst thing is when you go in and interview somebody like a set designer and they show you twenty-five drawings. By the end I'm like, *Throw*

some cold water on me. I'm already falling asleep. And by then the phone's rung three times and I need to go do other things. That goes for assistant art directors, graphic designers, art department coordinators, anybody. They have to show me the essence of their job.

But can they do the job and can everybody be happy together doing the job? That's the second part of it and that's critical. That's where everybody typically loses the job. Because they're so egocentric that they're going to yap on and on–what this project was, what that project was, and so forth. As opposed to saying, *What are you working on?* You know, they don't plug themselves into the environment they're sitting in for the interview. Usually when I'm interviewing somebody I'm working. If that's the case then talk about what we're doing. You'll have a better chance of being more immediate and being perceived as invaluable. So I'm really looking for someone who can work well with others. Have a sense of humor, be light about it, be involved. But at the same time I would take a sourpuss who's a Leonardo Da Vinci–don't get me wrong. But you know I'd probably think long and hard about it before I did it.

AS: For features that changes . . .

MN: It changes in a big way. For instance on *K19* I had a team in Montreal with an art director, I had an art director in St. Petersberg, Florida, I had an art director in Los Angeles. Art directors are a dime a dozen in those shows. So now you've got a big flock and every one of those guys has their own team.

So in a sense you're giving them autonomy. You're flying around as an ambassador for the script with the director so when you show up you're trying to pull in the herd to somehow focus on the real story or what we're going to do. And again the technical aspects of all those positions, you're assuming that they're doing those perfectly. And you'll know immediately if they're not. I'll get a phone call as fast as lightening.

AS: What would you say the attributes are that a production designer should have, in contrast to, say, an art director or set designer?

MN: I think that there's a lot of flexibility in that. I agree with what John Muto said, in that being a writer is a good background for being a production designer. You know I've been told that we're in charge of everything that's out of focus behind the actors. Which to a large extent is true. But there are moments when we break out of that and we establish clearly a visual character in the script that's distinct. I had a great moment watching K19 when I first saw that submarine out at sea–because I saw that's a character that I made. And it really was a character. It was about that boat.

AS: Some people talk about production design being visible or invisible . . .

MN: When you've created something where nobody notices it, the belief in that environment is what carries the story. There are shows where that's not the case. You know, a *Harry Potter* show is delicious with its detail and its environments. On

a TV level *Pushing Daisies* had elements that were delightful in and of themselves. You could pull the actor out and it would have still been a great moment. You know, the Pie Hole Restaurant. Kudos to Michael Wylie for coming up with that.

> "I'VE BEEN TOLD THAT WE'RE IN CHARGE OF EVERYTHING THAT'S OUT OF FOCUS BEHIND THE ACTORS.

AS: Say someone's just starting out and wanted to avoid any pitfalls . . .

MN: I hate to say it but it's true you should probably shut up and listen to the director. I think a new designer might tend to get out and think he's the greatest thing since sliced bread. The danger there is that very quickly somebody's going to realize that he's not the greatest thing since sliced bread. His talking is going to overshadow the conversation at hand. So the bottom line is that sometimes it's better to simply listen.

Often I'm very tempted to say, *You know, that should be a beige room, that should be a red room.* And then I'll stop myself and say, *Sleep on it. Think about it. Don't give everything at once.* Eke things out bit by bit as the ideas come through to you. Form them and really get behind them personally. Then come forward with them when you really feel they're solid ideas that have made it through at least a day. Unless of course you're a virtuoso. There are a few of those around.

AS: With the latest developments in the field of production design–with 3D and the ubiquitous greenscreen, how do you see your role as a designer changing?

MN: Well, basically my role won't change at all. I'm always trying to put a visual to the story. Whether you're going to use a computer to do that or if you're going to use screens on a stage and then do comps. You still have to shoot the plates. Bottom line is you're putting a visual to the story. And you put that visual to the story any way you can. You're talking to a director, trying to overlay your ideas with his thoughts. He's not thinking as visually as you are. That's your job. Your job is to come up with the vision of the show. I don't care what process you're doing, what the final output is. You're still imagining what that thing looks like. So it doesn't change my job at all. We were doing greenscreen and computers long ago and it hasn't changed a thing for me.

AS: Do you use SketchUp on your shows?

MN: We use SketchUp and we use virtual fly-throughs to present sets that are reasonably large investments in money, time, effort, etc. The key sets upon which we might hang an episodic show. It gives people who can't read drawings an opportunity to really see the set. I've found that helpful for the last few series. When everybody's on the same page there are no surprises later. I do this with the first set of a series but usually I'm going so fast I don't have the time.

AS: You hear rumors of James Cameron being challenging to work with. Was that your experience?

MN: No, as a director I don't find him any harder to work with than, say, John Avildsen, Ronald Neame, or Richard Fleischer. Those are gentlemen I've worked with who all have their own idiosyncrasies. So do I. As many people have said, if you know what you're doing and you're doing your job then you're going to be fine with Jim. If you're going about something the wrong way you're going to be exposed very quickly. So if you're just winging it, your longevity on one of Jim's shows is going to be rather threatened.

After *True Lies* there was an article and they quoted Jim as saying, *There are those people who think I'm an asshole and there are those people who think I'm an asshole with a vision.* And you know he was sort of jokingly putting people into two categories. The bottom line is, his focus is on the picture. If he's short with somebody it might be because he's trying to get to the story. That's fine. I should have enough chops and enough knowledge of what I'm doing to be able to see through that and do what I need to do.

AS: So story is a very important part of the job of the designer?

MN: It's everything. As far as I'm concerned it's everything. If I went down onto that stage floor right now and talked to one of the fifty or so workers that are here on the lot and I asked them what they think of Act III they're going to look at me like I've come from Mars. Whereas I'm going around in my head, *Jesus what am I going to do about Act III?* I have certain scenes that I have going through in my head that I have to get worked out.

And there are specific scenes that I'm working out right now. Right now we're doing this very high tech, high risk laboratory that's developing viruses that could end all mankind. And what do you do when you open that cleanroom door? You're retinally scanned and you walk inside. What do you do then? Well, the script says you walk in, you extract some virus samples from a safe and then you go in another cleanroom. But what's going on in the cleanroom? You're taking viral samples from what to what? What do you do? Oh, you're probably using human growth hormone. You're probably using human growth cells. You're probably transferring with a pipette from one element to another. You're probably analyzing things. Well, what would be visual? Maybe a screen. What's on that screen? Maybe some electron micrographs of viruses. What kind of graphic readouts would be there? Maybe there are temperatures. Maybe there are angstrom units of measurement. Blah, blah, blah, blah. The point is you should know what the process is. That's the story. What's the story between the words that has a visual counterpart?

That designer better get that stuff together because that actor's going to walk in there and ask, *What am I going to do next?* And the director's going to turn around and look to the production designer and say, *Gee, what should be on that table?*

Take a look at the script. It's got certain story beats in it–how are you going to push that along? The closer you can get to telling that story, the closer you can get to your production design making some real, pertinent statement.

> **IF I WENT DOWN ONTO THAT STAGE FLOOR RIGHT NOW AND TALKED TO ONE OF THE FIFTY OR SO WORKERS THAT ARE HERE ON THE LOT AND I ASK THEM WHAT THEY THINK OF ACT III, THEY'RE GOING TO LOOK AT ME LIKE I'VE COME FROM MARS. WHEREAS I'M GOING AROUND IN MY HEAD, *JESUS, WHAT AM I GOING TO DO ABOUT ACT III?***

AS: Does it involve a lot of research on your part?
MN: Yes. And thank God there's Google now because it's great. Now everybody's a genius. There are iPhone geniuses in the van. You know I refuse to do it within five minutes of a conversation. There's such an amazing access to information now and it's fantastic. The other thing you can do is take that information that you've done a cursory scan of and give that information to somebody who really does that job. You can become a genius very quickly.

AS: Like someone in that specific field?

MN: Absolutely. Like with Jim we went to JPL [NASA's Jet Propulsion Laboratory] all the time when we were doing the *Destination Mars* script. We flew to Houston. We went to NASA. We stayed there for days. We went into the greenhouses where they grew cultivars of projected plants to be grown on Mars. We talked with people who were developing the latest forms of thrust. We went into the wet labs where they're underwater and weightless and working on the tools that are needed for outside the ship and so forth. We had subcontractors up from San Diego who were working on habitats. There's a whole area of reality out there that you should tap into as a production designer.

> " I'D SAY FOR A NEW DESIGNER GET OUT THERE AND GO TO AS MANY CORNERS OF THE EARTH AS YOU CAN.

As Jim says, *Why are we using the rover? Because it's a car. Why is it a car? Because it looks cool.* And that's the bottom line. You have to take all of that and make it look cool. You have to make it look interesting. And there's a fine line in there. Between really cool and hokey.

AS: What's it like having your son in the business?

MN: Well, I have all the normal issues that a father has with his son. When you want your son to be the best at something. So of course everything he

does when he's younger, he probably did it exactly as you would have done it when you were his age. But of course you tell him that's not good enough. So that whole process goes on and pretty soon you catch yourself doing that and that's just a discussion of parenting.

But when he became my assistant art director it started to get really interesting. Particularly when I worked with Mr. Cameron and we were in my office together. Jim would come in quite often. There were so many set designers and art directors working with me on that project that we put Daniel in my office off to a corner at a drawing table. Jim would come in, talk to me, and then he'd go see what Daniel was drawing. Dan did drawings of the Mars Ascent Vehicle. Once you land on Mars you need a vehicle to get off Mars. When you work on something like that with Jim there's a lot of physics involved. There are a lot of scientific parameters that have to be met.

When we finally put the project on the shelf the producer called me and said that Jim had asked her, *Who's that kid that was working with Mike?* And she said, *Well, that's Daniel, that's his son.* And he didn't know. He thought that was any other set designer. That was a validation.

Getting something like the Mars Ascent Vehicle that has both the science and looks cool, that's a tough nut. So Daniel held his own. It was at those moments that I realized I had someone working with me who could be doing his own thing. And so very shortly after that he went off and started doing his own projects.

AS: Is there any set that you worked on that stands out as your favorite set?

MN: Well there weren't so much favorite sets as there were sets within wonderful locations. You know doing the Admiral Perry story in the Arctic [*Glory & Honor*] was exceptionally wonderful. Like taking a komatik sled and a snowmobile forty-five minutes out from camp to the place where I was building the lodge. You know in January when it's minus fifty? Those are fun projects. You're going along and the director's in a komatik sled behind your snowmobile and he gets dumped out and you don't know it. You come back thirty minutes later and go, *Christ, where's Kevin Hooks?* And then you find him and he's got a new perspective on Hollywood. That shit out there is real. You know the Inuit guide that takes you out in those locations has a gun. He's got the gun for the polar bears and he's got the gun for the seals in case he sees something to eat. I love going to places and bumping into another culture.

Shooting in Thailand was like that, in the hill tribe area of Chiang Mai and by Phang Nga and Phang Nga Bay. You know, the sea gypsies–those were amazing cultures and it was just delightful being there. Working there and building there. You go to the ends of the Earth. I'm in a very bizarre hotel in Phang Nga and I'm in the lobby and I'm thinking, *How the hell am I going to get an art department here?* And the guy who runs the hotel says, *Well, there's an art department leaving.* I'm like, *What?* It's Victor Kempster and he's been doing *Heaven & Earth* with Oliver Stone and he wants to sell all his drafting tables.

AS: Wow.

MN: Those surprises happen. Generally speaking, it's a wild ride. Now I love being calm in my backyard. I like getting off the road. I've been on the road a long time. I really appreciate my family and being home. But I'd say for a new designer get out there and go to as many corners of the Earth as you can.

POST

How involved are you in post production?

A compilation of excerpts covering the subject of post production, taken from the interviews in this book

Historically, there has been a disconnect between the design that goes on during preproduction and the design that goes on with visual effects when post production commences. These days more and more productions are hiring visual effects supervisors to be present during all stages of production, working closely with the production designer. And several of the production designers I interviewed came to the job from a visual effects background. They are well-versed in the magic that makes a great movie even better. But how do most production designers interface with these visual effects teams and are they satisfied with the current system?

GRANT MAJOR

The way I work is that I hand over to the visual effect supervisor a turn-key design so everything's been conceptualized and modeled in 3D as required. All research files go with that, all the texture files, color choices and everything else. For example, on *Mulan* the art department produced the complete visual effects set extension work that was required. Now, I expect some things to change and some things to be massaged as they go, but with all the information they've been given they have more than enough material.

The design needs to be cohesive. Everything in proportion to each other. It's important that we sort of stamp our personality and our techniques on the visual effects area. It's a tool, really. It's a tool for visually expressing time and place and what have you, so we need to take control of that.

PATRICK TATOPOULOS

More and more, a designer on a big project needs to know visual effects very, very well and needs to know how to work with the visual effects team. When you budget you need to know what needs to be done in CG. And you'll be creating 3D models that will be handed to the visual effects department. For example, with *Maleficent: Mistress of Evil*, the whole castle was designed by the art department all the way to the last little tower. People didn't necessarily know that we designed the castle because in the movie it's visual effects. But you need to make sure when you build the balcony for the facade of a building that the architecture and scale of the balcony fits the architecture of the rest of that building. So what do you do? You design the whole thing in 3D first.

I used to say the production designer is the person that designs the look of the movie and that VFX creates the effects. We have to be careful when we say that today because it's teamwork. Ultimately both visual effects and the art department create the look of the movie now. But if you give them enough tools, in the end it's still going to be the movie you designed.

The best way to do this right is to have a great relationship with the visual effects supervisor and their team early on. Don't look at it like, *Well, those guys are just going to do their own stuff.* No, those guys are working with you to make the best looking movie ever. So you work with them. The closer you work with them the more chances you have to make sure the vision carries across.

Often in post production the look changes not because the visual effects supervisor wants to change it or the director decides to change it. Sometimes it's simply because they don't have enough elements. And at the end they ask, *Should we call the designer to come back?* The studio says, *Well, we don't want to pay for the designer now.* But the visual effects supervisor will still call you directly if you're a collaborative person, and I've always been cool about this because I care too much. I tell them I'll even sketch something if they need it.

But sometimes they just do it on their own because they don't have time to look for you. That's why you need to design everything and model as much as possible. There's no way you design just what's to be built on stage. You have to do more than just the concept art today. Years ago when we did *Bram Stoker's Dracula* it was sketches first, then the *production designer* took all those elements and they drafted the sets. Then the matte painter and model makers would come look at what extensions were needed. Today, the art department requires 3D upfront.

SARAH GREENWOOD

I can keep an eye on [post production]. I do go in and have a look. For *Sherlock*, we did four weeks work with my illustrator and art director, setting them off into post. In an ideal world I should be on for the whole time with the team. In reality that's the last thing I want. That's not what I do.

JESS GONCHOR

I'm not going to design a whole movie and then turn it over to some visual effects company. They need to be respectful and understand what it is that everybody's worked so hard on. I'm involved not to the point where I'm reporting and going to work with the visual effects company every day. But when production's over and we see what we need then I'm going to generate some comps of what I think it should look like. And react to what has been done and put my two cents in.

HANNAH BEACHLER

[*Black Panther* director] Ryan and I made a pact that visual effects were going to be background as much as possible. *Black Panther* is maybe the only Marvel film that had as much building as we did. But there are certain things that you can't build. VFX came in maybe two months after I started so I already had illustrators going. We had illustrated and designed everything.

[My five hundred page bible] then went to the ILM and The Third Floor visual effects houses. What I would do in post is go into the Marvel offices and sit down with the visual effects supervisor Geoff Baumann. He'd say, *Okay here's what they've done with Golden City*, and I'd go through and say, *Okay, this needs to not be that. Let's go back and look at the city*. I had one person working on building Golden City in 3D. Which took about eight months. We dumped it onto a ginormous hard drive and that went to ILM so they had our 3D digital city.

When we created the palace in 3D we were able to go inside the models, so when we built the sets it matched when you're looking from inside the set at

How involved are you in post production?

the outside. And my art directors also built sets in VR so I could stand inside the set and walk around and say, *Okay let's move this here, move that there.*

We did the same thing with the Royal Talon fighter aircraft. That interior was all built. We built some of the exterior as well. And we built the front window using a huge piece of glass. It was really expensive and I was shocked they let us do it but because of the way Ryan wanted to shoot it, we had to. We designed all of the aircraft and we dumped all of those files to ILM and they did the VFX on them.

PATRICE VERMETTE

[Visual Effects] is a great tool. For instance at Lancaster House where we shot the ballroom scene after the coronation in *The Young Victoria*, the room was pretty darn big. We had a lot of extras but we needed to make it more impressive. So that's when visual effects comes in. Let's double the size of that room. Let's triple it. You bring references. Let's hang that picture on that wall there. There's good teamwork with visual effects. For *Westminster Abbey* it was impossible to shoot a real coronation so we did it on greenscreen.

Visual effects is an essential tool in moviemaking right now. Another good example is what Sarah Greenwood did on *Sherlock Holmes,* with set extensions. I saw the latest Tim Burton film over the weekend, *Alice in Wonderland*. I consider it really amazing production design. I think all types of film will still exist but with visual effects you can go the extra mile. Instead of showing just a quarter of the street because you only have enough money to dress that much well, you can shoot a bit wider and say, *Hey, let's have the rest.*

For example, it would have been impossible for the production to shoot the exterior we needed in Bavaria where you see mountains with a bit of snow on them so we added those mountains in post production.

There was also a scene that was supposed to be taking place on the Isle of Wight and I looked at Jean-Marc and said none of the locations we have are next to water. But when we were walking in the parking lot of a castle we realized we could actually shoot that scene right there. There were flatlands and a bit of mountains so we kept the mountains but we replaced the flatlands with water, in post. So that's why I can't stress enough what a great tool it is.

Daniel Novotny

A second generation production designer, Daniel Novotny made a name for himself with the insanely popular TV show *CSI.* It was both the most watched program on television and the most watched scripted show at various times in its fifteen seasons. He has worked non-stop since then, designing back-to-back episodics including *Gotham, The Arrangement,* and *Outer Banks.*

AS: What was your first introduction to the field of production design and art department in general?

DN: I was building models and miniatures in my dad's [production designer Michael Novotny] model shop. He made underwater effects for *Jaws 3D*–that was his first movie. I cut the foam and made latex molds, sharks, and plants. So I learned about fake plants–I learned about spraying them and painting them.

Then I was on a Barbie Doll commercial with my dad. I might have been ten or twelve. They were shooting into this little glass tank where Barbie was on the beach. They carved out the bottom, which was Plexiglas. It looked cool to me but when they got the camera set up they couldn't shoot it because of the glossy reflection on the bottom of the Plexiglas, underneath the water. So they had to empty out all the sand and put in black paper. The black paper got wet but it didn't matter because now they could shoot it. So I learned about coming up with art department solutions kind of young.

One of my dad's early production design jobs was when he was working for this visual effects company 4Ward Productions. For features sometimes they subcontract out these big visual effects shots, they'll give you a check for like three hundred thousand dollars and in return they get the sequence. You know that shot in *Terminator 2* where Sarah looks through the fence and imagines the explosion and it's like the end of the world? My dad was the production designer for that visual effects shot–just that shot. So that was the first time I realized that, as a production designer, he's actually not really making anything but he's still responsible for it. So he did all the drawings of all the palm trees bending over and all the houses being blown away and he designed the sequence. That was pretty cool. And over the years I just watched him work as an art director and as a production designer and saw the way the whole system worked.

AS: So you began by doing art department and then at some point you made the transition to production design?

DN: Yeah, well maybe it was because I had my son while I was in high school and I had to get a job. I was really good at drafting in high school–I was getting an A. I was like the best draftsman the teacher had ever met in his entire life! I mean I was like wicked good. And I would always get in class late, I was such a flop, but I was so good at it. And so I had my son and I remember my teacher said, *Well, let's get you a job.* So I started drafting. I started trying even harder and then my dad said, *Look,*

when you're done you can get a job as a set designer. So as soon as I graduated high school I got my first job as a set designer on the *Arrival*, a movie with Charlie Sheen. And I went to Mexico, I was eighteen or something–it was pretty cool. So I learned traditional set design. Proper set design. I went from set designer to assistant art director to art director then to production designer. I learned the draftsmanship skills first, but then in the off-time when I wasn't working on a movie as a set designer I was working in scene shops, non-union set shops building scenery or painting. You know in the non-union set shops you do everything, right? So I was sweeping floors, I was running cable, doing electrical work, it didn't matter, whatever. Set up Steeldeck, unload trucks, drive forklifts, whatever it took. But I could always draw and whenever there was a project that came in that required drawing I'd always get the cool jobs.

AS: Do you still sketch? After initial meetings with the director do you do a bunch of sketches?

DN: The process changes depending on how important the set is and how complicated it is. On a show like *CSI* in its tenth season, it's pretty much a smooth process. So if I say I'm going to give something, if I just say it and if it's not that complicated, no drawings are required. Because we always talk about it and we just do it. But if it's a real challenge or if it's something the director can't visualize or something the DP can't visualize or maybe I can't visualize, for whatever reason, I'll do more drawings and sketches. I usually don't do too many, just a few to explain what's going on. And then I'll give it to our set designer and he might do some plans. I have a digital set designer and often if there's a particular establishing shot that I want him to do, not so much for coverage, just a shot to establish the environment, I'll have him do a mock-up in Sketch-Up. I'll fly through it in SketchUp to show the director how I think it should be shot. They may do it or not but at least I put my two cents in.

> " YOU HAVE TO REMEMBER THAT THIS IS A BUSINESS ABOVE ANYTHING. AND THAT'S THE ONLY REASON WE HAVE A JOB. IT'S NOT THE BUSINESS OF SELLING FINE ART. YOU'RE GETTING PAID TO DESIGN SETS THAT NEED TO BE SHOT BY SOMEBODY, SO IT'S REALLY A BUSINESS ABOUT CREATING ENVIRONMENTS THAT CAN BE SHOT.

AS: You'll send the director a clip of that fly-though?

DN: Usually I'll convert it for the iPhone and then it just gets sent out. Usually I'll send it to a lot of people. I'll send it to the director but I'll cc ten different people.

AS: Do you find the DP's involved in a lot of that preliminary design?

DN: I include the DP in everything. Oftentimes I will talk to the DP first, just because we're friends.

We have two DP's and I'm close to both of them so I'll talk to them first and get them on board. We'll iron out all the kinks and if they have any ideas we can throw those in too. And then I pitch it to the director after the DP and I have already talked about what we think would look best.

AS: What size is your crew on *CSI*?

DN: On CSI I have an art director, an assistant art director, a set designer, graphic designer, an art department coordinator, and then there's the decorator, the shopper, the lead man and about five or six swing guys, and there's the construction coordinator, foreman, about four or five carpenters, the lead painter, and about four painters, then there's props–there are two propmasters, and there's a props buyer, and there is key on-set props, three other on-set props. It's a lot of people.

AS: Are there one or two *CSI* sets that stand out that you're particularly proud of?

DN: Yeah, we did a set that was a brothel. We built a brothel on stage, it was really cool. We did a white nightclub that was pretty fantastic. We've done a lot. The best photographs are on my website dannovotny.com.

AS: What was it about the brothel or those sets that made them cooler than the average set that comes up on *CSI*?

DN: Well for one, it was a twenty-five hundred square foot set. It was really big. And then the other thing was they shot this really cool Steady-cam shot through the whole set. It's on my reel. They did a really long walk and talk–ten or fifteen seconds long.

AS: It's always lucky to get a walk and talk through your set . . .
DN: Yeah, I know, it often doesn't happen like that.

AS: What are qualities that you think a production designer should have?
DN: You gotta be able to draw. You have to be able to tell somebody how something will look on paper. However you want to do that. Drafting is a key, key, skill. You gotta know about lenses, lens sizes. I think it's really important to know about the way that they're going to shoot something. If they're going to shoot it with a long lens or a wide lens. You gotta know a little bit about lighting. You gotta know how you're going to light your practicals, but also it's important to know how the DP is going to light it and where he's going to hide his lights.

Those are all things that you learn over time. But if a kid is just coming into the business, the important thing is you gotta know how to draw.

It's also really important to have a certain disconnect from what you think is right. A lot of production designers are artists before they're production designers. But you have to remember that this is a business above anything. And that's the only reason we have a job. It's not the business of selling fine art. You're getting paid to design sets that need to be shot by somebody, so it's really a business about creating environments that can be shot.

And if you think something looks good you have to sell it. They might disagree with you. They might hate it. They might think that what you're doing is wrong and you have to kind of roll with that and accept it. It's really not your art form. The movie is an entire production, the production design is just one element in it. There's acting, there are the sets, there's lighting, there's music, sound, the wardrobe, and it goes on and on but production design is only one piece of the pie.

> "MY DAD GAVE ME TWO WORDS OF ADVICE. WHEN I GOT THIS JOB HE SAID, *WHEN YOU'RE IN THE SCOUT VAN ALWAYS SIT IN THE MIDDLE, SO YOU'RE ALWAYS RIGHT IN THE MIDDLE OF IT ALL. AND WHEN YOU'RE IN THE SCOUT VAN DO WHATEVER YOU CAN DO NOT TO TALK ABOUT WORK. TALK ABOUT ANYTHING BUT WORK.*

AS: You were saying that knowing different lenses is important. How does that help you? How would that change how you're designing the set?
DN: Well, I wouldn't spend money on things that are not going to be seen in that lens. So if they're going to be shooting something and it's all about talking heads then I won't buy the expensive molding to put ten feet up in the air, you know? So for

me it's all about putting the money where the lens will see it. So if you're going to have a wide lens then it's all game but if you're gonna have a long lens then there's no point in spending money on places that you won't see. By spending money I mean on expensive paint, expensive molding, artwork, set-dressing, all of the above.

> **THEY KNOW YOU'RE GOING TO GET THE PRODUCT DONE. THEY WOULDN'T HIRE YOU IF YOU COULDN'T DO THE JOB. THEY'RE JUST GOING TO WANT TO WORK WITH YOU NEXT TIME BASED ON IF THEY LIKE YOU OR NOT. THE SKILL LEVEL IS JUST ELEMENTARY– DESIGNING GOOD SETS. THE SOCIAL- IZING PART MAKES PRODUCTION DESIGNING DIFFERENT THAN ART DIRECTING, AND ASSISTANT ART DIRECTING AND SET DESIGNING.**

AS: When you're crewing up are there certain attributes that you look for in the people that you'll be working with?

DN: They have to be really good politically. Especially on a TV show. On a feature you know you're going to work with a person for a few months and then you're going to leave. And with a commercial, really who cares because you're just going to be done with them in a week or two. But on a TV show when you're going to be working with someone for ten months it's really about finding

a good family member that's a good fit. On *CSI* in particular, the politics on this show are playground politics. Everybody's been there a long time so nobody really cares who you are or where you came from, they just care if you can get along with everybody. And then obviously secondary to that, or equal to that, is their skill, what they bring to the table. Everybody's got their own skills. Everybody's got their strengths and weaknesses. If one person's strengths are x and y then I'll make sure the other person has something else.

AS: Would you say production design should be visible or invisible?

DN: It depends on the movie. I think a film like *Harry Potter* or *Lemony Snicket*–I don't know how the production design on that film can be invisible. It really depends on the project. I mean take a film like *Dog Day Afternoon*. That production design was invisible, you couldn't tell that those were sets. Or a show like *American Beauty*–it was well shot but I think the production design was kind of invisible. Then a show like *Napoleon Dynamite* I don't think that that show was meant for the production design to be invisible. It was intended for you to really notice that everything was wacky and quirky, right? So I think it really depends on what the concept is, going into the project. I mean you have some science fiction films like *Star Wars* where the production design was much more invisible than it was on some *Star Trek* films, you know what I mean? The original *Star Wars* was so realistic–you looked at it and you couldn't even comprehend that those were sets, they looked real, they made sense. *Godfather* was invisible but *Pan's Labyrinth* was obviously not . . .

AS: Would you say a set can be a character?

DN: I think it can be a character in a film. If it's telling a story. Maybe you can argue whether it's a character or not, but if it's telling a story it's something important. If you don't want to call it a character call it something. Some sets are more influential than others, you know?

AS: You mentioned working with your dad in the beginning–are there any specific things that you learned from your dad?

DN: That's a good question. You know the production designer job in particular is a unique position. I believe that anybody can do this job. I don't mean to say that literally, but theoretically. It's really all about getting along. To me it's more of a relationship. It is a relationship with the people that are going to hire you. I mean anybody can design a set, and the director and the producers know that they can hire anyone to design the set. But who do they want to hire? Who do they want to be with?

My dad gave me two words of advice when I got this job. He said, *When you're in the scout van always sit in the middle, so you're always right in the middle of it all. And when you're in the scout van do whatever you can do not to talk about work.* Talk about anything but work. They know you're going to get the product done. They wouldn't hire you if you couldn't do the job. They're just going to want to work with you next time based on if they like you or not. The skill level is just elementary–designing good sets. The socializing part makes production designing different than art directing, and assistant art directing and set designing. It's about being the person behind the curtain.

Joseph T. Garrity

Among Joe Garrity's extensive credits are classic Christopher Guest films including comedies *Best in Show, Waiting for Guffman,* and *A Mighty Wind.* His ongoing career as a production designer feeds into his work at the film school AFI, where he heads up the Production Design department, inspiring the next generation of visionaries.

AS: Have you always been drawn to the art department?

JG: Most people who are artists figure it out when they're small. I drew as long as I can remember and then I got this little marionette puppet and I started to be curious about what kind of environment I could put this little thing into. So there was an interest in creating spaces where they weren't. And environments where they weren't.

And then stage crew in high school became a very interesting thing to me because I got into these group efforts. I liked the idea of working with oth-ers to create something. And the idea of putting a show on was very interesting to me too. At that point I wasn't a designer but I was part of con-structing the sets and painting the scenery and running the lights and being there to run the show and pull the fly system and all that. I really enjoyed it and thought that would be what I would do.

And then a movie camera was introduced to me, a Super 8 camera, when I was in high school. I got really into the idea of seeing things, not only where the audience sits in the chair and looks at a pro-scenium arch from one perspective and lighting focuses their eye, but instead I discovered I could choose how the audience sees things with my little camera. So I got fascinated with the language of film and telling the story that way, through this little machine.

AS: You made your own movies?

JG: I started to make little movies and then I went to college. I went into the film department at Temple University. They made documentary films so I was making documentary films but the theater department was connected so I was always over there helping with the sets and designing some smaller productions. I learned how to draft and I got serious designing the sets. Yet I loved the movies, the language of film, and when I said I wanted to combine these somehow someone told me about the American Film Institute. I applied to AFI and I wasn't accepted the first time but when I tried again I got in.

There was a production design department and I was one of two who were in it that year. We were busily working on shows and just learning by doing–which is a great way to learn. I got through and was noticed by a designer from one of the thesis films I did and I started working with them on a couple shows.

AS: You were working as an art director?

JG: I was assistant art director. My purpose when leaving the school was to go out as a designer primarily. I didn't want to go and be a PA for somebody and work up from the bottom. So I was lucky

enough to do non-union work in the 80s. Ten years of non-union work all over the country as a designer primarily. And then in 1992 I got grandfathered into the union on a Disney movie called *Son In Law*. Then I became a small fish in this bigger, different arena.

But it was a love of community, of working with a group of people towards a common goal that drove me and I always hoped that the movies had something to say. That they would not only entertain us but elevate, and inspire us by showing that ordinary people can do extraordinary things. Now and then you get to do movies like that, movies that mean something and entertain at the same time.

WE TURN WORDS INTO ARCHITECTURE AND FURNITURE AND COLOR AND WALLPAPER.

AS: Movies that resonate . . .

JG: Yes. I've been lucky to get a few of those. One out of every eight that you do might be something that's worthy and will be long-lasting and say something important. And production design certainly is by nature invisible. But a movie couldn't be made without an art department and a production designer. Every movie you've ever seen has had an art department and a production designer and a crew creating that space that allows that story to happen. And it's a visual medium. What's up there on the screen should say something.

AS: And help tell the story . . .

JG: Yes, and set the mood. Why do we make the choices we make? It should be from the script and from understanding the people in it, what the story is. What the writer's intent was. What the director's point of view is. He was chosen to make this movie because he convinced someone of his take on it. So that director should be able to tell me what that is. What drew him to this? Sharing that and having that conversation is what prep is all about. That prep time is so vital to a designer and to the director and the DP and to all the creative people.

AS: What does prep involve for you?

JG: It involves research–quickly researching whatever it is that you need to be knowledgeable about. Say a movie like *My Girl*. It was about the funeral business and mortuaries and embalming and the life of people that do that sort of thing. I knew nothing about it. So very quickly I had to meet and go and see and watch. Go down where the bodies go. Because we were going to recreate that as a set, the whole interior of the funeral parlor. It was a big old house. So I had to get up to speed on what the process is and what kind of people do that sort of thing, and why. So I'm educating myself first, to help educate the director second.

And that goes with every movie unless you're already an expert in whatever it's about. Most of us need that research period and then it's time to take that research and apply it to the story being told and to understanding the people in it. *Who are these people? What is their background? What's their back story?* Understanding that their story did not begin at the beginning of this movie–they had a whole life that led up to this time. *What's their religion? What's their sexual orientation? What is their connection to money and how do they spend it? What is the job that they do that maybe isn't addressed in the script but what do they do when they go away to work? Where did they go to college?* That helps with set dressing and how you can layer a room–when you understand the history of the people that are in it.

AS: You then discuss this research with the director?

JG: Absolutely. Everyone has to be on the same page and then, from all that conversation you begin to make choices and turn language, the script's language, into visual motifs and the visuals and color into architecture. We turn words into architecture and furniture and color and wallpaper. Those are our tools. The DP's tools are the camera and the lens choices and the filter choices and compositional choices and things like that. We all have different tools but we should all be unified by design approach or concept. We should all be playing in the same sandbox. We all have room but there's a wall–we can't leave the box and do our own thing.

So the design concepts–the do's and don'ts of this movie, the rules of how this movie's gonna look and why–are really essential. And to maintain it during production can be hard sometimes. It's supposed to be a dry movie and now it's raining so what do you do? Like *Chinatown* being about Los Angeles in a drought. If you look at it, everything in that story is yellow ochres and tans and off-whites. It's about what happens when the sun beats down on a landscape and there's no water. It's as simple as that and that's what the whole look of that film is about. And you'll see green grass only in the areas where people own water and are powerful. That's where the green comes through. And that's a concept, that's an approach to telling a story visually.

AS: Do you feel you have your own, emotional response to a script that plays into your choices?

JG: Absolutely and that has to jibe with the director's. A good director is open to interpretations and open to what people bring to the plate. We need to find the vision that we can all wrap ourselves around and that we're all in agreement to preserve as we go into this together. That's good collaboration. We stress that a lot here at the school because it doesn't always happen. You've got massive egos and controllers. People who believe that unless it's their idea it's not gonna work.

AS: It's not a guy painting in his basement . . .

JG: If that's what you want to do, you should paint. But in film, you have to be able to work and collaborate with talented people.

AS: You've worked consistently with Christopher Guest and his team. What was that like?

JG: It was great. He's a very neat guy and very quiet and talented and smart. I interviewed cold with him on *The Big Picture* which was his first as a feature film director. He was a weird interviewer, but it worked and he brought me back on all his feature films ever since. He and I were the right kind of merging of people. He's a quiet guy who doesn't want to be bombarded with anybody buttering him up. There's a certain quality of people that I think he likes around him. I fit that type and also I delivered the look that he wanted and that I wanted for those films.

> **SOME DESIGNERS ARE VERY QUIET AND JUST DO AS THEY'RE TOLD. THE BETTER DESIGNERS HAVE GREAT IDEAS AND SOLVE PROBLEMS AND COME UP WITH GREAT SOLUTIONS.**

AS: You collaborated on seven movies?

JG: It was *The Big Picture* and then *Attack of the 50 Foot Woman* for HBO and then *Waiting for Guffman* and then *Almost Heroes* which was a comedy with Chris Farley–it was his last film–not that successful but a big movie, and then *Best in Show*, the dog show one, and then *A Mighty Wind* about folk music and finally *For Your Consideration* which was the movie story he did. *The Big Picture* was the first one. We've done a couple of other things–pilots that never went anywhere. We've done a few things together–he's great.

AS: What are the best attributes to have if you want to be a production designer?

JG: Collaboration. And being adaptable. To adapt to change well is really important. If you're a super logical person it would make you go berserk.

You've got to be a little crazy. And you've got to also realize that there's a deadline. You've got to be good with deadlines. You've got to be good with budgets. And you've got to be a good people person because you've got to get up there and sell an idea and do that well. 'Cause there's a lot of money that people are going to let you spend to do something. And you want to be clear and excited and be able to stand behind your idea and sell it well visually. You've got to be a problem-solver too. You want to be the person who says, *Okay here's what we do.* There are directors that need a lot more hand-holding and there are directors that are going to be very, very in-your-face. So you've got to be able to adapt. Some designers are very quiet and just do as they're told. The better designers have great ideas and solve problems and come up with great solutions.

AS: Is it important to show up with those ideas in that first meeting?

JG: In the interview you're coming in reacting to something you've read and you bring in imagery. I'm not going to design any sets but I'm going to bring in something that gives the director a sort of visual sampling of what I got out of the film, while leaving it open at the same time. And then you have to be able to say, *I've read this and here's what really said something to me.*

You're interviewing the director as well. Because it's going to be an intensive series of months that you might be working together. Am I enjoying my conversation–will I enjoy this on multiple occasions at all hours of the day or night? And how you react to some of the peculiar problems that this particular script has will tell the director, *This guy knows what he's talking about and he's brought up things that I would never have thought about. You want to have some great ideas.*

Sometimes I've met directors that have elevated what I thought was something ordinary into something extraordinary from how they approached the material. Some directors can be really inspiring. They makes everyone around them better.

AS: Is it the same with DP's?

JG: Well there's something I've read in books called "the trinity" which is that the chief visualizers are the director, the DP, and the production designer. The DP is a vital person that you want on your team, on your side.

The title production designer began, as you probably know, on *Gone with the Wind* with William Cameron Menzies. Because that art director went above and beyond. He storyboarded the whole film and got himself networking with all the various departments. And that's why David O. Selznick created the production designer credit–you're designing the production.

The productions that are burned into our skulls, can you imagine how much design is part of the memory of these films? Some people think that they just walk into places and shoot and it's not the case at all. But the best review of good design is that there is no mention. Because it works and people believe. What we do and sometimes what the cinematographer does and what the costume designer does just seems to be natural and moves the story along. It keeps this belief system and helps transform us, an audience, to a place where we can believe this is really going on.

And then with period pieces and with the future, production design comes forward. That's what people tend to think is good production design but it's not always the case. There are great films where it looks like you just shot them, but in reality they were totally orchestrated.

AS: Are there films that you think of as representational of good production design?

JG: Well there are the classic ones like *Gone with the Wind* and *The Wizard of Oz*–those big things. I loved *All that Jazz*. The big movies that you remember. But films like *Ordinary People*–regular films–there are some that are just so spectacular. I loved a film called *Character*, a period thing that was just told so well through art direction and cinematography. There are so many others. In every film something wonderful's been done by an art department.

[Production designer] Bob Boyle's turned one hundred this year. He's a teacher here and has been for many years. He tells amazing stories about his beginnings and about coming from USC architecture school in the 30s and coming into the film business which was booming during the Depression. He came from an architectural background. He worked with Alfred Hitchcock and did *North By Northwest* and *The Birds*–all these fabulous films. He worked in Hollywood when it was the studio system and you could go to work in a world where people are making movies and the lumberyard's right there. Everything you'd ever need is within the boundaries of the studio.

There were supervising art directors who would keep the Paramount look of a movie. There were art directors who were assigned to certain pictures, but the supervising art director usually got the credit and the regular art director who ran the show never did, or got some kind of secondary credit. The supervising art director would get you started and then not be involved anymore. That was the one dark spot where people wouldn't get the credit that they deserved. But it was a great time to be making movies and you learned and collaborated with all your peers that were all on the lot. It was a kind of unifying time. Right now we're all out on our own–independents trying to find our own little projects. It's a very different time.

We're dealing with that here at the school where the tools are changing. We stress the importance of being able to use a pencil and actually sketch something out. Because you might be in a van, and the ability to draw is something that should never go away. And production designers should know how to draft because they're going to be looking at drawings. And these wonderful programs that we're teaching–Vectorworks and the Autocad programs and SketchUp and Photoshop and Illustrator, they are important tools. A designer who's going to survive in the years to come is going to be someone who has a handle on all these programs, even if they're not doing it themselves. But as all these things are changing there still is going to be a need for the person who has an idea and that's the designer.

There are a lot of people coming into this city every day wanting to become production designers and why are they going to get the job? It's luck, talent and timing. And some people spend their whole lives trying to do this but they are never there at the right moment. So much talent. And whenever I get I job I just thank God that I got one because I know how many people want it and never seem to get it. I'm really happy to have had the career that I have had, although I've always been in that world of five million to like thirty million dollars. So I don't know this *Lord of the Rings*, I don't know this *War of the Worlds* or *Indiana Jones*–I don't know these movies. I've never worked on them. We've had people come in the school that have, it's so interesting to hear about. But most of us are going to be making movies that are not these handfuls of gigantoid things, although we all talk about them and love them and want to work on them. Not everyone's going to have that opportunity, especially when you're just getting out of school.

AS: What size crews have you worked with?
JG: I would say . . . maybe twenty? You have a coordinator, you have an art director, you've got

a graphics person, you've got a set designer or two, you have a set decorator and a construction coordinator, a lead man, and you've got a scenic painter, and then their crews. But these are just the key positions. There are carpenters and painters. Four swing at least and you've got a shopper. Then you've got a prop department which has about two, three people. So you're at twenty. Easy. Usually that's kind of minimal. Fifteen to twenty for an average art department. But then you get more people when you're doing bigger things and you've got to bring the carpenters in, the welders and the plasterers. And there's illustrators and all these other things. Model-makers. It can grow. And it does when you do *Men in Black* and when you do *Ghostbusters*. When you do all these big movies you get hundreds of people working for you.

AS: Do you do your own sketches in the beginning?
JG: I find myself being architectural and I often create models. I do illustrations sometimes. For *Best in Show* I would do a sketch and give that to Chris to okay. You need to be clear. People need to understand what they're getting before they get there. And not be surprised. That's when we make changes, not when it's up and you want to make it three feet–

AS: Instead of ten feet.
JG: Right. Constant communication and collaboration is vital. If you can't collaborate and talk and keep the communication flowing, be actively

bringing people together to solve problems, then you don't belong in this business.

AS: What advice would you have for someone just starting out?

JG: Well, there's no right or wrong way. You talk to anyone who comes through this school and every single story's different. You've got to have passion for this and love being a storyteller. And you've got to be flexible and adjustable to anything that comes up. You've got to be persistent and not give up. You've got to really believe in what you're doing. Know when to fight and when to pull back.

And always be aware that people are watching you from the beginning because your reputation depends on what people are saying about you. Even if you're talented, if you're just not a good collaborator and you're a pain in the ass, most people don't want to go through a hellish experience to maybe get something good at the other end. People like working and going through difficult and challenging times with people who are passionate and are team players. This is not just about any one person, it's about people working well together through difficult and challenging moments.

And know that you're going to be in it for the long run. It's not going to be easy. It's usually 24/7 for a designer. Most people go to sleep and rest but a designer usually brings all that crap home if he gets home at a decent hour! If you want to have stability in your life this is a business that you don't want to be in! You're going to go through peaks and valleys of working and not working. And it starts over every time you finish a movie–then you've got to find the next one.

> " PEOPLE LIKE WORKING AND GOING THROUGH DIFFICULT AND CHALLENGING TIMES WITH PEOPLE WHO ARE PASSIONATE AND ARE TEAM PLAYERS. THIS IS NOT JUST ABOUT ANY ONE PERSON, IT'S ABOUT PEOPLE WORKING WELL TOGETHER THROUGH DIFFICULT AND CHALLENGING MOMENTS.

I've been lucky enough that this business has supported me financially and that I enjoy doing it. And I'm back at the school that got me here in the beginning. And the fact that they're paying me now, while I paid to be here before, is pretty great. I'm still working and I'm fifty-five years old and that's okay. I'm very happy with how things have worked out. And now I'm grading people's film design papers–it's pretty interesting to give back and to share the knowledge that I have. These kids get perspectives from our teachers who have worked in the business or are working in the business. And we're mentoring them with things that we've learned, so it's interesting to say the least.

Colin Gibson

Colin Gibson invented a fleet of road warrior vehicles while designing the movie *Mad Max: Fury Road,* essentially becoming a "War Boy" himself in the process. A far cry from his more traditional work on *Babe and Babe: Pig in the City,* the world he brought to life for *Fury Road* was brutal and unforgettable and won him his first Academy Award.

AS: Your collaboration with director George Miller on *Mad Max: Fury Road* was mind-blowing.

CG: There's nothing like collaborating with a towering imagination to give you a head start to mind-blowing. George showed me a room full of storyboards and no script and said, *This looks like it's right up your street.* I didn't know at the time that it was going to take quite so long! It was the year 2000, which was the same year as the Sydney Olympics and so it was either the Olympics or *Fury Road* and my back had been playing up so I took *Fury Road.* But it turned out to be slightly longer than a four year turnaround!

AS: What exactly did George show you in those first meetings?

CG: George, Brendan McCarthy, Peter Pound and Mark Sexton had initially built the story in storyboards rather than with words. There was nothing written, nothing in the way of dialog. There was also some enthralling concept art that Brendan had done, fantasy in the true sense of the word. The concept art was glorious but very, very fantasy and not especially up my street. I'm a little too much in love with physics. I like to define gravity and then defy it but I don't like to pretend it doesn't exist and CG my way around it. The reason I was brought in was in part to bring some rigour, physics and truth back to the action. Instead of my being an anchor on George's imagination I think the tension, like the tension in real world gravity, worked to our advantage.

But storyboards are terrifying things where in one storyboard there are two people filling the cabin of a car and in the next storyboard there are eleven and there still seems to be enough room for a football team.

AS: How did you first meet George Miller?
CG: George ran Kennedy Miller, which became Kennedy Miller Mitchell, which is a production company. I had done a couple of jobs for him in his capacity as producer. He was producing films and telemovies and the odd mini-series for television. I was meant to be on *Thunderdome* but had to absent myself at the very start of production shooting because my son was about to be born. They didn't talk to me for a while but then fortunately I was brought back in and I worked on *Babe* and then *Babe 2* and then just as George started work on *Happy Feet* he offered me *Fury Road*.

AS: On *Fury Road*, how many of the final set pieces and vehicles closely resembled the original storyboards?
CG: In the action and pacing, they were remarkably true to conception. Storyboards by their nature are not very detailed, however. One car looks pretty much like the next ten or twelve that are drawn in the storyboards.

Brendan McCarthy is a great graphic novelist and his concept art was beautiful but much didn't really fit within the rules that we started to impose. Everything had to follow the logic of the Wasteland where there were minimal amounts of fuel and water, a finite universe of salvage. If something didn't have a believable form and function or it didn't appear to be valuable enough to have survived, it was jettisoned and we had to find another way in.

Unfortunately hovercrafts the size of football fields or 747's welded to Amtrak trains being hauled across the desert by a dozen prancing semi-trailers didn't really fit with the notion that there's probably only two gallons of fuel left and is that the last pair of pantyhose in civilization?

> **THE REASON I WAS BROUGHT IN [ON *MAD MAX: FURY ROAD*] WAS IN PART TO BRING SOME RIGOUR, PHYSICS AND TRUTH BACK TO THE ACTION.**

AS: What was the process for creating one of the vehicles? After those initial storyboards would there be more detailed sketches done and then a trip to a scrapyard to find matching pieces?
CG: No, we inverted it. What I try to do with any job is to design the design process first. For this design process we decided we'd be true to the Wasteland. We designed the way they would have. We did the salvage first, asking, *What are we looking for and why are we keeping it?* That way we managed to get rid of the last forty years or so of the automobile

universe because nobody wants to go into battle with a piece of carbon fiber Japanese technology. Nobody wants to go in with computerized engines that you can no longer fix with a stick and some bubblegum. And nobody wants to bother saving anything that's as ugly as a Camry or a Corolla.

> ❝ **I AM A GREAT LOVER OF RUST AND PATINA AND HISTORY LIKE EVERY OTHER TRAGIC, SENTIMENTAL ART DIRECTOR.**

We figured the War Boys of the Wasteland had their own preoccupations. One of them was the guilt that you might feel at the end of civilization. There's all this great flotsam and jetsam washed up on the edge of the Wasteland that you're salvaging scraps from, that you just know must have been fantastic. This was one of the reasons that we worked in the theory that just because it's the end of the world doesn't mean that you don't try to make something beautiful. You try to re-purpose something that you know is beautiful even if it's out of context. Maybe it's just me but the tail fin of a '59 Cadillac is always going to be something worth salvaging.

AS: I heard you would avoid aging the vehicles with a lot of rust.
CG: Rust was one of the arguments that George and I had, because I am a great lover of rust and patina and history like every other tragic, sentimental art director. We love that post-industrial falling-apart

look. But George was nervous about going back to what he'd already done in the first movies and what had been devalued by decades of b-grade genre–the idea that you merely had to weld a piece of barbwire to a Camaro and call it the apocalypse.

Given our color palette we didn't want to go with the obvious bleach-bypass route. We let history and the world add a new fetish and bleach it for us. By going with beaten metal we kept a lot of the color out. We pared back a lot of the patina and rust but still kept it as a little bass-note. One of the things I wanted was black and given that there was no paint left we discovered that there was a beautiful sludge byproduct of petroleum cracking. We re-purposed that as something to plaster over the rusted metal of some of the vehicles. A lot of the Citadel vehicles that are black are actually an inch or two of this lovely thick, black pitch. And it also meant that we could smear in skulls and doll's heads and guns and assorted other fetishes. It also was logistically a wondrous thing. When you have the same War Rig going out for a hundred and forty-eight days and have it slammed into by eighty or ninety other vehicles it's handy not having to re-panel it every night. Instead you just smear some more of the black pitch over the top and then buff it back to continuity.

AS: Did the vehicles take on a life of their own?
CG: We worked on the theory that they were all characters. Some of them more than others had a genesis in the storyboards, the War Rig being one.

It was in sixty percent of the frames and had a lot more worked out in it. Peter Pound, who was the real revhead in the early storyboard process, did a lot of particularly great work in pre-imagining what the War Rig might be, and Nux's car as well. He loved cars and had done a lot of great work. But we didn't really start off with the designs, we started off with the salvage. We decided we'd be true to the way the War Boys would do it and we'd go out and find salvage with that love, that passion, that guilt, and that half-remembered wonderment. Like a Labrador peering at a toilet roll and thinking, *I'm not sure what this is but I'm sure it's fun!* we collected the salvage, we brought it back, and then myself, an art director, a steel worker, and a mechanic, would sit down and start writing the story of that particular character.

The storyboards would tell us, *This vehicle needs to have a crew of at least two people on it, it needs a flame-thrower, it's got eighty days of keeping up at eighty kilometers per hour over four different flavors of desert and when it does go, it needs to launch itself into the air, do a pirouette, burst into flame, and launch its crew in different directions.* We'd hit the salvage pile with great mechanics who would try to top each other with how to make it more grunty, bigger, and more beautiful. Mount iconic curves, buff, weaponize, add cup-holder and floor it.

AS: These were all created in Australia?
CG: The production had a roller-coaster ride. In 2002 we had sourced vehicles in Africa. In early 2003 we began manufacture of them all in Africa, but the project fell through at that stage for various geopolitical reasons. The odd invasion of Iraq, Mel Gibson's wife getting nervous about how many Muslims there may or may not be in Namibia. (I think there was only one, who ran a 7-11). It all fell apart and the next time round, (2009), we were planning to shoot in Australia. We built a workshop in Sydney and our original vehicle search was around Australia. A great art director and buyer, Laurie Faen, went out in one direction and I went in the other and we found various vehicles as salvage, purchased and brought them all back. We also bought some ex-U.N. and military trucks in England and Europe, and in America tracked down the Cadillacs and a pair of Kaisers, then shipped everything back home to the great big salvage build-your-own armada.

 MOUNT ICONIC CURVES, BUFF, WEAPONIZE, ADD CUP-HOLDER AND *FLOOR IT.*

AS: Would Stunts and Special FX come in and test out the vehicles?
CG: The Special FX team was working in the same workshop with us. We were hand-in-glove. We worked together from very early on, which is always my preference. That way we could build all the requirements into the vehicle as we went. I'm not big on specialization and particularly loathe it in those big-budget American films where you go and build something and then the Special FX guys

come in and build four versions of it that have to do something else but don't do it very well because they have nothing to do with the object you invented in the first place. We wanted to control that and we wanted to put all the money and effort into the vehicles that were characters, actors that could do their own stunts. That way we don't have to build four plastic versions of the one that had Velcro holding the seams together because we had actually built them to do what they needed to do.

> " LIKE A LABRADOR PEER-ING AT A TOILET ROLL AND THINKING, *I'M NOT SURE WHAT THIS IS BUT I'M SURE IT'S FUN!* WE COLLECTED THE SALVAGE, WE BROUGHT IT BACK, AND THEN MYSELF, AN ART DIRECTOR, A STEEL WORKER, AND A MECHANIC, WOULD SIT DOWN AND START WRITING THE STORY OF THAT PARTICULAR CHARACTER.

AS: How many months of actual paid prep did you get?

CG: I wish you hadn't said paid! It was basically a ten month process in Australia. But it varied–it was start and stop, studio and weather-dependent. It would start and we'd get five months and then we'd get another two. George was busy doing tap-dancing penguins and that kept him away from us for quite a while. Finally we got to a point where we were closing on a shoot date, and we went to Broken Hill where we were planning to shoot. P.J. Voeten,

producer and first AD, Guy Norris the stunt coordinator and second unit action director, and myself and our teams all went and had a great time shooting and testing the vehicles. We then sent the footage back to George who suddenly realized we were almost ready to go.

AS: Did all these vehicles ultimately need to go to Africa?

CG: We built a bit of an airstrip in Mundi Mundi, which is in Broken Hill outside Silverton. It's what we call the nearest outback to a city. But unfortunately the heavens opened up and the flowers carpeted the otherwise red desert and it turned into a beautiful horticultural miracle. You couldn't swing a camera without seeing pelicans and camels dancing in the background. It was time to go back to where we had originally intended to shoot in 2003. We packed everything onto a very large boat and headed to Namibia.

AS: And this was a large amount of vehicles . . .

CG: It was just under a hundred-and-fifty. There were eighty-eight characters that we built. Trucks, tanks, cars, motorbikes, etc. But we had doubles, triples, quadruples, breakaways, and so on. Close to a hundred and fifty objects plus containers of weapons, props, and some of the wardrobe that had already been made. A lot of the wardrobe was fabricated in Africa under the lovely and talented Jenny Beavan, while we set up the new workshop. Stunts came over and almost immediately we started testing out in the new African conditions, which were a little different to what we designed for. The harder underfoot plains of Broken Hill gave way to sandy riverbeds an awful lot softer under the tire and there was another ten or fifteen degrees of heat. So there was a bit of reworking, reorganizing and re-purposing. Adding the odd radiator, a hundred foot of garden hose, additional suspension and somewhere to store the sunscreen.

AS: Did you work with local crews in Africa? Did you hire a team of people when you got out there?

CG: The first time we were in Africa we'd only taken three Australians and one New Zealander with us. Everyone else was local or South African. But this time around because we'd already built all the vehicles and everyone who knew how they went together tended to be Australian, the bulk of the crew was Australian. But of course we hired Namibians, South Africans, some terrific English mechanics. We did have six or seven hundred people on set many of the days and were shooting in two or three different locations at a time. It was quite a big enterprise.

AS: Going back to long before you were working with these crews of seven hundred, how did you first get started in the field of production design?

CG: Some of us start out going to art school and some of the rest of us happen to be failed actors whose children start screaming for bread and shoes!

AS: You were one of the actors?

CG: Yes, I used to pretend I was waiting for my big break but no matter how tight the sweater I wore it still never happened, so fortunately there's been enough work in the art department to keep me going!

AS: Did you go to a theater school rather than art school?

CG: I did go to a theater school while I was at university, trying to find a way out of university once I discovered that it wasn't like school. In philosophy class you go to all the trouble of learning *I think, therefore I am*, and then you go back next week and some other philosopher's got some completely different theory. I needed to find something else to do and I did part-time acting classes and worked as an actor for a few years. I discovered that most of the places that I worked at as an actor I was also taking over the sets and the lighting and occasionally the production itself.

I found myself schlepping international shows around festivals in Australia and New Zealand and sort of redesigning them and repackaging them and that ended up being my new life. And then one time I took a beautiful Yugoslavian company to Melbourne as an outdoor show and it rained for two weeks straight and I was losing a fortune. I called an ethnic television station that had just opened in Sydney called SBS and asked them if they'd like to come and shoot. We had a free weekend before we opened in Sydney and I was in need of making some money. They came down and not only did I have great fun but I also made more money on that weekend than I had been making while schlepping thirty Yugoslavs around the Southern Hemisphere. Two weeks later I was offered a job as a props guy, not really knowing what a props guy was. It involved a cruise ship, *Love Boat in the Pacific*, and there you go–the rest is history.

AS: Were you working as a propmaster or assistant props?

CG: It was called Stand-by Props in those days, which meant you were standing by on set. It was unfortunate in the early days because I had a tendency to call *Cut!* whenever anything looked bad and while working on *Love Boat* a lot of things looked bad. I eventually broke myself of the habit of yelling *Cut!* to other peoples' productions and when I got back to Sydney I continued doing props. I then discovered all the things that prop people were supposed to do. Nothing that I knew very much about. For example, I needed a truck but I didn't have a driver's license and I needed tools but had never actually used any. And when you need to smoke up a hall and you don't have a smoke machine you do go through an awful lot of Camel unfiltered cigarettes!

AS: You went from props to Art Director?

CG: Yeah, I was never very good at taking orders. I think the only reason I became a production designer is I just got sick of other old men telling me what to do. Although it doesn't actually solve the problem because there's always a director or producers. But you've thinned out the ranks.

AS: What was your first experience as an art director, before you became a production designer?

CG: *Young Einstein.* Slightly odd-ball stuff. In the good old days when you were an art director you didn't have to just art direct, you got to also stunt drive and help the grips set tracks and rig cranes and light the odd set and to this day I'm still not comfortable with specialization. I like to give everybody a go with everything just to find out how you can expand the universe.

AS: Production designer Jack Fisk was nostalgic for the days of the art department being just four guys where everyone does everything.

CG: I'm all for him. I had a look at the *Art Stars* site and I fell in love with Jack Fisk for all of those reasons. We have a similar M.O. The disadvantage with a lot of specialization is that on too many gigs it's about coming up with shiny concept art and not really thinking through the problem. Something else Jack said that really rang true was that it's the parameters that make us what we are. It's what you haven't got that makes you come up with a new and exciting way to do it. Otherwise we all just go out and do the same thing over and over again.

Those of us of a certain age were never tested in battle. We haven't had a war to prove whether we're actually responsive and resilient enough. So instead we go and make a film. George Miller on *Fury Road* often referred to it as a battle. Although when he referred to me as the one he was doing battle with I guess it wasn't such a good metaphor!

AS: When you're hiring people for the art department what kind of qualities do you look for?

CG: Someone who doesn't look like they're pretending to laugh at my jokes! It never ceases to annoy me how many people it takes to make me look competent. I love to find people who are passionate about what they do and they make me passionate. Because I didn't go into this as a dyed-in-the-wool revhead, *God I just love V8's!* Like all the other jobs you do as a designer you become passionate. You become fascinated. You discover that whether it's outer space or scuba gear, you learn a new passion. And you can only do that by finding people who already have that passion who can help pass it on to you. In that way I'm a little vampiric.

AS: What would you say are the qualities required to be a production designer? Do you draw a lot?

CG: Here I have to plead the fifth and claim Jack Fisk back again. I draw badly. But I can also draw with words. I can draw with passion. I can sell anyone a used car if I have to. On this production there were those early storyboards done that had some detail. There was some concept art that we worked up for particular vehicles as well. But in general we wanted desperately to do it as though we were trying to build something that we only half-remembered. It was the idea of working your way out of that fog. It's Charlton Heston on that beach looking up and seeing the Statue of Liberty. *Fuck me, I've been here before!* We wanted that. And I guess I was there to bring the fog. The lack of lucidity. And the passion.

AS: What would you say are the differences between working as Art Director and as Production Designer? I noticed you've done both.

CG: Even when I was working as a props guy I don't think there was that much difference between the art department jobs. Obviously the responsibility comes back and stops with you and I like that. And I like being able to have the conversation at the top level with directors, with cinematographers. I like being able to share those ideas. Which is the only thing I miss. Otherwise I think it's pretty much the same thing. I'm always aware of logistics. I'm always aware of parameters. I always try to find a smarter, cleverer way to get to somewhere. Personally I think they ought to all be the same job and have the same job description. You just get to have arguments with slightly different people.

> " ON TOO MANY GIGS IT'S ABOUT COMING UP WITH SHINY CONCEPT ART AND NOT REALLY THINKING THROUGH THE PROBLEM.

AS: I heard you were working on a movie called *The Great Wall?*

CG: I was very fortunate to get parachuted into China to help with *The Great Wall.* One of the designers you've already interviewed, John Myhre, was working in China and they had yet to start on their exterior sets. And they were running out of time. I was lucky enough to be offered the gig. I've already been in, I had four months building exterior sets in China. Those have finished shooting and my work here, as they say, is done and I'm back in the unemployment line!

AS: What was it like to work with John Myhre?

CG: It was great. And John as I think you would have discovered from your interview is hugely enthusiastic, optimistic and a visionary chap. You can't help but have a good time sharing that with someone else.

AS: I remember he said there's nothing worse than hearing crew complaining on set—he knows we have the greatest job ever.

CG: You do have to wonder about some people. You get gaffers and they're complaining about how horrible it is and you keep thinking, *If not for the grace of God you'd be pushing a cable under a house, plugging in somebody's toaster.* So enjoy. We're a very lucky group. If nothing else it's always better than a real job.

AS: How involved in the actual production design is George Miller?

CG: If you sit down for a year or so and do two-thousand storyboards you definitely have a handle on what you want. But he gave us a great amount of leeway. He was also very busy doing tap-dancing penguins for *Happy Feet* at the same time. We'd get three month stretches where we didn't see him and we could move ahead making our own version of great progress. As Mr. Fisk mentioned I'd rather rebuild it again afterwards but at least be able to show what it could be. I

would, in my own fascist system, sort out which vehicle belonged to whom and George would come in and say, *No, I love this one so much it has to become this. I refuse to blow it up that early in the movie.* And then he'd tie it all back together with his rather incredible obsession and imagination.

AS: What would you say that you like most about designing movies?

CG: The chance to think about something. Sometimes we just don't think about stuff enough. What I love is you get to look at a script and you get to go into it as deeply as you allow yourself. And that gives you the chance to break it down and to start to understand how the component parts work and how they affect other people. I think it's a fantastic way to look at how we communicate and how we think, how we feel. And if you think about it enough and you have enough good people around you they can turn what could have been the bad poetry in your bedroom into something the whole world can share.

AS: When someone hands you a script what are some of the first things you do?

CG: I read it and then go back and start over again almost immediately. I break down the ideas that are in it. If it's a good script I can find three or four arresting images. You come up with those three or four arresting graphic moments and then you go back to the director or whoever's offered this to you and say, *What about this? This is how I imagine you could get that across. Does this tap into something?*

Then you start to come up with a visual language to go with the written language. I'm wedded to the word as much as I am to the picture. If you discover something that strikes a chord with you, usually it can echo with an audience as well.

AS: Do you always work with the same crew?

CG: Part of the great tragedy of working on a movie that I was first offered in the year 2000 is that sadly the crew changed. It changed a lot, more than I would have liked. But I do enjoy working with different people. I do like the idea of going to different countries. It was fantastic being in China and having only a local crew for the first seven weeks of the build. Obviously there are people who you know and love and who you're on a wave-length with. People who have saved your ass before and who you're always happy to have taking your back. But I'm also happy to go out and find out what other talents the rest of the world has.

AS: How was the crew in China?

CG: They were great. People fly in and they get nervous and they want to bring ten or fifty of their closest personal friends. But I found I was more than happy to make ten or fifty new closest personal friends. And obviously the talents are there. There's some fantastic moviemaking that happens in China. And even in countries like Namibia where there's very little filmmaking, that doesn't mean that the talents aren't there. That doesn't mean that there's not something that you can tap into. Drop me on a desert island and let's see what we can make the coconuts do.

AS: How involved are you with the CG aspect?

CG: Well, we don't have a choice anymore. We trumpeted loudly that we wanted *Fury Road* to be, if not the last of the great action films then the first of a new series of great action films. That we would try our best to avoid CG. But that didn't mean we were turning our back on half the crayon box and not coloring things in the smartest way. Both David Nelson and Andrew Jackson, the VFX supervisor on *Fury Road*, have taught me much. Everything from how you can improve something with CG but not make it a CG thing, to how you can use CG to make something safer that might have been unsafe. How you can add another five cameras and use CG to get rid of the evidence but still have those cuts to use back in the editing.

> **THOSE OF US OF A CERTAIN AGE WERE NEVER TESTED IN BATTLE. WE HAVEN'T HAD A WAR TO PROVE WHETHER WE'RE ACTUALLY RESPONSIVE AND RESILIENT ENOUGH. SO INSTEAD WE GO AND MAKE A FILM.**

You'd be insane to do without them unless you're Georges Perec, who decided to write a novel without the letter "e." You can always do that as an exercise in parameters, but CG is a fantastic tool. You just have to remember it's only a tool. Why does a dog lick its balls? Because it can. There are a lot of things that we can do now but that doesn't mean that we should. Because it will get tedious, hollow and empty. And if you can pull anything out of a hat nobody gasps anymore at that cute little rabbit.

AS: How closely do you work with the DP?

CG: A great DP, just like a great stunt driver or a great scenic, can make your work much better than you could ever imagine that it could have been. I'm always happy to work with a DP as much as humanly possible because they're the ones who finally capture the magic. You give them all you can, and smile as they compose and color and riff on the same storyline your team (and the costume team, the actors, the writer and the director, et al.) have been developing.

> " YOU DO HAVE TO WONDER ABOUT SOME PEOPLE. YOU GET GAFFERS AND THEY'RE COMPLAINING ABOUT HOW HORRIBLE IT IS AND YOU KEEP THINKING, *IF NOT FOR THE GRACE OF GOD YOU'D BE PUSHING A CABLE UNDER A HOUSE, PLUGGING IN SOMEBODY'S TOASTER. SO ENJOY.* WE'RE A VERY LUCKY GROUP. IF NOTHING ELSE IT'S ALWAYS BETTER THAN A REAL JOB.

AS: Do you spend time on set as shooting goes on?

CG: I've worked with some fantastic designers in this country and a lot of them are like, *We've made our sets, here's the keys. We'll be off on the next one, let us know how it goes.* I tend to like being a part of the shoot, making sure that the props, the sets, can still respond. Maybe it's an emotional problem. I just can't let go! I'd be there for every shot if there wasn't another set coming up tomorrow or the day after. That's usually what drags you away. That's why they make more hours in the day–so that you can be on the set and still go and get the next set ready without missing anything.

AS: After working in other countries how would you characterize the Australian film industry?

CG: I'm biased but I find the Australian crews are terrific. Partly because of my own proclivity to not be specialized. I couldn't understand going to Los Angeles and not being allowed into my own prop truck and needing teamster number seven to hand me the object from the box. It's a little more friendly here for those who want to keep control of what they're doing.

AS: For *Fury Road* did you watch *Road Warrior* a bunch of times? Do you use a lot of cinematic references?

CG: I try not to watch movies as reference. I watch movies to keep me plugged in to the zeitgeist. Not to the level that George does, he might as well be jacked into the internet. He's constantly aware of everything that's happening. I watch movies because we're all working in different vernaculars and idioms and I want to know as many adjectives and as many foreign languages as possible. But I never go out looking for filmic references that way.

I was offered a job not long ago where they sent me a glossy brochure of sci-fi wonderment telling me how they wanted to make a film that was unlike any that had ever been made before and the glossy brochure proceeded to show me various shots from *Alien* and *Star Trek* and *Star Wars*.

You need to be able to speak the language but you want to find a new way to put the words together otherwise you're just playing karaoke.

AS: Are there other places you get inspiration from?

CG: Books (novels more than coffee-table reference tomes). Art galleries. We have a great art gallery in Sydney called White Rabbit that specializes in Chinese art and the day before I was to head off to China, an exhibition opened by a Chinese artist who had deconstructed stolen pieces of the Great Wall. These pieces were stolen by local villagers and turned into hen houses and barbecues and he's re-stolen them back and rebuilt them as artwork versions of the same. That work was handy to be taking with me to China if just to say, *That's what the color of Great Wall bricks were in the 12th or 14th century. I wonder what ours will be like in the 11th?* There's always reference. Some of it's visual. Some of it's in words and words paint pictures too. I read a lot. There's a whole universe of reference, you just need to keep your eyes and ears open.

AS: Any advice for someone just coming into the business?

CG: You don't have to start as an art director. You don't have to draw. You don't have to go to art school. Like Jack Fisk, throw a hammer in the back of a ute and head off and the badlands will shape you.

FUTURE

How do you see your role changing?

A compilation of excerpts covering the subject of the future of production design, taken from the interviews in this book

Anyone worried about the future of production design and the invasion of green screens, LED walls and omnipresent CGI should read the following production designer's responses. They remind us that visual effects are just tools and that someone will always be needed to design the look of the film and have the inspiration and artistic vision to help tell the story visually. Even if movies transform into immersive virtual environments more akin to video games, there will always be the need for a production designer with taste and unending imagination to create groundbreaking worlds...

GRANT MAJOR

Good production design is all to do with the narrative. The narrative overrides all these other technical inventions that come along. The story's the most important thing but the story itself is a vessel and inside the vessel are characters. In the best stories these characters have perspective, they have backgrounds and have psychological requirements. Recognizing all these subtleties is tremendously important because human beings are a social species. We go to the movies to interact with other human beings, notwithstanding that they're projected on a cinema screen. Technologically production design's gonna move on, but the fundamentals of storytelling won't change. We still are creating environments and worlds within which we tell stories.

NATHAN CROWLEY

I've worked on a lot of very digital films and I remember the art department being terrified we're all going to be out of work. I was like, *What are you guys talking about? The most valuable tool you have is being creative and there are not that many people who are.* Our job is never going away because people want ideas. No one is going to replace the idea. Design is about ideas and taste. You can't replace that. That is why you're valuable. Design will never change. The Art Directors Guild has nothing to worry about. Because people will always want someone who comes in with a different way of looking at things. Just keep retraining. Keep up with technology.

GUY HENDRIX DYAS

Our industry is changing rapidly and it's normal for production designers to wonder what the future holds. I tend to be optimistic and not only because I have a background in VFX but because films will always need the contribution of artists and to me a green screen is a tool, it's not a craft, and tools can never replace crafts, someone still has to envision the environments for these stories to take place in.

MICHAEL NOVOTNY

Well, basically my role won't change at all. I'm always trying to put a visual to the story. Whether you're going to use a computer to do that or if you're going to use screens on a stage and then do comps. You still have to shoot the plates. Bottom line is you're putting a visual to the story. And you put that visual to the story any way you can. You're talking to a director, trying to overlay your ideas with his thoughts. He's not thinking as visually as you are. That's your job. Your job is to come up with the vision of the show. I don't care what process you're doing, what the final output is. You're still imagining what that thing looks like. So it doesn't change my job at all. We were doing greenscreen and computers long ago and it hasn't changed a thing for me.

EVE STEWART

I think there's a sort of backlash [against too many greenscreens] if anything. I find that people are asking for more and more in-camera. Of course the really big movies are going to stick to doing green but I find that there's actually more being put

FUTURE

in-camera and I think audiences get a bit tired of the kind of glossiness of the non-realism of CG. I think they like a bit of realism where they can connect. Definitely there's a back-lash at the moment.

DAVID WARREN

We should never get away from the fact that there are films being made every year that are normal films. That aren't great visual effects extravaganzas. Out of the movies that were nominated this year, the one that Patrice [Vermette] did, *Young Victoria*, probably had like ten visual effects shots in it–matte paintings and a little bit of augmentation. That was a film all shot on location. *Avatar* has two thousand visual effects shots yet both films were still nominated. So it's interesting that it's still just about taste and what looks good to the eye.

What Robert Stromberg did on *Avatar* is symbolic of the way that film design may go in the future. This bridge between visual effects and the art department is a very strong thing. Doug Chiang was the production designer on *Beowulf* and he was the visual effects design director for the first two *Star Wars* movies. But then Gabriella Pescucci did costume design for *Beowulf* and she's a real old hat. You have a very young, modern team designing the sets–these were guys that bridged with visual effects–but then for costume they brought in somebody who worked on movies in Italy. It's about how costumes flow, how stuff is cut, and how stuff holds onto the body.

But I think as time goes on people like Bob Stromberg bridging visual effects will become more and more common.

RICK HEINRICHS

The future of our industry has always been a big question in my mind. Are we going to continue to be able to be making the big feature films that we've been making in the kind of numbers that we've been making them in? And there's the brave new world of distribution over the internet. What are the sort of economies we are going to look at now if indeed we're going to be producing and designing films that are going to end up on a small computer screen?

As a production designer I love to build sets but when you're in a structure that doesn't allow you to build sets what are you doing? We're using a lot more digital and virtual sets. But it's life-sucking to work on a greenscreen set. The challenge is, *How do we make it a usable tool that is actually cool to work with?*

How do you see your role changing?

JOHN MYHRE

The fact is, there have been some amazing movies made that have been virtually all against bluescreen. But there's still somebody designing all that. There will always be production designers. And now we have these amazing new tools that can extend sets in the ways that we never have before. It's fantastic but it's still the same job.

K.K. BARRETT

Will we be thinking about 3D films in four years? It went away before. What I'm surprised at is that there are not more people making films for nothing. Because the technology is there. You could really make films for the price of the access to a camera. To be competitive you just have to have good stories. Engaging stories. And characters. And you need good sound. But all of those things are very obtainable for five-thousand dollars. And a lot of free time. But I think it's because there aren't enough good stories.

So I don't think it's about CG or not CG, or greenscreen or not. Those are just tools. They're not ideas–they're just tools. A hammer can lay sitting on a table but it's not going to help you unless you have something you decided to do with it. Tools are just tools. You have to have the idea and make something out of it.

EUGENIO CABALLERO

It will be different in certain ways but not in the most important way. We, as designers, are meant to create visual concepts for films. The tools that we use to transmit them are evolving. We don't use the same tools that we did twenty years ago. Or even fifteen years ago. There are certain things that were not even imaginable ten years ago in the digital world. But the most important thing is that all of these developments have to support your visual concept for a film. And those visual concepts are what we as production designers must continue providing.

MARK FRIEDBERG

My TV is 4K at home. You go to the movies it's 2K right now. Some people would say the quality of writing on TV right now is better than what you get in a lot of what's in theaters. To justify the economics of having a theater, the kinds of movies that get made are bigger and broader. That's just what's happening. Ang [Lee, director] said movies will become like Broadway. It used to be there was a dramatic theater on every corner. That's how people got their entertainment. And then TV happened and that stopped. Then Broadway became something that you could do twice a year that cost a lot and was an event. That feels a little bit like what's happening to cinema. But it's not just cinema. It's sports. The stands are empty. Because why go?

FUTURE

I can watch five games at home, in my underwear, and it costs me nothing. Or I can spend two hundred dollars and get on the subway and go to the Bronx and get beer poured on my head. It's a bigger issue than just cinema.

I live in New York and I can't function here in LA because I need to touch people. I need to bump into people. I need to be knocked down a little bit. I need that friction energy to live. That's how I'm raised. The world is not that way right now. We've retreated into our phone world and fortressed ourselves in there.

Technologically the theater's got to figure out how to do something that the LCD screen at home can't do if we're going to keep going.

KIM SINCLAIR

About ten years ago people started to say, *You guys'll be out of a job soon. It's all going to be digital.* And we were like, *Yeah right.* It's kind of gratifying that *Avatar*, which has the most digital content of any film ever made, also had the biggest art department I've ever put together. The live action part was eighty-eight days. With Jim the average day is a fifteen hour shooting day. That's quite a lot of shooting on practical sets. If you've got an actor it's a lot better if you can put a real background behind them. It's better for the actor, it's better for the director. Secondly, this process is pretty expensive. It's kind of wanton to say you can do away with the sets with digital ones or just greenscreens. That's a device on *300*, it's been done to give the film a look but I think it's a stylistic thing and I don't think it'll ever replace sets. The digital world allows you to do things you can't otherwise do. And if it allows you to do things you can't afford to do, that's well and good. But for the vast majority of dramas you're going to want people and you're going to want a set.

RICK CARTER

The job of production design is not going to be dependent on what we've had in this last epoch. Production design is not a static thing. Just the advent of computer imagery into the process caused a development that we've all had to adjust to, those of us who've been around for a while.

And here comes another change [with the coronavirus pandemic] and this one's going to be very, very trying but I think it will lead to great solutions. Designers will have to really help design the production, not just what it looks like. Designing the future will be a part of the production designer's role. We'll look up and in five years from now there will be a group of people who will have shown the way. And some of them will have been production designers that have helped fundamentally to shape how movies get made.

Some of it will become more virtual. Some of it will become more divided up into groups, bringing aspects of the movie together both in realtime and later. But how much of a "collage" can the movie sustain, so that it still feels like it's of a whole?

It's like when they first thought about going on location and they discussed how to integrate that with stage sets or back lots and still make it look whole. My mentor Richard Sylbert looked at me at one point and said, *It looks like you're going into the digital realm. And whatever it's becoming now, it's going to be different.* It has to evolve and the design challenges will evolve and I'm interested to see where it goes.

Acknowledgments

A huge thanks to the many people who helped make this book happen. It all started with my first visit to The American Film Institute where instructors Joe Garrity and John Muto agreed to be the first two production designers interviewed for my artstars.us blog. The blog took off from there and has been going since. Thank you to Joe and John and to all the readers who found value in the knowledge imparted and kept up with the interviews over the years!

Going back even further, I'd like to thank production designer Yvette Taylor for first introducing me to the field of production design and to my friend Nelson Cragg for DP'ing the first feature I designed and helping me to land the next few after that. Thanks also to Nelson for connecting me to his former CSI cohort Dan Novotny and through him Michael Novotny who were great interviews to add to this book. Yi Ju Hee of Neon Rated was a tremendous help by not only connecting me with Lee Han-Jun but also translating the interview and correspondence. Also thank you to Ellie of Neon Rated for connecting me to Yi Ju Hee in the first place.

I'm also grateful to William Anthony who joined me in the early interviews and photographed the designers. Thanks to everyone who helped connect me to these designers and also those who provided photos and clearances. I used the cleared photos to create the portrait illustrations. Rachel Aberly was a huge help facilitating interviews including those with Mark Friedberg, Adam Stockhausen and Guy Hendrix Dyas. Leonardo Manzo produced an amazing photograph of Eugenio Caballero and Aido Osuna helped with clearances. Thanks to Sarah Lopez who helped with Dennis Gassner clearances and Mimi Gramatky, former ADG president, who connected me to Rick Carter. And thanks to Shari Ratliff for connecting me to Rick Heinrichs.

Thanks to my wife Kristy Jennings for her amazing book design and to my artist daughter Pepper for providing infinite inspiration. And to my mother Anstiss Morrill and surrogate father Barry Koffler for proofreading and editing help!

Rest in peace legendary production designer Bob Boyle who was scheduled to be interviewed for Art Stars the week he passed, at age 100.

Tom Lisowski

Tom Lisowski designed the Liam Neeson thriller *Honest Thief,* the dark satire *The Oath* with Tiffany Haddish, and the Rob Reiner dramedy *The Magic of Belle Isle.* A New York native, he studied painting in Chicago and Berlin, and now resides in Los Angeles with his wife and daughter. Progressing from video game art direction to the world of feature films, his work has taken him around the globe, production designing features in China, the Caribbean, the Himalayas in the Kingdom of Bhutan, and coast to coast within the U.S. He won an Emmy for the *Entertainment Tonight* promo *Treat Yourself,* was nominated for a Best Art Director VMA on Tyler the Creator's *Tamale,* has received press coverage in *Variety* and *The New York Times,* and designed the Emmy nominated series *Youth and Consequences* (produced by Mark Gordon). He hosts the production design blog www.artstars.us

Index

Made in the USA
Las Vegas, NV
27 January 2024